KEEN
of
PHILADELPHIA

William Williams Keen Jr., M.D., 1902 oil portrait by William Merritt Chase
[Thomas Jefferson University]

KEEN
of
PHILADELPHIA

THE COLLECTED MEMOIRS
of
WILLIAM WILLIAMS KEEN JR.

EDITED BY W. W. KEEN JAMES
INTRODUCTION BY STANLEY M. ARONSON, M.D.

William L. Bauhan, Publisher
DUBLIN, NEW HAMPSHIRE

2002

Keen, William W. (William Williams), b. 1837.
    Keen of Philadelphia : the collected memoirs of William Williams Keen Jr. / edited by
W. W. Keen James ; introduction by Stanley M. Aronson.
        p. cm.
    Includes Index.
    ISBN 0-87233-129-6
    1. Keen, William W. (William Williams), 1837-1932. 2.
Surgeons–Pennsylvania–Philadelphia–Biography. I. James, W. W. Keen. II. Title.

    RD27.35.K44 A3 2002
    617'.092–DC21
    [B]

                                                                    2001043766

WILLIAM L. BAUHAN, PUBLISHERS
P.O. BOX 443
DUBLIN, NEW HAMPSHIRE
03444

Please visit our website:
www.bauhanpublishing.com

PRINTED AND BOUND IN THE UNITED STATES OF AMERICA

THIS BOOK IS DEDICATED WITH GREAT AFFECTION TO DR. FREDERICK B. WAGNER JR., WHO INSPIRES WITH HIS KNOWLEDGE, HIS HUMOR, HIS PERSISTENCE, AND HIS ENTHUSIASM FOR LIVING THE FULL LIFE.

Wand of Aesculapius

Contents

LIST OF ILLUSTRATIONS

Illustrations

ABOUT THIS BOOK

I'M KEEN ON KEEN—and for more reasons than mere kinship. In my youth, the icon who was my mother's grandfather was paraded before me with a frequency and earnestness that virtually assured that I would *not* try to follow in his Brobdingnagian footsteps. It did not help that his entire name, William Williams Keen, was affixed to my surname at my launching. By conviction and persuasion, his daughters (he had no sons) christened three other William Williams Keens, but, like them, I was not a firstborn and thus not dynastically inclined.

Not particularly keen on Keen as a role model, then, despite the occasional inheritance of trivial, though sometimes monogrammed, paraphernalia, what has brought me to my present state of enthusiasm? How did I become keen on Keen?

He left a record.

In 1912, five years after retiring from surgery, he began writing "An Autobiographical Sketch" for his four daughters. Completed in November 1915, it told of his childhood, his college years, his courtship and marriage, and the emergence to prominence of his career. Still in vigorous good health (apparently to his surprise), and never comfortable with any traditional notion of retirement, he again took up the pen in January 1916, and provided many more anecdotes from his life and times.

With the arrival of Keen's eightieth birthday a year later, he may have viewed this milestone as an appropriate point for closure and for the assembling of his recollections. In any event, that summer copies of the unedited composition titled "Reminiscences for My Children" were given to his daughters. A measure of formality was added to the somewhat casual production (typewritten sheets on legal-size stationery) by means of a cloth binding with each daughter's name handsomely embossed on the cover.

About a decade ago, my brother Wynne and our cousin Frank Freeman decided to widen the distribution of the four copies to include the known descendants, photocopying the original pages (but reducing them to the more standard letter size) and adding an index for easier access to the plethora of names, family and other, in the text.

I was delighted with the opportunity to prepare the index but appalled at the poor quality of the print, so that the text was frequently illegible. Suddenly seized with the notions that our great-grandfather's life spanned the virtual midsection of the life of the Republic (from the end of Jackson's administration to the end of Hoover's); that the stories of his life and career were likely to resonate just as well with people who were *not* his descendants, both in and out of the medical fraternity; and that the country at large ought not be denied this national treasure, I converted his "Reminiscences" into *The Memoirs of William Williams Keen, M.D.*, which I published in 1990.

Brown University (where Keen graduated in 1859, became a trustee in 1873 and a fellow in 1895) has a collection of his books which he donated over a lifetime, distributed among the Sciences Library, the John D. Rockefeller Jr. Library, and the John Hay Library for Special Collections. In addition, the letter has also become a repository for a Keen archive, much of it donated by his descendants long after his death. One item of the Keen listings in the computerized catalogue cites "approximately 35 linear feet of scientific papers (manuscript articles, pamphlets, reprints); autobiographical notes; memorabilia; family papers and correspondence; professional correspondence; diplomas and certificates; military orders and passes; clippings; photographs and glass photographic plates; calling cards" these ranging from 1861 to 1930.

It was in the midst of cataloguing the thirty banker's boxes of this material, beginning in 1993, that I became keen on Keen. This first extended exposure to the man and his work confirmed what I had heard virtually from my days in the cradle, as well as what I had learned from his own reminiscences: William Williams Keen was a model of industriousness and a model of integrity. These models seemed compatible with my somewhat stereotypical notion of what was expected of the Victorian bourgeoisie, though in this case with a fervent Baptist cast.

A MODEL OF INDUSTRIOUSNESS

William Williams Keen Jr. was the sixth of eight children born to his parents, but he was raised virtually as an only child. His brothers, George Budd Keen and Charles Burtis Keen, the only other survivors of the eight, were half a generation older. (The disparity in ages is manifest in the 1849 daguerreotype (on p. 4), which was made only a few months before the death of the youngest son, Baron Stow Keen.) Life was tenuous, and one can imagine that Will, born when his father was forty and his mother was thirty-three, was precious indeed. His words bear ample witness to a close, loving, and supportive family, and his life bore witness to his striving to justify his parents' great faith in him.

This mostly meant hard work—which he loved. He excelled in school, in college, in surgery, and in teaching, and all by dint of "diligent," "painstaking," "thorough," "unstinting," and "untiring" effort—his words, all. Only five feet four and a half inches tall (he stood on a box at the operating table), he was determined not to treat his physical stature as a drawback. He seemed to thrive on competition, and when he felt himself to be trailing in a race, again and again found that by an extra measure of hard work he could come in first.

Energy seemed to be the key. Keen was tireless, as a husband, father, doctor, churchman, and as a citizen and patriot. There was household help, of course, but when his wife died prematurely, even in his grief he recognized and accepted without question his augmented role in raising his four children. I previously described the private record, the reminiscences he left for his family that are the text of this book and its predecessor. Yet it pales in significance to the prodigious output for the world at large: books, essays, letters, medical monographs, and abundant miscellanea. The mental and physical stamina required for such productivity must have been exceptional. The hours of even a long lifetime seem insufficient; there clearly was no waste. He made several chronological autobibliographies, and at each stage his output was phenomenal.

A MODEL OF INTEGRITY

If Keen's industriousness was a factor of his privileged position in a close-knit family, his integrity was a factor of his lifelong affiliation with the Baptist Church. In his professional life, this integrity undergirded the standards he maintained at the table in his surgical teaching clinics. He operated with courage and order, and with a missionary zeal. He seemed to thrive on the arduous, on extra preoperative preparations and study, as well as on postoperative evaluation and description for the record. As soon as asepsis and antisepsis were made known during Lister's 1876 visit to Philadelphia, they became Keen protocol, despite the additional work entailed. He was gratified to reflect on the fact that a large number of the estimated ten thousand students he taught became missionary doctors. And he always gave thanks to God for the happy outcome of his ministrations.

In his personal life, his integrity was manifest in several arenas. First, marriage was sacred and perpetual, and if one partner died, the survivor would remain faithful to the vows and rejoin the departed in Heaven.

Second, the money he earned was not an end sought for itself but the means by which he could make greater contributions: providing medical libraries with rare or historic books and documents; helping to restore war-torn facilities with donation of his personal instruments; publishing at his own expense the books and tracts most likely to be useful; expressing his gratitude for God's gifts by contributions of service and financial support to his church. When money was directed toward his family, it was intended for their education, growth, and comfort (in its original sense of strength), rather than for luxurious living or lavish display, and his estate was devised for their security.

Although a daughter described his drinking a bottle of ale somewhere in the Far East during their 1901–02 trip around the world, and he records drinking beer when stranded at the Bulgarian frontier, Keen was a prohibitionist long before Prohibition. Sacramental wine on sacramental occasions was the only acceptable alcoholic consumption, a view that was supported by distressing first-hand evidence from patients of the abuses precipitated through overindulgence.

In view of Keen's very vocal ministry for abstinence, readers of the *Philadelphia North American* must have had a good laugh when in 1921 his picture mistakenly appeared at the top of a column captioned PUSSYFOOT JOHNSON SEES U. S. TRULY DRY WITHIN 3 OR 4 YEARS. (William Eugene Johnson earned this sobriquet by his ability to sneak up on Prohibition violators.) He and Johnson were on the same side, but Keen never "pussyfooted" about anything.

His personal behavior was always appropriate, never compromised. His humor, both professional and personal, was decorous, a social lubricant, and never calculated to give offense. (Humor among the medical fraternity can seem bizarre to the laity sometimes, but it must serve as a useful release for those intimately involved in life-and-death issues.) He was embarrassed at double entendres and avoided venues where they might be expected to appear. As an Anglophile and consistent with the norms of his time, he found the Irish a suitable butt for humor, but certainly would have adjusted his attitude to today's mores.

Keen had a strong sense of self and self-worth, but true to the values of his age, which called for equilibrium, he maintained a counterbalance of modesty.

As a citizen and patriot, he celebrated what was glorious—or at least right, reasonable, and just—and excoriated what was mean, miserable, wrong. He urged correction for those matters needing it, addressing his comments directly to those with the power to make the changes he saw fit. This included successions of executives (among them, Philadelphia mayors, Pennsylvania governors, and U.S. presidents), legislators and jurists. He did not equivocate but clearly believed that integrity among elected officials should be at least as strong as his own.

One dictionary defines *gadfly* as "A persistent, irritating critic, a nuisance, and "One [who] acts as a provocative stimulus; a goad." From Keen's hundreds of published letters to the editor, he could be seen as either, depending on the reader's point of view.

As it turned out, the binding and presentation of Keen's "Reminiscences for My Children" in 1917 was merely a convenient pausing point. (He could hardly have foreseen that he would live another fifteen years.) The memories continued to pour forth, and additional loose sheets almost equal in volume to the original were discovered during my cataloguing of his papers at Brown, under the lid of one of the four original volumes.

If Keen had stopped with the "Reminiscences," we never would have had his accounts of the confrontation with his mentor, the legendary Dr. Gross; of his preoccupation with the perfidious Kaiser and his responsibility for the Great War; of President Wilson's "treason"; of the fifth triennial Congress of the International Society of Surgery, over which he presided in 1920 at age eighty-four; of his touring the war ruins in France and Belgium; of his trip to Campobello for consultation over the stricken Franklin Roosevelt; or of dozens of other intriguing recollections of people and events. His innate curiosity evoked a vigorous correspondence with top authorities in many fields, his sense of wonder never left him, and his passion for the involved life never cooled.

This volume includes all of the new material brought to light, much of it blended in with the earlier accounts. He himself issued a caution sometimes overlooked by other aging storytellers. At eighty-eight, he said that the reminiscences "have been written at various times, and on re-reading them, I find that I have, in several instances, repeated in later manuscript what was already in . . . earlier manuscript. I do not want to take the time and trouble to hunt out such duplicates and adopt the one which would be . . . preferable."

The title, *Keen of Philadelphia*, is twice apt. First, it reflects the habit among the world's top surgeons of referring to one another by surname and principal venue: Halsted of Johns Hopkins, Fitz of Boston, Czerny of Heidelberg, Langenbeck of Berlin, Moynihan of Leeds. More important, Philadelphia was the venue for Keen's entire life, not just his surgery. Born and raised there, he was away only for ten years of schooling. He returned and dug in, raised a family, and died and was buried there. He clearly was "of" Philadelphia.

With such a sure sense of his place in history, he must have expected that a fuller account of his life story would eventually emerge for the world at large. A full-scale biography awaits only the experienced pen of a visionary writer who can be so touched by the life of this compressed capsule of energy as to become also keen on Keen.

W. W. Keen James

INTRODUCTION

Biographies typically speak in two voices: in the first are the words and reminiscences of the subject of the biography, sometimes plainspoken and faithfully rendered but sometimes a willful selection of carefully sanitized utterances. In the second are the author's interpretive interjections and commentaries. The final biography may therefore range from scholarly history to fanciful fiction.

How can a biographer manage to capture the authentic life of his subject while preserving both its vitality and accuracy? How can he transport the reader into the time, place and ambience inhabited by the subject? How can the social priorities, struggles and even language of the subject's era be faithfully rendered? How, finally, can a biographer avoid contaminating the text with his own wishful interpretations?

Mark Twain, realizing the difficulties of composing an honest appraisal of a person's life, declared: "Biographies are but the clothes and buttons of the man—the biography of the man himself cannot be written." To be trustworthy, Winston Churchill observed, the biography of a public personage should be compiled from discarded memoranda, hastily scribbled letters and pages of secret diaries. And Arthur Balfour was convinced that an authorized biography was little more than sterilized propaganda unless it was written by an avowed enemy: only then could it be a faithful rendition of the life of the subject.

Perhaps, then, the only truthful biographies are autobiographies, but here, too, difficulties arise. Most autobiographers, particularly those who believe themselves to have gained a tenuous foothold in history, will be wary of being needlessly candid. Posterity, they fear, may not look kindly on the disclosures resulting from an unsparing honesty.

This memoir represents a thoroughly faithful portrait of a gifted man and the age in which he lived. William Williams Keen maintained voluminous records of his exceedingly busy life, and in his eighth decade he assembled a compulsively honest account of his varied activities for the benefit of his family. Keen's recollections are assertive, painfully frank, sometimes chronologically disjointed, often uncompromisingly judgemental, but doubtlessly authentic. Keen's words have been written by a man of such implacable faith in his personal rectitude and his relationship to his Creator that he could afford the luxury of scupulous honesty.

Keen was an extraordinary man who left an awesome paper trail. Of course there have been conventional biographic essays on Keen's life. Many authored by Keen's professional colleagues or former students, these commentaries have been appropriately respectful, often adulatory; they portray a person in his Sunday best. These past efforts have been accurate only to the extent that they provide a chronological listing of Keen's public accomplishments.

Fortunately, the Keen archives have been preserved, and contain an abundance of historical information in documents, memorabilia and memoirs. Keen James is one of the first to explore the many papers generated by his illustrious great-grandfather. Mr. James has now distilled these writings into a memorable volume. The editing is the product of Keen James's industry. The words, intimate thoughts, and expressed priorities are all those of William Williams Keen, M.D., of Philadelphia.

And what manner of man was W. W. Keen? He was, as Keen James observed, a man who left a record; a record of such size as to dismay but ultimately gratify the most diligent of biographers. At age 75, much like an elder Moses (whose eye, according to Deuteronomy, "was not dim nor his natural force abated"), Keen wrote an extensive memoir for his daughters. Four years later he amplified upon this informal document with further anecdotes, remembrances and relevant correspondence. His archives at Brown University occupy some 35 feet of library shelving.

Churchill observed that one of his political opponents was a modest man because he had so much to be modest about. Keen, on the other hand, was an unusually endowed and integrated individual who contributed materially to this world but was not falsely modest about his unceasing stream of contributions. He meticulousy documented his achievements, not from vanity but from a love of order and precision.

Keen was a man of limitless energies, a diligent worker in the Calvinist tradition. Through unstinting, unflagging effort, he succeeded in each of the major tasks that circumstance had placed in his path.

Keen was a man of stern principles and unwavering convictions. His religious beliefs, strongly held and emphatically expressed, extended well beyond the customary Sabbath piety. Honorable behavior in daily business, in professional activities, in interpersonal relationships, in marital commitment, in personal obligations, for him were all one moral fabric. His ethical integrity allowed him to affirm, without arrogance, that the path he chose was the correct one. As a surgeon at the operating table, he once declared that there were two choices: his way and the wrong way.

Keen was witness to and an active participant in a third of this nation's history. He was born on the last day of Andrew Jackson's tenure as president and died during the depths of the Great Depression in the waning months of Herbert Hoover's administration. Keen saw active service as a battalion surgeon in the Battle of Bull Run during the Civil War, and also served in the Army in World War I (records indicate that he was the only commisioned officer to have served in both of these armed conflicts.) With Halsted, Gross and a few others, he was one of the acknowledged founders of modern American surgery. His patients included presidents from Grover Cleveland to Franklin D. Roosevelt.

He was friend to such leaders of medicine as Weir Mitchell, Oliver Wendell Holmes, William Osler and Joseph Lister. More than ten thousand medical students, principally at Jefferson Medical College, learned the rudiments of surgery and the principles of ethical practice from Keen's lectures and bedside conferences.

Where does one find the real W. W. Keen? Certainly he was honored during his lifetime by scores of universities, prestigious societies and grateful governments. But the honor, and responsibility, that involved him most profoundly was his election late in life to the presidency of the American Baptist Missionary Union. Keen was a God-fearing man; his greatest admiration was reserved for those of his professional colleagues who answered a higher calling to labor as medical missionaries. The travails of the resolute Dr. David Livingstone, who once declared: "I shall open up a path to the interior or perish," represented for Keen the highest that man could hope to achieve. Livingstone was his model of a life well invested. In later life, seeking his personal "path to the interior," Keen traveled the world in support of the many medical missions implanted by his church in Africa, Asia and Oceania.

Was there, Keen speculated, a sacred mission worthy of pursuit beyond the conventional teaching of the gospel? He answered this in his 1906 presidential address to the Baptist Mission Union, declaring: "The ravages of disease . . . inevitably caused attempts [by our missionaries] to teach the first principles of sanitation often combined with elementary medical treatment; and hence the medical missionary, the hospital, and other agencies, sought to ameliorate the physical sufferings . . . of the heathen world. In other words, there has been an evolution in missions as inevitable as it is desirable."

Keen derived immense satisfaction in having trained the scores of physicians to travel to distant lands as medical missionaries, carrying with them the precious gifts of anesthesia, vaccines, aseptic surgery and the general principles of public health and sanitation. He took pride in the 379 hospitals, 783 dispensaries, 67 medical and nursing colleges and 533 orphanages and leprosaria established and supported by the churches of this country. And it pleased Keen deeply that his cherished church was vigorously supporting the right of women in India to be educated. His personal commitment to a woman's right of access to higher education may be found in his decades of earnest teaching at Philadelphia's Women's Medical College and in his trusteeship at Vassar College.

Keen saw no conflict between his religious convictions and his vocal advocacy of Darwin's writings and experimental vivisection. In his address to the Baptist Missionary Union, he declared that "ignorance is the handmaiden of superstition and vice," and he considered the existence of illiteracy to be a major sin. He declared that education, in company with cleanliness, was next to godliness.

Others recognized Keen as an outstanding patriot, as one of the fathers of modern surgery, as America's first brain surgeon, as the author of hundreds of significant medical articles and textbooks, and as teacher to generations of young physicians. Keen viewed himself as a medical evangelist striving to fulfill his fervent belief that a human life, to be purposeful, must aspire to the virtues of honesty, sobriety, frugality and industry.

In this volume, Keen James has provided us with a faithful distillation of the writings of his eminent ancestor. Read these pages and you will surely enter the world of W. W. Keen.

Stanley M. Aronson, M.D.
Brown University
Providence, Rhode Island

Keen
of
Philadelphia

I

—••⟨ ⟩⟨ ⟩••—

The Early Years

BEGINNINGS

I WAS BORN JANUARY 19th, 1837, at No. 232 South 3rd St., then a residential part of the city.[1] The house is still standing (1912)[2] but has been long occupied only for business purposes. Adjoining it on the north, I well remember, was the Willing Mansion,[3] which stood at the front of a large garden extending to Willing's Alley and from 3rd to 4th St. In the garden were a number of large trees, which were the favorite haunt of the swarms of bees from my father's garden at the rear of our own house. One of my very earliest recollections is of his being called out of church to hive them.

We lived on South 3rd Street till I was a little over six years of age. My parents had eight children, of whom five died when thirteen years of age or under. I was the sixth child. There was an earlier William, and at my birth I too was named William. There was an earlier Susan, who died before I was born, and the child next younger than I was also named Susan. I just remember her (she died when I was five). The eighth and last child was a boy named Baron Stow, after a warm friend of my parents', Baptist clergyman Rev. Dr. Baron Stow, of Boston. My dear father and mother had one overwhelming grief, when two of their children, the first William and the first Susan, died of scarlet fever on successive Sundays.

My older brothers, George and Charles, were not strong, and it was thought that a trip to Europe would do them good. They sailed from New York, and all of us, except for seven-year-old brother Baron, went over to see them off. To go to New York, passengers had to take the Walnut Street ferry to Tacony, where the railroad terminated. The journey could be made in less than a day—about four hours, I think. A trip to Europe in the 1840s meant more preparation than that for a flight to the Pole does now.

On our return from New York, we found that Baron, who had been left in

3

Keen family. Left to right: Will; Charles Burtis Keen (brother); Susan Budd Keen (mother); Fanny Louisa Colladay Keen (George's wife); William W. Keen (father); Baron Stow Keen (brother); George Budd Keen (brother) [Daguerreotype by Langenheim Bros., Philadelphia]

the care of Aunt Anna Reeves, had been taken ill with "croup" (which is now known as diphtheria). I remember how my parents would walk the floor with him at night, even Michael the coachman taking his turn, while the poor child gasped for breath. After ten days, the little fellow died, choked to death. The moment George and Charles heard of Baron's death, they returned from Europe, but it took a long time for the letter to reach them, and their return could not be made in less than two weeks' time. (They went both ways by a side-wheeler.) My mother and father were prostrated by the death of their "Benjamin," but eventually they derived some comfort from the daguerreotype of the entire family which we had taken before our trek to New York.

The daguerreotype was a wholly new invention at the time, and we had to sit still for fifteen or twenty minutes, I think. The only firm in Philadelphia which took such pictures was the Langenheim Brothers, whose studio was in the present Stock Exchange Building, at 3rd and Dock Streets. My nephew Frank Keen has the original, still in excellent condition.

While living on Third Street, I remember clearly, we were members of the old

First Baptist Church, then in La Grange Place, directly adjoining the old Christ Church, whose chimes summoned us to worship. I especially well remember the Sunday school and its circle of seats for the scholars, the teacher occupying a chair placed in a break in the circle. I also remember Rev. Dr. George B. Ide (whose daughter later married my brother Charles), preaching in his sonorous voice from the high pulpit, behind which hung a red pleated curtain. General Duncan, with his long white hair and (as I learned later) his new wife, sat just in front of us. Long after we moved to West Philadelphia, my parents kept up their warm friendship with the old stand-bys there: Mrs. Keyser, Mrs. Inglis (née Keyser), Miss Mary Hallman, the Wattsons, Hansells, Butchers, and many other household names and faces from my childhood. Deacon Wattson was the great-grandfather of Howard Butcher Jr., my son-in-law, and Washington Butcher was *his* grandfather.

Before she moved into our house, in her last years, my grandmother Budd lived on the north side of Pine Street, west of Third. I was constantly running around there. The ice cream man had one "freezer" of lemon and one of vanilla, which he used to trundle around in a wheelbarrow. He would scoop out a "cent's worth" (a generous tablespoonful) into a small wine glass, with which was furnished a little spoon, both glass and spoon being washed "clean" in a pail of water that accompanied the freezers.

Then too, I recall the "A.P."s, delicious cookies made on 2nd below Chestnut, I think, by a certain **A**nne **P**age and embossed with her initials.[4] They don't make such ice cream or such cookies any longer—although I sometimes have a dim suspicion that an aging palate may have something to do with this idea.

When I was about five or six, the "Millerite" excitement began. Followers of a man named William Miller were led to believe that 1843 would see the Second Coming of Christ and that Judgment Day was at hand.[5] Some even put on their white ascension robes and went out to George's Hill, prepared to ascend. I heard it talked about at the table and thought there was little hope for such a little sinner as I was. I slept in a trundle-bed, which was slid under my parents' four-poster during the day and drawn out at night. The windows of the bedroom faced south, so the moon was visible. I can vividly recall lying awake in my bed, anxiously watching the sky, and remember the fright I repeatedly felt whenever the clouds near the moon grew thinner and the light grew brighter and brighter. I looked expectantly at the rifts in the clouds to see if the Lord was not appearing then and there on His great white throne.

Then again, I remember well the great comet of 1843, with its long narrow tail, a sight which filled me with curiosity and wonder, and, I suspect, not a little fear. Youth is always ignorant and credulous, and credulity easily culminates in superstition.[6] This, I suppose, was the origin of my fear. My parents regarded it, I am sure, with entire equanimity.

My mother once sent me to the drug store, and while I was waiting for the prescription to be filled, I saw something which I took for candy and helped myself. It tasted pretty good, so I took another, and then another, and then bought a box of them, which I proceeded to eat on the way home.

But the tempting things had ipecac in them, and pretty soon it began to get in its work. Oh, how sick I was! Everything came up except my boots, and I was sure I was going to die. After that, whenever my father gave me any money, he used to say, "Now don't buy any bronchial trochies with it, will you?"

I didn't hear the last of it for fifteen years.

My father's health having suffered from his grief at the second Susan's death, in 1842, as well as an attack of erysipelas, he was advised by his physician to move to the country. So in May of 1843, he bought the lot at the southwest corner of 37th and Chestnut, where the Presbyterian Church now stands. It had an old stone house, facing Chestnut, and a stable at the Sansom Street end of the lot. In this house there was a fine Dutch oven, in which many good things, such as bread and pies, were baked, and many a succulent offering roasted, such as the little pig which was always served with the traditional lemon in its mouth. It (the oven, not the pig) was lined with fire-brick, then filled with wood and fired. It was set deep and solidly in the wall, as I remember, and was over two feet wide and over three feet deep. When all the wood had been reduced to ashes, the oven was swept clean, the pies or meat were placed inside, and the door was tightly closed. (Our neighbors also borrowed the use of it, from time to time.)

We lived there for some three or four years and then moved into the house which my father built on the middle 300-foot lot of the 500-foot square on the north side of Chestnut between Margaretta (36th) and Park (37th). At the time, the lot had been an open and unfenced pasture where young men and maidens gathered for summer evening frolics. It measured about an acre and a half, extending over 200 feet back to Ludlow Street, where he built a stable and a coach house, a hothouse, a hot and a cold grapery.

We had both a flower garden and a vegetable garden, where Father raised strawberries[7] and blackberries, in addition to potatoes, peas, lima beans, beets, cabbage, lettuce, corn, asparagus, and other vegetables. He also kept a cow and some chickens, so I had *almost* a real country life. When Michael, our gardener, farmer, coachman, ostler, and general man Friday, was digging potatoes, it was great fun for me to partially spit the useless little potato nubbins on the point of a sharp stick and launch them far into the air.

Michael Montague was for many years an institution—the "Fuller" of that day.[8] He was a faithful and industrious Irishman, as may be judged by his multifarious offices. After many years, he developed a rare and curiously slow pulse (down even below 40), and, at rare intervals, epileptic attacks. I am surprised now that we did not appreciate the danger of his driving a pair of spirited horses. One day, Hattie was paying a call at a house near 20th and Chestnut, when two gentlemen walking by saw that the lines had fallen from Michael's hands and that he was lying limp on the seat. Investigating, they discovered that he was dead, apparently having choked to death in a fit. What a fortunate escape for Hattie that it had not happened while they were in transit!

Michael was succeeded by Conrad, a German and an excellent farmer. My only recollection of him is of his reply to my father, when he told him he ought to be married: "No, Mr. Keen, de vimun is qveer tings. I tink I von't haf much to do mid 'em."

(My rough sketches of the house and grounds at 3621 Chestnut leave much to be desired, but they are, in general, fairly correct.[9] I am not quite certain of the topography to the north of the greenhouse, or of parts of the greenhouse itself.)

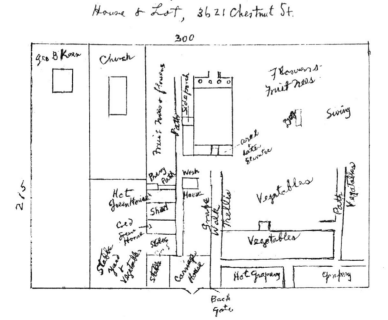

House and lot plan of Keen's childhood home

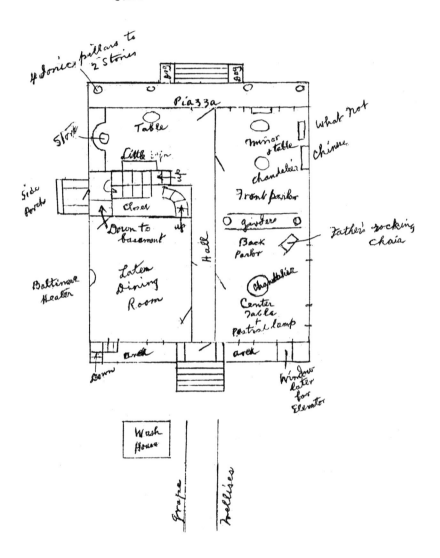

First floor of Keen's childhood home

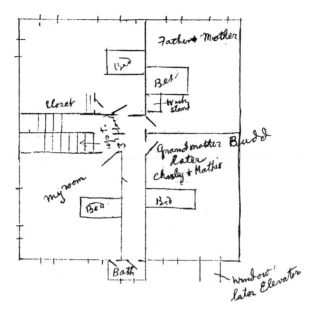

2ᵈ floor 3621 Chestnut St.

Second floor and basement of Keen's childhood home

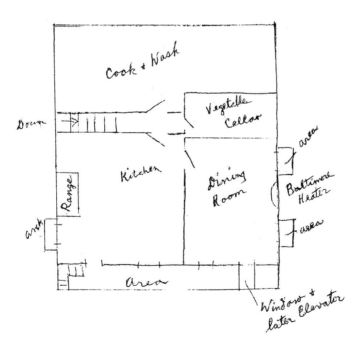

Basement 3621 Chestnut St.

We were accustomed to spending many evenings in pleasant talk and village gossip, on our piazza. On each of the two cheek blocks[10] there was an iron greyhound, which children were always eager to mount. To the west of the house, standing four-square and facing south, there was an iron Saint Bernard, which served as a base for games such as "prisoners' base" and "I spy." Farther out, there were ten or fifteen fine trees, chiefly oak and chestnut. Among them was one fine persimmon. My unwary mouth soon taught me the virtue of watchful waiting for the well-ripened (and then delicious) fruit.

The trees were the noble remnants of the primeval forest which once covered the whole territory. The woods began in earnest, where some mild hunting could be done, at 40th and Pine and extended for a long stretch out to what is now 50th Street and Woodland Avenue (then called Darby Road) and beyond.

At the front of our grounds we had some beautiful flower beds, two large magnolias (*M. conspicua*) and another (*M. glauca*) to the east. When in blossom, they were indeed beauties. A large copper beech grew a little to the south and east of the side porch and was highly ornamental. We had scattered at various points some excellent pear trees, which Father imported from France. (I remember my boyish excitement and pride over our "French importation.") There were also peach, cherry, plum, apricot, nectarine, and other fruit trees, plus trellises and espaliered grape and Lawton blackberry vines.

Father was very strict in some things and very unconventional in others. He *never* allowed us boys to come to the table in our shirt sleeves, even in the hottest weather. But when the streetcars were installed on Chestnut Street, following the construction of the Chestnut Street bridge over the Schuylkill, in the late '60s, father would hail an approaching car in a stentorian voice. In those days the cars stopped at any point where they were hailed, rather than only at the intersections, and he would occasionally carry two small bouquets and give them to the conductor and the driver "for their wives or sweethearts."

When my own young family was settled at 1619 Chestnut, he would bring a basket of fruit, flowers, or vegetables to our house, two or three times a week. As he entered, he always hooted, which sent the children scurrying into hiding. His pretended searching for them on the upper shelves of closets, while they were bursting with suppressed laughter on the floor, and the final shouts as he at last discovered them, who of us can forget? How much pleasure it gave us all!

He had a blithesome spirit and was full of fun. Once, at 3621, Michael found a nest of field mice, while digging potatoes. Mother was one of the few who had a quilting frame, and she was hosting a quilting party in our parlor for friends from the old First Baptist Church, Mrs. Wattson, Mrs. Washington Butcher, Mrs. Standish Hansell, Mrs. Keyser and her daughter, Mrs. Inglis, and others. Sitting around the quilting frame, they were busily at work when Father came in and, opening both hands, dropped the mice in the middle of the quilt. Then such a screaming and scattering—and such fun afterwards!

Father usually wore a diamond breastpin in his shirt front, his only piece of jewelry, so far as I can recall.

We always had roast beef (and always "the finest piece of beef we have ever had on the table") for Saturday dinner, which was served cold at Sunday dinner so as to give the cook as little work as possible on the Sabbath. Father collected the scraps from our plates, at the end of the meal, cut them up very fine, then salted—and especially peppered—them well. After dinner, we usually strolled around the garden, stable, graperies, and greenhouse, and the table-scraps were given to the chickens. They all got to know this routine so well that the moment he appeared and *clucked* once or twice, they were thick around his feet, eager for the feast.

One late spring morning, when the vines in the grapery were growing rapidly, I noticed the tender young shoots and marked on the trellis the exact point of one shoot. This was just before church. About two hours later, I again marked the point, noting that it had grown one and three-quarter inches, nearly a sixty-fourth of an inch per minute. Using a good magnifying glass, I could literally have *seen* it grow. I have often been sorry that I did not repeat this kind of observation a number of times, to determine the maximum rate of growth, not only in grape vines but in other plants as well.

George's boys, in Father's later life, were often a source of annoyance to him, on account of their pranks. Father was very proud of his fine grapes and was constantly sending them to the sick, or to friends. Regularly every autumn, he would take a specially fine large basket of his most choice bunches to one or more monthly meetings of the board of directors of the Western Saving Fund. On one occasion, when the grapery was locked, two or three of the boys crept through the open ventilators in the front, lowest section. These were simply boards on hinges, and the opening was just wide enough for them to squeeze through. They reached up to every bunch in the house and picked off the *one lowest* grape that completed the apex of the bunch. Father was really (and justly) incensed and banished them from the house and garden for thirty days. As fruit was then very abundant, the punishment certainly fitted the offense, which was not very damaging but certainly most irritating.

(Possibly some of my own daughters' pranks, at the expense of their grandfather and uncles in Fall River, may have been parallel in forgivable iniquity.)

Summer evenings we usually spent on the piazza, when George's family, the McLeods, Cousin Jane Burtis, and a number of other friends, would drop in. I well remember the evenings when we adjourned to the basement dining room for cookies and ice-cold watermelon or cantaloupe. We often went around to Mrs. Burns's, on Market above 36th, for her ice cream and cake. One time, Charley said, "Mother, they have lemon and strawberry. Which will you have?" Her prompt reply, "Vanilla," produced laughter for years afterwards.

One of our early horses was a fine bay named "Prince." Father thought we could afford a pair (and our first carriage took four). Mother and I would spend a day in Kensington, from time to time, visiting Uncle Burtis, who had married a sister of my father's. He had some large mills, and their clattering machinery was a wonder to my youthful eyes and ears.

Helen was the daughter of my uncle, Charles Keen, and his first wife. His second marriage was not the success that it might have been, though there was never any quarrel. Charley ('the Count') and "Tillie" (Matilda, after her mother) were the children of that marriage to Mrs. Frick, who had two daughters by *her* first marriage. Our visits there were always formal and constrained.

Aunt Anna Reeves (the mother of Mary Banes) had been long separated from her worthless husband (as I was told; I never saw him) and lived near Uncle Charlie's house on a small street (Ellen St.), in what she facetiously called a little one-eyed house (that is, with only one window to accompany the door at the street level). She occasionally would spend a day with us, especially when the corn was ripe. (Father would often trick her by sneaking his cobs onto her plate and then point out her gluttony.)

When Father was trying out a new horse to replace Prince, who had aged so that he had to be shot and turned over to the glue factory (we had no zoo then), Baron, who was not much over five years old, proceeded to cut all the hair off this strange horse's tail. (Fortunately the horse kept his hooves to himself, while this barbering was going on.) While a new tail was growing, that horse was the queerest looking beast I ever saw. I do not remember whether or not he was provided with a caudal toupee, but my father had "to pay" for him, of course.

There were no means then known of cold storage, or even of canning. The preserving of strawberries, peaches, pears, green grapes, and other fruits—and the making of currant, grape, or other jellies—was a regular occupation of every housewife in the appropriate season. Will and Sam Colladay (Fanny's brothers), or John and Louis Evans, or some other boys, and I, were sure to be on hand at such times, especially when the green grapes were being preserved. Bread spread with the "skimmings" (or "scum," as my daughters insolently call it) was fit for a king. Our faces glistened with pleasure, when such culinary treats were announced, and soon after were sticky and plastered over from ear to ear with sweet delight.

When the tumblers (and I) were filled, then came my job of helping Mother to cover them. We cut out a round piece of rather thin writing paper, dipped it in a saucer of pure brandy, and laid it on top of the jam, jelly, or preserve. It was my special duty to cut larger round pieces of more substantial paper and paste one over each tumbler, later labeling the lot. (There were none of the modern patent jars, in the earliest days.) It is surprising how effectual this method proved to be. It was rare that more than two or three of all the two or three hundred tumblers would ferment.

We usually had only two household servants, a cook and a maid who served as chambermaid and waitress. The latter function was not very burdensome, since the meals were not served in courses. She had only to place the meal on the table, remove it, and bring on the dessert. We did our own reachin', as a rule. The cook was paid $1.50 a week, the maid, $1.25, and since the basement kitchen adjoined the dining room, much labor was saved.

Later, when there were only Father and Mother, or those two and Helen Keen Weir (a dear, good cousin who took care of the house as Father and Mother grew more feeble); or still later, when Mother was an invalid and confined to her room, and there was Father and Miss Savage (the housekeeper), and occasionally me, the "little" room (as we always called it) at the northeast corner on the first floor was used as a dining room.

Our house at 3621 was furnished comfortably but plainly. I have indicated on the floor plan the various chambers, and in my sketch of the parlor, I have indicated where the principal pieces of furniture stood. There were two beautiful glass chandeliers in the front and back parlors, and it was no easy job for Mother, when house cleaning, to wash every one of the pendant triangular crystals, with an octagonal glass star above each crystal. My first memory of the solar spectrum was from my observation of those crystals.

One night, my father nearly shot my mother. (He was subject to dreams and would sometimes talk and even cry out in his sleep. I often heard him.) Our village had little or no protection at night. The streets were not lighted. There were no watchmen on duty at night, or at least I do not remember hearing about any, for we were an orderly community. Burglaries, therefore, were a rude shock to us all. My father bought a loud watchman's rattle[11] and a pistol. The latter he kept under his pillow. Our only light at night was a taper—a wooden button pierced by a short wick, which floated on the surface of oil in a simple tumbler. It is even possible that this taper, always used in time of sickness (since it was dimmer than a candle), was not lighted, so that the room was almost totally dark.

At any rate, my mother was moving quietly around the room, in the middle of the night, when my father suddenly awakened, and in his dazed condition, half awake and half asleep, seized his pistol and was on the point of shooting the "burglar" when she sank down at the foot of the bed, screaming with terror. It was a close call.

Our beds were all four-posters, of which one or two were of mahogany and handsomely carved. They were high enough to allow a trundle bed to be pushed under in the daytime. Valences hung on all sides of the bed, except at the head, to conceal the trundle bed. Curtains at the head and foot were looped up or tied at the middle, for almost every bed.

Our house was only one of three buildings on this lot. At the eastern side of the lot, my father later built a house for my brother George and his family. Between that house and our own, he gave a fifty-front-foot lot to the First Baptist Church in West Philadelphia. This later became the Epiphany Baptist Church, which still later merged with the Berean Baptist Church to become the present Chestnut Street Baptist Church, having moved beyond 40th Street.

My father later converted our stable into an excellent dwelling, but as I recall, when he gave it, rent-free, to our church for a parsonage, the village was greatly scandalized. But he insisted that, inasmuch as the Founder of Christianity was born in a stable, it was logically fit for one of His ministers to live in one.

My father organized the First Baptist Church in West Philadelphia, and he was its main support. It was into this church that I was baptized, in 1850, when thirteen years old. With my brother Charles, I entered into all its Christian and social activities. Charles served for over thirty years as church organist and music director, and for many years he was also the superintendent of the Sunday school.

My father *bought* back the lot on which the first building stood, when the new church was built. This second church was begun not long before the Panic of 1857, but Father was determined that it should not fail. He begged a considerable amount from his friends, sold his own carriage and pair, sold the grapes from his graperies, and in general curtailed family expenses wherever possible and "gave the money to the Lord." Such sacrifices are as rare as they are admirable. After my father's death, the place was bought (and is still occupied) by the Pennsylvania Home for Indigent Widows and Single Women.[12]

Later, after the death of both parents, my brother Charles placed a brass memorial tablet on the wall of the second church edifice, at the southeast corner of 37th and Chestnut, com-memorating the services of our parents to the Church. This, I am told, is to be removed to the Chestnut Street Baptist Church before the building at 36th and Chestnut is torn down. I would like this to be seen to. *It is now* (1915) *in place.*

I remember one amusing incident there. The church building had a basement vestry or lecture room, two steps below the level of the ground, which was used during the week, the auditorium for Sunday services being above it. John Francis, the colored sexton, discovered from his seat at the back of the room, one Friday evening, that the ladies were drawing aside their skirts and moving away from the middle aisle. The cause of the disturbance was an inoffensive toad, who had entered the door at the rear and was on his way to the pulpit. John decided to remove it by means of a dustpan and brush. First he placed the pan behind the toad and tried to sweep him with the brush, backwards into the pan. Mr. Toad hopped with ease over the approaching brush. After two or three vain endeavors, John decided upon a rear action, instead of a frontal attack. So he placed the pan in front and tried to take him in the rear with the brush. Mr. Toad simply hopped over the pan as easily as he had cleared the brush. The first series of failures had gotten most of us giggling, but the second fiasco resulted, willy-nilly, in an outburst of loud laughter, and the prayer meeting was at an end.

The toad in church seemed to indicate the rural character of West Philadelphia, which was called "Hamiltonville," after William Hamilton, who occupied a large yellow mansion and lived in considerable grandeur,[13] but who had died before we moved there. We usually referred to the area as "the village." The houses were quite far apart. From building line to building line, all of Chestnut Street was grass save three bare furrows, one worn by the horses and two by the wheels. No paving, no sidewalks, not even boards to walk on—and very disagreeable in wet weather.

West Philadelphia was entirely independent of "the city," which was limited by Vine and Cedar (now South) Streets and by the two rivers. The only bridge over the Schuylkill was at Market Street, and the only means of reaching the city were by walking or by having one's own carriage. It was a great event when, to accommodate the businessmen, a "bus" regularly went to the city in the morning and returned at night. We boys used to call its driver "Santa Anna," after the defeated Mexican general, because each of them wore a wooden peg leg. There was a current legend that, when teased beyond endurance, our Santa Anna would suddenly detach this wooden leg and hurl it, with great precision, at the nearest offender.

The first murder trial I remember, as a boy (and I read every word of the newspaper accounts), was that of Professor John Webster, who taught Chemistry at Harvard until he was convicted and hanged, in 1850, for killing Dr. George Parkman, of Harvard Medical School.

As far as I can remember, the only houses on Chestnut Street from the Schuylkill River to the present 40th Street—beyond which were woods and farms—were Joseph Keen's house at 32nd; the Newton Grammar School, below 36th; Mr. Colladay's house (his daughter Fanny, a descendant of David Rittenhouse, was married to my brother George), at the northwest corner of 36th and Chestnut; Rudulph Evans's house, between 36th and 37th, opposite our second home; our first home, at 37th and Chestnut; two residences between 37th and 38th; Miss Ellen Price's residence on the north side of the street and occupying the entire lot from 38th to 39th; and the Academy, just east of 40th Street. Just nine buildings in all, in the ten blocks.[14]

A notable event was the establishment of a winter course of lectures at the Academy. Though I was old enough to go, my memory retains nothing of the lectures, though it records the fact that I headed the family procession, carrying a lantern in order to find the pitfalls, either by its aid or by falling into them. On re-reading this, I recall distinctly a lecture read in the Academy by Mr. James Allen, of our Church. He was a well-educated Englishman, and I remember the deep impression made upon my young mind by one phrase he used, "looking through nature up to nature's God." I had never heard it before, nor did I know that it was a quotation,[15] but the felicitous and poetic idea and wording impressed me very deeply.

The house that my father built in 1846-47 was my home until I settled into practice in the city, in 1866. It was a large house of wood, two stories high, with an attic and a basement kitchen and dining room. It had four large Ionic columns extending from the piazza to the roof, and it stood on the north side of Chestnut across the street from the Rudulph Evans house. He was a brother of Dr. Thomas Evans, later the well-known dentist in Paris,[16] and John, his oldest son, and I were boon companions.[17]

Many times since then, John and I and our families have met in Paris. Only recently (1909-11) have he and his wife both passed away. When I was studying in Paris, in 1864-65, his uncle was very urgent that I should settle in Paris to practice. He promised me his support, an important factor since he was an influential figure at the court of Napoleon III, as well as in French and American society. But I decided not to stay there. What a different career I should have had, had I accepted! Providence has been very kind in helping me to decide these recurring questions, and, as it seems to me now, always rightly.

The amusements and the reading for boys and girls, in those early days, were far less varied and extensive than those of my children and grandchildren. We boys played hoops, town-ball, "I spy," tag, shinny (or hockey), and prisoners' base; and the others swam, rowed, and skated. We coasted on our sleds, and occasionally, when there was snow enough, we had sleigh-rides. Others also fished or went out to shoot birds, in the nearby woods. I was never very strong, as a boy, and was hampered by being nearsighted, as well as short of stature. More inclined to books than to sports, I never learned to swim, fished but little, and scarcely ever used a gun. (It should be pointed out that none of us got more than two weeks of summer holiday from school.)

The girls played at tag, grace hoops, battledore, and shuttlecock, but it was not considered lady-like for them to swim or skate, and rarely to row. Our mixed sports at picnics (and rather rare evening parties, which began by eight and were over by ten) were Forfeits, "Pussy wants a Corner," Post Office, Hunt the Slipper, Jerusalem, and Copenhagen, the last of which degenerated into a boisterous series of almost athletic contests for a kiss.

Our reading was practically confined to *The Thousand and One Nights, Robinson Crusoe, Gulliver's Travels, Swiss Family Robinson,* Bunyan's *Pilgrim's Progress,* and *Sandford of Merton.* The "Rollo" books were published when I was a grown-up boy and were, so far as I can recall, the first of the distinctly "children's" books. There was no St. Nicholas or anything approaching the modern Christmas in scope.[18]

GENEALOGY

My father, William Williams Keen, after whom I was named, was born on September 4th, 1797. He would have been born in Philadelphia, except that, because of the yellow fever epidemic in that year,[19] his mother had taken refuge in her father's home in the nearby countryside of Tacony.

He was a lineal descendant of Jöran Kyn, a Swede,[20] who arrived in New

Sweden aboard the *Fama*, in 1643, in the retinue of Johan Printz, the first governor of New Sweden. (Printz was a man of great weight in the community, as he is said to have tipped the scale at 400 pounds.) The colony was dispatched to the New World by Oxenstierna, the chancellor to Gustavus Adolphus.

At the south entrance to Philadelphia's City Hall, there are two bronze tablets, the one on the right commemorating the settlement of the Swedes, and the one on the left, the settlement of the Dutch, who followed the Swedes. Jöran Kyn is cited as one of the prominent citizens of the Swedish colony. Few would recognize him as my ancestor on account of the spelling. When the Dutch succeeded the Swedes, they sacrificed the spelling in order to preserve the pronunciation. In those early days, people wrote little and talked much—a habit not yet lost—and *Kyn* in spoken Dutch would have been pronounced "Kine"; so the Dutch authority changed the spelling to *Kien*. The oldest deed in the possession of the family (1676) is for 300 acres of land bought by "Hans Jurianson (i.e., the son of Jurian—or Jöran)[21] Kien of Delaware River, husbandman." The "annual quitrent for the 300 acres to be paid to His Majesty's representative in America" was "three bushels of good winter wheat."

Originally, the family were Swedish Lutherans. In the Gloria Dei Lutheran Church,[22] the oldest adult grave is that of my great-great-grandfather, John Keen. It is on the west side of the path running south from the south (or side) door of the church. The Swedish congregations and the English people and clergy interchanged for many years, but in 1845, it became the Old Swedes' Episcopal Church.

One branch of the family settled in Oxford Township, north of the old city of Philadelphia, and a number of that branch are interred in the cemetery of Trinity Episcopal Church. A still larger number of the family are buried at the Pennypack (now Lower Dublin) Baptist Church, in Bustleton.

The substantial stone house built and occupied by John Keen, still stands at what was—and still may be—known as "Keen's Lane," near Tacony. *(This is an error. Gregory Keen informs me (1925) it was pulled down many years ago.)* In 1797, when the city was visited by its second epidemic of yellow fever, my grandmother and a sister-in-law took refuge in this old family residence, as previously noted. A child was born to each of them: my father, William Williams Keen; and Rebecca Keen, daughter of Isaac and Sarah (Knowles) Keen—who was later Mrs. Rebecca Miles.

(At my mother's funeral, in 1873, "Cousin Becky" Miles not only appeared but also returned to the house to spend the night. We children[23] were indignant at her intrusion on my father's grief at such a time, but it proved to be the greatest blessing to him. Though elderly and quite deaf, she got to reminiscing with him about old times and old friends, and this took him perforce away from his sorrow. Two weeks later, she gave me an old family deed, old wills, and other family documents, which I have passed along to [my daughter] Corinne.)

My great-grandfather Matthias Keen was twice married. His first wife was Mary Swift, and his second wife was Margaret Thomas. The latter was a Baptist, of Welsh descent, and evidently a woman of great force of character: She not only converted *her* husband from the Episcopal Church to the Baptist, but she also persuaded him to leave the bulk (possibly all) of his property to her children only. I have no idea how much this amounted to, but the evident injustice of it caused a breach in the family that was not healed until 1843, when we moved to 37th and Chestnut, in West Philadelphia. Nearby on Chestnut Street (where the Drexel Institute of Technology now stands) lived Joseph Swift Keen, the grandson of Matthias and Mary Swift Keen. He and my father completely ignored the old quarrel, and the families became friends again. Joseph's son Gregory is the author of *The Descendants of Jöran Kyn of New Sweden.*

My mother was a descendant of Rev. Thomas Budd, who was an Oxford M.A. and the vicar, successively, at Montacute and Martock, in Somersetshire. Under the influence of George Fox, he became a Quaker and in 1663 was imprisoned in Ilchester, where it was expected he that he would recant his opinions and return to the established church.[24] Little did the court know that Budd was made of sterner stuff.[25] He adhered steadfastly to his beliefs and died in prison seven years later. I am proud to reckon such a "jailbird" as an ancestor. In 1910, Florence and I visited Ilchester, Montacute, and Martock. Ilchester, although the county seat and on the main direct road between London and Exeter, has languished since Jeffreys' day. The inhabitants believe, so we were told, that this has been the result of the "Bloody Assizes." The jail has long since disappeared, not one stone left standing upon another. All the records, too, have disappeared. The old courthouse alone remained, and of this I had a photograph made.

Thomas Budd's two sons emigrated to New Jersey, and many of their descendants still live there. Budd's Lake[26] is named after them. I have in my desk a number of papers tracing their descent and other facts pertaining to the family. Prominent among those published are *The History of the Budd Family* and *The Early History of the Provinces of New Jersey.*

My mother's mother, Susannah Budd, born in 1769, was the daughter of John Britton. She married George Budd on November 29th, 1792, and died on December 22nd, 1848, when I was almost twelve years old. As a widow, with all her faculties unimpaired, she lived with our family for many years, at 3621 Chestnut Street.

Her father had a considerable farm, separated from Valley Forge by the crest of a moderate ridge. *(The fine old house is still standing* [1915]. *We visited it two or three years ago, and Corinne took some photographs.)* I have often heard her tell how, in the dreadful winter of 1777, when she was eight years old, Washington came to her father's farm a number of times seeking food for his men and fodder for his horses. Though he had none of his own, he was very fond of children, especially little girls. My grandmother used to tell me, with justifiable pride, how he would pet and caress her, chucking her under the chin, and so forth. I judge from the miniature portraits that she must have been a very attractive child.

This recollection demonstrates two things: It shows how young our nation is, and it testifies to my own age to realize that there is only one person between George Washington and me.

KEEN'S EARLY EDUCATION

When we moved to West Philadelphia, the first school I attended was the Newton Grammar School, on the south side of Chestnut Street below 36th, then not only a grammar school, but with primary grades down to A, B, and C. From there, in February of 1849, when I was just twelve years old—the age limit being twelve—I entered the Central High School, then on Juniper Street below Market. Its principal was, as I later found out, a fine and scholarly man, though we found him to be cold-mannered and un-genial. His name was Dr. John S. Hart, but we young idiots, with the perversity of pupils the world over, dubbed him the "Juniper Street Humbug."

It was here that I first discovered I was nearsighted. In the Newton School, we had been seated according to rank, and I had a desk in the front row, near the blackboard. But when we entered the Central High School (located where Wanamaker's now stands), we were seated alphabetically, and *K* in my class came far back. I could no longer see anything written or drawn on the blackboard. I was advised by my teacher to go to McAllister's (later Queen and Company), then the only optician, I suspect, in the city (on the south side of Chestnut and east of 10th). I well remember old Mr. McAllister, with his tray of spectacles, putting one on me and bidding me look at the bricks of the houses opposite. Whether I could see distinctly, and without discomfort, the lines of mortar between the bricks was the standard by which my glasses were chosen.

Not altogether a bad plan, until the advent of Ezra Dyer, of Harvard, who had just come back from Europe, where he had learned more accurate methods by which to test letters and lines. He was for some years the only man in Philadelphia who could scientifically fit a person out for the proper glasses. If I recollect it rightly, the correction for astigmatism came somewhat later.

One of my fellow students, though not my classmate at the high school, was Ignatius L. Donnelly, whose fantastic title for his Commencement address, I remember, was a poem entitled "Love and Whiskers." He later became a well-known scholar, warmly taking the position that Francis Bacon was the real author of Shakespeare's plays.

When Lajos Kossuth, the Hungarian patriot, visited Philadelphia, in 1849 or 1850 (having escaped after the failure of the Insurrection of 1848, when all of Europe was in political ferment), and was to be received at Central High School, a number of students presented themselves as candidates for the honor of delivering an address of welcome.[27] With true freshman impudence—I'm not sure but that I ought to say "true Keen temerity"—I wrote out my masterpiece. I did not know what form my exordium should take, but I remember I began my manuscript well down at the middle of page one and then consulted my pastor, Rev. Dr. E.M. Levy, as to a suitable, and as I deemed necessary, rhetorical introduction. Alas for the vanity of human wishes! What a wet blanket was thrown over me when he thought that only "Illustrious Sir" should be enough to occupy—but surely not to fill—that yawning, yearning space. And when my speech and I were rejected in toto, I believed that I had been unjustly relegated to an undeserved oblivion.

However strange it may seem, I survived this dreadful blow and spoke my first little piece in public (saving some earlier appearances on the Sunday-school stage), in the Musical Fund Hall in February, 1853, receiving the wholly undeserved degree—Heaven save the mark!—of Bachelor of Arts, at age 16.

My father's early education had been very meager—though it was supplemented by extensive reading. He was a man of great intelligence, force of character, and breadth of view, and he was determined that his children should have the best possible education available, if they were willing to avail themselves of his generosity. He offered me a college course, and I eagerly accepted his proposal.

Before deciding whether to go to the University of Lewisburg or to Brown,[28] I visited the former in June of 1853. I went as the protégé of our pastor, Deacon Wattson, who was a member of the Board of Trustees at Lewisburg. The following account of my journey may be of interest.

The Sunbury branch of the Pennsylvania Railroad was not yet completed. At Harrisburg, we had to leave the railroad and proceed by boat, on the branch of the Pennsylvania State Canal that ran along the Susquehanna River. Approaching the mountains, we were passed through thirty-nine locks in the forty miles. It was lovely June weather, and the company, consisting almost wholly of Baptists, included a large number of well-known clergymen visiting the university for Commencement. Among us were quite a few young folks of about my own age, and we had no end of merriment, in the soft summer air of sunset and the full of the moon (we had embarked late in the afternoon). We told stories, sang, and often walked from one lock to the next.

The cabin had curtained berths on each side and a long dining table in the middle. When we sat down to supper, the captain, at the head of the long table, rapped on the table with his knife-handle and said, "Will the Rev. Dr. Dowling say grace?" Unfortunately, it had not occurred to him to forewarn the reverend gentleman that he would be called on to ask the blessing. We all bowed our heads and waited . . . and waited. Everyone knew that Dr. Dowling was on board, but still the grace was unsaid. At last, we glanced furtively up and down the table and discovered Dr. Dowling in a most perplexing and embarrassing plight. Dentists of those days made artificial teeth for show but not for mastication, and Dr. Dowling had taken out both uppers and lowers and put them in his trousers pockets. They seemed to be the most elusive teeth ever possessed by any man, but finally they were seized and installed, shielded by the corner of a napkin. Then, red-faced as a boiled lobster, he arose and said grace, offered amid an audible titter, which was temporarily prevented from becoming an outburst of laughter by our respect for the Cloth. As soon as he sat down, many tried to save his feelings by making some inane but supposedly facetious remark to furnish a reason for the irresistible laughter to which we finally gave way.

We disembarked at about four in the morning (at all events, in the early pre-dawn) on the bank of the canal. The young folks then walked the three miles to Lewisburg, while carriages were provided for our elders.

On my return I informed my father of my preference for Brown. My selection was made chiefly on account of the great reputation of President Francis Wayland, who in 1850 had introduced a new system, in which students were offered elective courses, for the first time, and modern science was placed on a par with the humanities.[29] (*He thus antedated President Eliot's work at Harvard by many years.*)

However, taking stock of my achievements thus far, I found that I was far behind in the entrance requirements for college. Accordingly, my father enrolled me in the school of Professor E.D. Saunders, on 39th Street above Market (where the Presbyterian Hospital is now), where I spent two years on Latin and Greek. Looking back at the matter, I find it clear that if I had gone to one of the great "fitting" schools of New England, such as the Phillips Academy in Andover, Massachusetts, or the one in Exeter, New Hampshire, I would easily have accomplished more and better work than I did in my time with Professor Saunders. He lacked system and accuracy and worked in a sort of helter-skelter way. Still, I did fairly well.

BROWN-BRED

When I entered Brown, in September of 1855, I was measured alongside of the boys who knew every rule and every exception in the Grammar of the Latin Language of Andrews and Stoddard, and the First Greek Book of Albert Harkness.[30] I thought I had had a fine "fitting," but when pitted against the Phillips Academy boys, I found I "wasn't in it," not at all in the same class with them. I had to buckle down to hard work, to put my nose to the grindstone, and to begin almost at the very beginning.

Earnest study for the purposes of obtaining an education was more the fashion in those days than these.[31] Athletics were poorly developed, and as a result, the health of the students was by no means as robust as at present. I took part in the then simple football games, in which everybody played, and in 1858 we started a college rowing club. Our "shell" was housed on the Seekonk River, and Adoniram Judson and I each had a wherry, i.e., a light lapstrake[32] boat rowed by one man. The day I turned twenty-one saw my first venture in the financial field, and I made a dismal failure of it. I borrowed one hundred dollars for three months at six percent to help pay for our rowing club boathouse, and for this I gave a note to old Rev. Dr. Alva Woods, a rich but mean old skinflint.[33] When the three months came around, the club failed to pay me, and I could not scrape together the hundred dollars, so I had to ask for an extension. I paid it later, interest and all, and thereby rehabilitated myself and avoided going into involuntary bankruptcy!

In Providence, I became a teacher in the Sunday school almost at once and in that first year had mounted a top hat, as became a college man. One Saturday that winter, a cold drizzle had frozen on the trees so that on Sunday morning the sight was splendid. On my way to early Sunday school, I was going down Waterman Street, which is quite steep and has a curve featuring a narrow and rather deep gutter. The pavement, alas, was almost a sheet of ice, and just as I reached the curve I tried to step over the gutter. At the same time, I raised my hat to greet some young ladies I knew, who were going uphill on the opposite sidewalk, and down I went, with top hat, umbrella, Bible, and I going in four different directions. Naturally, the girls couldn't help bursting into uproarious laughter, which they never bothered to repress or conceal. I picked up myself and my impedimenta, in confusion and in great heat, and made my way to the church, not, it may be imagined, in exactly a Sunday school mood.

Professors Lincoln and Angell and their wives were very kind to me at Brown. They rather took me under their wing and made me feel at home in their homes. Lincoln was superintendent of the Sunday school, and this naturally drew us together. As Angell was only seven years my senior (though I always thought of him then as *far* older than I), and had very recently been married to Professor Caswell's daughter, and as I knew the young people of the Angell and Caswell families very well, I became quite intimate there.

Judge Greene (author of *Old Grimes*) and Mrs. Greene had three daughters. Mary and Sarah became my two most intimate young lady friends, and these friendships have lasted through all our lives. The oldest sister, Mrs. Potter, a young widow and later the wife of ex-governor C.C. Van Zandt, I knew much less well. The elder of the other two married Samuel Eastman, of the Class of '57; the younger, who is still living, married Rev. Samuel Duncan, of the Class of '60.

I was drawn to Brown by that magnet, Francis Wayland, who in 1850 had introduced his "New System," by which Science was placed on the same level as the Classics, and which allowed for electives. When Dr. James [Burrill] Angell became the president of the University of Michigan, in 1871, he introduced Wayland's ideas and methods. Nearly all of the present great state universities in the West were modeled after the Michigan pattern, so Brown was responsible, in no small measure, for the intellectual development of these noble institutions.

[James Rowland] Angell, one of my favorite teachers at Brown, was Professor of Modern Languages. Think of it! He taught French and German all by himself. Now, in 1925, there are over a dozen teachers of various levels, and Italian and Spanish have been added to the French and German. Angell, as a man of broad culture and high ideals, influenced me socially and personally, as well.

The entire faculty consisted of only twelve men, including the Registrar, Mr. [Lemuel H.] Elliott, who was commonly known as "Pluto."

The three men on the faculty to whom I owe the greatest intellectual debt were Lincoln, Chace, and Gammell. Lincoln's felicitous translations, his exact scholarship, and his broad views of what studying Latin meant (far more than a mere textual rendering) were most inspiring. He never pardoned inaccuracy or slovenliness in our translating: If it was not right, it was, in his own words, "precisely wrong."

Chace was a master in the exposition of Science. He taught Physiology, Geology, and Zoology and made them so fascinating that I could hardly wait from one recitation to the next. He was more esteemed by the scientists than by the theologians, for even in that early day there were Fundamentalists. He was thought of as a bit of a heretic, but they never attempted to bring him to book.

Gammell taught History, and in the right way, making it not merely a chronological record of dates and events but an unfolding of human development. He was always aware of the latest developments, especially in European history, and he made it so interesting that we were both taught and charmed. I have loved the subject of History ever since.

Each of these men encouraged questions, independent thinking, and reasoning, so that our minds were not only stored with facts but also were developed in the broadest way. Our essays[34] with them—and with Dunn, Professor of Rhetoric—were splendid training and to them I have always attributed my ability to successfully explain scientific facts to nonscientific readers. Many people have said to me, after having read various articles published in popular magazines such as *Harper's*, that they have enjoyed the lucid explanations so that they could readily understand what I was writing about. Then, too, in my lectures, I have followed the same method and gotten similar results. Whenever I want to explain a subject, I first try to reduce the elementary facts to the simplest possible statements. Then, proceeding one step at a time, from the now known to the as yet unknown, to show the natural development of the matter.

(My large scrapbook of Brunoniana, in the John Hay Library archive, should be consulted.) There is also a published list of the books I borrowed from the library, while an undergraduate, as assembled by librarian Harry Lyman Koopman. The two debating societies, the Philermenian and the United Brothers, also had fairly good libraries of current books, and I used them quite as much as the university library.

My friendships among college mates included not a few in classes other than '59. For example, I knew (but very slightly) Richard Olney, of '56; Eastman and Goodwin, among others, of '57; I knew John Hay, '58, quite well, and that friendship lasted until his death; Duncan Gordeon, Kirke Porter, and others, of '60; Tom Caswell, of '61; and a few in later classes. In my own class, Poinier (my roommate for two years), George Porter, and Adoniram and Elnathan Judson were close friends. Naturally, my companions were chiefly among the fraternity of the Alpha Delta Phi.

My college life was very happy, though we were always eager to hear from home. A student was postmaster and stood at the door of Manning Hall to hand out the mail as we came from prayers. I plodded along with my studies, being especially interested in mathematics, to which I attributed my love of order and precision. I abominate disorder—on my desk, in my office, in my wardrobe. I took the first prize in an extra examination for each of the first three years in college. (If there had been a Mathematics course in the senior year, I would have taken it, as well.) The winner in this competition was awarded a prize of ten dollars, which in my college days was by no means a despicable sum, and so I rather patted myself on the back, confident that I had answered every question correctly.

Professor Alexis Caswell was the Professor of Mathematics. He took our papers and decided who had passed the best examination. He died in 1877, but his older son, Dr. Edward Caswell, in going through his father's papers, not long after his death, actually found my three prize-winning examinations and sent them to me. Why the dear old teacher ever kept them, I cannot imagine, but I am very glad he did, for they gave my pride a sad jolt. The papers were bloody with the many corrections made in red ink. My wonder was how much bloodier must have been the papers of the other contestants![35] It has been a good lesson to me ever since—now nearly fifty years.

One amusing adventure, in 1858, was the trip to Barrington, where I was to give a lecture. Lizzie Sears (daughter of President Barnas Sears[36]), the two Greene sisters, Addy Judson, and Sam Duncan accompanied me as my guests, and we drove there from Providence, a distance of three or four miles. We started in ample time, and with a driver who "knew the way." All went along merrily, for a time, but when darkness came on, in the short winter day, the driver confessed that he was lost. Farm houses were very scarce, but I saw a light at last, quite a distance back from the road. I jumped off and hastened across a rough-plowed field, for we could not find any entrance road towards the light. The first thing I knew, I had run up against a sapling, which bent before my impact but, acting like a spring, recoiled and threw me sprawling. I had on an evening suit, and not only was it covered with dirt, but the legs of the trousers were badly torn, and the swallow-tail coat was ineffective as a covering.

Learning the correct road (and also that we were far out of our way), the driver then plied the whip, and we finally arrived, half an hour late, just as the audience had begun to disperse. They were good enough to return, and while they were being seated in the church, the girls of our party pinned up the rents and brushed off the dirt as well as possible. I gave my lecture. I did not roam about the platform, you may be sure, but stayed by the friendly and welcome shelter of the pulpit. In the front-row seats just below me were five enemies of my comfort and equanimity, who led the applause at every opportunity and otherwise plagued the life out of me. My chief subject was the Canterbury pilgrims, and I ended up with the first alleged "poem" I ever attempted. I have the manuscript in my desk, but I hope you *won't* read it.

Another funny—but at the time mortifying—incident happened when I asked one of Mrs. Buel's girls to go with me to a lecture by Henry Giles. When I arrived at the house, Mrs. Buel told me that "Pa Buel," as we boys always called him, had been taken ill, and she asked if I would allow her and two or three of the girls to follow us two, under my valiant protection. Just why a woman of fifty or so, with not two or three but, to my consternation, five girls needed my protection was not clear. But as I wanted to be in her good graces, on account of the girls I wanted to call on, I assented. With seven ladies getting ready, naturally some time elapsed. We went afoot, as it was quite near—and my pocketbook had been stepped on by an elephant.[37]

When we reached the hall, every seat was occupied, and the late-comers had begun to occupy chairs in the middle aisle and at the very front. The only way to get these chairs was for me to bring them from the space under the platform. Four trips did I make, emerging in the face of the entire audience, holding aloft a chair in each hand—and then *da capo* and *da capo* and *da capo.* I suspect my face was red, from both the exertion and from rage. Needless to say, I did not *wholly* enjoy Mr. Giles's wit and wisdom; nor do I even remember the subject.[38] After escorting my "harem" back to the school, I returned to my room, which I found full of the boys, who cheered when I entered and shouted out such taunts as "How many will you take next time?" and "How did you enjoy it?" Never again did I repeat the performance, but even today, some old graybeard at Commencement will poke me in the ribs and ask what I thought of Henry Giles's style.

Also in 1858, I saw the most magnificent sight in the heavens that I have ever seen, Donati's Comet. Every night for weeks, as I walked from my room (No. 23, University Hall) and across the middle campus to Deacon Bates's for supper, I saw that glorious spectacle. The tail extended over nearly one-third of the heavens and spread out in a wide fan-shaped curving triangle, far more splendid than the comet in 1843.[39]

I had never studied with a view to winning college honors, and when I received my appointment for the Junior Exhibition, I was not a little astonished—and I must also confess greatly pleased—to find that I was given the "Latin Salutory." This meant that I was at the head of my class and that, unless my work suffered in the following year, I would be given the Valedictory. Then for the first time, and all through my senior year I really worked for honors, as I didn't want to miss a prize so nearly in my grasp.[40]

During my senior and graduate years, I earned some money by my own labor, for the first time in my life. I coached a classmate; I reported lectures for the *Providence Journal* (preserving my reports in the scrapbook which I presented to the library at Brown, some years ago); and I played the melodeon in the New Brown Street Baptist Church. No money I have even earned since has been so sweet to me as this. At Christmas, in 1858 and 1859, I gave to my parents and my brothers presents bought by money I had honestly earned. It was a new and real joy to me.[41] After that, I had no opportunity to earn again until I entered the Army for a month in 1861, and later, in May of 1862.

2

—••ɛ)ɛ ɜ••—

My Career

A NEW DIRECTION

ROM MY EARLIEST CHILDHOOD, and possibly even before my birth, my father had dedicated me to the Lord. I never knew the time when he—and I too—did not fully expect that I should enter the ministry. When I went to college, it was to prepare me for that sacred calling, but as time went on, I found myself insensibly changing my mind. I became more and more convinced that I was neither "called of God" nor fitted for the ministry. By my senior year, when I had to make the decision whether or not to enter a theological seminary after graduating, I felt so strongly about this that I consulted Professors Lincoln and Angell, who advised me to talk with my father at Christmas vacation. It was a very hard task for me, and a still harder one for him, I'm sure. I knew it was a great blow to all his years of hope and longing.

I put the matter plainly before him and told him why I had changed my mind, stating that I wanted to study medicine. Never did I respect my dear father more. He did not hesitate for a moment but said that if I felt that God had not called me to preach, I ought *not* to do so. Never a word of persuasion, entreaty, or command did he utter. His self-control and self-denial amazed me, for I knew how deep-rooted was his wish, cherished for over a score of years. If I wished to study medicine, he said, I should have the best education he could give me. The matter was settled between us. But between him and God I know that there must have been a sore outpouring of his soul. It must have cost him many a tear and the deepest sorrow. But once it was settled, it was settled once and for all; he never discussed it again. I am happy to add that perhaps a dozen times in later years, he said to me, "My son, I think you have found your niche."

He concurred in my desire to spend a resident graduate year at Brown, studying the branches of learning leading up to Medicine, as well as courses in general culture—especially English literature. This last was most fortunate, for, from the time I began to study Medicine until now, I have had little leisure time for literature.

I left college in June of 1860 and in September enrolled at the Jefferson Medical College. The faculty there, with Gross, Pancoast, and Dunglison, among others, was far stronger than that of the University of Pennsylvania. In addition, my mother's sister had married Dr. Thomas Mitchell, Professor of Materia Medica and Therapeutics. He was weak as a professor, I am sorry to say, but his advice to me on one point, to enter the office of Brinton and Da Costa as a private pupil, was invaluable. Had I not done so, I would have graduated without ever having looked through a microscope, ever having personally examined a patient, or ever having written a prescription.

A still more fortunate result of my going into their office was that I made the acquaintance of Dr. Weir Mitchell, and on this wise, I started my studies in Brinton's office (1005 Walnut Street, where the Jefferson Medical College Building now stands) on the first Monday in September. Two or three days later, I was sitting at one of the front windows with Gray's *Anatomy* in my lap and a skull in my hands, beginning the study of the bones. Gray's book was new, and I could not have imagined that my name would eventually appear on its title page as editor. The afternoon sun was hot, and I had the Venetian blinds slanted so as to exclude the direct sunlight. Suddenly the slats were changed to a horizontal plane, and, as I turned my head to see who was there, I saw a pair of eyes looking at me and heard a voice outside say, "Doctor, don't you want to help me with some experiments on snakes?" To have attained the degree of M.D. in two or three days naturally flattered me, and snakes, of course, were very attractive to me. I jumped up, laid down book and skull and, going to the front door, I opened it and saw a rather tall and slender young man, who introduced himself as Dr. Mitchell.

That was the beginning of a friendship that has endured for over fifty-two years (1912), without a cloud as big as a man's hand coming between us. I helped him all through my college course in Medicine and was associated with him for a large part of the Civil War, in the special Hospital for Diseases and Injuries of the Nervous System. When I returned from my study in Europe, in 1866, I assisted him in his later researches on snake venom. Still later, I was his colleague at the Orthopedic Hospital and for a long time did all (or nearly all) of his neurological surgery. I count it the most fortunate event of my professional life that I came early under his stimulating and elevating experience. I owe him a debt of gratitude I can never repay.

S[ilas] Weir Mitchell *[Library of College of Physicians of Philadelphia]*

PARIS, 1864–65

In Paris, I lived at 41 Boulevard de Sebastopol (which later was changed to Boulevard St. Michel), rive gauche, with Dr. W.J. McNutt. He was from the eastern provinces of Canada and later became a very prominent gynecologist in San Francisco.

My teachers were, first and foremost, the celebrated Nélaton, who had recently invented an instrument called the Nélaton probe. This long probe, tipped with unglazed porcelain, was successfully used by Italian surgeons to determine whether the hard substance at the bottom of the wound in Garibaldi's foot was bone or bullet. (The bullet of those days, as large as the last joint on a large thumb, was the *minié*, a leaden ball named for its inventor, Claude Étienne Minié.) Inserting and rotating the rough porcelain tip of the probe, the surgeons discovered, from the small black spot which revealed the lead, that the foreign matter was a bullet. (Bone would have made no telltale mark.) It was removed, Garibaldi soon recovered, and Nélaton's fame was spread far and wide.

He always operated in an overcoat, covered with a white linen apron, and with the cuffs turned up—but soiled with the blood from earlier operations.

Père Velpeau, then in his eighties, I think (old, certainly), was an excellent clinician but, like Nélaton, of the Old School.

Chassaignac, he of the primitive *écraseur*, was also a good teacher, but not equal to the first two. The *écraseur* was a wire loop which grasped the base of the part to be removed. The wire was gradually drawn up through a tube and crushed its way through the base. This barbarous relic died out before long.

A son of Pouchet, the principal opponent of Pasteur, was my preceptor, but I was convinced that Pasteur had the best of the argument on spontaneous generation.

My neighbor in the lecture room was a Nubian as black as the ace of spades, but in no way objectionable personally.

    N. B. (Feb. 2, 1927)

    While in Paris, I bought a fine skeleton, which hangs in a case of black walnut. There are also two paste-board boxes bought in Paris. One contains every bone of the head, disarticulated and separate. The other contains a skull sawn in different directions to show the natural skull cavities. There are also some other loose bones in the walnut case. This whole outfit for the study of anatomy could not be replaced today for less than six hundred dollars. I give it to Walter J. Freeman, Jr., M.D., on the condition that he shall lend *it to any of my descendants who study medicine for their use while studying medicine.*

                                                    W.W. Keen

VIENNA, 1865

In Vienna, I often dropped in to listen to Hyrtl, the wonderful anatomist, whose two books, *Zergliederungskunst* ["The Art of Dissection"] and *Handbuch der topographischen Anatomie* ["Manual of Topographical Anatomy"], were books out of which not a few other books have been made. One had to go early (to a lecture on *Anatomy!*) to get a seat, or if late, to stand in the topmost row. He was a Hebrew with a knowledge of a dozen or more languages, and whose learning in history, art, archaeology, and other areas made all of them tributary to his lectures and books.

In 1874, I bought his two cases of the dissections of the ear for the Mütter Museum of Philadelphia's College of Physicians (one of which is reproduced in the fourth edition of my book *I Believe in God and in Evolution*). I also bought his wonderful collection of the skulls of many races, as well as his equally wonderful injections of all varieties of placentas. His "corroded" preparations were invaluable. Different colored wax, in the artery (red), vein (blue), and duct (yellow), was immersed in solution of weak acid, which gradually ate away the tissues, leaving the colored wax of the artery, vein, and duct. One preparation, the arterial system of a new-born child showing the systemic and foetal circulation, was the only one broken in transit!

I heard Hebra on Dermatology and Syphilology (he was a master), and Schuh, who was a rather poor professor of Surgery. The brilliant Billroth, who was soon to succeed Schuh, was still Professor of Surgery in Zurich, so I missed him.

I also attended Skoda's lectures on Medicine, often at six in the morning.

BERLIN, 1865–66

In Virchow's lecture room, a continuous miniature railroad, loaded with microscopes with various labelled slide preparations, passed from student to student while he lectured. My horizontal microscope, which was *handed* from student to student, in the Philadelphia School of Anatomy, was the best available substitute for Virchow's railroad. Now (1920) we have the epidiascope, with illustrations for all of us to see simultaneously and be described and commented on by the lecturer—a far better plan.

Virchow was but little taller than I and weighed much less. He was not only the father of modern pathology, but also was an archaeologist, friend, and fellow worker with Schliemann at Troy. In addition, he was a leader among liberals in the Prussian Landtag. (There was no Reichstag until after the unification of Germany, following the war.) While I was a student in his laboratory, I asked him if he could provide me with a ticket to the Landtag. He very kindly gave me one when there was to be an interesting debate in which both he and Bismarck were scheduled to speak.

Bismarck was, of course, his chief adversary, and what a contrast he was, large and burly, as became the "man of blood and iron," and a most emphatic speaker. He was quickly becoming the leading figure in Prussia, following the Austro-Prussian War, and was soon thereafter to become the foremost statesman in Germany, if not Europe, following the Franco-Prussian War.

Virchow was slight of figure and under medium height, and a quiet but convincing speaker. When he spoke in parliament, it was much as he spoke to us students on science. He fearlessly held his ground in the debate.

As I remember, Bismarck won the battle over the more logical but more legalistic Virchow, though whether by force of character, manner, or circumstances, I do not remember. He finally was challenged to a duel by Bismarck, though somehow the duel never was fought.

While I was a student of Virchow, there was a severe outbreak of disease, caused by trichinae, in Hedersleben, a small town not far from Berlin. (Dr. Joseph Leidy, of Philadelphia, had discovered trichinae years earlier, but their life history had not been studied with care.) A local butcher had mixed the meat of three hogs, one of which was later found to have been infected, from which he had made a large number of sausages. All those who ate of these sausages suffered, and a number of them died.

Virchow sent Cohnheim, his first assistant (and later a distinguished pathologist), to investigate the epidemic at Hedersleben. Returning to Berlin with some of the infected meat, he fed it to animals and worked out the whole pathology of trichina poisoning, elucidating the life history of trichinae in animals and in man.

Gurlt, in Berlin, was an excellent surgeon. In his clinics, as a commentary on Virchow's work, I saw him remove a large fatty tumor from a man's shoulder. It revealed, on section, many trichinae, explaining the mystery of the restaurant deaths in Hedersleben. His patient was one of a school committee who had met for an inspection. Those of the committee who ate raw sausage for lunch at the restaurant were taken very ill with inflammation in the abdomen and various organs, and all died except for Gurlt's patient. Nothing was known of trichinae in Germany, at that time, and naturally poison was suspected. A thorough chemical analysis of all the remaining food from the committee's lunch revealed no poison, but the restaurateur was ruined and forced to emigrate.

Von Langenbeck was the head of the University surgical staff, a fine operator and an excellent clinical teacher. In spite of his diagnostic ability, he sometimes made mistakes. I saw him amputate a breast for cancer, one time. Cutting across the specimen after the operation, he revealed that the cancer was actually an abscess. He looked at it a moment, then turned to the class and said, "Gentlemen, I never made such a mistake but once before."

In 1890, when Von Bergmann was his successor, after the operation on Crown Prince Frederick, I was inspecting an exhibit of surgical instruments with Von Bergmann's first assistant. I was struck with the size and clumsiness of some tracheotomy tubes and asked, *"Für Tieren?"* (For animals?) *"Nein, für Menschen."* (No, for people.)

The Germans seem to confound bigness as identical with greatness. Witness that dreadful monstrous monument commemorating Leipzig.[1]

LONDON, 1866

On my way home from the Continent, I spent nearly a month in London. The surgical opportunities for a stranger were very meager there, certainly nothing to compare with Paris, Vienna, or Berlin.

On the other hand, I had the happy privilege of hearing a debate between Gladstone and Disraeli. Mr. Charles Francis Adams was still our Minister there (we had no ambassadors at that time), and I had asked him for a ticket to the House of Commons. (I have often wondered at my good fortune, in this, but suppose it was because there were few Americans in Europe, so soon after the close of our Civil War.)

It was a memorable evening, for Mr. Gladstone was to move the second reading of his Reform Bill of 1866, in a speech of some two hours. In his Life of Gladstone, Sir John Morley says that this speech was one of his best ones. He impressed me deeply with his advocacy of great moral principles of righteousness and justice. He was eminently an eloquent philosopher, applying great principles to the case in hand. With his flashing eyes, earnest manner, and wonderful voice, he held us spellbound to the very end.

During the whole of Gladstone's speech, Disraeli, on the bench of the Opposition, sat with his top hat drawn down over his forehead and his arms folded. He scarcely moved and seemed almost asleep. But the moment Gladstone stopped, he jumped to his feet, put his hat on his seat, and spoke, as I remember, for no more than twenty or thirty minutes—but it was brilliant. Without a scrap of a note, he never hesitated for a word or a phrase, but poured forth a torrent of words of invective, sarcasm, and attack on the bill, in short, pithy sentences which seemed like stiletto thrusts. Yet he impressed me as an opportunist ready to overcome his opponent, not by confuting his great moral principles but by the tricks of the orator.

The story is told that Dizzy was once asked the difference between a calamity and a misfortune, to which he replied that if Mr. Gladstone should fall into the Thames, it would be a misfortune, whereas if someone pulled him out, it would be a calamity.[2]

In any case, it was a rare privilege to have heard these four great men—Virchow and Bismarck in Berlin, Gladstone and Disraeli in London—men who molded the destinies of empires, and even of Mankind.

The general impression I was left with, possibly tinged with my later knowledge of their careers, was that Gladstone was a man convinced of the righteousness of his cause, dead in earnest, and determined that he could and would convince his listeners.

Disraeli, on the other hand, seemed to be a political gambler, who was adroit, resourceful, and often successful. One example of his extraordinary ability as a phrase-maker was his allusion to Gladstone as a "sophistical rhetorician, inebriated with the exuberance of his own verbosity."[3]

His often splendid retorts included this reply to an opponent in Commons who had twitted him with being a Jew (in itself a testimony to his ambition, pertinacity, and ability, that he should be Prime Minister of England). In his loftiest tone, he said, "When, sir, your ancestors were barbarians, mine were priests in the temple of the everliving God." Nothing could be finer than that.[4]

PHILADELPHIA

The Philadelphia School of Anatomy

In June of 1866, I opened my office at 107 South 13th Street. In October, Dr. R. S. Sutton, the head of the Philadelphia School of Anatomy (which was founded in 1820) wished to sell the goodwill and the fixtures of the school and remove elsewhere. After talking with my warm friend, Weir Mitchell, and with Dr. Agnew, under whom I had studied anatomy in the same school, I bought it.

The purchase price included the lease, seven pupils at ten dollars each, a dozen dissecting tables, and half a dozen cadavers.

At that time, the University of Pennsylvania was on the lot at 9th Street, extending from Market to Chestnut, and the Jefferson was at 10th and Sansom. My Dissecting ticket was accepted by both schools on a par with that of their own Demonstrators of Anatomy. For nine years, I had a very successful career as a private teacher of both Anatomy and Operative Surgery.

I had to live a hand-to-mouth existence, learning anew the anatomy of each lecture until the preceding midnight, dissecting the next morning the part to be lectured on, giving my lectures at 7 P.M., and spending the evening with my pupils in the dissecting room.

If a student dissecting a leg asked me a question of its anatomy, when my own studies had progressed only as far as the arm, sometimes I could mask my ignorance by the expedient of helping the student with the dissection. If that was impossible, then I boldly confessed that I myself was only a beginner and had to learn my anatomy all afresh, for I had not dissected or studied anatomy since I had graduated, five years earlier. I think I gained the students' respect and confidence, by this honest confession of my own ignorance.

I had never attempted anything like this before, but I took as the subject of my first lecture, "The Ligation of the Femoral Artery." Fortunately, I had decided to speak extemporaneously, the method I always followed subsequently, as well. I first demonstrated its surgical anatomy and then demonstrated the procedure for its ligation, especially warning the class of the danger of the ligation of a vein. In those days of sepsis, such an accident might easily occur in the small incisions then in vogue: "Double the length of the incision and double the danger" was the maxim.

I had hardly spoken for four or five minutes when my supply of saliva gave out, and it seemed to me that I should never be able to secrete more. As soon as I concluded the demonstration, I hustled the "subject" out of the room, for I had the sneaking suspicion that I had tied the vein, contrary to my own warning. As soon as I was alone, I dissected the parts and found my suspicion verified. To save face, lest even my janitor would despise me, I removed the ligature from the vein, placed one on the artery, and never disclosed my mistake until many years afterwards, when I could afford to do so.

Of course, I had few—and often no—office patients, and therefore I had time for hard study, and study hard I surely did!

By the end of the first session, I had twenty students. Each year saw my classes grow larger and larger, until my lecture room was overcrowded. In 1875, I was obliged to close the school, as the Government took the property—and also that of the University of Pennsylvania—for the present post office. The University moved to West Philadelphia. I could depend only on students from the Jefferson, if I fitted up a new property, but this entailed a financial risk which I did not feel it wise to incur.

One of the sessions of the School of Anatomy I opened with an address on "The Early History of Practical Anatomy," which taught me more than my lecture taught my listeners, since I had given a good deal of time to its research. Even today, I find it quite interesting. When I closed the school, in 1875, I published its history, a serious and valuable record of the good work done in the sixty-five years of this "School of the Prophets," from which came many of our distinguished teachers.

Other teachers of anatomy have opened anatomical and surgical schools with the same name, but even though they have the legal right to use the name, they are in no sense a continuation of the original Philadelphia School of Anatomy.

Jefferson Medical College

In the meantime, the Jefferson had organized a summer course by lecturers outside the regular faculty, and from 1866 to 1875, I had an appointment as a Lecturer on Pathological Anatomy. This was the first recognition of this branch of scientific medicine in any important medical school in the United States. I made it chiefly a course in Surgical Pathology, for there was not time for more, and based my lectures largely on Virchow's *Cellular Pathology* and Billroth's *Surgical Pathology*, both new books at the time, and both full of meat. This enforced study was most useful to me later, as Professor of Surgery, in that it laid a foundation for me in pathology without which I should have taught surgery much less effectively.

At Jefferson Medical College, in 1873, the Chair of Anatomy, which had become vacant by the resignation of Professor Joseph Pancoast, was to be filled. I worked as hard as I could to obtain the post, for which there immediately arose a very warm contest, the other candidates being Drs. William Pancoast, William Forbes, and John Brinton. I may say that the profession-at-large recognized that, if ability and success as a teacher had been the determining factors, I deserved the place. (Among my letters are the relevant letters of recommendation.[5]) But Professor Samuel David Gross, though declaring that I was the best teacher among the candidates, finally threw his influence with the trustees for Pancoast, who was thus elected. I do not *know* the reason for his action, but it was generally understood that in return for this, the influence of the Pancoasts, father and son, would be thrown to Dr. Samuel Weissel Gross for his father's chair, when *that* became vacant, likely to occur soon in view of the elder Gross's age.

This was the greatest disappointment I ever experienced, professionally. I had worked very hard to fit myself for this chair, and I *knew* that I could fulfill its duties acceptably. Later, when the Chair of Therapeutics became vacant, so good a man as Professor Jacob Mendez Da Costa urged me to accept election to it, assuring me that it would be undisputed if I would accept. I declined, on the ground that I was not fitted to teach that branch of Medicine, and that if I accepted, my teaching would be perfunctory, and therefore obnoxious to me. (At that time, I never even thought of—much less less did I aspire to—the Chair of Surgery, feeling it to be far above my abilities.) After my defeat for the Chair of Anatomy, it seemed to me that all my hard work had been for nothing, and that there was no prospect of my ever having a successful career as a teacher.

Sixteen years later, in the spring of 1889, the younger Samuel Gross, who with John Brinton had succeeded to the Chair of Surgery, unexpectedly died of pneumonia. This was less than a year after the meeting of the American Surgical Association, at which I presented my early brain cases.

Shortly afterward, Minis Hays called on me and said that members of the faculty had asked him to determine whether or not I would be a candidate for the vacancy. I told him frankly that I would be willing to have my name considered, but on two conditions. First, that if nominated, I should certainly be elected. Second, that for my election there should be no need of any personal canvass of the trustees, though I would, of course, be willing to call on each of them as a matter of courtesy. These conditions having been met, I made a call on each of the fifteen trustees, selecting a time when I was virtually certain that they would not be at home, so that I should only leave my card but not be exposed to a personal interview. I was elected to the vacancy and at once began my preparation for the important and arduous task before me.

To the analytical method which I learned at Brown I attribute my success as a teacher. I always tried to reduce a problem to its simplest known terms and then proceed, step by step, to the more complex and the unknown. Often, I have tingled from head to foot, when, suddenly, in the midst of a lecture—like a spark struck at a blow—a happy apposite illustration, phrase, or argument has occurred to me, and I have been all aglow with enthusiasm. I was always in dead earnest, in my efforts to make clear to my students, and to impress on them, the great truths of surgery. Every lecture was a new subject, on which I had read the latest literature. I never tired in my efforts to turn out the best doctors, so far as my department was concerned. I never spared time, labor, or painstaking preparation.

In consequence of the fact that the Chair of Surgery had been divided, my salary, during all my service as Professor of Surgery, was only half of the four thousand dollars paid to professors in other chairs. My clinical work in the hospital required from one to three hours every day (I never delegated this work to assistants, save in minor cases that were doing well), and my clinics usually lasted three to four hours, so that I gave far more time to my duties than several of my colleagues, while receiving only half their pay. But I scorned the idea of asking for more, or of calling the attention of the trustees to the inequality, if not the injustice.[6]

Moreover, a considerable part of my salary I gave back to the college for various objectives, such as the J.M. DaCosta Laboratory, Donation Day, and the Y.M.C.A., for example. In addition, I always bought my own instruments and appliances (including the first Trendelenburg chair in Philadelphia).

We had no projectoscope or epidiascope, in those days. In my Philadelphia School of Anatomy, I had bought a portable hand microscope:

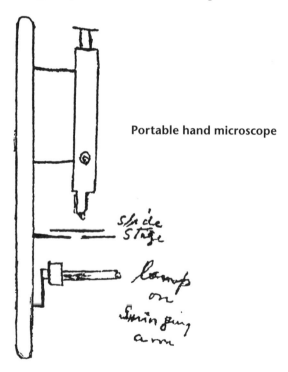

Portable hand microscope

slide
stage

lamp
on
swinging
arm

I brought this to the Jefferson, together with a large number of expensive microscope injections, which I had imported from Thiersch, of Leipzig. All of my drawings and plates were paid for out of my salary. When I retired from the Jefferson, I left all of these things to the college, except for a number of my instruments. These, a very large and expensive collection, I donated to the ladies of the Emergency Aid, in 1915, to be sent to the hospitals in Belgium and France. And I had my microscope put in first-class order, in 1912, and sent it to a Baptist mission hospital in China.

In January, 1907, having turned seventy, I resigned my chair after having taught for forty-one years in all, the last twenty-three having been devoted exclusively to surgery—five in the Woman's Medical College and eighteen in the Jefferson. In all, from 1866 to 1907, I estimate that I have had over ten thousand students in anatomy and surgery.

I may say, without vanity but with what at least I please myself with thinking is a proper and just satisfaction, that I have had a more than usually successful career, both as a teacher and as a surgeon. If unsolicited honors, American and European, be a test, I have had far more than my abilities deserve. They are a satisfaction to me, partly as a recognition of my half a century of unstinting work, but chiefly because they will be a source of pleasure, and a just pride, to my descendants.

A list of the positions I have occupied, and of the honors so generously given me, and of the books and papers I have written or edited, will be found in the drawer of the table in the front office.[7] They are also presented, to a limited extent, in *Who's Who in America*. Of two of the highest professional distinctions, one European and one American, I only learned while traveling around the world in 1901-02. In 1901, I was elected one of the eight honorary fellows of the German Surgical Society, the largest and most prestigious surgical society in the world. I am the only surgeon who, up to 1914, when Halsted was elected, had ever received that honor. And in 1902, I was elected president of the Sixth Triennial Congress of American Physicians and Surgeons, to be held the following year. This is the blue ribbon of the American profession, and the list of its presidents is a distinguished one:

1888–John S. Billings	1903–W.W. Keen
1891–S. Weir Mitchell	1907–R.H. Fitz
1894–A.L. Loomis	1910–E.L. Trudeau
1897–William H. Welch	1913–William C. Gorgas
1900–Henry P. Bowditch	1916–W.S. Thayer

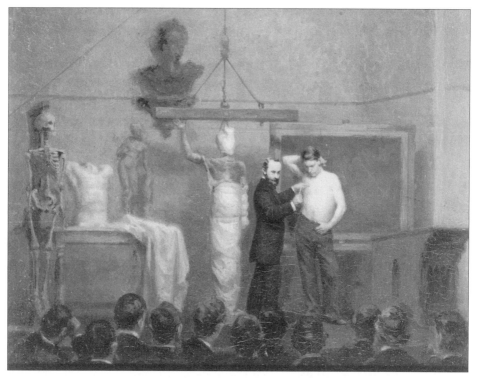

Anatomical Lecture by Dr. William Williams Keen, by Charles H. Stephens, c.1879
[The Pennsylvania Academy of the Fine Arts]

The Pennsylvania Academy of the Fine Arts

In between my two appointments at the Jefferson, I was offered and accepted the place of Professor of Artistic Anatomy at the Pennsylvania Academy of the Fine Arts, which had just moved from Chestnut above 10th to its new home at Broad and Cherry.[8] I occupied this position until 1890, when I resigned.

One of the first things I did was to test all of the students, forty or fifty, men and women, for color-blindness. I placed on a table twenty-five or thirty hanks of wool, representing as many different hues of color. I then picked out a hank of apple green and tested each student alone, by his or her selecting half a dozen hanks to match. Not a single case of color-blindness was noted among the women, who quickly and accurately selected the proper hanks. Color-blindness is exceedingly rare in women. Of the men, however, two were somewhat uncertain, and one man selected several different colors, one of which was a bright scarlet. When I explained his error, he said, "That explains the problem I had in finding a red cow, on my father's farm, when she wandered into the green bushes." He abandoned colors and restricted himself to black and white—and with some success.

The anatomical lessons at the Academy were most congenial and delightful. The students were in earnest, and I threw myself with enthusiasm into the work. My course consisted of about thirty lectures,[9] combined always with demonstrations on a living model.[10] I also used a cadaver. On one side, the muscles were exposed *in situ* by the dissection away of only the skin, superficial fascia, and fat. On the other side, each muscle was dissected down to its attachment to the bones. I hung the cadaver upright, by two iron hooks inserted into trephine openings in the sides of the skull, so that cadaver, skeleton, and living model were all in the same vertical position. No mental transposition from a horizontal cadaver to a vertical skeleton and living model was necessary.[11]

On the living model, by voluntary, active, and resisted movements—and by the galvanic battery (especially for the facial muscles)—the action of the various muscles was constantly demonstrated. One outcome of these lectures was my paper "On the Systematic Use of the Living Model in Teaching Anatomy," which I read at the International Medical Congress in London, in 1881. This in turn led to a delightful acquaintance with Professor Cunningham who taught Anatomy in Dublin, later in Edinburgh.

The Pennsylvania Museum and School of Industrial Art

From 1878 to 1882, I was also Professor of the Anatomy of Animal Forms as Applied to Decorative Art, in the Pennsylvania Museum and School of Industrial Art.

Finding that there was no entirely satisfactory book written on the subject of artistic anatomy, I started to write my own. Those written by artists had too much art and not enough anatomy, and those by anatomists, too much anatomy and not enough art. I think I still have a considerable portion of the manuscript, but my surgical practice, essential to my financial needs, was absorbing more and more of my time, and I finally had to relinquish the hope of finishing the proposed book, a great disappointment.

These excursions into artistic and decorative anatomy were delightful by-products of my anatomical work. They broadened my conception of the uses and value of anatomy and brought me into intimate personal acquaintance with both officers and students in the two institutions. Not a few of my old pupils, especially in the Academy, have become distinguished painters, sculptors, and illustrators.

With the death of Dr. Lenox Hodge, in 1881, the Demonstratorship of

Anatomy at the University of Pennsylvania became vacant, and both Weir
Mitchell and William Pepper were very eager that I should succeed him. I
should then be in line, before long, to succeed Dr. Joseph Leidy, Professor of
Anatomy, who could not be expected to remain much longer in active service.
They did their best, as Mitchell told me, but for some reason which neither they
nor I understood, Leidy and Agnew, Professor of Surgery, both opposed my
election. What a fortunate escape for me! As fortunate as my defeat in 1873 for the
Chair of Anatomy at the Jefferson. Pepper's subsequent letter said that he could
not help "in telling [me] how deeply I regret having lost the chance of securing
as an associate . . . one who has won such a brilliant reputation as a teacher—and
one for whose abilities and character I have the highest respect."

When the Medico-Chirurgical College was started, in 1882, I was also urged
to become one of the faculty, but I declined, as I did not like the ideas or ideals
of the men at the head of the enterprise.

The Woman's Medical College of Pennsylvania

Also between my two appointments at Jefferson Medical College, from 1884
to 1889, I was Professor of Surgery at the Woman's Medical College, having
lectured there on regional surgery for a year or two. I found the students in
dead earnest, hard workers, and diligent. They were careful and exact dissectors
and soon overcame their natural repugnance to handling a dead body. Their
emotional nature was at once a help and a hindrance. It gave them enthusiasm,
but at the same time it made inroads on their sleep and mental poise, especially
at examination time. As I once said to them, half of them were taking coffee
to keep themselves awake while cramming, and the other half were taking
bromides to put themselves to sleep.

When I was asked to accept the Chair of Surgery, women doctors were
decidedly at a discount. Very few men (prominently, Dr. Ellwood Wilson and
his first assistant at the Lying-in-Charity, Dr. Albert Smith) were friendly to
them and warmly advocated their admission to the county medical society.
The large majority were partly neutral or, more commonly, actively hostile.[12] I
sought the advice of several clear-headed friends as to whether I should accept
the appointment. They were doubtful, as a rule, but not averse to my accepting
the post. I myself felt that the stage had passed when only strong-minded freaks
constituted the majority of students, and that a goodly number of young women
who had to earn their own living had a right to study and practice medicine.
If so, they should have the best possible instruction. If I could give them such

instruction, I felt it my duty to do so. Despite the certain unpopularity of the position, I accepted the chair and never regretted my action. In fact, it enabled me to try my wings in Surgery, in clinical extemporaneous teaching, and in operating before a body of criticial students, all of which fitted me for the more important place at the Jefferson.[13]

My five years' training, in both didactic and clinical teaching, were invaluable to me. But I never worked so hard in my life, reading textbooks and medical journals; card-cataloguing every important paper and all my own clinical cases for ready reference; and rewriting my notes, for I always lectured extemporaneously.

Early Patients

The Civil War broke out on April 15th, 1861, just after the close of my first course at the Jefferson Medical College. Practically all of the young doctors who served in the Jefferson surgical clinics entered the Army, and their places were filled by the students of the second course. There was no examination at the end of the first course, but a comprehensive one on all of our studies, at the end of the second, to determine whether or not we should be graduated. Both of these courses were called "years," but after deducting generous Christmas holidays, they were practically sessions of about four and a half months—from October to February.

George Porter, my classmate at Brown, was also my classmate at the Jefferson, and our knowledge after a single course of lectures was rather scanty. At about eleven o'clock, one day (the clinic began at noon), a hurry call came to an accident case, and Porter and I responded. We found a quite elderly woman who had tripped on the carpet, fallen on the floor, and lay on the bed suffering greatly. She could not move, especially her left leg. Was it a fracture of the neck of the thigh-bone or a dislocation at the hip? Porter and I together manipulated that leg by flexion, extension, rotation, and traction, with one holding the patient and the other holding the leg. (I am sorry every time I think of this case for the pain that we in our ignorance inflicted on that poor woman.)

We finally went into an adjoining room to consult with each other. I said, "George, I don't know whether it is a fracture or a dislocation, and since we *must* leave now for the clinic, don't you think it best to consult with Dr. Gross?" George agreed, so we told the family that we would return after the clinic but now must go back to our duties. When the clinic ended, we laid the case before Gross.

"Was the woman young or old?"

"An old woman, Sir."

"Was it a slight fall or a heavy one?"

"A slight fall. Tripping on the carpet, she fell to the floor."

"As she lay on her back, did her toes point upward or outward?"

"Outward, Sir."

"My God, have I been teaching you to the best of my ability and you don't know that if the patient is old, the fall a slight one, and the toes are in eversion, it is absolutely a sure diagnosis of a fracture of the neck of the femur?"

It was a sure rebuke, but as I have written, we had had only one course of lectures, and among the maze of things to be remembered, this particular condition had not been etched upon our brains.

For the purpose of so etching it on the brains of my own pupils, I have told this story almost every year, to the great benefit of their future patients.

Also clearly recalled from my days as a student under Professor Samuel David Gross was the following incident. I had become one of the "quiz masters" on Surgery, and of course I attended every lecture and took notes of anything he taught that was new or unusual.

One day—I remember neither the date nor the subject of his comment—he set the class laughing at me by some unclean joke which he made at my expense.

I rose at once and left the room.

The next day, he sent for me and tried to excuse himself. But I immediately replied, "Professor Gross, I am a young man and just starting out on my career. To be an efficient and successful teacher, I must have the respect of my students. Your remarks yesterday inevitably would cause them to lower me in their respect. I must ask you to apologize to the class at your next lecture, or I will cease to attend your lectures and to quiz on Surgery—and I will explain explain to my class why I have done so."

He tried to laugh it off, but I was firm, though respectful.

The result was that he did apologize to me in front of the class at his next lecture—and he did it handsomely.

In the end, it was really a benefit to me, for it showed that I would maintain my self-respect, even with the acknowledged chief of the Jefferson faculty and of American surgery.

I entered the Army after having had only one term at the Jefferson. On other hand, I had had some rather unusual advantages, at first in the private anatomical room of Dr. John Brinton, my preceptor. With the cadaver provided there, I had the opportunity to do a good deal of extra dissection, to do all the standard amputations, and to go through a course of ligation of all the principal arteries.

In addition, I was a pupil in the joint quiz class of Brinton and Dr. Jacob Mendez Da Costa (his brother-in-law, incidentally), and in the office of the latter I had had many opportunities to look through a microscope, to personally examine patients, listening to the heart and percussing the various viscera, and so forth.

Since these practical experiences were not a part of the regular course in Medicine at Jefferson, which consisted almost entirely of lectures, I was very much better equipped than most first-year students for Army medicine.

I was sent immediately down to Alexandria, where my regiment was in camp. We had morning sick-call, of course, and I was also available at any time for sudden emergencies. I had over me the surgeon of the regiment, but he was rarely in evidence in the camp.

The first patient ever under my care was an Army officer, a patient of my preceptor, Dr. John Brinton. I sat up with the officer all night, prepared to arrest any hemorrhage from an arrow wound inflicted on him in one of our many Indian wars. The arrow had penetrated a little below the eyeball, and the point had wounded an important artery. After Dr. Brinton had operated on him, there was always the possibility of a dangerous hemorrhage. It was a very uncomfortable night for me—much more than for the patient. He recovered without any aid from me. It was only a case of watchful waiting.

As soon as possible after the beginning of the war, Professor Gross had written (in about ten days) a brief text-book on military surgery (which the Lippincotts had on sale just a few days later). One day when I was reading the earlier parts of this brief epitome in my tent, a man came running up to say that one of our soldiers had accidentally discharged his rifle while cleaning it, and the ball, which had entered his right chest, had not emerged. (The soldier, typically a greenhorn with military matters, as well as with his weapon, had not withdrawn the load from his rifle before cleaning it.) The surgeon was absent, and so I was immediately called to attend the case. I was very careful not to run, but to walk, because, first, I did not want to appear as scared as I actually was, and second, I wanted to think over the case and decide what I ought to do, for I had not reached "Wounds of the Chest" in Gross's little book.

As soon as I got there, I inquired how the wound had been inflicted, and I then undressed him, following what I thought was the right process. I wanted to find out whether there was hemorrhage, either external or internal. I found that there was a very moderate oozing of blood from the wound and that percussion showed no dullness over that part of the lung. This suggested that there probably was no accumulation of blood in the chest. Additional evidence of moderate hemorrhage was that the expectoration was only tinged with blood rather than being pure blood. I was wise enough not to introduce a probe, for it should be remembered that this event was years before any knowledge of bacteriology or of Lister's antiseptic methods.

I decided to dress the wound with simple cold water and applied it by means of a bandage. To my surprise and gratification, the man progressed steadily and was recovered in time to be marched to the Battle of Bull Run.

I made a great reputation as a wonderful surgeon, among the men in the regiment, a reputation wholly undeserved.

My first amputation was of a hand just above the wrist. I made a circular sweep around the forearm, a little above the wrist. This severed quite a number of blood vessels and produced a severe hemorrhage, which scared me. We had no hemostatic forceps, in those days. Each blood vessel had to be seized by a small hook and tied, with one end of the ligatures cut off short and the other left long. Of course, the presence of several ligatures would prevent the healing of the entire wound until they rotted away.

I hastened to tie them as quickly as possible, fearing that the patient might bleed to death before I could tie them all.

Hemorrhage is the chief test of a surgeon. Feeling the warm blood flowing over his hand and knowing that death will soon follow unless the vessel or vessels are secured, may easily unbalance the surgeon's judgment, at first, so that he will not be able to think clearly and act with coolness and promptness.

In time, I overcame my fright, and having mastered the hemorrhage again and again, even in the most difficult cases, I became sure that I would win out. In my later operations, I was as cool, even with the most profuse hemorrhage, as I had been frightened in the earlier ones—and especially in the very first amputation.

In our operations before Lister taught us antisepsis, we were very much averse to making long incisions. I well recall a paper analyzing the various factors of danger in abdominal cases. The author included a cautionary table showing the percentage of deaths in incisions of two, three, four, five, and six inches.

The length of an abdominal incision is a very minor matter today. The rule is enough elbow room to afford a full view of the abdominal content, but never beyond what is necessary.

Surgical Confreres

In the 1890s, I made a serious effort to intiate a movement for an international surgical congress. I corresponded with Billings, Czerny, Kocher, Gussenbauer, von Bergmann, Durante, and other leading surgeons in the U.S., Germany, France, Great Britain, and Italy. They all approved of the idea, and it would have materialized but for the position of the British surgeons. They had no surgical society with scientific meetings or published transactions. The Royal College of Surgeons of England is charged with (1) the examination of students, along with the Royal College of Physicians and the Society of Apothecaries, and the granting of degrees in Medicine; (2) the care of the Hunterian Museum; and (3) the oversight of certain funds for stated courses of lectures on surgical subjects. Their honorary fellows are from all civilized countries. Their fellows number in the hundreds and their members and licentiates, several thousand. To include all of these was impossible; to include some and exclude others was equally impossible. I finally had to abandon the scheme.

About 1902 or 1903, the Belgian Surgical Society took the bull by the horns and organized such a congress. They invited certain surgeons, in various European countries and North America, to meet in 1905 in Brussels. Kocher was chosen first president and Depage the secretary general. The Congress was a great success. The delegates were entertained with lavish hospitality. (Florence and Dora accompanied me.)

The Third Congress was held in 1911, with Championnière presiding and Depage again the efficient secretary. I was unable to attend.

The Fourth Congress, in April of 1914, was held in New York, with Depage now the president. I had feared that it might not be the success we wished for, and that the European surgeons would not attend in great numbers. But it again proved to be a success, largely due (from the social aspect) to Drs. Harte and LeConte, of Philadelphia. The day before it adjourned, I was asked if I would accept the presidency of the Fifth Congress, to be held in 1917 in Paris. I objected that I would be too old (over eighty), but their desire seemed so sincere, and they were so urgent that I consented. I was elected unanimously.

On the first of August, the Great War (of which not the faintest suspicion existed in April) erupted, and I do not know if the Congress will ever be held. The unfortunate animosities aroused by the war would seem to indicate that it could not be held in Paris, or any other capital of a belligerent nation. When the war is over, I propose writing to the Brussels International Surgical Society to see if it is possible to arrange for a Congress to be held in Switzerland or some other neutral country.

LANDMARK CASES

Brain Surgery

When I had just finished my intensive study of the nervous system, in May of 1887, a hospital patient, Theodore Daveler of Lancaster, sought my advice. Had he come a year, or even three months, earlier, I should have lost *a great opportunity in my life—and a turning point in my surgical career.* During the twenty-five years since my graduation in Medicine, I had had a successful career as a teacher (1) in my private anatomical school, (2) in the summer school of the Jefferson, (3) as a lecturer on pathological anatomy, and (4) in the position I held at the Woman's Medical College. But my anatomical hopes had been blasted by my failure to obtain the Chair of Anatomy at the Jefferson; and my position at the Woman's Medical College, though of great value in training me as a teacher of surgery, was relatively inconspicuous, in the large world of surgery.

Daveler came to see me at St. Mary's Hospital just at the criticial time. Earlier, I should have been unable to make a correct diagnosis, and my future would have been totally different; later, I should have been only one of many brain surgeons.

My diagnosis was a brain tumor in the left motor area. The first modern operation for a brain tumor had been done in London, in 1884, by Godlee. I had witnessed Weir's operation in 1885 or '86, but I had never before had a case under my own care and, of course, had never done an operation. I was not willing, therefore, to trust my diagnosis without a consultation. Drs. Mitchell, Wood, Lewis, Harlan, and Oliver kindly saw the patient with me. They all concurred that the diagnosis was not clear enough to warrant so serious an operation as opening the head. I was too distrustful of my own diagnosis (though I still believed it to be the correct one) to operate, in the face of such an adverse judgment. So I sent Daveler home with directions to follow the treatment advised by the consultants, adding that if he was not better in the autumn he should come back to the hospital, and I then would be willing to operate, on my own responsibility.

He returned in the fall, and after a minute and painstaking review of all the facts, and now with the concurrence of the former consultants, I operated on him, on the 15th of December. Never shall I forget my delight, and my dismay, when I removed the trephine button from his skull. There lay the tumor, just where I diagnosed it to be, but it was larger than the opening I had made—an inch and a half and a *very* large opening in those days of half-inch trephines. Another button was removed, but still more bone had to be removed by bone forceps, before the tumor was entirely disclosed. It was seven and a quarter by six inches in circumference, and only two or three tumors larger than this had theretofore been removed. My heart sank within me, at the prospect of even attempting its removal, but no other course was possible. I passed my little finger around its margin and peeled it out as easily as one scoops a hard-boiled egg out of its shell with a spoon! I expected a serious hemorrhage to follow, but the amount of blood lost was not great and was readily stopped. What a sigh of relief escaped me when the last stitch was tied, the wound dressed, and the man put back to bed—alive!

As I long since learned, I mismanaged the after-treatment. But he not only survived the operation itself but also my bungling care, which was due to my total want of experience. In 1912, twenty-five years after the operation, he is still living.[14] The tumor was a fibroma, and not being malignant, has of course never returned.

Naturally, the successful removal of a brain tumor, especially so large a tumor, at a time when such American operations were few in number, attracted a great deal of attention. Almost immediately, two other brain cases, involving epilepsy resulting from injuries, were brought to me, and I operated with successful results in both cases.

In September of 1888, the First Congress of American Physicians and Surgeons was held in Washington, under the presidency of Dr. John Billings. Horsley and Ferrier were my guests in Philadelphia, immediately after the Congress, in which brain surgery was the leading topic. These two doctors, who had done so much to advance it in England, were both present as guests of the Congress and lent it added distinction. The general discussion on this relatively new field of surgery was participated in by Charles Mills, Roswell Park, David Ferrier, Victor Horsley, Allen Starr, E.C. Seguinn, Robert Weir, and myself.

In the separate meeting of the American Surgical Association, I reported my three cases and had the three patients present as exhibits (along with the tumors and the portions of the brain tissue removed), in connection with the paper I presented. I especially remember that Ferrier told me that when he heard the account, in one of my cases, of the motion induced in the arm by the electric stimulation of a particular area of the brain, he almost jumped from his seat: It was the first confirmation in the brain of man of his experiments on the brains of monkeys. This paper, and the successful cases described in it, was the beginning of my work in cerebral surgery.

Just after Christmas of 1888, Dr. George Strawbridge referred a four-year-old boy to me at the Woman's Hospital. The diagnosis was an inoperable tumor of the cerebellum which caused increasing hydrocephalus because it prevented the escape of cerebrospinal fluid in the lateral ventricles. The boy had been totally blind since Christmas, with a choked disc in each eye, the swelling of the optic nerve measuring 2.3 millimeters on one side and 1.8 on the other. He suffered greatly from constant and severe headache, and the chief indication was to relieve the poor child from pain, even if his life could not be saved.

On January 4th, using a method I first devised, I tapped one ventricle, reaching it from a small trephine opening above the ear, at a depth of one and three-quarters inches. I inserted a few strands of horsehair as a drain, which allowed two to four ounces of fluid to escape daily into a copious antiseptic dressing. A week later, I substituted a small rubber tube for the horsehairs, allowing the freer flow of four to eight ounces a day.

On February 8th, I tapped the opposite ventricle, inserting a drainage tube there also. On two occasions, using a fountain syringe raised only a few inches above the boy's head, I washed out the ventricles from side to side, passing eight ounces of a warm boric-acid solution into one ventricle, from which it freely escaped by the tube on the opposite side. The moment the warm solution began to flow, the boy lost his irritability and settled down into a position of evident comfort.

He lived for fifty-two days after the first tapping. The first tube had been in place for almost that length of time; the other, for two weeks. The first tube was removed, cleansed, and replaced at least thirty times, without discomfort to the child or injury to the brain.

The post-mortem examination disclosed a sarcoma of the cerebellum on the right side, just as diagnosed. There was no inflammation around the track of the drainage tubes. The septum between the two ventricles had not been harmed by the removal and replacement of the tubes. The boy's mental condition was unimpaired until a week or ten days before his death.

In addition to these drainage tubes, we probed the brain six times, in as many different places, in the hope that we might find the tumor and possibly remove it. No evidence of these additional punctures could be found at the post-mortem examination.

It was one of the most unusual, and most satisfactory, cases of brain surgery I have ever done, and as a result, I made a careful study of the surgical anatomy of the ventricles, laying down systematic rules for the formal operation of tapping the lateral ventricles. The operation is now a well-recognized procedure.

In the years that have passed since then, other and far abler surgeons have done more and better work, as I most gladly testify. But while they have the joy and the rewards of their extensive and important discoveries and improvements in diagnosis and technique, they could never have felt the thrill of those relatively few surgeons of my own age and generation who were among the "first that ever burst into that silent sea." [15]

The First Diagnosis of a Wound of the Sympathetic Nerve

As Executive Offier in the Saterlee Military Hospital, in 1863, it was my duty to assign new patients to the various wards. One day, a new patient entered and stood by my desk, waiting for me to finish a letter I had been writing. I looked up and instantly observed that his left pupil was of normal size while the right one was contracted to a pinpoint. "By George," I said to myself, "he is Dalton's cat."

I must explain. *Dalton's Physiology* was a textbook I had studied at the Jefferson. In the chapter on the sympathetic nerve, he related Brown-Séquard and Bernard's experimental researches, which included the cutting of this nerve in the neck of cats and rabbits. [16] Up to that time (1851 or '52); all that was known of this nerve was its anatomy. Little was known of its physiological or pathological functions.

In the neck of both man and animal, it is a slender cord, about as large as medium-weight sewing thread, and it lies just outside of the carotid artery and jugular vein. It is easily accessible for experimental research, but it had never, until then, been divided. In cats and rabbits, its division was followed by a great contraction of the corresponding pupil, by a reddening and heat (which was easily observed in the ear) on the same side as the operation, by a slight falling of the upper eyelid, and also by sweating on that side.

In spite of the doubtless many cases of its division in man, by bullet, sword, or bayonet, no observation of such a division had ever been made. The missile or weapon inflicting such a wound almost inevitably produced a quickly fatal injury, either to the spinal cord in the neck or in the severing of the great blood vessels close by.

Dalton had not only described the effects which followed the division of the nerve: He also presented a picture of a cat so affected. Had he merely stated the observed phenomena, it is very probable that I should have read and soon forgotten the statement. But the picture, with the cat's strange appearance, made a strong and distinct impression on my mind which did not fade.

This is a lesson which teachers should not forget. Illustrations, however rude, fix the facts in the mind as mere verbal descriptions can not. This is especially true of a picture drawn on the blackboard at the moment when students are able to watch it evolve before their eyes. Even in my own unskilled hand, a sketch growing on the blackboard has often been far more effective than completed pictures, no matter how elaborate or artistic. The many things seen all at once, and in mass, often obliterate the memory of details. A picture seen in its genesis and growth is not easily forgotten.

At any rate, this patient, who was instantly Dalton's cat, pointed to his right neck, when I asked him where he had been wounded. I transferred him at once to Mitchell and Morehouse's Special Hospital for Injuries and Disorders of the Nervous System, and a few days later, I was ordered to the same hospital as their junior assistant. We studied this case most thoroughly and recorded it fully in our *Gunshot Wounds and Other Injuries of Nerves.*

In the winter of 1864-65, when I went to study in Paris, I gave a copy of this book to Claude Bernard, drawing his attention to the history of this particular case. Quite naturally, his enthusiasm knew no bounds, since it was the first confirmation in man of the similar effect he had produced through laboratory experimentation on animals. Only those familiar with medicine can fully appreciate how profoundly important has been the discovery of the function of the sympathetic nerve, in anatomy, physiology, pathology, medicine, surgery, and therapeutics.

INCOME AND PROFESSIONAL FEES

(Written in January, 1916)

At my father's death, in 1886, each of his three boys—George, Charles, and I—received one third of his estate, which was about $50,000 each but netted eventually only about $30,000 each.

I was given the house at 217 Chestnut Street, at a valuation of $40,000. It was rented at $3,000, but this gradually fell to $1,200. In addition, I owed my father $10,000, which he had advanced me for living expenses in the early and lean years of my practice and teaching. The house was finally sold for about $20,000, so that my net inheritance from his estate was a little over $30,000.

Father Borden, through no fault of his own, failed, in 1877.[17] His failure carried down sons-in-law Walter Paine and George Durfee, and sons Jefferson Jr. and Spencer.[18] For quite a while it looked as if sons-in-law George Dean and I might have to support Father and Mother Borden.

The only amount my dear wife Tinnie received from her father was the equity in 1729 Chestnut Street, which amounted to about $21,100, as there was a mortgage on it of $17,000. At his death, she received somewhat more—how much, I never knew, or at least don't remember. Father Borden paid the interest on the loan up to the time of his failure, when I had to assume it. It was a heavy burden for me.

He was so trusted that he had borrowed a considerable sum on his note and purchased, at the sale of his holdings, some of the best mill stocks in Fall River, as well as some real estate in Olean, New York, on which oil was discovered not long afterwards. This greatly increased the value of the property and enabled him to repay his friends, retain the family homestead, and live in modest comfort there for the rest of his life.[19]

Professionally I may be said to have had an unusually successful career, but financially, though I have been a very active surgeon, my income has never been continuously very large. It has been disproportionate to the great amount of work I have done. The most irksome time of the year was when I had to send out my bills, for I was always at a loss to determine how much my services were really worth—and how much the patient could afford to pay. I always had to screw up my courage to send out any bill for over $1,000, or even $500.

It has always been a real delight to me to give to deserving objects, especially to those with which I was personally connected, and I have given freely. This has created an impression of much greater wealth than I have ever had. The same was true of my father. After his death, a cousin said to me, "I suppose you will now retire from active practice, since you have plenty to live on!"

That I shall leave my dear children comfortable—as far as human foresight can go—free from any danger of want, though far from "rich," according to present standards, is due almost wholly to my own endeavor to save something each year, by carrying all the life insurance I could afford, and by making careful—and in several instances very lucrative—investments.

Visiting the Casino in Monte Carlo, in 1892, we saw W.K. Vanderbilt, who looked quite old and seemed half demented. He sat there for a long time with a small pile of silver and gold, seldom playing but poring over his figures, calculating his chances, speaking to no one, and holding his hand over his money in the most miserly fashion. It is a pitiful sight to see people seemingly so crazed by greed of gain.[20]

In one instance, on what seemed good judgment at the time, I invested a very considerable amount in public utilities in the West, managed by Rhodes, Sinkler & Butcher. The unexpected and violent Panic of 1907-08 came very near wrecking the whole business, in which case I should have lost very heavily. The anxiety and faithful watchfulness of Howard Butcher Jr. (my broker and a son-in-law) finally—and by a very close margin—saved the day. I can never be too grateful to him for all that he did and suffered, during those anxious days and nights, while [daughters] Florence, Dora, and I were enjoying ourselves in Europe, with but slight appreciation of the terrible ordeal he was going through. He wrote me only what he was obliged to tell me, concealing the heavy burden he was carrying so as not to worry me any more than was necessary. My respect and affection for him were greatly enhanced—and in fact unbounded—when I learned the facts. Only long after my return did they leak out, little by little.

Fortunately, the tide turned, and in a brief time most of those properties were sold at a good profit—though others also at a loss.

Our trip around the world, in 1901-02, and our eighteen months in Europe, in 1907-08, did not encroach upon my capital. In each case, our traveling expenses, apart from purchases, were nearly paid for by life insurance policies, and the balance by my income from my investments. In fact, my capital increased somewhat, during those long trips, for a part of my income was added to it. Of course, had we not taken those trips, my capital—in money—would have been increased far more than it was; but my—our—capital in pleasure, information, and culture, far more than the money, would have been deplorably less.

I lost a good deal of money in the Michigan Lake Superior Power Company, but so far as my good judgment at the time went, and my knowledge of the people who were at the head of it, I cannot blame myself—although I regret it.

The largest loss I have ever had was in the Real Estate Trust Company. Knowing the directors, Weir Mitchell, Edward P. Borden, John H. Converse, Joseph deForest Junkin, and others like them (and a better, more upright set of men could not be found in Philadelphia), and trusting the president, Frank K. Hipple, as I would my own brother Charles, I gradually added to my holdings, until I had 250 shares of the stock. I was receiving 12%—$3,000 a year—in dividends. On January 1st, 1906, I inventoried the stock on my balance sheet at $325 per share, or $81,250. Then, in the summer, while Florence, Dora, and I were in the Canadian Rockies, came Hipple's suicide. The company was saved from absolute bankruptcy by the skill of George H. Earle, Jr. and by the splendid self-sacrifice of the directors. But on January 1st, 1907, I inventoried my 250 shares at the nominal figure of $10 per share, instead of $325, a loss of nearly $80,000. In addition, the $3,000 a year cut from my income was a very severe blow to me at the time.

At present (January, 1916), the common stock—and all mine is common—is quoted at between $32 and $35. When it will resume dividends is very uncertain. *(Note, April 1926: By a curious irony of fate, the Pennsylvania Sugar Co., established by fraud and by Segal, with Hipple's help, is now a very profitable asset of the Real Estate Trust Company. The latter has been paying 7% for two or three years, and its value is over $200 per share. The final value will be much above its present value.)*

On the other hand, my investments in other trust companies, and in the Stetson Hat Company, have been very fortunate. The best ultimate investment I have ever made, in my opinion, was the purchase of 1727, 1731, and 1733 Chestnut Street (and I later bought 1721, 1721½, 1723, and 1725).

Some thirty or more years ago, I was offered (twice, in fact) 1727 for only $16,000. The only trouble was that I didn't have the $16,000. The lot was unimproved, but in the then state of my finances, I did not dare to borrow to buy and build, lest it should swamp me. In 1910, I had to pay $70,000 for it, in order to protect the light of 1729 on the east side, for any buildings higher than the present ones—which have greatly reduced my light—would have been a disaster for our home.

Hardly had I bought 1727 (my name was not known in the transaction, of course) than 1731 and 1733 were offered to me, at about the same price. I did not hesitate a moment but bought them both. The present rentals bring in practically little or no return on the investment, but in ten or fifteen years—1925 to 1930—it will be a different story, and I am willing to sacrifice my own present income for the ultimate benefit of my children and grandchildren.

These four properties, 1727 to 1733, cover a lot 79' by 120', a lot large enough for a large building by itself. But with the corner, which is 44' by 120', they become a lot 123' by 120', a splendid corner property for a very large and lofty building. By 1925 or 1930, I believe these four properties will easily be worth an average of $150,000 each, or $600,000 in all—and possibly more. *(Note, April, 1926: Eventually, I bought 1729, for $60,000, and later sold everything from 1721* *to 1733 inclusive for $975,000. To finance it, I had to borrow $250,000, so the net return to me was $725,000. Could I have waited two or three years, I could have sold them for far more, but the burden nearly broke my financial back as it was. The proceeds of this, and of Point-No-Point, I have placed in a trust fund with the Aldine Trust Company for my children, whose income is thus assured for all their lives, beyond any peradventure, in even more than comfort. Besides this, I made a trust fund for them with the Girard Trust Company, in 1919, of securities (all gilt-edged), which in five or six years have increased over 50% in capital value.)*

As to my professional income, the largest gross income for any one year—and only one (1900)—was a little over $55,000. In only one other year did it ever exceed $35,000. From 1890, the year after my election as Professor of Surgery, to 1905 were the fifteen years of my largest professional income. In six of those years I received, gross, between $30,000 and $35,000.

The mythical fee of $75,000[21] never materialized, alas!

The largest fee I ever received, $10,000, was for two consecutive and difficult cerebral operations which, after long convalescence, saved the young man's life. The mother, a wealthy woman, never objected to the amount of the bill, but delayed and postponed and delayed, paying in installments only, until after several years, I obtained the final payment only after putting the case in the hands of an attorney and threatening suit.

Twice I have received a fee of $7,500, once for a very difficult brain operation, and once for a fulminating attack of appendicitis—for which I operated at 3 A.M. Both of these cases involved wealthy people, and both, like the $10,000 case, were out of town and required repeated, time-consuming visits. Never were fees more willingly paid, especially in the latter case. I did not see the parents in that case for several years, but when I did meet them, at a reception at the Carnegie Institution in Washington, their gratitude for my saving the life of their son was almost embarrassing.

I have received probably three or four, possibly five, fees of $5,000 each, but most of my fees have been from $2,000 down, the number of cases increasing as the amount of the fee diminished. The great majority have been from $100 to $1,000—and not nearly so many of the latter as of the former. Yet I have been told that I had the reputation of charging enormous fees! If I had done so, my balance sheet would show a very different picture than it does. I suppose that my financial books would show at least $100,000 justly due me which has never been paid. Only two or three times have I ever sued for a bill—and always won. I have received my best and richest fees from the poor, whom I have served without money and without price. For years after 1865, many of my old Army patients sought me out for a handshake and a hearty "God bless you!" When my daughters read the many letters of gratitude—which I have recently re-read with many a heart thrill, they will agree with me as to the best rewards of my long and active surgical life.

INVITATIONS FROM ABROAD

I have had several invitations to go elsewhere than Philadelphia as a professor of surgery, but none of them were sufficiently attractive to tempt me even to consider them.[22]

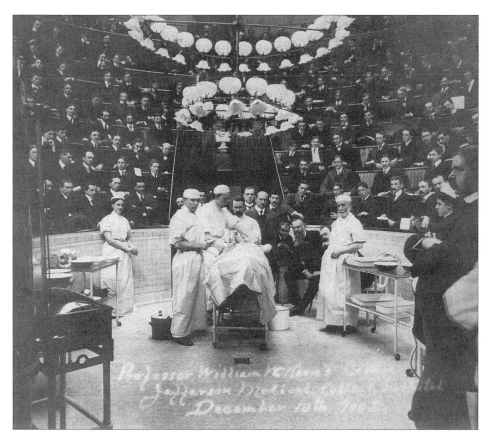

Professor William W. Keen's Clinic, Jefferson Medical Hospital, December 10th, 1902, **by Edgar Newton Fought (Seated closest to and peering around Keen are visiting Viennese surgeons Prof. Dr. Adolf Lorenz and Dr. Friedrich Mutter.)** *[Historical Collections, the College of Physicians of Philadelphia]*

San Francisco

Early in March of 1880, I received the following letter from San Francisco, with its offer that, however attractive, I declined. (It was from a man with whom I had shared quarters while studying in Paris, in 1864-65.)

> *Friend Keen:*
>
> *...I am appointed one of a committee to fill the [surgical] chair, and upon my representation of your qualifications, the committee have asked me to write to you and ask you if you would like to leave the sleepy old town of Philadelphia and come out here to accept the Chair of the Principles and Practice of Surgery in the Medical Department of the University of California. Our regular term begins June 1st. You would like California, no doubt. I do not believe I over-state the matter when I say you can expect to get a practice of $20,000 per year. And with the prestige you would naturally have from coming here to occupy the Chair, you would not be long in making yourself a practice.*
>
> *Your old friend,*
>
> *W.J. McNutt*

Boston

In November of 1882, Oliver Wendell Homes resigned as Professor of Anatomy at Harvard. At the request of some of the faculty, Dr. Weir Mitchell submitted a proposal to me to take Holmes's place for a year, and if my teaching proved satisfactory, that I should be appointed to the Chair. This was a very proper condition, and a test I should have welcomed most heartily, as I had been teaching Systematic Anatomy since 1875. Boston was only an hour away from Fall River, my dear wife and I had many Boston friends, and the Harvard atmosphere was very attractive, as well. But I should have been obliged to relinquish an increasingly successful practice and devote all my time to the duties of the Chair, at a time when I had a growing interest in surgery. In addition, I had a wife and four daughters, for whose support I was almost entirely dependent upon my earnings, and the $3,000 salary was so meager as to preclude my seriously considering the proposition attractive, much less the possibility of accepting such a position. I was convinced that it would be far wiser for me to remain in Philadelphia and devote myself exclusively to surgery.

Chicago

In 1891, when Dr. Charles Parkes, Professor of Surgery at Rush Medical College, died, my good friend, Dr. Nevins Hyde, Professor of Dermatology in that flourishing school, came to see me, on behalf of the faculty, and offered me Parkes's chair. He was most kind and urgent and stated that in Chicago, I would have a professional income of $100,000 a year in less than five years. After due consideration, I declined the promotion. I was over forty and had gained a satisfactory and growing surgical clientele; my family ties were strong; my friends, medical, scientific, and social, were many and warm; and my religious associations were most agreeable. To break away from all these and go to the West (as Chicago was then considered) would be a mistake for which no amount of money could compensate. The latter makes a living; the former makes a life. Unquestionably I should be far better off than I am now, pecuniarily, had I gone to Chicago or California; yet I shall leave my children a sufficiency, I think, and the last thirty years of my life have been far more satisfactory to me from every other aspect.

SPEAKING IN PUBLIC

I have always lectured extemporaneously, having before me only a few notes as an outline of the lecture, so as to be sure to preserve a logical order, and also so as not to omit or repeat. But on more formal occasions, I wrote out my address and read it.

In writing such addresses (and my scientific papers), I always followed a regular routine. First, I gathered all my material and drew up a skeleton of the address, with chief headings and a more or less full list of subheadings, making brief notes of the topics and facts and arranging them in the order in which I intended to present them. My secretary put markers at all the desired pages in the books or journals to be consulted. After mulling over the matter for some time, I dictated or sometimes wrote a rough sketch to my secretary. (In an evening, from eight to ten o'clock, I could usually dictate about three thousand words, the equivalent of four pages of *Harper's Magazine*.) My secretary then typed this copy, with about double the usual space between the lines. I went over this several times, erasing, adding, transposing, and editing in general. Time permitting, I preferred to lay aside this sketch for some days and then attack it afresh. The manuscript was usually a tangled mess, which had to be deciphered by my secretary. She then made a fair copy, in duplicate. I read over the carbon copy with great care, only for the purpose of correcting the English, since the arguments and facts had already been corrected in the rough copy. When the carbon copy was satisfactory, I embodied the corrections in the original, which I would use for the formal reading.

The original was typed on sheets of rather stiff paper, the size of letter paper, and on one side only. As I read each page, I slipped it behind the last page, and so was never annoyed by having a manuscript which would easily bend over and thus be difficult to read.

Once, at the opening of the winter session at the Woman's Medical College, when I was on the program to make the "introductory" address, I picked up my manuscript from my office desk and went on my way in peace. In consequence of the method I have just described, I was, of course, familiar with both the substance of my lecture (including, to a large extent, its exact wording) and with the sequence of the ideas to be covered.

I read freely, that is to say, not bound to my text. Being nearsighted, I used spectacles with the lower half cut away. By looking through the upper half, I could look at my audience, an important means of keeping in touch with them. By looking underneath the lenses, I could glance at my manuscript and, by catching a word or phrase, could immediately look up and into the eyes of my listeners.

After I had read a number of pages of my address, on this occason, I partly displaced the sheet from which I was reading, so as to slip it behind the others, quickly exposing the next sheet, and I saw, to my consternation, that the next sheet was Page One! In picking up my manuscript from my desk, I evidently had taken only part of it, inadvertently leaving some four or five sheets, strange to say.

That the human mind *can* do two things at once I then found to be both true and *very* useful. While reading the last four or five lines, I debated what I should do. Only two courses were open to me: first, to confess the fault and stop abruptly; or second, to continue extemporaneously. I promptly chose the latter course. Never was I more glad that my method of preparing an address had made me so familiar with the text.

I turned the last sheet to the back and proceeded extemporaneously, deceptively glancing at my manuscript, from time to time. When I had spoken, as I judged, about the amount that would have occupied a page, I slipped the uppermost sheet to the back and so continued, sheet by sheet, until I reached my conclusion. But that hot sweat covered my face, and that my mental tension and activity were most strenuous, for those few minutes, were mild statements of fact. I am convinced that I succeeded in my venial fraud.

Carbon Copies

The International Medical Congress was held in Berlin in 1890. Cerebral surgery was the most important field of progress, but such a new field that many parts had been imperfectly explored, and some not explored at all. I happened to have had several cases involving the opening of the lateral ventricles, and one on irrigating the ventricles from side to side across the entire brain.

Deciding to prepare an elaborate paper on "The Surgery of the Lateral Ventricles" for the Congress, I spent all of my spare time for an entire year collecting every relevant case or paper. I searched systematically, first of all exhausting the resources of the College of Physicians of Philadelphia. Then I went to Washington and, with the invaluable help of the index catalog of the Surgeon General's library, and the *Index Medicus*, going back to the days of Paré and the old black leather books, I investigated the older literature, in many quartos and Latin folios, every case from the Middle Ages down.

No one had as yet written an important paper on this subject, though many cases had been reported. My paper, when completed, involved some eighty pages of typewritten manuscript, and, I may say without vanity, it was a most valuable contribution to the subject.

Of course, no paper of such length could be read *in extenso* at the Congress, so I made a four-page written abstract. Immediately after reading this résumé at the Congress, I placed it—and the full paper—personally into the hands of Dr. (now Professor) Eduard Sonnenberg, of Berlin, who was the Secretary of the Surgical Section and responsible for the publication in the *Transactions* of papers presented at the Congress.

In those days, few doctors had secretaries, and carbon paper copies were just beginning to be used. Possibly they did not exist until later. In any case, I had only the original lengthy manuscript and no copy.

The following summer, while vacationing in the Adirondacks, I received a cable from Ernst von Bergmann, the chairman of the Surgical Section: "If you don't forward your manuscript at once only a Referat can be published."

I immediately cabled: "Manuscript and *Referat* handed to Sonnenberg by myself immediately after reading the paper."

I followed this with a letter to von Bergmann, with a full account of the facts, and to Sonnenberg. The latter never replied at all, and von Bergmann wrote that my manuscript could not be found. I was in despair. I had no carbon copy of the original paper. I could sympathize with Carlyle, whose manuscript of one whole volume of his history of the French Revolution was burned up by a careless housemaid who lighted a fire with it, but I did not have the undaunted industry with which he re-wrote it. I had not the courage or the time to re-write the paper. A year had passed since my search through the literature. I had other things to do. I was forced to let the abstract be published, rather than the original.

From then until now, I have never received any letter of explanation—or apology—from either von Bergmann or Sonnenberg. A year's labor thrown away. And in the intervening twenty-one years, no one has ever as thoroughly tackled the subject in any complete paper.

Twice since then, in Berlin and in Paris, I have been assigned to escort Frau Sonnenberg in to dinner. On each occasion, I confess to having taken a rather malicious pleasure in making myself as agreeable as possible to *her* while remaining frigidly formal and polite to *him*. I have scorned to allude to his carelessness, and he has never been manly enough to confess his fault.

In 1914, at the Fourth Congress of the International Surgical Society, in New York, I am not sure whether he nominated me or seconded my nomination as President of the next Congress, but I responded to his brief, but quite eulogistic, speech with thanks but not effusion.

But I learned my lesson and since then have never written *anything* of consequence without retaining a carbon copy.

Yellow Journalism

One Wednesday evening, I read a paper on the massaging of the heart following chloroform collapse. I had collected for this paper all of the then-reported cases and added two new ones: one of my own (fatal), and one of Dr. Igelsrud (successful), of Tromsø, Norway.

Next morning, I was called up by the editorial office of the *New York Evening Journal*, one of Hearst's newspapers. The reporter said he had understood that I had made a great discovery and "had brought the dead back to life." He wanted the full particulars for the paper. I replied that they were quite right, except that I had made no great discovery and since my patient had not recovered, I had not brought the dead back to life.

I added that I could not give them any information whatever, as I was averse to the publication of professional cases in lay journals, and that when my paper was published, it would then be public property and they could get the facts and make any comments they saw fit. I also requested that nothing be published about this case.

About an hour or so later, the same editorial office called again and said that they had not understood whether my patient had died or recovered, to which I replied that he had died two years ago and was still dead.

In that very afternoon's *Journal*, they published about a third of a column, with banner headline, proclaiming Dr. Keen's wonderful discovery and his bringing back to life a man who had died. They even reported having interviewed this man, who described his sensations, etc.

I was furious at such obviously conscious mendacity and wrote a highly indignant letter to Mr. Hearst himself, commenting that he could hardly have learned to lie so outrageously while at Harvard. The paper's managing editor replied that Mr. Hearst was attending to his congressional duties in Washington, that they were extremely sorry to have misstated the facts, and that their columns were open to any communication I might wish to make. I responded that I had never bought a copy of a Hearst paper, much less printed anything in one, and that I declined to do so now.

In 1907 or 1908, while in Rome, I saw that Hearst, in order to influence the election in New York, had sent a long telegram to the *Times* accusing a political opponent of lying. It was timed so that there was no possibility of a reply in the New York papers before the election. I could not resist the temptation: I wrote to the *Times* and described Hearst's lying in my own case, and they published my letter.

Another illustration of the persistence of a newspaper in spreading false news is the following incident.

In May, 1912, while I was abed with an injured knee, Dora was climbing Mt. Blackburn, in Alaska, and at about eight o'clock one evening, a reporter of the *Philadelphia Press* called to see me. He sent up word that he wanted to ask about a dispatch they had just received stating that two fellow climbers had left my daughter Dora and returned to Kennicott, leaving her marooned on the mountain and in danger of starvation. I had him come up at once, of course. The dispatch turned out to be an inquiry from the Western Press Association, in Seattle, asking if the report was true. I told him it evidently was false, for I had had a letter from Dora only two days before, in which she said she was taking five weeks' provisions. The date the men had left Dora was only two weeks from when she had started; if the two men could get back, so could she, so she could hardly have been marooned; and if the Seattle people wanted to know what was going on in Alaska, the place to inquire was Kennicott, not Philadelphia.

I especially requested, therefore, that he *not* publish the dispatch, and he promised to suppress it. The next morning, there was the dispatch, printed in full, without a word of my explanation, and I began to have inquiries from all sides, along with letters of sympathy and alarm. I wrote the editor to complain of the breach of faith. He replied that the reporter had no authority to suppress a dispatch and that these decisions rested with his superiors. He made no excuse for printing false news, nor any apology for the anxiety and pain which its publication caused me.

THE AMERICAN PHILOSOPHICAL SOCIETY

In the spring of 1907, having reached the age of seventy, I resigned my chair in Surgery at the Jefferson, and from then until the following October, I absented myself completely from the scene by means of an extended trip to Europe. In January of 1908, I was notified that I had been elected president of the American Philosophical Society.

As I learned after my return, I had been proposed for the presidency a few years earlier, on the resignation of General Wistar. The only other name put forth at that time, so far as I was able to determine, was that of Dr. Edgar Smith, provost of the University of Pennsylvania, and Dr. C.C. Harrison asserted positively that Dr. Smith, and not I, must be elected. After Dr. Smith resigned, there was no further opposition to my nomination.

My election was all the more complimentary in that it was known that I was not to return to America until the fall of 1908 at the earliest. I had been informed of my proposed election and had consented to serve, though of course I had done nothing to promote it.

It was the highest scientific honor I have ever received. To sit in the chair which had been occupied by Franklin, Rittenhouse, Jefferson (this last for eighteen years), and their distinguished successors, was far above anything I had ever dreamed of. Though I had been elected to membership in 1884, I never took an active part in the society, though I served on the council for three years.

While still abroad, I laid my plans for a vigorous administration in various ways, and as soon as I returned, I threw myself into the work with all the ardor I could command.

The meetings were held twice a month, on the first and third Fridays from October through May. On my arrival, only a few days before the first of October, I found that on October 2nd, A.E. Kennelly and Walter L. Upson were to present a paper on "The Humming Telephone," and that E.B. Titchener and W.H. Pyle were to present a paper on "The After-Images of Subliminal Colored Stimuli," but that no other speakers had been provided.

I was fortunate in immediately securing Dr. E.O. Hovey, of the American Museum of Natural History, for October 16th, the first meeting at which I personally presided. He read a very interesting paper entitled "A Contribution to the History of Mt. Pelée, Martinique." In New York, I also secured Dr. Alexis Carrel, of the Rockefeller Institute, who presented a paper on November 6th entitled "Recent Studies in Transplantation of Organs in Animals." On November 20th, Mr. Rosengarten read a paper on "The Early History of the American Philosophical Society," and Professor T.H. Montgomery followed with a paper on "The Recapitulation Theory of Embryologists."

Meantime, I had gone to Washington, where I spent several days interviewing our own Washington members, as well as the heads of some of the scientific bureaus of the government, and obtained several promises of additional papers. All of those I saw, whether members or not, were most kind and cordial, and their cooperation gave us a little breathing room.

On the first of April, 1910, we decided to hold only one meeting a month, and that was to be on the first Friday. In the beginning, when life in Philadelphia was simple and engagements were few, the meetings were held every Friday evening, as is still the case with the Royal Society. But with the increasing complexity of modern life in a large city, when everyone has many interests and many engagements, the Society wisely has been led to schedule less frequent meetings.

I have found excellent support from a number of our members, and we never have missed a meeting; nor have we ever been without a speaker, except twice, as I remember, on those occasions when the meeting was scheduled for the first two or three days of October, when we could hardly expect to gather an audience. On the two occasions when our expected speakers failed us, on account of illness, I filled the breach myself.

We have had a number of special meetings when we were addressed by especially distinguished speakers: Hon. Charlemagne Tower; Signor Guglielmo Ferrero, of Rome; Sir William Ramsay, who on the first of November in 1912 presented to the society the first photograph ever taken showing the paths of individual electrons; Professor J.C. Bose, of the Presidency College in Calcutta, who demonstrated electrically the similarity of rhythmical impulses in plants to the nervous impulses in animals; and on April 23, 1909, we commemorated the fiftieth anniversary of Darwin's publication *On the Origin of Species*, with addresses by Mr. Bryce, the British ambassador, Professor Goodale, of Harvard, and Professor Fullerton, of Columbia.

Besides monthly meetings, some fourteen years ago, at the instance of Dr. Minis Hays, the Society, which at that time had fallen into an almost somnolent condition, inaugurated a general meeting for all our members. This has been a great success and has re-established the Society in the dignity and importance to which it is rightly entitled. These meetings are usually attended by about a hundred members, and the papers read are of the most important character. By an amicable arrangement with the National Academy of Science, the two societies meet in the same week, dividing the time equally between them so that, as many persons are members of both, they can attend both meetings with the outlay of time and money for a single journey.

Beginning in 1912, the Saturday afternoon of the general meeting has been given over to a symposium on some topic of general interest, viz.:

      1912   Stellar Spectroscopy
      1913   Wireless Telegraphy
      1914   The Physics and Chemistry of Protoplasm
      1915   The Constitution of Matter
      1916   International Law

This last one was of exceptional interest. It was organized by Professor John Bassett Moore, who introduced the subject. He was followed by the Hon. Charlemagne Tower, Professor G.G. Wilson, of Brown (now Harvard), Professor Philip M. Brown, of Princeton, and the Hon. David Jayne Hill.

At various general meetings, there have been presentations of medallions: for example, one of Hooker and another (with a fine steel engraving) of Darwin. In 1913, my portrait, painted by Robert Vonnoh, was presented by Mr. Rosengarten and received by Professor Pickering.

In 1906, the Society arranged a splendid celebration of the bicentenary of Franklin's birth, and the meeting was a remarkable success in every way. Congress authorized a special medal to be struck,[23] and while I have one of the copies in bronze, the original, in solid gold, was presented to the government of France.[24]

The Society has held three memorial meetings, following the death of each of three distinguished members: in 1909, in honor of Henry Lea; in 1912, in honor of Howard Furness; and in 1914, in honor of Weir Mitchell. A number of other organizations took part in each, and there were notable addresses.

Our dinners are unique. Always printed on the menu is an appropriate quotation, perpared by various members such as Shakespearean scholars Horace

Howard Furness, père et fils, or Dr. Holland, Professor Gummere, and Professor Schelling, with prominence given to other Elizabethan writers. The last, in 1916, featured a number of legal quotations and was prepared by Hampton Carson. The toasts are always four in number: "To the memory of Franklin"; "To our sister societies"; "To our universities" (or "To our institutions of learning," depending on the speaker); and "To the American Philosophical Society."

One dinner will always stand out in my memory for the most distinguished and brilliant speeches I have ever heard. On my right sat Ambassador James Bryce, an Englishman who had written the best book on the American commonwealth;[25] and on my left sat Harvard president Lawrence Lowell, an American who had written the best book on the government of England.[26] Both they and Henry Smith Pritchett, trustee of the Carnegie Foundation for the Advancement of Science, spoke, and spoke admirably. But the gem of the occasion, and the best after-dinner speech I ever heard, was by President Francis Patton of Princeton, on Benjamin Franklin. He used not a note and hesitated for not a word—and the word chosen was always the right word. He was logical, witty, learned, and, in fact, everything that was brilliant and fascinating.

At the April dinner of 1912, I presented to Mr. Charles Burr the Phillips Law Prize of two thousand dollars. His essay was chosen out of nine, by a notable panel of judges including diplomat Joseph H. Choate, of New York; Jacob M. Dickinson (late Secretary of War), of Tennessee; John C. Gray, Harvard Law School professor; Henry W. Rogers, dean of the Yale Law School; and professor of international law James Brown Scott.

The subject was "The Treaty-Making Power of the United States and the Methods of its Enforcement as Affecting the Police Powers of the States." Mr. Burr wrote the best essay ever written on the subject, according to all good judges, and from it has arisen a large and remunerative practice in international law, I am told, and he deserves it.

The committee who selected the subject consisted of [Pennsylvania] Chief Justice Mitchell and four other lawyers. Several topics had been submitted for consideration, and the one chosen was the topic I had suggested. I proposed it because I had felt deeply the weakness of the United States in dealing with injuries to the persons and property of aliens, particularly in Louisiana, California, and states in the Northwest.

Burr's essay showed clearly the supreme power of the United States as to treaty rights. I sent copies of it to ex-presidents Roosevelt and Taft, to President Wilson, Secretary of State Bryan, Senator Elihu Root, and many others. It was acknowledged by everyone except Mr. Bryan, who, judging by his policy in foreign affairs, I conclude has never even opened it.[27]

We have had as members ten presidents of the United States. Roosevent and Taft were elected to membership while in the White House, and the other eight had been members for a number of years prior to their election. It has always been with pleasure and heightened esteem to meet with Mr. Taft, at the annual dinner meetings, at one of which the establishment of a National Seismological Bureau was proposed, and at another, the re-establishment of the Army Canteen. When Mr. Wilson was sworn in, in 1913, a committee consisting of Messrs. Root, Woodward (president of the Carnegie Institute), Walcott (secretary of the Smithsonan Institution), Tittman (superintendent of the Coast and Geodetic Survey), General Greely, and I, were directed to present to the President (who had been a member since 1897) a congratulatory address. In subsequent conversation, alluding to the fact that he was the eighth member of the Society to enter the White House, I told him that I sometimes even shook in my shoes myself.

On my 75th birthday, in 1912, Florence invited all the local members of the Society—as well as the members of the Franklin Inn Club—to come in and greet me at home. The occasion was a most delightful one.

The Commonwealth of Pennsylvania owned all of Independence Square and the buildings on it (which the city later acquired from the state), and in 1785, the state donated the site on 5th St. to the Society, which erected its buildings in 1787. By 1911, we were convinced, after much debate in several meetings, that we ought to move. The reasons were several.

With the westward expansion of the city, our original site is now far out of the way; our building is not fire-proof (and could not be made such), so that all our treasures are in danger of being completely destroyed, along with collateral danger to Independence Hall itself; our walls are already weighted to the limit of safety, so that we have had to store ten thousand volumes in a nearby fireproof building; and we have outgrown our building: We need a reading room and a relic room, both to be open to the public.

The first vote for removal came at a special meeting in May, when the votes were 57 to 7 in favor. At the June 2nd meeting, the vote was unanimous. On November 29th, 1911, we also voted to accept a contract with the city, which would give us a lot on the Parkway at 16th and Cherry, in exchange for our old lot and building. The contract was obtained one year later.

The main stumbling block has been the lack of funds. When the stock exchange moved from 5th and Chestnut to Broad and Walnut, the brokers (and others) naturally followed. This left us with only one tenant, instead of four, who had occupied the lower rooms, which we could not use for our own purposes. Our income from these rooms had been $5,500, but we now get only $1,500—which is likely to be further reduced when the current lease expires.

The burden of raising the money has fallen on my shoulders, to a large extent. I have had a hard time. The depression of 1913–14 made it impracticable for me to obtain subscriptions, and now that prosperity has returned and the war profits are being made, the endless appeals for the victims of the Great War seriously interfere with my success.

Still, to date (May 1st, 1916), I have raised fifty thousand dollars for the building fund, with a contingent subscription of ten thousand dollars by Messrs. Alba Johnson and Samuel Vauclain, which will be added to every ninety thousand I raise, up to $650,000. For publication funds, I have obtained $13,500 in endowment, and from Dr. C.F. Brush, of Cleveland, a donation of ten thousand dollars for our general support.

I also have some prospects which I hope will materialize. I have been twice to New York, with no result, and once to Boston, with a yield of six hundred dollars. If my life is spared, I hope to attain our goal of $750,000, a tidy little sum covering $300,000 for a building, $250,000 for the endowment, and $200,000 for the promotion of research. If I don't get it, it will not be for want of persistent work.[28]

Among the names of those who have died since I became president, are the following. They indicate the resplendent names on our roll of membership:

Wolcott Gibbs	Charles Francis Adams
Simon Newcomb	Samuel Dickson
Henry C. Lea	James T. Mitchell
Anton Dohrn	Sir James A.H. Murray
H.P. Bowditch	Frederick W. Putnam
F.A. March	Lewis Boss
Jacob H. Van't Hoff	Horace Howard Furness
Rear Admiral George W. Melville	W.W. Goodwin
Sir Joseph D. Hooker	Rt. Hon Joseph Lord Lister
Jules Henri Poincaré	John S. Billings
Lester F. Ward	Rt. Hon. Lord Avebury
Sir William Henry Preece	Alfred Russel Wallace
Silas Weir Mitchell	B.O. Peirce
Sir David Gill	W.S. Holden
W. A. Wright	August Weismann
Charles S. Minot	Rear Admiral Alfred Thayer Mahan

THE COLLEGE OF PHYSICIANS
OF PHILADELPHIA

Having been nominated by Dr. Weir Mitchell, I was elected a Fellow of the College of Physicians of Philadelphia in 1867. Prior to that, I had attended some of the College meetings down in the "picture house" of the Pennsylvania Hospital, between 8th and 9th on Spruce. (This building was so called because it was erected for the purpose of publicly displaying Benjamin West's painting *Death on a Pale Horse*, which is now in the possession of the Pennsylvania Academy of the Fine Arts.) In 1863, the College moved to the building at the corner of 13th and Locust.

When I was first elected, Robert Bridges, assistant to Dr. Bache (who was the professor of Chemistry at the Jefferson), was the librarian. The library was open for one or two hours a day, and only one or two days of the week, instead of, as now, from ten till six every weekday, with extended hours for two evenings in the week.

The entire library, when we moved, was carried in three or four wagon-loads. The early meetings of the College were pretty dull, for we had a series of reports on meteorology and the effects of weather on health, which could better have been read by title and printed for those who wished to consult them. After the move, however, the library and the college took on a new life. A great source of encouragement was Samuel Lewis, who had such a bad stutter that he never entered into practice, though his means allowed him to live in comfort and have considerable to spare. He started the Lewis Library, for which he was constantly buying books. It has been a large and important part of the college library for years.

In 1900, I was elected president. There is always a contest over the vice-presidency, but the winner is automatically elevated to the presidency three years later. I resigned in 1901, as Florence, Dora, and I were embarking on a two-year trip around the world, so I was not able to serve the third year of the usual allowable term in office.

On my election, I found that we had only ten or fifteen thousand dollars in endowment funds for the library. This made it impossible for us to purchase any books, as the money was used up in bookbinding and in the subscriptions to journals. As president, I got busy and raised about sixty thousand dollars in various funds (including a five-thousand-dollar contribution of my own), whose purpose was the purchase of binding and books for the library, plus $2,500 for a building fund.

In 1882, at the insistence of Weir Mitchell, the college established the directory for nurses. Dr. Sinkler and I joined Mitchell as the committee to organize this directory. We worked hard over it, and it became a great success from the very start. From then until now, it has paid about two thousand dollars a year into the treasury of the College, exclusively for the use of the library, so that as of now, it has produced over sixty-eight thousand dollars. I retired after long service as chairman of this committee and was succeeded by Dr. James Wilson. The directory has been a great boon to physicians, to the sick, to those who have met with serious accidents or emergencies, and to the nurses themselves.

Our quarters at 13th and Locust finally became so crowded with books that they were sometimes stacked two or three deep on the shelves, and it was simply impossible not to make a radical change. A number of the conservatives, especially Arthur Meigs, bitterly opposed moving, and there was a great division of opinion over the matter. They wished to buy the adjoining building lot and to put an addition on the existing building, an addition that would have been inadequate. Dr. Mitchell and I, with help of some of the younger men, held out for complete removal. After several years of debate, we carried the day by a large majority. Even then, the feelings ran so high that it almost severed some early friendships, which was absurd.

We bought a lot on 22nd Street above Chestnut for eighty thousand dollars. The adjoining lot was bought by Mr. Eckley Coxe, Jr. for forty thousand dollars and given to the college, a donation engineered by Vice-president Dr. Sinkler, in spite of being ill at the time. (Little did we dream that it was to be his last illness.) No better service was ever done the College than this. The adjoining lot had been occupied by a stable but was then bought by a syndicate of gentlemen whose purpose was to transform it into a garage, which, filled with barrels of gasoline and motor oil, would have presented a serious fire hazard, not only to us on the north but still more to the church on the south, which was much closer. The building was pulled down and the lot made into an attractive garden as a memorial to Dr. Sinkler.

During my lifetime, two members of the College have served as president for two terms, Dr. Weir Mitchell and Dr. Jacob Mendez DaCosta, both Jefferson graduates.

Mitchell was a great force in the College for many years and was its greatest friend, giving not only money but also gifts of all sorts of curios, rare books, pamphlets, and manuscripts. Most important of all was his personal devotion and the spirit which he infused into nearly all the members. Our later presidents have done much for the College, in raising and giving money, and in obtaining additions to our bibliographical and medical treasures.

November 10th, 1909, was a proud day, when we opened the new building and, following the president of the college, in walked Mitchell with Andrew Carnegie, who had just donated a hundred thousand dollars.[29]

The building cost about three hundred thousand dollars, and the rooms were furnished by the descendants of deceased fellows—especially officers—of the College. In addition, we have had some notable gifts, especially the bequest, just received, of Dr. Lewis Duhring. He has willed us five thousand dollars for a special fund, the income to be used for the purchase of books on dermatology, plus one-fifth of his residuary estate, which amounted to about two hundred thousand dollars. This now gives us an endowment of three hundred thousand dollars for the library alone.

I suppose that our real estate is worth about five or six hundred thousand dollars, and our invested funds something over a hundred thousand. Our library, with more than 110,000 volumes, is probably worth about $150,000, since our collection of incunabula alone amounts now to nearly two hundred volumes worth a large sum. Our entire worth probably comes close to $1.5 million, quite a contrast to when I was first elected a Fellow!

As late as 1866, when Dr. Ezra Dyer first settled in Philadelphia, he was the only man who could scientifically prescribe a pair of glasses, and so strong was the prejudice against specialists, in those days, that Dyer's (and later Dr. William Thomson's) friends thought it wise to postpone for some years proposing them for fellowship in the College of Physicians, lest they should be black-balled. By contrast, in 1910, Dr. George E. de Schweinitz, purely and simply an ophthalmologist, was elected *president* of that same college.

In 1876, while preparing the Toner lecture on "Surgical Complications of Typhoid Fever," I had to get two large dry-goods boxes full of books from Washington for my research. If I had to do the same work today, I doubt if there would be more than half a dozen volumes that would not be available in the library of the College of Physicians.

3

—••◦ɛ)ɛ ꒧◦••—

On the Road

ABOUT 1855, my father and mother went as far as the Mississippi for the first time. Father had given my brothers George and Charley money to start them in business but (naturally) never had given me anything.[1] In St. Paul, a bustling, thriving city, he found a nice lot on 4th Street which he bought for $400. In 1864, I sold it for $10,000. This gave me the means to defray my expenses for 21 months in Europe.

By the early summer of 1864, the Confederacy was evidently on its last legs (so at least I thought).[2] Kirke Porter was going to Europe for the benefit of his health and urged me to join him.

We crossed from Philadelphia to Liverpool on the sailing ship *Tuscarora* of the Cope Packet Line. Her sister ship, the *Tonawanda*, had been captured by the *Alabama* (Confederate pirate) and bonded, I think, for $250,000 to be paid on the recognition by Europe of the Confederate government. We and the captain's daughter, a girl of about fifteen or sixteen, were the only passengers. Our captain kept a *very* vigilant watch for any smoke and when it was discovered, he ran away from it as fast as he could.

We were driven off course by storms, as far south as the Bay of Biscay, so that the trip to Liverpool took twenty-one days. As we neared the English coast, we met another American ship and were told of the sinking of the *Alabama* a few days before. What a shout we set up! Kirke and I studied French during our transatlantic crossing, but as we had no teacher, our pronunciation was doubtless hair-raising, and our sentences probably violated all the rules of grammar. As gold was at three hundred and every shilling meant seventy-five cents, we were as economical as possible. After a month in England and Scotland, we crossed to Holland and went up the Rhine to Switzerland. Among other places, we visited the falls of the Giesbach, which were quite famous for their colored illumination at night by means of lamps behind the falls. Of course, electricity has vastly improved all of that.

At lunch, we wanted to order sandwiches and rolls. Since our small pocket dictionary did not contain either "sandwich" or "roll," I described the former by pantomime of bread, butter, and ham until the waitress understood, but rolls knocked me out.

I searched the dictionary in vain, but I finally made an attempt to ask the waitress for some *rouleaux de pain*, and strange to say, they actually appeared. As she placed them on the table, she said, with a smile, *"Voilà, monsieur, vos rouleaux de pain."*

The next morning, as we left the hotel, it seemed as if all of the waitresses in the hotel were gathered to see us—and to giggle over our *rouleaux de pain*.

We finally reached Paris early in October. There I settled down to work, while Kirke returned to America. In particular, I worked under Nélaton, Velpeau, Maisonneuve, and Duchenne de Boulogne, as well as a number of the *chefs de clinique*.

After a hard winter's work in Paris on French and Medicine—especially surgery—I took a holiday in Italy, spending Easter week in Rome. The monarch of the States of the Church, in 1865, was Pope Pius IX.[3] He and the cardinals were constantly met in the streets of Rome, he in white, with six horses, postilions, and footmen; they in scarlet and with four horses. I heard the *Miserere* in the Sistine Chapel on Good Friday, and was just back of the *Guardia Nobile* when the Pope passed up to the high altar on Easter Sunday, carried in the *sedia gestatoria*. He blessed me (among some thirty thousand of the devout) from the balcony, and later I saw the illumination of the dome of St. Peter's and, for the last time, the gorgeous fireworks on the Pincian Hill.

In 1866, instead of a united Italy, as now, there were Sardinia; Lombardy and Venice, under Austria; Parma; Modena; Tuscany; the States of the Church; and the two Sicilies—seven frontiers, with seven visas or passports; seven customs houses, searches, and often duties; and seven different currencies—to the joy of the money-changers and the sorrow of travelers. (In those days, the only two countries in the world where a passport was not required were Great Britain and the United States.)

In May, 1865, I settled in Vienna for the spring term in Medicine—and also to get some German. I boarded with a German family, consisting of parents, several children, and a niece, Fräulein Victorine. She and I could communicate in French, but we agreed to exchange service for service: she was to teach me

Keen during study-tour in Vienna and Berlin, 1865

German and I was to teach her English. Within a very few days, she confided to me that she was *verlobt* and offered with pride to show me the letter that her fiancé had written to her uncle, asking for her hand. As I never saw it, I suspect that one or the other had objected. Soon, the sentimental gave place to the practical, and the first two phrases she asked me to teach her in English were *Je vous aime* and *Donnez moi un baiser.* It was difficult for her to master the English letter *V,* and her first efforts, in a fetching way, produced "I luf you" and "Gif me a kiss." I did not respond to either enticement.

From July to October, my brother Charles and I traveled through France, Switzerland, Italy, Germany, Sweden, and Norway. Early in October, he left for home, and I settled in Berlin for the winter, with Langenbeck, Virchow, and Gurlt, among others.

While a student in Berlin, I wanted to buy a good edition of the tales of Baron Munchausen. I asked for the book in a bookstore, but, forgetting that the title should be pronounced "Munch-howsen," I pronounced it as if it were an English word, for it had, of course, become anglicized.

"*Bitte?*" (Pardon me?), asked the clerk.

I repeated the name of the book.

"*Was meinen Sie?*" (What do you mean?), he asked.

I repeated the name slowly and explicitly. A gleam appeared in his face, as he finally comprehended my meaning, and he explosively exclaimed, "*Ach! Munck-hausen.*" I got my book forthwith.

I had a similar lesson in Frankfurt, when I asked for the address of the Rothschilds' bank, but pronouncing it *Roth-child*, in the English way. Following a conversation something like the one I had in Berlin, my guide finally understood what I meant and exclaimed, "*Ach! Rote-shild,*" and I got my money.

The banker's name, like that of the champion braggart, had become so completely "naturalized" that, even after my Berlin experience, it took a second rebuke to cure me.

By February of 1866, due to over-study, I broke down with an attack of insomnia. After a month of idleness in other things (but of constant work to get well, at Dr. Beni-Barde's Hydro-Therapeutic Establishment at Auteuil) I recovered, attended to a few last things, and went to London for a farewell visit, and to see a bit of English surgery.

In May, I returned to Philadelphia, crossing with Henry Lippitt (the future Governor of Rhode Island) and Professor N.P. Hill, my old teacher of Chemistry at Brown (and later, senator and millionaire), on the final voyage of the *Scotia*, the last side-wheeler of the Cunard Line.

THE OPENING OF THE KIEL CANAL

In the summer of 1895, I went to Europe about five weeks in advance of my three younger daughters, who came over to meet me later. I used this time for a round of visits to different surgical clinics in order to study German methods. I had arrived in Hamburg a few days before the opening of the Kiel Canal, which took place on a Thursday, Friday, and Saturday. I went to Kiel on Monday morning and spent that day and the two days following in von Esmarch's clinic. (I learned a great deal, during those three days. Bier, now the successor of Langenbeck and von Bergmann, in Berlin, was then his first assistant.) I had written to him some weeks in advance, asking him if he would kindly engage suitable quarters for me, as I was entirely ignorant about the local hotels. In reply, I received a letter from the Princess Henrietta von Schleswig-Holstein, Gemahlin von Esmarch. She had gone herself to see a friend, a Frau Peterson, who kept a small but very nice boarding house and arranged for a bedroom and a salon, where I was made very comfortable. For the entire week, I was invited to one meal every day in the von Esmarch home. During the three *Feiertagen* at the end of the week, we had Prince Henry's band under the window, during mealtime. Von Esmarch also had obtained fine seats on the tribune, from which I could see everything.

All the court was in Kiel, during the last three days of the week, and I met several of those in the court circle. I particularly remember a bright and entertaining young countess, a bride of about twenty-five, whom I took in to dinner, on one occasion. Never were my ears on more tension than during that meal. She spoke in German at the pace of a racehorse, and I felt sure that my occasional *"Ja wohl"* or *"Gewiss"* came in at the wrong places. It was a comfort to me to turn to the princess, on whose right I sat, and have a little conversation in respectable English.

The celebration was wonderfully well organized. Each had directions as to his toilette, as well as to the boat on which he was to go to the end of the canal—some distance from Kiel itself. No spectators were put on boats where they could not be accommodated with seats.

At the actual canal opening, the Hohenzollern boat came first. On her deck were many colorfully costumed and distinguished-looking people. On the bridge were perhaps a dozen of the highest ranking admirals and generals, and on the *Überbrücke* stood one alone, the Kaiser, who was eminently *IT.* He was dressed in the white uniform of the *corps de garde*, with a bright red sash across his chest and his silver helmet, surmounted by the Prussian eagle, on his head. He looked every inch a king. He saluted, from time to time, and as he passed through the canal into the open water, salvos of artillery (three thousand guns in all) greeted him, to which were added innumerable bands and lusty cheers from the great multitude. It was a most inspiring sight.[4]

TWO FORTUNATE ESCAPES
FROM GREAT DANGER

The Jardin in the Mer de Glace

Kirke and I, travelling in Switzerland, formed an agreeable acquaintance with a young Englishman and made an excursion to the *Jardin*, on the first day of October.

We reached "the garden," an oasis surrounded by glacier ice between two points of land, without noticeable trouble, and we lunched and rested there for an hour or two. It was a hot day, and while we had crossed *to* the garden at eleven in the morning, by the time our guide started us across Talafre Glacier to reach land again, it was one or two in the afternoon. The ice was dripping, and sodden from the summer sun, and we had to cut steps for ourselves. Half-way across, we suddenly found ourselves standing on a projecting piece of ice that seemed insubstantial. As we four hikers weighed perhaps over six hundred pounds, the danger of the ice's breaking off was very great. In fact, we were not very encouraged to watch a similar but smaller projecting ledge break and fall perhaps forty or fifty feet, breaking into a thousand fragments.

Cautiously, and farther apart than before, to distribute the weight, we crept on, step by step. When we stood again on terra firma, we breathed a prayer of thankfulness for our escape.

(We ought to have reported our guide for his carelessness but did not. In addition to ignoring conditions, he had not thought to bring rope for the outing.)

The Shoshone Falls of the Snake River, in Idaho

In 1897, Florence, Dora, and I took our summer holiday in the Northwest and in Alaska. Among other places we visited were the splendid Shoshone Falls.

The river has eroded a deep canyon for itself of over a hundred feet deep and two or three hundred feet wide at the ferry. The ferry itself is two or three hundred feet above the falls and is crossed by a flat-bottomed, barge-like boat with a large drum in the middle. A steel rope, stretched from bank to bank, is wound around the drum, and with a crank handle the boatwoman turns the drum, working the boat from shore to shore.

When we were about half-way across, a furious wind suddenly rushed down the canyon, pushing our boat directly downstream toward the falls and making a V of the wire rope, with the apex at the drum. The party on board consisted of us three, our driver, the boatwoman, and two horses and a carriage. The tremendous pull on the rope made it impossible to turn the drum, though the driver and I tried to help the woman. So there we were, stalled in midstream, our lives depending on the strength of the wire and the security of the fastenings on both ends. Our situation seemed desperate.

The tempest, which *seemed* to last an hour (though it was probably less than five minutes) subsided and we reached shore—and later returned—safely. Never were five people more grateful for a wonderful escape.

SPEECH AT THE ANNUAL DINNER OF THE BRITISH MEDICAL ASSOCIATION, MONTREAL, SEPTEMBER 2, 1897[5]

[Recorded by B.M.A. secretary]

Dr. Keen said that in the absence of Professor Bowditch, who was also expected to respond to the toast, he now found himself called upon to make two speeches, at two o'clock in the morning. He would promise them, however, that the two speeches should be short.

The organization of that meeting did credit to the profession of Canada, and above all to the profession of Montreal. He only hoped that in Moscow they had a Roddick, an Adami, a Bell, an Armstrong, a Shepherd, and so on; he might go through the whole list of officers. They had also admired the learning gathered in the association, which met not for the purpose of hoarding trade secrets, but of casting them broadcast over the whole world. They had found in Montreal a most unbounded hospitality, a hospitality as royal as the mountain that had given its name to their city, a name which now graced their first citizen. They had found in Montreal a friendship as spontaneous as the clear crystal springs that flowed from their mountains and as broad as the acres of their great wheat fields, the granaries of a nation. He was sure he was the spokesman of every guest, nay, of every host also, when he said that the hardest tie to break would be that which bound them to one who was peerless as a benefactor to mankind, under every sun and in every clime, not only in the last years of the waning century but in all centuries to come, around whose head the gathering years were weaving a chaplet of honours intertwined with reverent love, Mr.—Sir Joseph—Lord Lister.

Nor did they forget the land to which their departing friends would go. It was historic ground, the land of Hampden, of Pym, and Harry Vane and John

Milton, hallowed by the blood of Roundheads and Puritans, hallowed by the fires of Smithfield and Oxford, in the glorious struggle for liberty; and as in this jubilee year of a glorious reign some of them would rest by Canadian firesides and others go to dear Old England, their cousins across the border, Britons only by one or two removes—for did not U.S. spell not *you* nor *me*, but *US?*—as they waved a last farewell, would join with all their hearts in singing "God Save the Queen."

SITTING IN THE SEATS OF THE MIGHTY

I was appointed one of the seven official government delegates to the International Medical Congress, in Paris. Also in Paris, in 1900, was the International Exposition, or World's Fair. Daughters Florence, Dora, and Margaret were with me.

One day, we agreed to separate after breakfast and meet for dinner. I went to the Congress, Florence and Dora went to the exposition, and Margaret stayed at home. In the morning, Margaret received an invitation addressed to me to which a reply was requested. Though written in English, it was signed *"Jacques"* and conveyed an invitation from the President of the Republic to occupy his box at the opera, that evening. Margaret accepted at once, expecting that my daughters were included. At the Congress, I met Dr. Jacobs, of Baltimore, the secretary of our government delegation—and the "Jacques" of the invitation. He explained to me that the President had courteously placed his box at the disposition of the seven official delegates.

I returned to our rooms rather early, explained the facts to the girls, and arranged that we should dine at the hotel where one of their friends, Dwight Merrick, was staying, ask him to dine with us, and then go along to the opera. All went auspiciously. I had bought four tickets in the orchestra for the young people and managed to leave the dinner table a little early so as to be in my place promptly.

I had been given no ticket, so I presented my visiting card at the ticket office and explained the invitation I had received. With no hesitation, I was handed over to a much be-medaled man who conducted me to the President's box (formerly that of Napoleon III). After a few moments, I was joined by Dr. Robert Weir, another delegate (and an old friend of mine from the 1862 days at Antietam-Frederick, Maryland). We sat there looking and feeling superior, as if accustomed to sitting in the imperial-presidential box, and condescending, from time to time, to cast a benevolent downward glance on my daughters and Merrick.

We sat through the first act of the opera, which was *Les Huguenots*, but we thought it odd that none of the other American delegates had arrived. Deciding to explore, we searched the corridors and foyer, but in vain. We finally went out on the large terrace in front of the opera house and spied the others in close consultation. They beckoned us to join them, and then we learned, to our consternation, that the invitation was not for the *Grand Opéra* but the *Opéra Comique*. We flew to our places, gathered up our belongings, and fled to the more appropriate theater.

What a complication it would have been if another guest—or even the President himself—had appeared in our loge while we were there! How embarrassing, and even inexplicable it would have been! Happy indeed were we to have been spared such humiliation!

I have often thought since then how extraordinary it was that we two could have penetrated to the President's box, without tickets and without authority. We have always said that we passed because of our honest and handsome faces.

The *Opéra Comique* performance was poor, and we soon left. Picking up Florence, Dora, and Margaret en route, we went to the home of Professor Lannelongue, the president of the Congress, who was giving a reception for the foreign delegates. I presented "M. Jacques" to Margaret, and ever since then, Jacobs has been our M. Jacques.

This last reminds me of a photograph of *Jacob Wrestling with the Angel*, which I bought in 1865, when I was studying in Berlin. The legend is printed in German, French, and alleged English, as follows:

> *Jacob mit dem Engel ringend*
> *Jacques luttant avec l'Ange*
> *Jack wringing with the Angel*

PERSONAL INCIDENTS OF TRAVEL IN PERSIA, BOKHARA, AND THE CAUCASUS

How Keen and His Daughters Escaped Imprisonment in Persia

In 1902, Florence, Dora, and I were traveling in Persia. At about this time, a Mme. Humbert, along with her brother and sister-in-law, M. et Mme. d'Aurignac, had perpetrated an enormous swindle, amounting to millions, and were being sought all over the world. The French government heard that they had been seen in Persia and telegraphed their minister to arrest them on sight.

As there are fewer than half a dozen places of entry and exit in Persia, the minister telegraphed to each of these, among them, Enzeli. The consul there replied that the three persons wanted had escaped on a steamer the night before. *We* were the three suspects! I said that we had two ample means of disproof: first, our passports; and second, hearing us speak French would be the convincer. It was bad enough to travel in Persia outside a prison. What it would have been inside a Persian prison one could only imagine. We doubtless should have had abundant reason to long for Persian insect powder, most appropriately named. We were blissfully ignorant of all these facts until told of them by Mr. Lloyd Griscom, who was the minister to Persia when we were there, and who mentioned them to me in 1903, while en route to his new mission as ambassador to Japan.

A Persian Play

While in Teheran, we visited the palace and the lovely gardens of the shah's brother. Being tired, I sat down in the shade of the front of the palace while the girls walked around it. They were gone for quite a long time, and I went to find them. I discovered them in conversation with a lady they introduced to me as Mme. X, a Parisienne and governess to the palace children. As soon as they told her they were from Philadelphia, she fell upon their necks, in her joy, and said that her daughter had married an American dentist practicing in Baku, and that her grandson was a draughtsman in Cramp's shipyard.

In a few minutes, she went to her apartment and brought us a large diamond ring, which she asked us to carry to him (how confiding!), which we did. Nothing was a trouble to her and she laid herself out to please us. Just then, it was Bairam (the Mussulman Lent), and the chief of police was giving a play to his friends to which Mme. X said she would try to get us admitted. (There were no tickets for sale.) The same play was repeated elsewhere, and in Isfahan, even Mrs. Griscom had been refused admittance. The play lasted ten afternoons and cost the chief the equivalent of ten thousand dollars.

Mme. X got permission from the chief's wife, a special friend, to admit Florence and Dora (to what, I did not know, except that it was some sort of show), and I was left outside. But in a half-hour or so, I also was asked to enter, along with my Armenian servant. The tent was about as large as a circus tent. There was a latticed enclosure (a), where the wife of the chief, Florence, Dora, and some other women could watch the play unveiled. In the center was an oval stage (b), about three feet high, fifteen feet long, and ten feet wide. Around the

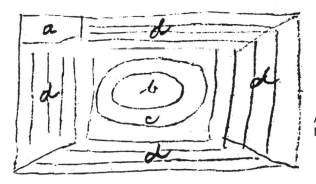

Arena plan for
Muslim passion play

stage was a passageway (c) about ten to twelve feet wide, for camels, soldiers, and others in procession. The rest of the tent was occupied by rising rows of seats (d), as in an amphitheater.

When I entered at the top (I was the only infidel out in the open seats), I saw a high pole in the middle of the stage and a boy with a rope around his neck suspended from the pole. My first thought was that we were witnessing a Persian execution. In a moment, however, he began to make a speech, reading from a slip of paper, and my fears for his life were appeased.

Then followed different actors on the stage, each of them furnished (by an old man) with a slip of paper with his speaking part. There was much banging of shields with ineffective swords, and some other action intermingled with various recitatives, some hideous music by a band, and marching and counter-marching in the passageway.

Finally, the crowd seemed overcome with what I thought, at first, was laughter, but I discovered to be profuse weeping and sobbing. Even my Armenian servant was wiping his eyes and gulping down his sobs. Never have I seen such universal passion and religious fervor. I verily believe that if I had exhibited any disdain or unbelief, this crowd of excited, fanatical Mohammedans would have readily attacked me, if indeed they would not have torn me to pieces in their wrath.

The play was the tragedy of "The Life and Death of Hassan and Hussein," the sons of Mohammed.

Florence and Dora, in the women's box, witnessed everything through the lattice. They can relate their experience with coffee beans and other spices, with the narghile[6] (through which each took a whiff), the mouthpiece of which was not even wiped clean when handed to them by the hostess, much less a fresh mouthpiece offered to each.

They also had a new experience on our return by boat from Enzeli to Baku. Their stateroom (the only first-class one) was invaded, willy-nilly, in the middle of the night, by a Belgian woman who carried only one small bag. She rose first, in the morning, and Dora found, to her astonishment, that the woman had borrowed her hairbrush and comb. Later, in the presence of the woman, she carefully washed them, as a hint, and stowed them, the next night, under her pillow. Florence, thinking that the rebuke had been sufficient, did not take the same precaution, and in the morning she was furious on finding that the woman had used *her* toilet articles, including even her *toothbrush!*

The Russian Railroad From Krasnovodsk To Samarkand

Returning from Persia to Baku, we crossed the Caspian Sea directly eastward, thence to Krasnovodsk, where we took the railroad to Bukhara and Samarkand, a distance of nearly a thousand miles. In that entire journey, except for the few population centers of Kizyl-Arvat, Ashkhabad, Mary, Bukhara, and Samarkand, the landscape was a continuous sandy desert, the sand being thrown up in billows by the wind and engulfing everything in its way. Yet at one time it must have been well-watered and fertile, for Alexander led his vast army the entire distance to Samarkand.

At Geok-Tepe, the train halted for twenty minutes while we visited a fort (a mile or so square) with immensely thick mud walls. It was in this fort that the Turkomans so long resisted Skobelev until 1876, when they were practically all slaughtered indiscriminately—men, women, and children. This so cowed the Turkomans that they never since then have lifted a finger in revolt against the Russians. Opposite the fort is a small museum, with many relics of the fight—and a large equestrian portrait of Skobelev.

We were met at Bukhara by a Swedish missionary (speaking excellent English), whose acquaintance we owed to Mr. Koop. He spent two days of great interest with us and then refused, not only for himself but also for his work, a contribution that I tried in vain to get him to accept.

By permission of the Russian governor, we visited old Bukhara, one of the oldest trade and cultural centers of central Asia, which is some five or six miles from the new city, centered around the railroad station. The bazaars were a never-ending delight, and I especially remember seeing a hair clipper made by Brown & Sharpe, of Providence, Rhode Island.

The ark, or citadel, is a spacious and quite imposing mud fort, the residence of the finance minister, who is also—and this seems to be his primary function—the chief falconer. (The emir lives in a town some twenty miles away.) Our guide obtained an audience for me. The girls were not allowed to enter the fort, but watched a snake-charmer outside for the twenty minutes, or so, of my audience.

The room in which I was received was about fifteen by twenty, with a mud floor (though the mud walls were covered by exquisite silk rugs). There were European chairs and a table on which was served sweetmeats and other courses, ending with boiled mutton. The falconer/finance minister was a large man of about sixty, who wore a large snow-white turban and a robe stretching from his neck to his heels. This latter was light pea-green, of satin, and covered with large stars, so woven as to show a sheen that was absent in the rest of the robe. He looked very grand, indeed. He was dignified, courteous, and kind, and when he heard that I was from America, I was quite sure that he had no idea of what America was, or where it was situated.

We next visited the nearby dungeons of the prison. Through a small door, the only avenue for any light, we saw a score or more of filthy, abject-looking, poor wretches with fetters on wrists and ankles. They looked half-famished and devoured voraciously some long Persian loaves of bread we gave them. (Each loaf was about six feet long, six inches broad, and an inch thick.) Below their prison, reached by a hole in the floor, was a second dungeon, of inexpressable horror, the same in which, in the 40s, the two English officers were eaten alive by vermin and finally died. It was perfectly horrible.

In Bukhara, the men are the birds of fine plumage. The colors of their robes, white, yellow, purple, red, green, are astonishing. Great splashes of color on a white background. I brought back some samples to show what they are like.

Samarkand, the furthest point reached by Alexander, has some of the remains of his palace, though almost entirely buried in the sand. The bazaars here too were a delight, but the chief object of interest was the tomb of Tamerlane.

The mosque is surrounded by a square wall with minarets at the four corners. Two of them had already fallen; a third was leaning far over and has since fallen; and the fourth will doubtless follow. The mosque proper has a beautifully fluted dome, which, like the walls, was once covered with beautiful blue Persian tiles. A large number of the tiles had fallen off, and there were many fragments on the ground. (I have always been vexed that I did not appropriate two or three.) Among the Mohammedans, one "acquires merit" by *building* a mosque, but repairing one is a work of supererogation.

Our journey back to Krasnovodsk and Baku was marked by amusing—and annoying—incidents. From Krasnovodsk to Tashkent, then the terminus of the railroad, it is twelve hundred miles. The year we were there (1902) was the first time that the train had a first-class car on a daily basis. Previously, a first-class car and a restaurant car were included only three times a week. The first-class car had three compartments with four berths each. Florence and Dora occupied half of one compartment; I took a lower berth in the other.

One of my companions, a Russian officer, was resplendent in his gray overcoat with scarlet facings. But when he removed the coat (the thermometer measured about 103°), his once-white uniform was dirty, to a degree. When he went to bed, I understood the reason for the notice which had puzzled me the first time I rode in a Russian car: PLEASE REMOVE YOUR BOOTS WHEN YOU GO TO BED. It seemed to me a superfluous injunction, but my officer, making a pillow of his overcoat, and not even hiring a sheet or pillowcase, threw himself on the bed with his boots on—and with spurs attached.

In the middle of the night, I was awakened by an altercation in which I heard Florence and Dora's voices, so I got up to take a hand in the game. I discovered that, the other compartments being full, the conductor was insisting on giving the third berth on their compartment to a man. They vehemently objected, in English, French, and German, but apparently in vain. I concluded that if any man was to go into their compartment, it should be me; so I gave the intruder my berth and took a lower in their compartment. Later still, another woman was assigned the remaining berth. We lived in harmony for three days.

Breaking The Imperial Bank Of Persia

When we reached Rasht, I wanted to draw enough money to take us into Teheran and out again. I took my letter of credit on Brown, Shipley & Company to the Imperial Bank of Persia and asked for fifty pounds, forty pounds in notes and ten pounds in currency. The Indian babu at the desk told me he could not cash the draft, because the bank manager had gone to Enzeli with the British ambassador, who was on his way to the Coronation, in London. When I was told he would return in three days, I pleaded that we wanted to start for Teheran the next day. He shrugged his shoulders and continued to deny the request. I then bethought myself that, just before leaving Baku on the eastbound trek, I had drawn a considerable amount of Russian gold and asked him if he could change that. He promptly replied, "With pleasure." I then gave him five hundred rubles and asked him to let me have the amount as indicated. He was gone a long while and finally came back with forty dollars in Persian notes, all the bank had, and two hundred ten dollars in currency.

Persian currency, for all practical purposes, consists of krans (i.e., crowns), worth about ten cents, and tomans, worth about ten krans. In theory, the tomans are struck in gold and the krans in silver, but in actuality, the gold is never seen and the silver only rarely. The krans were coins about the size of our nickels, but so debased that the handling of a few of them made the fingers black. In addition, the tenacity of the metal had been largely lost, so that when the die came down, it made a very poor impression, and the margin of the coins were often split radially. (I have two or three of them in a small coin box in the parlor.)

The clerk brought me over two thousand of these vile krans, in two great linen bags which so weighted down the pockets of my sack coat that I was afraid the fabric of the coat might give way. I had to hold them up with my hands. The counting was laborious and soiled my hands badly. Fortunately, I got rid of about a thousand of them at the posting station, where I paid for a landau into Teheran and back. When we reached the city, I went directly to the posting station to see if we could get a better landau, for this one was so bad that we declared we would never go back in it. We feared we should break down at any moment, and a breakdown in that desolate country would be serious business. When we saw the array of dilapidated coaches available, however, we gladly re-engaged the one in which we had come. Fortunately, it did not break down before we had returned to Rasht.

THE BULGARIAN FRONTIER

We left Constantinople for Genoa, by way of Budapest and Venice, to take our steamer home. There were six of us: three of my daughters, Dr. D., of Providence, a friend, and I. We had exactly one extra day to catch our boat. Leaving in the evening, by the Orient Express, we were due at the Bulgarian frontier at seven the next morning. As I always woke up early, I took all of the trunk keys, so that my daughters could sleep as long as they wished. We had had a pretty strenuous time in Constantinople—and during the whole summer, in fact. The only other first-class passengers in the *wagon-lit* were a family of three from Wilmington. The son was a young businessman who had spent three years in St. Petersburg and, fortunately for me, as it turned out, was able to speak Russian.

At the frontier, we stopped at what could only charitably be called a station. It consisted of two small wooden buildings, one for disinfection and the other for the storage of disinfected baggage. On a hillside about a quarter of a mile away were some barracks for passengers who might have to be quarantined. About three miles beyond that, on flat, open ground, lay the village of Hebibchevo, which consisted of a small collection of almost identical two-story houses, irregularly spaced and fringing both sides of its one street.

I had given our passports to the conductor, and soon after the train had stopped, I heard an official calling for me. He was a quarantine officer, who had just arrived the day before from Sofia, where he as a professor of Bacteriology at the university.

"You come from Russia?"

"Yes, from Moscow to the Crimea, thence to Constantinople."

"You will have to be quarantined for two weeks."

"For what reason?"

"Because there is the plague in Russia."

"But the plague is only in Astrakhan, and we have not been within five hundred miles of Astrakhan."

"My orders are to quaratine everybody coming from Russia."

Finally, after much expostulation and debate, he agreed to allow all of our party, and the H. family from Wilmington, to proceed to Budapest, on condition that all of our baggage be left for twenty-four hours for disinfection.

Neither the young Mr. H. nor I was willing to turn over all of our possessions, unguarded, to strangers, so we stayed behind. The impatient railway officials and the other passengers, having already been delayed fifteen or twenty minutes, at last departed for Budapest, almost a two-day journey. The members of our party had absolutely no baggage, save for toilet articles. They later told us that when they arrived in Budapest, tired and dusty, they went straight to bed, while their clothing was being washed, since they had not a single change.

Meantime, Mr. H. and I had more than a dozen trunks, in addition to as many more pieces of hand baggage. The doctor proceeded to disinfect all this baggage by unpacking and placing everything in the large, deep drawers of what might be described as a huge bureau. The bottoms of the drawers were pierced by large auger holes, and the fumes from the sulphur being burned below were supposed to disinfect everything in the drawers. Fortunately, we were able to rescue the ladies' hats, gloves, and photographs from impending destruction. There being so much baggage, the bureau had to be filled three times.

As to the trunks themselves, they were sprayed inside and out—and inefficiently—with a little carbolic-acid solution and then dried in the sun. How to get everything back in the proper trunk and handbag, and to the proper owner, was a problem. Finally, I made a list: Things from A's handbag went into the top drawer front, to the right; those from B's, into the second drawer rear, to the right; and so on. When it came to re-packing the trunks, especially the ladies' hats, I said to Mr. H. that as soon as we turned these trunks over to the ladies, "you and I had better take to the woods." I thought it was polite flattery, when they later declared that they couldn't have done it better themselves.

The tedious process of unpacking, labeling, disinfecting, and re-packing occupied the whole morning, during which we had not had a bite to eat. The doctor took us in a canvas-covered wagon, with no springs, over the three stony miles to Hebibchevo. Steak and potatoes (which were cooked—that is, burnt and smoked—over an open wood fire) and black bread were set before us, along with nothing but two-pronged iron forks. Calling for a knife with which to carve the meat, I was provided with what might be called a cutlass, or even a scimitar, but it served the purpose. The doctor warned us against drinking the water, and the wine was bad, so we had to be content with poor beer. The sun was fiercely hot (the temperature seemed to be in the nineties), and so, hungry, thirsty, and tired, we were not in a very placid state of mind.

We passed the afternoon in a short nap, on the straw in the wagon; an inspection of the town industries, including blacksmithing by one of the women; and a tiresome, two-mile walk to visit a neighboring gypsy camp—though they had vanished before we arrived. We also conversed with the doctor, whose French was distressing but comprehensible. Recalling the complete bacteriological laboratory at the Jefferson Medical College, I was amused at his assumption that we in America were ignorant of the science of Bacteriology. But he had the self-satisfied attitude of superiority, and this was a good example of his knowledge about America.

After supper, which was a repetition of the noon meal, the doctor offered to take us back to the station, but remembering the testimony of our aching bones from the morning ride, and noting that the moon was bright, we thought that the road would be marked well enough for us to venture forth on our own. We lingered for another hour and then started out. We had not been on our way for more than ten minutes when we confessed to each other than we had lost our way and decided to return to the village, which we found, though with some difficulty. Even then, the houses were so similar that we could not tell which was our "hotel," and there was not a light to be seen, as everyone had gone to bed.

We finally roused people in one house (whether or not the right one), and a head protruding from the second-story window evidently asked what we wanted. How fortunate it was that Mr. H. could speak Russian, for, using a kindred Slavic tongue, they understood him and provided us with a small boy as a guide. With his help we reached the station, though we were suddenly stopped on the way by a soldier. He let us pass, though reluctantly, after the boy explained who and what we were.

On arrival, I asked the doctor for my suitcase to get out my toilet articles. He shrugged his shoulders and, pointing to the storehouse, said that the suitcase was locked inside and that the guardian with the only key was in Hebibchevo for the night. That settled conclusively the question of nightclothes, toothbrush, soap, and hairbrush.

As we were being led to the barracks where we were to spend the night, I noticed that we were being followed closely by a soldier carrying a rifle. When I asked the doctor why this guard, he said, "You don't seem to realize that we are on the Turkish border, and that at any moment, but especially at night, we might be attacked by the Turks." A soothing nightcap, indeed.

Mr. H. and I only half-undressed, but we soon fell asleep and slept soundly until six in the morning, when we were roused to our very brief and limited toilet. At seven, we were back on the next day's Orient Express for Budapest. Fortunately, we could now obtain a good breakfast in the diner, and we did it full justice.

The *wagon-lit* was not quite full, but we were out of luck, for our sleeper tickets were valid ony for yesterday's train. In spite of our elaborate explanations, the conductor would not accept them for *his* train, so we had to buy new tickets. It is only just to add that, on arrival in Budapest, we sent a reclamation to the chief officer of the sleeping-car company, in Brussels, and the cost of our extra tickets was eventually refunded to us.

If the porters were astonished at the paucity (or rather, the absence) of baggage when the rest of the two parties had arrived the day before, their surprise must have been even greater at the excessive baggage appraently required by two mere men, unadorned with an entourage of servants. We just caught our steamer at Genoa, after a most uncomfortable night on an accommodation train with no *wagon-lits*, which was the only train we could take, there being no through express trains on that route. We were thankful to have started out with one day's leeway, and grateful that our Bulgarian Professor of Bacteriology was lenient enough to keep us only one day, instead of two weeks.

His ideas of disinfection were evidently as imperfect as was his knowledge of the state of medical progess in America. But we forgave him and hope that he has won distinction in the present Balkan War.

I'm not sure but that in the long run, we have had so much fun in recounting our experiences that we are almost glad that we were quarantined.

THE BABYLONIAN CYLINDER

When on a camping trip from Tiberias to Damascus with Florence and Dora, in 1902, we usually arrived in camp at about four o'clock and found the tents up, a bath ready, and, in due time, dinner. Neighboring peasants often gathered around our camp, curious to see such exotic travelers. One afternoon, camping on a shoulder of Mount Herman, we were surrounded by quite a crowd. One of them offered me a copper coin and a Babylonian cylinder. I paid him a Napoleon (20 francs) for the two.

I immediately recognized the coin as Tyrean, for the Greek name *Tureon* was very legible, and the prow of a ship was depicted on the reverse. (Tyrians were well known as very early navigators.) An expert numismatist later dated the coin to about 300 B.C. After reaching home, I had it mounted as a scarf pin and gave it to Walter Freeman, the husband of my eldest daughter, Corinne.

The cylinder was an inch long and half an inch in diameter. It was hollow and made of hematite, a very hard iron ore. It was covered with cuneiform script and three figures. Small particles had been chipped off in four places. The man who sold them to me said that he had dug them up on his own farm, and I suspect that he had neither the intelligence nor the tools to have cut the

Keen posing with "a Babylonian cylinder, which is on my watch chain–a rare find"
(Postcard mailed from Carlsbad in August of 1902)

cuneiform characters nor the three figures. On our return to Philadelphia, my friend University [of Pennsylvania] Professor Morris Jastrow Jr. readily interpreted the figures and read the inscriptions.

The cuneiform inscription was an identification of two generations, "_____ son of _____," though I forgot to make a note and can no longer recall them.

The three figures were (1) the owner of the cylinder, who is carrying a kid (the fore-legs are easily visible) to (2) the priest, recognized by his dress, in order to sacrifice it to (3) the God of Thunder, recognized by a symbol held in one hand. I have compared this cylinder with others in museums in Constantinople, Paris, and London, and have seen several duplicates depicting the priest and the God of Thunder.

This cylinder served as the signature of its owner and was rolled on wax or clay affixed to letters or legal documents.

As a small loose object like this would easily be lost, even if put away in a box, when we reached Moscow, on a later leg of our journey, I had a bar inserted which was held in place by a cross at each end, and suspended from my watch chain by a short gold chain. If the links of the gold chain wear too thin, I would have them thickened.

I asked Dr. Jastrow as to the cylinder's probable age, and he estimated that it dated to about 1000 B.C., to which I replied, "Why, it's a bit older than I am."

THE MULTIPLIED MISHAPS OF
A TRIP TO PANAMA

In January of 1905, the Pan-American Medical Congress was scheduled to be held in Panama, followed, a few days later, by an American Congress of Hygiene, in Havana. A Washington doctor, who did not himself finally go with us, organized a party of over forty doctors—and members of their families—for the trip. He inspected and arranged for the Italian ship *Athos* to take us from Baltimore to Panama and Cuba, then return us to Baltimore via Jamaica. (The ship was regularly engaged in the banana trade between the Port of Baltimore and Jamaica, and on the return trip, we were to take on a cargo of bananas.) Dora and I engaged passage and left Philadelphia on the 26th of December, at seven in the morning. (It was not an agreeable hour of a dark winter's day, but we were anticipating warm days in the Caribbean.) We arrived in the city at nine and drove directly to the pier, as it behooved us not to miss our steamer. Though scheduled to sail at eleven, the *Athos* was not at the pier, but earlier arrivals had spotted her coming up the bay from a shipyard where she had been undergoing renovation. She arrived at about noon.

The day was cold, a drizzling rain was falling, and a blanket of fog soon covered the waterfront, so that one could only dimly see anything a hundred feet away. The ship had narrow decks and only one salon, which was to serve as dining room, social hall, smoking room, reading room, writing room, and conversation room. The door, of necessity, was constantly open, and there was no steam in the pipes. This cheerless room was surpassed only by the dreary and disheartened passengers themselves.

We soon sat down to lunch, a meal that augured so ill that we made a combined raid on the best grocery store in the city and supplied ourselves with coffee, canned milk, canned meat, sardines, biscuits, preserves, and other comestibles. Fortunately, Dora also bought a good coffeepot. Investigation of the ship showed but two bathrooms, and each tub was so repulsive that a deputation visited the captain and were promised two new ones, of which only one arrived.

Meantime, other troubles arose, with the cook's wife and the engineer's wife: One fell ill, and the other committed suicide. A new cook and a new engineer had to be procured. There was time for these emergencies, since the captain announced that because of the fog, we could not sail till the next day. Some of us spent the evening in town, with friends, at a hotel, or in various places of amusement, though some were discouraged and gave up the trip entirely.

We set sail the following morning, and then the troubles came thick and fast. On the second day out, the electric-light apparatus gave out, so that we had only candles, lamps, and lanterns. There was no electrician on board, but one of the stewards knew a great deal about electricity and was excused from dining-room duty in order to repair the dynamo. As we had only two stewards to begin with, this left only one man to look after the forty of us. We looked after ourselves, in fact, and didn't mind doing our own "reaching."

In the corridors and other places, kerosene lamps were set on the floor. If a storm arose, which was a likely event in the winter season, this seemed to expose us to danger from fire. Looking around, we found no fire buckets, no reels of hose, no posted lists with the names and places assigned to the crew members in the event of fire or other emergency, and no provision for a fire drill. As the son of one of the owners was on board, we called his attention to these facts, whereupon he took us to the roof of our composite living room, assuring us that there were a dozen fire buckets. True enough, there were twelve buckets, but one of them was partly full of water and the other eleven absolutely empty.

We then called on the captain, who objected to the ringing of a fire alarm for a fire drill because, he said, "nobody would know what to do." Both the humor and the danger of his reply were evident to us, if not to him, but he finally promised to have such a drill, post the necessary notices, and so forth. The notices were posted, but as they were in English, while the crew knew only Italian, their usefulness was not very apparent. The fire buckets, though fairly inaccessible, were at least filled, and we had a fire drill the next day. The bell rang, and the crew ran. An ancient hose lying on the deck was screwed to the pump, and an attempt was made to turn on the water by an iron lever with a square hole in the middle. The lever promptly broke in two, and it was ten or fifteen minutes before another was found. How long it would have taken in the panic from a *real* fire was not clear. Even when the water was turned on, the hose leaked so badly that the captain started the crew sewing on a new canvas cover.

These several shortcomings suggested to us than an examination of the lifeboats would not be amiss. Of these there were three, in addition to an ordinary large rowboat. Not one of these had any water aboard and two of them had no food. On the third we found a large square can, the lid of which was rusted off, and the contents of which, once presumably hardtack, had compacted into a sodden, pasty mass resembling Gorgonzola cheese in looks and surpassing it in odor. In one boat was an unmounted compass; in the others, none at all. I cleaned out an empty sardine tin and filled it with the Gorgonzola biscuit paste for later use.

By this time, the electric light was going again, and we had two stewards once more, but two or three days later, it broke down again, and the electrical steward had to be excused once again for auxiliary duty.

Our misfortunes had become a daily joke, instead of merely an annoyance. Our fellow-passengers were pleasant companions and full of merry jests and quick repartee. But by the time we passed Cuba, on our way to the Isthmus of Panama, the blower broke down, and our speed (if our rate of progress could be described by such a misnomer) fell to four or five knots, under natural instead of forced draught. It was evident that we should be late to the Congress, or possibly miss it entirely, so we resolved to hold a mock congress of our own. The official Mexican delegate represented Dr. Amador Guerrero, the president of the Republic of Panama, and welcomed us in perfervid Spanish. To this, Dr. Ramon Guiteras, as president of the Congress responded, also in Spanish, if I remember rightly.

We were all dressed fantastically. I made a chapeau out of some stiff paper

**Keen, aboard the *Athos*, costumed as "Major La Garde"
(note fearsome "sword")**

and stuck a borrowed feather in it. I borrowed also a green sash, from one of the ladies, and fiercely flourished a table knife as a sword. I represented the chief medical officer on the Isthmus. One of the ladies had carved a medal in wood, with **A** on the obverse and **K** on the reverse. This, by vote, was hung around my neck on a ribbon as a decoration of honor, the speaker declaring that **A** was for *Athos*, that swift vessel of renown, and **K** was for the worthy recipient.

Dr. McDonald declared later, in a very witty speech, that this interpretation of the symbols was wholly off the mark, and that the **A** and **K** stood for Antikamnia.[7]

After the effervescence of the dinner and the speeches, we really settled down to work and read and discussed our papers, which, by a generous laxity, were later included in the printed *Proceedings* of the Congress.

Before we reached Colón, our indignation at the danger from the inadequate appointments of the ship caused us to draw up and sign a protest. This, together with a statement in full of the dangerous conditions found, we signed and mailed (with my sardine tin of Gorgonzola paste) to Mr. Metcalf, the Secretary of Commerce and Labor. We accused the inspectors of gross laxity in allowing a ship so badly equipped to sail from any port in the United States. After our return, Mr. Metcalf sent a paper to each signer upholding his inspectors(!) I confess that it was a double (though grim) satisfaction, when I wrote to him a year later and included the announcement of the fatal loss of the *Athos*, and in the following June, when we sat on the same platform at Yale, he received only an honorary A.M., while I received an LL.D.

We reached Colón at last, but had been so long delayed that people were anxious for our safety, and a revenue cutter was about to start out to hunt for us. But there was more trouble. Nobody had been notified that we would need a berth at the dock, in addition to a special train to Panama City. (The regular train had already gone.) The captain rowed ashore, finally, and arranged for a train, on which we left at about noon. We stopped at Gatun, the Culebra Cut, and one or two other places on the way, and reached the city just as the Congress had closed. The only part in which we participated was the final dinner. We also were received by President and Mrs. Amador Guerrero, and the next day we returned to Colón and left for Havana.

We reached Havana just as the Hygienic Congress was adjourning, but we assisted in the ball at the presidential palace, that evening, and went on to Matanzas the following day. We visited a large sugar mill there and were greatly interested in sugar-making.

In view of the poor equipment and the unseaworthiness of the *Athos*, we abandoned her, not being willing to trust Dora and myself in a possible storm off Hatteras. We waited three or four days and returned to New York on a Ward liner.

Only four of the original forty passengers continued on the *Athos*. She went to Jamaica, and misfortune continued to follow her. When they dropped anchor in the harbor of Kingston, the anchor chain was so weak and rusted that it parted, leaving a $250 anchor at the bottom of the sea. As they started for home, a severe winter storm set in off Hatteras. They were driven far out to sea, fortunately, as the wind was offshore. Had it been onshore, she would undoubtedly have been wrecked. They had to shut off the steam from all the cabins and the living room, as it was all needed for the engine. Even then, they were able to make only three knots. For two or three nights, the four nearly frozen passengers did not dare to go to bed for fear of foundering. The voyage being prolonged by the storm, and provisions running low, the crew broke into the stores, and for some time, the bananas in the cargo hold were the principal diet. Many of these were wet by the sea and rotted, producing an extremely disagreeable and nauseating odor.

Reaching Baltimore at long last, cold, starved, and disgusted, the passengers united in employing counsel to prosecute the lessee of the vessel for obtaining money under false pretenses. Even if no accident befell us, the best rate of the ship was wholly insufficient to have landed us in Panama and Cuba in time for our congresses. We were told that in our absence, the firm had been merged into the Fruit Trust and we could get no damages, either by suing the owners of the vessel or the firm that had leased it and made the contract with us.

The later history of the ship was just such a tragedy as I had envisioned when we abandoned her at Havana. Just one year later, she sailed from Cape Breton and was never heard from again! She doubtless foundered during some storm and went to the bottom with passengers and crew.

I sometimes wonder how Secretary Metcalf felt when he received my last letter, with this evidence that our protest from Colón, unfortunately, had been more than vindicated.

MY LITTLE ITALIAN SPEECH
AND HOW IT GREW

While spending the winter of 1907–08 in Italy, we took Italian lessons, in Florence and Rome. I was persuaded that the ability to speak a language is attained only by practice from the very start (as a child learns to walk, in spite of many falls). Thus, I began to speak, or try to speak, Italian when I attended the Italian Surgical Society, even though I had had only a few lessons, and of course there were many grammatical and verbal stumbles and falls.

After one of the meetings, I was invited to luncheon by Professor Durante, president of the Society. His daughters were the only ladies present, and after the luncheon, they both joined the gentlemen in the drawing room, where cigars and cigarettes were served along with the coffee. I stumbled along in Italian as best I could, with one of the daughters aiding my unsteady steps with welcome suggestions, and without betraying the least amusement at my mistakes. Finally, I wholly upset her gravity, and the humor of my mistake made me join in her laughter, with me but not at me.

I immediately recognized and corrected my mistake. I wanted to ask her if she smoked, but instead of using the verb *fumare* ("to smoke"), linked the noun *fumo*, ("smoke") I coined the word *fuocare* (which doesn't exist), linking it with the noun *fuoco* ("fire"), for my inquiry. That blunder seemed to make us at once the best of friends.

While in Rome, Dora, Florence, and I had three teachers who gave us each a daily lesson. We changed around each day, but with each teacher had a continuous course. This had some advantages, as one teacher would emphasize grammar, another, punctuation, and the third, style, while the three, with slightly different voices, accustomed our ears to the subtle variations of spoken Italian.

We wrote exercises daily and, like schoolchildren, had them returned to us after the teachers had made the corrections, usually in red ink. But how bloody mine were! One day, I must have reached the zenith of inaccuracy. The teacher handed back my exercise and said, "Really, Dr. Keen, this is so bad you must do it over," which I did with great meekness—and some success.

When I described my misfortune to the Misses Pierce and Lawrence, they were not a little amused by my seeming apprehension that if I repeated my poor work, I should be kept in by my teacher.

While I was one of the managers of the American Baptist Publication Society, I became familiar with the self-sacrificing and successful work of the Italian Mission Church, in Rome, and I frequently attended service there on Sunday morning. One morning, after I had been studying the language daily for over two months, the minister asked me to say a few encouraging words to the little congregation, adding that he would be glad to serve as interpreter.

I had the hardihood to say that I should like to attempt to speak in Italian. I was sure that I should never have a more sympathetic or forgiving audience than this one, and if I broke down, he could come to the rescue. This seemed to please him. I spoke for three or four minutes, telling them in the simplest (and no doubt boldest) Italian how and what I knew of their early trials, congratulating them on their success, and conveying to them the best wishes of their American friends for a rich blessing from Heaven. I was very sure that my intentions were better than my Italian, but they seemed to understand me, at least, and I did not break down.

On returning to the hotel, I said not a word to the girls about my adventure. Three or four days later, Florence was a patient of Dr. Webb, an American dentist, who congratulated her on the very successful Italian speech her father had made, at the Baptist church on Sunday. She responded to this with, "Oh no! That couldn't have been Father." And so was the Scripture fulfilled that a "prophet is not without honor, save . . . within his own house."

Repercussions of that squib of a speech were remarkable. Not long afterwards, Miss Lillie Frishmuth (our opposite neighbor in Philadelphia) wrote to Florence from Switzerland and asked her to congratulate me on my Italian lecture. A month or so later, Mr. Penniman wrote to me from Philadelphia to say it was currently reported that I was giving lectures in Italian. And at the June meeting of the board of fellows at Brown, in 1911, Col. Robert Goddard alluded to those lectures when describing me as an accomplished Italian scholar.

"How great a fire a little matter kindleth!"

I have since told my friends that if they were to hear that I had been offered the chair of Italian Language and Literature, at the University of Rome, they were authorized to say that I had declined the offer.

Since the above was dictated, I have heard two further amusing exaggerations. In one, Miss Mollie Coles followed me, in my Italian lessons with Signora X, who told her that after my hour was over she was quite exhausted.

The second was still worse. The report ran that, after Queen Helena had received Florence, Dora, and me, during which we had a brief conversation with her (especially about her children), she said she had never met Americans who spoke such excellent Italian.

Such exaggeration reminds me of a report I had from Dr. George Spencer, one time. In Burma, in December of 1901, I broke my left collarbone by a fall from my horse. I was able to discard my bandages and splint only upon leaving Bombay. In Cairo, twelve days later, I operated on Miss Margaretta Taylor for appendicitis. Someone telegraphed the news to America that I had operated with an arm in a sling. Spencer told me that he saw the operation announced in an Indianapolis newspaper, including the news that I had operated with *both* arms in a sling.

THE PEPYS LIBRARY

In 1923, when I was last in England, Florence and I went to Cambridge, where we took luncheon with Professor Clifford Allbutt. He passed away soon after that, so that the only personal recollection I have is that he was most gracious, as well as delightful in his conversation, in spite of his very marked deafness.

While in Cambridge, we sought out Professor G.H.F. Nuttall, who had been on the faculty at Johns Hopkins, a number of years ago, but was now the curator of the Pepys Museum and Library at Magdalen College, Cambridge University. I learned from him that *Peeps* was the proper pronunciation of the name, and that some of the family are still living in the vicinity of Cambridge. In his will, Samuel Pepys left his library to the University with the following stipulations: First, the bookcases which held the collection were to be re-erected in Magdalen and the books arranged precisely as he had them. (He arranged his books by height, and where a book was shorter than the rest of those on the shelf, he put a false bottom under it so that it would conform to the uniform height.)

Another provision was that if ever a single book were missing, the entire library should be diverted from Magdalen to King's. For one hundred and twenty-five years after his death, two fellows of Magdalen and two fellows from King's counted all the books annually. Having performed this solemn duty and never having found a single volume missing, they very sensibly took the view that this was a great waste of time, and since then, the librarian has kept a hawk's eye on the collection to be sure no volume was missing.

The library holds some very important papers of state which had come to him in his role as Paymaster of the Navy under Charles II. Among them is a book of watercolor drawings of every Navy vessel, from the largest to the rowboat, together with a list of the officers and the ranks of the vessels and the numbers of the crew, plus the number of shot (both of solid stone and of iron) for the guns. (Of course, the Royal Navy had no explosive shells, in those days.)

There are also a number of autograph letters, of both Charles II and Queen Elizabeth. Her signature is legible but by no means beautiful. High school children would do better.

4

—••⟦ ⟧••—

Citizen Keen

1860

MY LIFE HAS COVERED all of the later phases of the slavery question, which finally ended in civil war. From about 1852, when I was old enough to take a personal and intelligent interest in public affairs, I was saturated with the debate over the one burning issue of the day, human slavery, one's owning of human beings as one owns cattle.

James Ford Rhodes, in his *History of the Civil War* (1917), shows with wonderful clarity how the slavery question permeated all levels of society, precipitated much discussion, and considerably affected personal relations; and how it would not down, even though again and again it was thought to be settled through compromise. The reason it would not down is that it was far more than merely a political question. For many years, the admission of a slave state had to be counterbalanced by the admission of a free state (and with the constant threat of having five slave states made out of Texas). Political questions had to be tested by their relationship to the slavery issue. If slave owners were not satisfied with a piece of legislation, they claimed the right to secede. The South considered that the United States was a confederacy of member states; the North believed that the United States was one indivisible nation.

Slavery involved enormous economic considerations, with millions of dollars at stake in the transporting and buying and selling of human beings. The South believed that what was property in Georgia should also be property in Massachusetts and in every other state or territory. On the floor of the U.S. Senate, Robert Toombs of Georgia declared that the day would come when he would call the roll of his slaves at the foot of the Bunker Hill monument.

But it was above all a moral question. This aspect of it was the source of the tremendous influence of Harriet Beecher Stowe's *Uncle Tom's Cabin.* As southerners now acknowledge, its moral influence was pernicous on the slave

103

owners, manifest in the increasing population of mulattos, quadroons, and octaroons, as well as in the occasional reports of some overseers who beat their slaves with the same passionate cruelty that leads owners to beat their horses.

Education of the blacks was prohibited. And if they were freed, they became liable to arrest as vagrants, from which they might be sold back into slavery. Dr. Booker Washington's autobiography, *Up From Slavery*, illustrates very well how hard the slave life was.

How far unreasoning passion went among the abolitionists is well shown by an incident in my father's business life. The property of one of his debtors in Virginia was seized, when he became bankrupt, and was sold by the sheriff at the insistence of some other creditor. Most of the man's property consisted of slaves, three or four of which fell to the lot of my father, in settlement of his claim. They were all old and unable to work. My father was bitterly opposed to slavery, but what could he do? He would not sell them; he could not free them, unless he transported them north, and that would break up their families. So he accepted them, held them as his slaves, and supported them till they died.

One Sunday when he was in Boston, he went to the Baptist Church presided over by Rev. Dr. Nathaniel Colver, an old and cherished friend. Dr. Colver, who knew all of the facts and motives as to my father's slaves, came to him in the pew, between the morning service and Communion, and said to him, "Brother Keen, I cannot allow the deacons to serve you with the bread and wine because you are a slave holder."

In 1856, when I was a college sophomore, Preston "Bully" Brooks, a Congressman from South Carolina, assaulted Massachusetts Senator Charles Sumner on the floor of the Senate and nearly killed him. The attack grew out of one of the many ante-bellum debates on salvery (though it was not made while the Senate was in session). A wave of horror (in the North) and of rejoicing (in the South) swept over the land. Indignation meetings to denounce this outrageous assault on free speech were held all over the North, and the one held in Providence was attended by the entire college.

The preliminary speakers were vehement and denunciatory and aroused the crowd to fever heat. Then Dr. Francis Wayland, the president of the university and clearly the first citizen of Rhode Island, rose to address us. His bulk, his leonine head and shaggy, beetling eyebrows, and his commanding personality caused a hush throughout the hall, following tumultuous applause as he mounted the platform. He began in a subdued voice, then proceeded in a calm, clear, and reasoned speech which convinced every listener. Finally, rising to his full height, with uplifted hand he said, slowly but emphatically, as the impressive climactic conclusion of the matter, "Fellow citizens: I was born a free man and, so help me God, I never will be made a slave!"

Naturally, pandemonium ensued. Everyone shouted himself hoarse, hats and caps filled the air, and for a long time, nothing was to be heard but the repeated cheers of approval. The words were simple, but the sentiment was one that appealed to every man present. Moreover, they had been spoken by the man who was the calm, cool reasoner, not given to appealing to passion, though when he did, his appeal went to the deepest depth of every man's heart and soul. It was the finest effect I have ever seen or heard, similar, it has always seemed to me, to that splendid appeal of Wendell Phillips to those "pictured lips" on the walls of Faneuil Hall.[1]

Slowly but surely, the forces on both sides of the question girded themselves for the conflict. The great debates in Illinois between Lincoln and Douglas were followed with almost breathless interest all over the country. In November of 1860, the brand-new Republican Party (which had nominated Fremont in the previous presidential election and polled a respectable number) nominated Lincoln. The Democrats were split into two factions, one of which nominated Breckinridge and the other, Douglas. A fourth ticket, backed chiefly by those who would pour oil on the troubled waters and compromise yet again, named Bell of Tennessee and Everett of Massachusetts.

When Lincoln was elected, the threats of secession grew louder and more insistent. As it was later shown, such madness was not taken as seriously as it should have been.

But oh, those *dreadful* days from November until the firing on Fort Sumter, the following April, who can describe them! We rushed for the newspapers every morning to see what new treachery had been perpetrated on the country, and we thanked God every evening if the day had passed without the uncovering of some new traitor. It seemed as though everybody suspected everybody else.

Buchanan, who was weak (though honest), admitted that a state could not legally secede, but if one *did* secede, he apparently believed he had no right to coerce her to stay. His cabinet was composed chiefly of southerners who turned traitor. Toucey of Connecticut, Secretary of the Navy, dispersed our ships all over the world; Floyd of Virginia, Secretary of War, divided our petty army into small garrisons all over the South, where most of our arms and munitions were stored; and Cobb of Georgia, Secretary of the Treasury, sent our gold and silver into the South, where it could readily be seized when secession was declared.

General Winfield Scott, a Virginian, stood by the Old Flag, but General R.E. Lee, also a Virginian, stayed with the Old Dominion. The Army and the Navy were disorganized throughout, and nobody knew whom to trust. It seemed that every day, this that or the other officer, senator, representative, judge, or other well-known figure deserted his post under the Union. Each such defection saddened us unutterably. The forces of disunion were rampant, and Buchanan and his cabinet either declined to do anything to stem the tide or else gave it active support.

Finally, when Cobb resigned, after having done all the harm he could, Buchanan brought in John Dix of New York (he and his like were later called "War Democrats"). When a treasury official at New Orleans reported that a mob was threatening to pull down the American flag, Dix telegraphed, "If any man pulls down the American flag, shoot him on the spot." "Thank God!" we all cried, "at last we have a man in the cabinet." This dispatch went through the nation like an electric shock, and we all took courage.

Along with everyone else, the medical students at the Jefferson were deeply stirred by the conflict. A large proportion of the students were southerners, who proceeded to make themselves unpleasant neighbors by trying to bully us northerners. One big chap from Richmond who sat near me was particularly offensive and intended, I was told, to do personal violence to me. For some six weeks, therefore, I carried a revolver and let the fact be known among my fellow-students that I intended to defend myelf. No further insults followed.

Finally, the whole body of southern students (perhaps thirty to fifty per cent of our total) left the Jefferson and were immediately received with open arms in the Medical College at Richmond, where they had to pay no additional fees.

From day to day, things went from bad to worse. More defections in Congress, in the Army, in the Navy, in the civil service, and in various government departments. The gloom deepend daily. Our despairing feeling was expressed in the question, "What will finally happen?"

Mr. Lincoln came to Philadelphia and raised the flag over Independence Hall (formerly the State House for the Colony of Pennsylvania). George Porter and I joined the rather sorry-looking cavalcade on horseback, as it met the president-elect at the Kensington depot, and escorted him to the hall. From there, he went openly to Harrisburg, but then, owing to threats of assassination while passing through Baltimore, he was transported at night, incognito, to Washington, through arrangements made by Thomas Scott, a vice-president of the Pennsylvania Railroad. What a sigh of relief followed when his safe arrival there was announced in the morning papers!

His inauguration, on the fourth of March, his splendid address, and the steps he took to preserve the authority of the United States, are all matters of record.

Never shall I forget that excited Sunday of April 14th, when Sumter was surrendered. George Porter, my brother Charles, and I walked, after church, in to the Continental Hotel, which was a major headquarters for news. The lobby and the streets were filled with an excited mass of people, and personal violence was freely offered to anyone with southern sympathies. I never in all my long life have sensed such deep feeling, such enthusiasm over the defense of Major Anderson, or such determination as witnessed in the expressed idea that if war was wanted, we were steadfast in our belief that it should *be* war, for as long as it took, to abolish slavery and save the Union. We did not get home till about 1 A.M. (afoot again), when we found the whole family breathlessly awaiting our return.

The next day, the papers were filled with the account of Lincoln's call for seventy-five thousand men, and the community went wild. No business was done. Edition after edition of the paper was issued and devoured. The first troops to go to Washington were a Pennsylvania company (possibly a regiment?), then the Massachusetts 6th and the Massachusetts 5th, then the New York 7th, and so on.

A cloud had been lifted. We felt that we now had a *man* in the presidency.

The rest is history.[2]

CIVIL WARRIOR

In my bound volume, *Addresses and Other Papers,* I have related some of my "Surgical Reminiscences of the Civil War,"[3] and in one of the copies I have recorded some other facts as to how I entered the Army. I think I have also filed some later data among my papers, but I cannot lay my hands on them at present.

I have just come across some of my old Civil War orders, letters, and clippings from the Charlestown (Mass.) *Advocate,* written, as I remember, by the Chaplain, Rev. Mr. De Costa, though not signed by him. Under date of July 7th, 1861, I find that he wrote from the camp of the 5th Massachusetts Volunteers, near Alexandria, Virginia, "We have also a new Assistant Surgeon,

Dr. W. W. Keen, of Philadelphia, who will undoubtedly prove a valuable acquisition to the regiment."

I had been sent down to Washington by Dr. Brinton, one of my preceptors, to replace another old student from his office. When I presented myself, I was not required to show my diploma, or any other voucher for my being medically equipped for surgeoncy with the infantry. They simply handed me my commission. We were three-months men, and as we had volunteered in late April, we were mustered out on August first. I then returned to my medical studies at Jefferson Medical College, graduating in March of 1862.

In May, after a real examination, in which I passed first and my classmate from Brown and the Jefferson, George Porter, passed second, we were both recommended for the Regular Army. The commission soon arrived, but on mature consideration, as I had decided not to make the Army my career, I returned it and asked for a temporary commission as Acting Assistant Surgeon. These were usually known in the Army as "damned contract doctors," but as they included all of the leading civilian physicians and surgeons (Weir Mitchell, George Morehouse, John Neill, William Keating, and other men of that stamp), we felt no pricks of conscience in the sobriquet, but were amused by it.

At that time, I did not foresee in the least that the decision not to enter the Regular Army was to be one of the turning points and a deciding event in my career, since it brought me under the sway of the master mind of Silas Weir Mitchell. Had I been in the Regulars, I should very soon have had an independent and very responsible position in a hospital or in the field. I never would have been made an assistant and, as it proved, an associate to Mitchell and Morehouse, two other "contract doctors."

Surgeon General Hammond was an intimate friend and collaborator in experimental physiology with Mitchell, who had suggested the establishment of a number of special hospitals, such as for the eye and ear, or for the heart. Among these was one for diseases and injuries of the nervous system, to which Mitchell and Morehouse were assigned.

Shortly after their appointment, Mitchell asked for my transfer from the Satterlee Hospital as what might be called the junior member in the medical firm of Mitchell, Morehouse, and Keen. What good fortune for me so soon after graduation! Practically, I might have been called their resident, yet they generously included my name with theirs on the title page as joint author of the book *Gun Shot Wounds and Other Injuries to the Nerves*, and of various papers, on an equal level with them, so far as the public was concerned. Their work carried my name all over the country—and abroad.[4] They might easily have printed all that I wrote and simply named me in the preface as their assistant. But throughout his career, Mitchell was scrupulously generous in giving credit to young men for any work they did for or with him.

A scheme of work was drawn up and certain subjects were assigned to each of us, the name of the one who actually wrote the paper being first in order. The other two read the manuscripts, which were then discussed by all three. I took almost all the notes in longhand, on reams and reams of paper. Mitchell and I wrote the papers assigned to us, but while Morehouse discussed his with delightful learning and acumen, his *vis inertiae* was such that he never put pen to paper. Finally, that pile of my laboriously handwritten notes, at least three feet high, was destroyed by a fire in his office. He never wrote a line.

Yet I do not grudge the hours and hours spent in digging out those minutes of the histories of these soldiers. I learned how to take histories, what was essential and what incidental, how to follow the lead of a casual word, the significance, sometimes, of a transient symptom. Most men would have been satisfied with the record that "A.B." was wounded on _____ and entered on the _____ Hospital records and the date of hospital admission, along with the fact and locality of his wound(s) and the symptoms and physical signs observed.

But not Mitchell! "What was your bodily attitude when you were wounded? Did you fall to the ground? How far were you able to walk before you fell? Did you bleed profusely? About how much blood did you lose? Could you move both arms and both legs? If not, what loss of motion did you observe? Did you suffer severe pain? If so, where and how severe was it? Did you lose consciousness, and was that from the loss of blood, or from shock, or from the pain of the wound? How long do you think you were unconscious? How do you know it was so long?" Every particular and every possible symptom or physical sign was elicited. What splendid training did I thus receive! How Mitchell's methods became ingrained in my very nature! How fruitful were those months of labor! How God led me in ways that I knew not of!

Our first work was at the Christian Street Hospital (the old police station) on Christian Street near 10th, but after a few months, we were all transferred to the Turner's Lane Hospital (at what is now 20th and Columbia, but was then open country), where most of our work was done. An old mansion house was occupied by the staff, and the tent barracks were erected around it. It was there that we really laid the foundation of modern neurological surgery, as embodied in the little book already mentioned.

During most of my service in the Army, I was an agent of the Army Medical Museum in Washington, for which I collected specimens from the hospitals in Frederick, Maryland (and later, in Philadelphia), and forwarded. My own notes and specimens fill many a page and furnish many an illustration in the six splendid volumes of *The Medical and Surgical History of the War of the Rebellion.* The circular on "Reflex Paralysis" was an important publication, which set forth a novel theory of shock which only lately has received the attention it deserves. It is a very rare pamphlet now: I gave one copy to the College of Physicians and have another one in my library.

In 1910, I joined the Loyal Legion and wear its button with pride.[5] My oldest male descendant will always wear it, I hope, and remember how much honor and patriotism it stands for. We in the Army—or at least I—did not fully appreciate the fact that we were making history, and so I kept no journal, which I now *deeply* regret.

At this point, I am reminded of a question posed by one of my children, when she was very young, as to whether I had been a surgeon in the Revolutionary War. When I recalled the fact that from 1776 to 1837 was a period of only sixty-one years, the question is not so odd after all. Throughout my own life, the Revolution has always seemed as far off as the Middle Ages. How greatly our perspective varies!

I also took part in the World War as a commissioned officer. So far as I know, I am the only person in the entire Army who served as a commissioned officer in both the World War and the Civil War. My former pupil, Surgeon General M. W. Ireland, tells me that he believes that this is true. I am well aware that I have no business, at nearly eighty, to be in the Service at all. But it came about this way.

In 1909, Surgeon General Torney, with a rare far-sightedness that does him the greatest credit, organized the Medical Reserve Corps so that, in case of war, he would have a body of partly trained men from whom he could at once obtain additional medical officers. I volunteered for the Officers Training Corps (O.T.C.), as soon as I learned of the project. My commission as First Lieutenant is dated December 28th, 1909. Nobody then thought anything about age, or of active service, as no one took seriously the idea of war. No one objected to me on account of my age, and I certainly didn't propose to object to myself. Once I was in, no one wanted to turn me out. As the Corps was originally constituted, members could decline to serve for any good reason and were not obliged to serve abroad unless willing to do so.

Major William W. Keen, Medical Reserve Corps, U.S. Army, 1917

On April 11th, 1917, just five days after we declared war on Germany, the O.T.C. was abandoned, and as many members as chose to were automatically transferred to the Officers Reserve Corps. These men, in contrast with their predecessors, were bound to go wherever ordered, including Mexico or overseas. It was at this time that I was promoted to Major, although I have never known either who suggested this promotion or by whom the promotion was officially confirmed.

In 1918, when all distinctions between Regulars, Volunteers, Militia, and the National Guard were abolished, I was officially in the Medical Reserve Corps, U.S. Army. When we were all merged into one Army, I wrote to Surgeon General Gorgas saying that if he thought I should resign I would do so, but that "it would break my heart." He replied, "Don't resign till I tell you to."

I have never been under pay and have had no special orders for service. My chief value to the Army, according to what several medical officers have told me, while seeking recruits among the doctors, has been as a stimulating example. When Majors Jump and McLean were traveling over the country, urging doctors to volunteer, they told me that one of their strongest appeals was, "Aren't you husky young fellows going to volunteer, when Dr. W.W. Keen, almost eighty, was among the first to do so?" They tell me that this fetched them, again and again.

Besides this, I am a member of the National Research Council and of the Council of National Defense, attending their meetings, from time to time. For the former, I wrote my *Treatment of War Wounds*, with all royalties going to the Council for their Division of Medical Research.

I also have travelled considerably to make addresses at the meetings of the two National Councils, in addition to medical organizations, in Philadelphia, Baltimore, Washington, Cincinnati, Chicago, Boston, and Providence.

In my Washington address before the Council of National Defense, I suggested that, based on our population, an American army of fifteen million men would compare with the present proportionate army of the Allies. I sent a copy of this address to Dawson Williams, editor of the *British Medical Journal*, who wrote me that my statement had been cabled to Great Britain and had been extensively commented on in the Press.

At that dinner, there were "only two or three speakers to follow me," as Dr. Franklin Martin announced when calling on me, but when I sat down, several of those men whispered to him to adjourn the meeting, whereupon he announced, "We have had the benediction. The meeting is adjourned."

AN IMPOSSIBLE WAR[6]

Mr. Toastmaster, My Lords, Ladies and Gentlemen:

The chairman and other speakers have all very naturally, and very rightly, referred to the captivating idea of celebrating the completion of one hundred years of peace between Great Britain and America.

But there is an earlier instance of the splendid magnanimity of Great Britain to which no one has alluded tonight, and to which scant justice has been done by anyone in the past. In 1876, we celebrated one hundred years of our national independence with an extensive and most successful universal exposition, in which all nations joined. Each nation erected a building to house its commissioners. Among the foremost, in the extent and value of its exhibits and the importance of its official building, was Great Britain. Without British aid, the exhibition would have been shorn of much of its luster. At the close of the exhibition, this British building was presented to the City of Philadelphia. It still stands, in full view from the Belmont Drive in Fairmount Park, a mute but eloquent witness to the magnanimity of a great nation. To assist, not grudgingly but heartily, in making such a celebraton by another nation a great success, in an incident unique in history.

Recall the startling facts: We were celebrating a war which began at Bunker Hill and ended with the surrender of Cornwallis at Yorktown. We were the victors, and the British were the vanquished. Yet a century later, they joined with us in celebrating our victory and their defeat. I challenge you to find a parallel event in the world's international relations. A war with a nation so magnanimous as to celebrate their own defeat and to treat us not as foreigners but as transatlantic brethren ought to be, and *is*, an impossible war.

Think, gentlemen of the British delegation, of the great gifts you have bestowed on us! Chaucer and Bacon, Shakespeare and Milton, Hampden and Burke, Jenner and Lister! How many memories cluster around each name! Recall too what we in turn have given to you: Washington and Lincoln, Longfellow and Emerson; Henry Lea and Howard Furness; and the blessed sleep of ether!

It is not unbecoming in me, on this occasion, to vaunt my own profession. The three boons, vaccination, anesthesia, and antisepsis—an everlasting trinity of benedictions—and all three, thank God! sprung from Anglo-Saxon loins, have already done more to mitigate suffering, prolong life, and promote human happiness than all the warriors, from Genghis Khan to Napoleon, have done to produce suffering, destroy human life, and make the earth a desert.

Your civil liberty and orderly processes of law, gentlemen, have found congenial soil in America, and we have even bettered your religious liberty by totally severing all relations between Church and State.

I repeat, then, my assertion that a war between such kindred nations is impossible, unthinkable. It would be a crime against humanity!

I have spoken of the action of Great Britain in 1876 as an unparalleled instance of magnanimity. But it is to remain without a fellow for only a few weeks more.

Six weeks from now, on the field at Gettysburg, hallowed by the blood of heroes of Lincoln's immortal address, the soldiers of the Blue and the Gray—those who, after fifty years, are still living—will meet again. There, on the very spot where they had done their utmost to slay one another, a half-century ago, with clasped hands they will bow their heads over the graves of their brave comrades and breathe a prayer of thanksgiving for peace. Show me, if you can, another such meeting on any other battlefield!

But while there never has been such a one before, permit me to express the fervent hope that there *may* yet be another.

A few days ago, as president of the American Philosophical Society, I signed a remarkable address. Its signers consist of presidents of fifty-five scientific, educational, and philanthropic institutions in the United States. The address is beautifully embossed on vellum and is to be presented to the German emperor on the 15th of June. It extends to his Imperial Majesty our collective congratulations on the completion of twenty-five years of his reign, and especially that it has been a reign of unbroken peace!

I cast a forward glance, and in the near future—only seven years away—I see the year 1920, exactly half a century after 1870! What a glorious augury it would be for the peace of the world, for the Golden Age that is sometime sure to come, if France and Germany could then again meet on the field of Sedan, not in armed conflict but to celebrate the *liberté egalité et fraternité*, which should never again disappear from the earth!

Then would we be able to sign, not "Peace hath her victories no less renown'd than war,"[7] but "Peace hath her victories *far more* renown'd than war."

5

—··⊰ ⊱··—

Author and Editor

AUTHORSHIP LAUNCHED

THE GOOD FORTUNE I had of falling at once under the stimulating influence of Weir Mitchell at the beginning of my medical studies is largely responsible for my later career: I was immediately stirred into authorship.

My first work was in reports of cases during the Civil War, many of which may be found in the *Medical and Surgical History of the War of the Rebellion*.

I later published some clinical charts and revived Flower's *Diagrams of the Nerves*.

In 1875, I wrote a *History of the Philadelphia School of Anatomy*, a serious and valuable record of the good work done in the sixty-five years of the school, from which came so many of our distinguished teachers. I had owned and operated the school since 1866, when I was newly returned from my studies abroad.

In 1897, while laid up with an injured knee, I spent the summer in bed in the Keene Valley of the Adirondacks, where I wrote *The Surgical Complications and Sequels of Typhoid Fever*, published in 1898 by Saunders. It is still (1915) the only book on the subject. Though its statistics are no longer valid (they are greatly improved), its principles remain intact. I think I have never seen any complication or sequel, except typhoid abscess of the breast, which is not described in this book. In my enthusiasm I had twenty-five hundred copies printed! They cost me $1,098.49, for I paid all the costs and got a small royalty. The book is still debited in my ledger with $403.48, the price of an unrequited love.

In 1898, I edited *The Bi-Centennial Celebration of the Founding of the First Baptist Church of the City of Philadelphia, 1698–1898*, to which I also contributed some of the writing. I worked for nothing and "found myself" with the history, but I spent at least a hundred dollars on it.

In the October 24th issue of *The Outlook*, in 1903, I published a paper on "The Cheerfulness of Death," which the American Baptist Publication Society later

Keen's granddaughter Polly (Mary Louisa Butcher), demonstrating for his book *Animal Experimentation and Medical
Progress* that laboratory work is not necessarily sadistic.

republished as a little pamphlet. It has been a great comfort to many, and nothing
I have ever written has brought me so many kind messages and letters.

In 1905, Saunders published a volume of my *Addresses and Other Papers*. I
think I printed a thousand copies, at a cost of $1,010.66 (which my contract, in
the safe deposit vault, would show). It was another instance of unrequited love,
for it is still debited with $443.22—once again on a royalty basis. (*Note*, 1926:
Fire has destroyed the unbound sheets.)

I hope to publish a second volume of *Addresses and Other Papers*, and also one
or two of the more important surgical papers I have written. There might even
be material for three volumes.[1]

In 1914, Houghton Mifflin published my *Animal Experimentation and Medical
Progress*.[2] My contract was made *early* in the year, and the Great War, I flatter

myself, is largely responsible for the small sale. In fact, the war has killed it. The edition was one thousand copies—and on a royalty basis, I paying all expenses. It has cost me $1,140.97 so far, and is still debited with $837.98. But in view of the good it has done, I am glad I published it.

EDITORIAL RESPONSIBILITY

I have always taken very seriously my duty as an editor, for example in *The American Health Primers*. This was a series of twelve small volumes on subjects pertaining to health, which I edited for Lindsay & Blakiston.[3] (I did not write a single volume.) As editor I was very vigilant, as I deemed it my duty to be, in seeing that the text of each volume was of the best quality. One volume was so slovenly and utterly inadequate that I returned it to the writer and obtained an excellent volume on the same subject by another author. The first author and his two sons became my bitter enemies for years. The sons paid me a visit with the intention of attacking me physically. Fortunately, Fuller[4] was within call. I rang for him, and on his arrival, I turned them out of the house and slammed the door. (They were both stronger and taller than I.)

This series was republished in England by Ward and Locke, under the title *Ward and Locke's Long Life Series*. The English publishers omitted my name as editor and the names of the twelve authors, substituting "by eminent members of the medical profession." The text was so revised that all evidence of its American origin was obliterated. I sent a copy of one volume, with its English counterpart, to the *Lancet*, with a protest against such plagiarism, but never received a word in return against such a scandalous outrage. I let the matter drop.

Gray's *Anatomy*

The one appalling disaster of my life occurred in 1886. On July 12th, my darling wife was suddenly taken from me, leaving me with four daughters to whom I had to become both father and mother. My personal grief almost crushed me. Had it not been for my children, I should not have cared to live.

By the autumn, I found that my grief was threatening to impair both my health and my ability to care for my dear girls. I could scarcely sleep, whereas prior to that dreadful loss, I had always been a sound sleeper. (Since that time, I have been unable to sleep, as a rule, over five or six hours—often less, occasionally more.) I became despondent, and I even feared a settled melancholia might come on.

One day, while I was in this condition, Philadelphia publisher Henry Lea proposed that I take on the editing of the New American Edition of Gray's *Anatomy*. This essential reference work had had a wonderfully successful history. It had been practically without a rival for over thirty years, but it had been allowed to fall behind the times. Lea offered me four hundred dollars, which I accepted. I would have done it for nothing, for I felt that I was in such a mental condition that congenial and absorbing work was just what was needed to bring me out of myself; to compel me to think of something else beside my grief; and so to help me do my duty to my dear children, as well as to myself.

I gave to the work all my spare time for a year—hours every day. When I came to the chapter on the nervous system, I found that I too, like the book, was hopelessly behind the times. I had not been teaching systematic human anatomy since 1875, when I closed my anatomy school. Meanwhile, the physiological, pathological, and surgical anatomy of the nervous system had been forging ahead by leaps and bounds. I resolutely put my nose to the grindstone, spending two months or more catching up. Then I revised, and largely re-wrote, those chapters. The new edition was published in 1887.[5] I was paid four hundred dollars; and the book opened the "door of opportunity" for me. As it was a necessary textbook of practically every medical student in the country, the appearance of my name on the title page made me known to the entire profession (especially for the future), and thus it was of great value to me in my surgical work.

It is a pleasure to me to tell my children that this edition, even now, after twenty-five years, is still sought, though it has been long out of print. And Henry Lea's son, Charles, said to me, only two or three years ago (1908 or 1909), that it was the best edition of Gray's ever published. (In 1893, I re-edited Gray from the 13th English edition.)

When [daughter] Margaret was nine or ten years old, she said that she had been unable to tell her schoolmates if I had edited Gray's *Anatomy* or Gray's "Elegy."

BOOKS AND INCOME

American Text-Book of Surgery

In 1892, Saunders published the first edition of *American Text-Book of Surgery, for Practitioners and Students*, a single volume of 1,209 pages selling for seven dollars per copy. By 1903, the fourth edition had appeared, and out of forty-four thousand copies printed, more than forty thousand have been sold, netting me a clear profit of ten thousand dollars. I think it is not going too far to assert that this book marked a new epoch in surgical texts and surgical teaching in all of the English-speaking world. It was new in the point of view from which surgery was envisaged; that is, from a bacteriological and antiseptic standpoint. The very first chapter was on "Surgical Bacteriology," and bacteriology and antiseptic or aseptic surgery were expounded and reinforced throughout the book. In addition, extraordinary emphasis was placed on the style of the English used.

My medical training had been long and thorough, beginning (almost in reverse order) with the practical training of field surgery in the Civil War, after one meager year of medical-school lectures. Following the collection and cataloguing of specimens for the Army Medical Museum [during the war] and two years of study and observation, in the great European teaching hospitals, I built up solid credentials in anatomy, in dissection, in illustration, and in research into medical literature, ancient and modern. I simultaneously refined my technique in both surgery and the teaching of surgery, so that when I was elected to the Chair of Surgery at Jefferson Medical College, in 1889, I was superbly well equipped to take the obvious next career step and pass the torch by means of the written word.

As soon as I was elected, I carefully examined every surgical textbook in the English language, British as well as American. I found none that was satisfactory, large enough to give fairly thorough knowledge, yet small enough to be practical, for busy students in the lamentably brief medical course. All contemporary textbooks were especially deficient in that they taught nothing of surgical bacteriology, then the new but rapidly growing science. Since my colleague in the Chair of Pathology was skeptical as to the role of these "bugs," as he disdainfully referred to bacteria, I felt it to be of the utmost importance that this subject should be at the foundation of a new textbook.

This was the genesis of the *American Text-book of Surgery*. I immediately took steps to organize a corps of thirteen professors of surgery in our leading medical colleges, assuring both its financial and professional success, in spite of the portentous number of authors.

Dr. William White, Professor of Surgery at the University of Pennsylvania, consented to serve with me as co-editor. We divided the subjects among the authors as appropriately as we could, following correspondence with each of them, and adopted a wholly new plan of authorship. Galley proofs of each chapter were submitted to all thirteen authors, with the request that he read, criticize, suggest improvements, and return them to Dr. White and me. Every line of it was read by both of us in manuscript and in proof, and fully discussed, whenever either of us questioned the statements made or advice given.

After the revised proofs were received, we submitted the entire work to Mr. McCreary, the most accomplished and best proofreader I have ever known and the first reader for our publisher. He read the entirety from the literary point of view, correcting not a few blunders and suggesting more felicitous wording where appropriate. Naturally, we were careful never to change the authors' *teaching.*

The galley proofs of the entire work were sent to each author with a request that he once again read, criticize, and return them to the editors. All serious criticisms and suggestions were then referred to the author of the chapter concerned. The result was a homogenous whole, in careful English and representative of the best surgical thought of the profession, in the United States and Canada. One of its particular features was that, as *all* of the authors had revised and made suggestions for *all* of the chapters, the book appeared with the thirteen names on the title page, though no single author was indicated for any specific chapter.

Saunders often commented later that the book became the foundation for his success as a publisher. He intuitively saw the possibilities in the new method and expanded the idea, publishing several medical *American Text Books,* including Dr. William Pepper's two-volume *American Text Book of Medicine.* Ours was a very successful publishing experiment, passing through four editions—the first in 1892, the fourth in 1903.

Few readers could realize the hours which Dr. White and I spent on the original edition and on each revision. The greatest tribute to our work is the fact that no subsequent English or American textbook on surgery was issued that was *not* based on Bacteriology, Antisepsis—and later, Asepsis.

> *NOTE: I have recently gone over the principal text books published prior to 1892, in English, French, German, and Italian, and while some mention antisepsis or speak of Lister, very few enter into antiseptic methods. They are "tinged" with bacteriology and antisepsis, but how wholly different they are from the* American Text-Book of Surgery, *which was founded on our modern knowledge. The first real textbook of surgery founded on bacteriology and antisepsis was that of Mansell Moullin, of Glasgow (1891), but by that time, the printing of our* Text-Book *was well advanced. Its scheme was devised and its outline completed in 1889–90.*

Keen's Surgery

From the time of that publication forward, a large number of books by American authors have been published, and we are now independent of Europe. Besides textbooks in one or two volumes, a considerable number of systems of surgery and medicine have been issued. The most successful is *Surgery, Its Principles and Practice*, so I am told. Saunders published this series of six volumes (1906–1913)[6] of which nearly fourteen thousand sets have been printed—including review copies for professors of surgery—and nearly twelve thousand sold. At seven dollars per volume, the net profit to me has been, again, about ten thousand dollars. This has been considerable compensation to me as editor, but the authors also have shared in the pecuniary success. Indeed, Dr. Robert Lovett told me last summer (1915) that he has received more for his chapter on orthopedic surgery than for any other chapter he has ever written, adding, "in fact, more than from all the others put together."

As editor of *Keen's Surgery,* I declined to allot two or three chapters to distinguished surgeons who wished to couple the name of an assistant with their own. I knew that it meant that the work would be done by the assistants, and that the surgeons' own names would give professional standing to the chapters. I meant that every chapter should be written by the man whose name stood as the author. In only one case was I deceived. One surgeon, accepting my invitation, had an assistant write the chapter, inserting his own name and suppressing that of the real writer. I only discovered it many years later and have always had a contempt for the man who stooped to the meanness of claiming credit (for the chapter was an excellent one) for another man's work.

In another case, a chapter ostensibly written by a distinguished surgeon was so far below what I knew he could write that I returned the manuscript to him, telling him that it was unworthy of his reputation and that I was sure he had had an assistant write it. I asked him to write another chapter, and in due time he sent me one that was excellent. Happily, the incident caused no break in our friendship. He always alludes to the incident as "the chapter which you and I wrote." Sensible man.

In a third case, an excellent chapter was written in very poor English. I changed the faulty style into good English but was most careful *never* to change the *meaning*. This author "kicked" and said that his chapter should appear as he wrote it. I asked him, "What is an editor for? Is he simply to be a conduit to carry the chapter from the author to the printer? My idea of an editor's duty is a far larger and wider one." He finally accepted the altered text, and again I am glad to say that he is still my highly esteemed friend.

I was ever on the alert to detect and correct any obscure text, or any uncouth or faulty English style, and as the volumes appeared, I had the satisfaction that not a few reviewers commented on the excellent English of volume after volume. I felt that this was my vindication, and naturally it gave me much pleasure.

As chapter after chapter reached me, I read every word of the text, and wherever I thought there might be an error in a prescription or in teaching, I always corresponded with the author, asking him to read his text on page ____, line ____, to see if that was what he really had meant to teach. He was directly responsible for the teaching or the operation, the remedy or the dose, and not I. If on reflection he stood by his text as written, in it went, absolutely in his own words, but in quite a number of cases, the authors revised their statements.

I have still in my files the volumes of correspondence.[7] Editing *Keen's Surgery* was no light task. It covered about fifteen years. Before a word was written or an author invited, I spent three months in drawing up a syllabus of each chapter and by so doing avoided repetition. For instance, I indicated to the author on the "Surgery of the Neck" whether or not he was to include the full treatment, or only incidental mention, of the surgery of the blood vessels, nerves, the spine and cord, lymphatics, etc., *in* the neck. The result was that there was very little overlapping. In making up this syllabus, I was greatly indebted to Chalmers DaCosta, whose critical judgment as a distinguished author was most useful to me.

In drawing up my syllabus, I was very careful to allot what seemed to me the relative number of pages according to the importance of the topic. In one case, when I received the manuscript, I immediately returned it to the author, telling him that he had sent me a book when I had asked for a chapter.[8] If I remember rightly, his manuscript was about three times the number of pages I had allotted to it. When I received it back, it was still considerably over twice the length it should have been. I took my blue pencil, therefore, and went over it page by page and sentence by sentence. It was the hardest work that I ever did, as an editor: It was extremely difficult to cut out phrases and sentences—and sometimes paragraphs—and yet leave the text so that it would read smoothly as good English, as well as good surgery. This cost me almost more work than all the other chapters put together. When it appeared that it was still many pages longer than I had planned, I had to let it go. I am glad to say that no one ever detected (or at least wrote that he detected) my blue pencil.

UNDERGRADUATE ESSAYS[9]

[Prepared for Professors Chace (*), Dunn (†), and Gammell (#)]

1. "The Character of Lady Macbeth" (Read before Alpha Delta Phi, Dec. 19, 1856).
2. "The Office of Theories in Physical Science" (Sept. 28, 1857).*
3. "Water Considered as a Regulator of Temperature" (Read in class, Oct. 12, 1857).*
4. "Extensive Reading, an Aid in the Formation of Style" (Oct. 13, 1857).†
5. [Not found.]
6. "The Gesta Romanorum" (Oct. 27, 1857).†
7. "The Lightning Rod" (Nov. 9, 1857).*
8. "Literature, the Immortality of Speech" (Nov. 10, 1857).† [See No. 26]
9. "The Atlantic Telegraph: the Difficulties in its Construction; the Probabilities of its Success" (Nov. 30, 1857).*
10. "The Trial of Sir Thomas More" (Speech, Dec. 2, 1857).†
11. "Three Uses of the Telegraph, in Respect of Transits, Longitude, and Velocity" (Read in class, Dec. 14, 1857).*
12. "Criticism on a Passage of [Goldsmith's] *Deserted Village*" (Dec. 15, 1857).†
13. "Nitrogen: Its Character and Offices" (Dec. 28, 1857).*
14. "The Genius of Handel" (Speech, Dec. 30, 1857).†
15. "The Requisites of a True Classification" (Read in class, March 8, 1858).*
16. "Swiss Character as Developed by Swiss Scenery" (Speech, March 17, 1858).†
17. "The Final Cause of the Diversity of the Animal Kingdom" (March 22, 1858).*
18. "The Mechanism of the Human Spine" (Apr. 5, 1858).*
19. "William Penn" (Speech, Apr. 7, 1858).†
20. *"De Memoriis Fori Romani"* (Exhibition speech [in Latin], May 1, 1858).
21. "The Excito-Motary System of Nerves" (May 10, 1858).*
22. "Men of Science, Citizens of the World" (Speech, May 19, 1858).†
23. "The Office and Ministry of Pain" (May 24, 1858).*
24. "The Character of Cardinal Wolsey in Shakespeare's *King Henry the Eighth*" (June 1, 1858).†
25. "The Ear" (June 7, 1858).*
26. "Literature, the Immortality of Speech" [See No. 8]
27. "The History of Civilization as a College Study" (Oct. 6, 1858).#
28. "The Conversion of Constantine" (Oct. 20, 1858).#
29. "An Imaginative Sketch of the Feudal Times" (Nov. 17, 1858).#

MEDICAL BOOK CHAPTERS
AND MAGAZINE ARTICLES

1. "The Minister in His Medical Relations," in the *National Baptist*, May 11, 1876.
2. "Christianity and the Bodily Wants of Man," in the *National Baptist*, June 8, 1876.
3. Original papers No. 100, 101, and 102, "Surgery of the Brain" and "Surgery of the Spinal Cord," in *Buck's Reference Handbook*, vol. 8, and No. 103 in *Keating's Cyclopedia of the Diseases of Children*, vol. 3 (1889).
4. "Surgery of the Spine," in Dennis's *System of Surgery*, vol. 2, pp. 787–866 (1895).
5. "Surgery of the Head," in the *International Encyclopaedia of Surgery*, vol. 7 (1895).
6. "Surgery of the Nervous System," in *Dercum's Text-Book of Diseases and Injuries of the Nervous System*, chapter 33, pp. 957–1006 (1895).
7. "The Use of the Röntgen or *X* Rays in Surgery," in Dennis's *System of Surgery*, vol. 4 (1895).
8. "The Advantages of an Academic Training for a Medical Career," Phi Beta Kappa address at Lafayette—and in an emergency at Brown, the original orator being ill. Published in the *Brown Magazine*, April 1896.
9. "The Use of the Röntgen Rays in Surgery," in *McClure's Magazine*, May 1896.
10. Section on Surgery, in the *Year-Book of Medicine and Surgery* (1896 and 1897).
11. "Thyrotomy and Laryngectomy," in Kyle's *Diseases of the Nose and Throat* (1899).
12. "The Cheerfulness of Death," in *Outlook*, October 24, 1903.
13. "Recent Surgical Progress: A Result Chiefly of Experimental Research," in *Harper's Monthly Magazine*, April 1909.
14. "An Account of the Festival Held at Upsala, May, 1907, in Commemoration of the 200th Anniversary of the Birth of Carolus Linnaeus," in *The Aesculapian*, vol. 1 (1909).
15. "What Vivisection Has Done for Humanity," in *Ladies' Home Journal*, April 1910.
16. "New Surgery," in *Harper's Monthly Magazine*, July 1910.
17. "Portrait," in *Cosmopolitan*, December 1912.
18. "Do Warts and Moles Result in Cancer?" in *Ladies' Home Journal*, March 1914.
19. "The Influence of Antivivisection on Character," in *Scientific American Supplement*, June 1914.
20. "Before and After Lister," in *Science*, June 11–18, 1915.

21. "Address at the Dedication of the Mitchell Memorial Building of the Philadelphia Orthopaedic Hospital," in *Science*, August 25, 1916.
22. "The Inveracities of Antivivisection," in the *Journal of the American Medical Association*, November 4, 1916.
23. "Fight Against Infection," in *North American Review*, July 1917.
24. "The Surgical Operations on President Cleveland in 1893," in the *Saturday Evening Post*, September 22, 1917.
25. "The Story of Three Tablets" [commemorating George Washington De Long, James Markham Ambler, Jesse Willliam Lazear, and William Martin Wightman], in *The Military Surgeon*, January 1918.
26. "The Red Cross and the Vivisectionists," in *Science*, February 22, 1918.
27. "Anti-Typhoid Inoculation," in *Science*, May 17, 1918.
28. "Military Surgery in 1861 and 1918," in *Annals of the American Academy of Political and Social Sciences*, November 1918.
29. "Seven Decades in Medicine," in *Yale Review*, January 1919.
30. "Autobiographical Address," in *Science*, February 11, 1921.
31. "Dinner in Honor of Dr. Keen," in *Science*, February 11, 1921.
32. "Portrait," in *Scientific Monthly*, March 1921.
33. "Great American Surgeon," in *World's Work*, April 1921.
34. "Truth About Vivisection," in *Science*, September 16, 1921.
35. "Message of Hope," in *Woman's Home Companion*, December 1921.
36. "The Surgical and Anatomic Evidence of Evolution," in *Science*, June 9, 1922.
37. "Erobic," in *Science*, March 23, 1923.
38. "Louis Pasteur," in *Yale Review*, April 1923.
39. "Aerobic," in *Science*, May 11, 1923.
40. "Memories of Sixty Years," in *Science*, August 17, 1923.
41. "The Value of Medical Research to Mankind and to Animals," in *South Atlantic Quarterly*, July–October, 1923.
42. "Some Social Nuisances," in *Scientific Monthly*, March 1924.
43. "The Supreme Court and Senator La Follette," in *Outlook*, October 29, 1924.
44. "Freeing Mankind from Disease," in *Collier's*, November 8, 1924.
45. "Portrait," in *Literary Review*, November 22, 1924.
46. "Personal Experience in Three Epidemics of Smallpox," in the *Saturday Evening Post*, February 28, 1925.
47. "The Scientific Accuracy of the Sacred Scriptures," in *Science*, December 11, 1925.
48. "Human Tails," in *Science*, June 11, 1926.

49. "The Conquest of Scarlet Fever," in *Woman's Home Companion*, November 4, 1926.
50. "Antivivisectionists' Methods," in *Hygeia*, January 1927.
51. "The Early Days of Anti-Vivisection," in *Science*, January 14, 1927.
52. "What It Costs the Doctor," in *Atlantic Monthly*, January 1928.
53. "An Anti-Vivisectionist Screed," in *Science*, March 15, 1929.

MEDICAL MONOGRAPHS

I have published over three hundred fifty articles in medical and other journals. Among them, these are some of the most important:

No. 1 "Reflex Paralysis from Gunshot Wounds" (1864) was published in conjunction with Drs. Mitchell and Morehouse, as were: **No. 2** "Gunshot Fracture of Superior Maxilla, and Wound of Internal Maxillary Artery; Ligature of the Common Carotid Artery; Paralysis with Convulsions of Opposite Side, After 35 Days; Death, After 41 Days; Abscesses of the Brain" (1864); **No. 3** "On Malingering, Especially in Regard to Simulation of Diseases of the Nervous System" (1864); and **No. 6** "On the Antagonism of Morphia and Atropia, Founded on a Series of Experiments" (1865).

No. 16 "A Case of Universal Hyperostosis with Osteoporosis (1870), written with Drs. J. Ewing Mears, Harrison Allen, and William Pepper, deals with a remarkable, and in my own experience, unique case.

No. 18 "Masked Fracture of the Articular Surface of the Tibial Malleolus in the Ankle Joint and Amputation of the Leg" (1871) was on a new diagnostic sign of a sprain fracture.

No. 20 "Necrosis and Removal of the Entire Petrus Portion of the Temporal Bone" (1871) described a very rare instance of necrosis of the entire petrous portion of the temporal bone resulting from an injury similar to one described in *Hamlet*.[10]

Nos. 29 and **30** "Gunshot Wound of the Brain, with Remarks on the Anatomy of the Retina and the Optic Commissure in the Light of This Case with Additional History and a Chromolithograph" (1870), written with Dr. William Thomson, described a pathological demonstration of the anatomical distribution of the optic nerve in the retina, a demonstration which was accepted as final by Flint, in his five-volume *Physiology*, and, I believe, by most later writers.

No. 45 "Experiments on Laryngeal Nerves and Muscles of Respiration, etc., in a Criminal Executed by Hanging" (1875) demonstrated the innervation of the internal and external intercostal muscles, by experiments on a criminal who was executed by hanging.

No. 56 "A Case of Cholecystotomy, with Remarks" (1879), an early paper describing and advocating cholecystotomy, was followed by **No. 65** "Cholecystotomy with a Report of Two Cases. With a Table of All Reported Cases and Remarks" (1884); and **No. 72** "Case of Cholecystotomy" (1885).

No. 61 "On the Systematic Use of the Living Model in Teaching Anatomy" (1881) was a method commended and adopted by Cunningham (of Dublin, later of Edinburgh).

No. 63 "Etiology and Pathology of Dupuytren's Contraction of the Fingers" (1882) was my first paper on Dupuytren's contraction. Later papers were **No. 99** "Dupuytren's Finger Contraction; Operation by Removal of the Contracting Band by Open Wound; Immediate Cure Without Reaction or Pain"(1889); **No. 100** "Dupuytren's Finger Contraction" (1889); and **No. 295** "A New Method of Operating on Dupuytren's Contraction of the Palmar Fascia, Together with the Successful Use of Neural Infiltration in Such Operations" (1906).

No. 73 "Stretching of the Facial Nerve. Report of a New Case, with Remarks, and a Summary of Previously Reported Cases" (1886) was on stretching the facial nerve in *tic convulsif.*

No. 74 "A Case of Perityphilitis which Apparently was Recovering, but which Imperatively Demanded Operation as Early as the Sixth Day" (1886) was an early case of appendicitis; other cases were cited in **No. 132** "Four Operations for Appendicitis: Three Recoveries, One Death from a Very Small Concealed Abscess" (1891).

No. 75 "Uncompleted Nephrectomy: Calcareous Vessel Mistaken for a Calculus by the Needle Test: Operation Abandoned on Account of Adhesions; Death; Autopsy; Primary Encephaloid of the Kidney" (1889) was the first instance of nephrectomy for a gunshot wound of the kidney.

No. 76 "Spontaneous Aneurysms in Children" (1890) described two cases of aneurysm at ages 18 and 8, a very rare condition in the young.

No. 82 "Death from Early Septicaomia Following Puncture Wound of the Toe by a Splinter: a Lesson in Septic Surgery" (1888).

No. 86 "Exploratory Trephining and Puncture of the Brain Almost to the Lateral Ventricle, for Intra-cranial Pressure Supposed to be Due to an Abscess in the Temporo-Sphenoidal Lobe. Temporary Improvement: Death on the Fifth Day; Autopsy; Meningitis with Effusion into the Ventricles, with Description of Proposed Operation to Tap the Ventricles as a Definite Surgical Procedure" (1888);

No. 88 "A Preliminary Report of a Case of Tapping and Irrigation of the Lateral Ventricles" (1889); **No. 89** "Tapping and Irrigating the Lateral Ventricles of the Brain" (1889); and **No. 90** "Specimen from a Case of Tapping and Irrigation of the Lateral Ventricles" (1889) first described and formulated the tapping of the lateral ventricles as a definite surgical operation.

No. 87 "A Case of Hysterectomy" (1888).

No. 94 "Successful Case of Nephrorrhaphy for Floating Kidney" (1889); **No. 114** "Nephrectomy..." (1890); and **No. 118** "Nephrorrhaphy" (1890) described early cases of nephrorrhaphy.

Nos. 101 "Surgery of the Brain" (1889) and **No. 102** "Surgery of the Spinal Cord" (1889) were among the very early papers on the surgery of the brain and spinal cord. They were followed by thirty-six other papers, each dealing with intracranial surgery in one of its many phases. By consulting them, one can see what I accomplished in cerebral and spinal surgery. This group of papers is by far the most important work I have done, surgically speaking. The first case opened up the door of opportunity for me, and I entered in. I was so far in the lead that even better men later could not catch up in reputation, at least for many years. A stern chase was indeed a long chase.

No. 104 "Deformity from Prominent Ears Cured by a New Method of Operating" (1889) de-scribed a new operation.

No. 109 "Removal of the Hand-Centre from the Cortex Cerebri in a Case of Focal Epilepsy" (1890).

No. 115 "The Surgery of the Lateral Ventricles of the Brain" [résumé only] (1890) was an elaborate paper (the 38th on cerebral surgery) that cost me a year of incessant labor and was lost, by unpardonable carelessness, so that only the abstract, which I had read at the Tenth International Medical Congress, was published in the *Transactions* of the Congress.

No. 124 "A New Operation for Spasmodic Wry Neck. Namely, Division or Exsection of the Nerves Supplying the Posterior Rotator Muscles of the Head" (1890).

No. 130 "A New Method of Tenotomy, by which the Tendons are Lengthened to a Definite Extent, Instead of the Present Haphazard Method" (1891).

No. 135 "Nephrotomy for Calculous Pyelitis. Nephrectomy Rightly Decided Against Because of the Small Percentage of Urea; an Apparently Almost Destroyed and Useless Kidney Found to Secrete over Four and a Half Times as Much Urine as the Other Kidney; Death" (1892). This showed what an apparently useless kidney was capable of doing.

No. 137 "Amputation at the Hip Joint by Wyeth's Method" (1892) described what is, so far as I know, the only case of amputation at the hip-joint for a large sarcoma, in a woman five months pregnant. She recovered, had her baby, and resumed her missionary work in Brazil, and though she lived on for some years, she eventually died from a recurrence.

No. 138 "On Resection of the Liver, Especially for Hepatic Tumors, with the Report of a Successful Case of Resection for an Adenoma of the Bile-Ducts, and a Table of Twenty Recorded Cases of Hepatic Operations" (1892) was the first case in America, I think, of the removal of a tumor from the liver. Further examples were cited in **No. 147** "A Report of the Later History of a Case of Resection of the Liver, and of the Later Discovery of its Coccidial Origin" (1893); **No. 201** "Removal of an Angioma of the Liver by Elastic Constriction External to the Abdominal Cavity, with a Table of Fifty-nine Cases of Operation for Hepatic Tumors" (1897); and **No. 222a** "Report of a Case of Resection of the Liver for the Removal of a Neoplasm, with a Table of Seventy-six Cases of Resection of the Liver for Hepatic Tumors" (1899).

No. 139 "Arterio-Venous Aneurysm of the Common Carotid Artery and Internal Jugular Veins; Double Ligature of Both Vessels; Recovery" (1892) was the most difficult operation I ever performed in the neck. A similar but less difficult case was **No. 160** "Ligation of the Common and External Carotid Arteries and the Jugular Vein, for Arterio-Venous Aneurysm of the Internal Carotid and Jugular, with Division of the Optic Nerve on the Opposite Side, the Result of a Gunshot Wound" (1894).

No. 143 ". . . Fecal Fistula Caused by Appendicitis" (1892) described a most extensive operation.

No. 145 "Ectopic Testicle with a Very Short Pedicle in the Inguinal Canal Combined with Inguinal Hernia, Twisting of the Pedicle with Haematoma of the Epididymis and Beginning Gangrene Discovered by Operation; Pyogenic Cocci Found; Recovery" (1892) was one of the earliest papers describing gangrene of the testicle, which resulted from the torsion of the spermatic cord.

No. 151 "An Ovarian Tumor Weighing 111 Pounds Removed from a Child of 15, Whose Weight was 68 Pounds" (1893).

No. 157 "Case of Suprapubic Cystotomy in which the Bladder was Distended with Air Instead of Water, and Four Hundred Ninety-five Calculi Removed" (1894).

No. 165 "Operation Wounds of the Thoracic Duct in the Neck; with a Résumé of the Two Prior Recorded Cases and Two Additional Cases" (1894).

No. 166 "Amputation of the Entire Upper Extremity (including the Clavicle and Scapula), and of the Arm at the Shoulder Joint. With Especial Reference to Methods of Controlling Hemorrhage. With a Report of One Case of the Former Amputation and Four of the Latter" (1894) was an elaborate paper dealing with the control of hemorrhage in the arm, clavicle, and scapula.

No. 170 "Extensive Thoracoplasty by Schede's Method" (1895) was a case of the amputation of the shoulder girdle. In it I reported also a case of extensive thoracoplasty by a new method, which I later discovered had already been done by Schede. I naturally gave him credit in my published paper. **No. 210** "Schede's Operation for an Old Empyema; Cathcart's Drainage; Recovery" (1898) describes a similar case.

No. 174 "Nerve Suture with the Report of Six Cases of Wrist-Drop; a Successful Operation for Suture of the Musculo-Spiral Nerve Three Months After its Complete Division" (1895) was followed by **No. 207** "Two Cases of Wrist-Drop from Injury of the Musculo-Spiral Nerve from Fracture of the Humerus" (with Dr. W. G. Spiller) (1898); **No. 245** "Six Cases of Secondary Operation for Wrist-Drop from Injury to the Musculo-Spiral Nerve by Fracture of the Humerus: Very Little Improvement in Four Cases, Complete Restoration of Function in Two" (1900); **No. 255** "Two Successful Cases of Secondary Suture, One of the Posterior Interosseous Nerve and One of the Median and Ulnar Nerves" (1901); and **No. 259** "Successful Intraneural Infiltration of the Median and Ulnar Nerves During an Operation for Dupuytren's Contraction of the Fingers" (1903).

No. 187 "The Treatment of Traumatic Lesions of the Kidney, with Tables of 155 Cases" (1896) was an elaborate paper on renal traumatisms.

No. 193 "Resection of the Sternum for Tumors, with a Report of Two Cases and a Table of Seventeen Previously Reported Cases" (1897).

No. 197 "Treatment of Cancer of the Rectum, with a Report of Twenty-five Cases" (1897).

No. 203 described one of the earliest cases of primary tuberculosis of the breast (1897).

No. 213 "The Cartwright Lectures on the Surgery of the Stomach. 'Gastrolysis, Gastrotomy, and Gastrostomy'" [Lecture I] (1898).

No. 216 "A Case of Appendicitis in which the Appendix Became Permanently Soldered to the Bladder like a Third Ureter, Producing a Urinary Fecal Fistula" (1898) was an extraordinary case.

No. 219 "The Technique of Total Laryngectomy" (1899) described an improved method of laryngectomy. **No. 220** "Two Unusual Cases of Surgery of the Trachea"

(1899) was written with Dr. W. S. Jones.

No. 237 "A Case of Multiple Neuro-Fibromata of the Ulnar Nerve" (1900) was written with Dr. William G. Spiller.

No. 239 "Nephrectomy for a Large Aneurysm of the Right Renal Artery, with a Résumé of the Twelve Formerly Reported Cases of Renal Aneurysm" (1900). This was by far the largest renal aneurism ever operated on.

No. 246 "A Case of Ligature of the Abdominal Aorta Just Below the Diaphragm, the Patient Surviving for Forty-eight Days: With a Proposed Instrument for the Treatment of Aneurysms of the Abdominal Aorta by Temporary Compression" (1900). This was the longest survival period on record. It was the twelfth such operation performed. I proposed and figured an instrument for the temporary compression of the aorta.

No. 248 "The Progress of Surgery in the 19th Century" (1901). This was one of a series of similar "Century" papers printed in the New York *Sun*, in the first months of the 20th century (i.e., in 1901) and later republished by Harper and Brother under the title *The Progress of the Century.*

No. 262 "The Duties and Responsibilities of Trustees of Public Medical Institutions" (1903). This has been reprinted by Dr. J. McKeen Cattell, in a volume entitled *Medical Research and Eduction* (1913).

No. 273 "A Case of Interilio-Abdominal Amputation for Sarcoma of the Ilium, and a Synopsis of Previously Recorded Cases" (1904). Written with Dr. J. Chalmers DaCosta, this described a new method of interilio abdominal amputation of the leg and one half of the pelvic girdle, a technique which Kocher embodied in the later editions of his *Operative Surgery.*

No. 275 was a paper on the massage of the heart, following a chloroform collapse, with notes of twenty-five similar cases.

No. 276 "Enormous Mixed Tumor of the Parotid Region; Reaching to the Clavicle and Weighing about Seven Pounds; Operation; Recovery" (1904).

No. 279 "The Danger of Allowing Warts and Moles to Remain Lest They Become Malignant; with Twenty-five Illustrative Cases" (1904); This paper drew the attention of the profession to a little-considered yet serious danger and evoked great interest. This was one of the most useful papers I ever wrote, though Osler's comment to me was, "From brain tumors to warts and moles: the first evidence of senility." A subsequent paper was No. 326 "Do Warts and Moles Result in Cancer?" (1914).

No. 297 "The Service of Missions to Science and Society. Presidential Address Delivered before the American Baptist Missionary Union, Dayton, Ohio, May 21,

1906," with references to original authorities, described what missionaries have done.

No. 299 "Tumors of the Carotid Gland" (1906), written with Dr. John Funke, was an exhaustive study of the subject.

No. 301 "Sacrococcygeal Tumor (Teratoma) With an Opening Entirely Through the Sacrum, and a Sinus Passing Through this Opening and Communicating with the Rectum, the Sinus Resembling a Bronchus" (1906), written with Dr. W.M.L. Coplin, described the only case on record, so far as I know, of such an anomaly. The patient (Helen White, my great-great-niece) is now a finely developed girl. The tumor was removed and the sinus successfully closed.

No. 303 "The Symptomatology, Diagnosis, and Surgical Treatment of Cervical Ribs" (1907), with histories of all the recorded cases I could find, was the most important paper on this subject up to that time. All the later papers I have seen have recorded only later individual cases.

No. 305 "Severe Burn on Top of Head at Seven Months of Age, Followed by Necrosis of Entire Osseous Cap of Cranium. At Fourteen Years of Age Detachment of the Entire Calvarium by Circular Craniatomy for Epilepsy and Defective Mental Development" (1907) recorded an extraordinary and I think unique case.

No. 333 "The Dangers of Ether as an Anesthetic" (1915), the last paper in this present list, was the Ether Day address, October 16th, 1915, at the Massachusetts General Hospital.

FOR THE RECORD

[Keen occasionally wrote comments, on letters and papers (whether incoming or on carbon copies of outgoing). These remarks were addressed to no one daughter in particular, nor even to any daughter at all. They sometimes give the effect of having the last word in matters disputatious, but it is likely that he simply wanted to reveal for posterity his opinions, thoughts, and feelings: The record would otherwise seem incomplete. In any number of instances, he recorded his participation in, or the outcome of, surgery, in each case confident that he had done the best that any surgeon could have done. He also indulged in the seemingly obsessive-compulsive editorial behavior of making additions or corrections in grammar, spelling, or syntax, even though this editing was not intended for the eyes of another. His comments, in this section, are set in boldface italics.]

Princeton biologist E.G. Conklin, wrapping up a letter (1924) concerning evolution and religion, said, "I rejoice in all the honors that have been heaped upon you." Keen added in the margin: *23!*

Bowman C. Crowell, associate director of the American College of Surgeons, expressed delight (1927) in the receipt of Keen's portrait photograph. Keen's comment was, *He asked for it.*

Next to the signature (1912) of South African Kendal Franks, Keen has penned his opinion, *An Admirable Surgeon.*

When William Anderson established priority in a surgical procedure that Keen believed he himself had pioneered, Keen added a footnote (*Of course he antedated me*), authoritatively signed, *W.W.K.*

N.P. Hill, writing from Denver (1880), thanked Keen rather profusely for his suggestion that a "liberal gift" to Brown would be welcomed. Keen's footnote (35 years later): *Never a stiver!*

Referring, in 1922, to a "reprint telling of my experiences at the second Battle of Bull Run," Keen parenthetically penned, *I was also at the first.*

To the typed "Synopsis of Portion of Military Record of Dr. W.W. Keen," and, continuing the third-person synopsis, Keen wrote:

> *In November 1923, the President of France conferred upon him the Decoration of the Legion of Honor with the rank of Officer.*
> *On November 24 [1920], the University of Paris conferred upon him the Degree of 'Doctor, honoris causa.'*

Keen also left a separate handwritten memo explaining the honor: *"This is the continental equivalent to an Oxford D.Ch. or Cambridge LL.D. Only 5 Americans [Woodrow Wilson, Nicholas Murray Butler, A. Lawrence Lowell, Albert Abraham Michelson, and Elihu Root] have been awarded this honor prior to 1920.*

Notified of his election to honorary membership in the Pennsylvania Academy of Science, who requested a brief biography for their *Proceedings*, Keen recorded that he *referred them to* **Who's Who.**

1923 Univ. of Paris honorary doctorates, November 24, 1923. *Left to Right:* Prof.
Salverda de Grave, Univ. of Amsterdam (Letters); Prof. Radais, Doyen de la Faculté
de Pharmacie; Prof. Keen, Philadelphia, U.S.A. (Medicine); Prof. Roger, Doyen de la
Faculté de Médecine; Prof. Golgi, Pavia, Italy (Medicine); Recteur Appell de l'Univ.
de Paris; Prof. Thomson, Cambridge Univ.(Science); Prof. Wilmotte, Univ. of Liege
(Letters); Prof. Brunot, Doyen de la Faculté des Lettres; Prof. Molliard, Doyen de
la Faculté des Sciences; Prof. Berthelemy, Doyen de la Faculté de Droit. *Not shown:*
Prof. Arrhenius, Univ. of Stockholm (Science); Prof. Scialoja, Univ. of Rome (Law);
Prof. Torres Y Quevedo, Univ. of Madrid (Law)

On the printed invitation to the sixteenth annual Phi Beta Kappa dinner at the
University of Pennsylvania, Keen scratched the query *Where's my hat?* (He was
79.)

An ad for Brotherhood Wines ("Recognized Standard for Use in Sickness"), underscored with the slogan, "The Wine Says the Rest," was juxtaposed with a publisher's
ad for a "photo-etching from life" that featured a portrait of Keen (along with an
offer of an artist's proof signed by Dr. Keen for $10.00). Teetotaler Keen made the
ironic comment, *Evidently the portrait of a well-known wine imbiber.*

Advised that "Mrs. Greene's Irish pamphlets" were on sale, Keen wrote *Never.
W.W.K.*

Cyrus Curtis said there is no "legitimate reason why his *Public Ledger* should not accept paid advertisements for Hearst magazines. Keen (who feuded with Hearst) commented: *I differ.*

A Quaker child's plea for Keen's autograph, to be used for raising money to help Hoover's mission in Europe, evoked this note: *I sent him a <u>letter of course.</u>*

A letter from the husband of a patient assures Keen of his confidence that everything that possibly could have been done for his wife had been done, to which Keen appended, *Brain tumor: I declined to operate as it was inaccessible, in my opinion, alas!*

On a broadside appealing for aid to malnourished Belgian children, Keen noted, simply, *My committee.*

In its December 31, 1917, edition, The Philadelphia *Public Ledger* published a front-page article captioned YARD BY YARD FORECAST OF LAUNCHINGS IN U.S.: ONLY 2,000,000 TONS OF SHIPS CERTAIN IN 1918, evoking a Keen letter to the editor protesting against this information's "giving comfort to the enemy by disclosing authoritatively our weakness." Editor John Spurgeon replied that it seemed "vital to the interests of this country and its Allies that we should not go along for a year under false pretenses. Keen noted in response that *the Ledger had done just right, in view of the facts disclosed.*

According to a story (published in the newspaper) by painter Robert Henry, an artist was escorting Keen through a picture exhibition, when the physician stopped in front of the portrait of a middle-aged man.
   "Do you know this man?"
   "Yes."
   "Is he dead?"
   "Yes, he has been dead for some months."
   "Well I would wager that he died from heart disease."
The artist, struck by a skill that could make a diagnosis from a picture, inquired into the death of the portrait's original and found that the man had indeed died of heart disease the winter before. Keen's comment in the margin: *Absolute fabrication, W.W. Keen.*

The Philadelphia *Press* of March 9, 1912, had a news item captioned JEFFERSON MEN OF '62 CELEBRATE ANNIVERSARY, which included the statement that "Fifty prominent physcians and surgeons, including Dr. W.W. Keen and Dr. S. Weir Mitchell, were present." Keen added the notation, *Such is fame! The dinner was in my honor [and] given by the Jefferson faculty in 1912.*

A statement in the *Ledger,* concerning grassroots support for a Hoover candidacy, declared that the movement at the University of Pennsylvania was given a big boost by a committee formed by Dr. W.W. Keen and several members of the University faculty. This prompted Keen's appended note: *This is erroneous. The movement had no relation to the University of Pennsylvania except that two of the faculty were among those who met at my house.*

Following the signature of a Dr. Jacobson, Keen has added *[Worth all his seniors put together].*

Mrs. Charles Garttner, of Easton, Pennsylvania, submitted an essay in a contest responding to the question on how to run U.S. foreign affairs, an essay which consisted entirely of: "Protect our own while dealing with others, treating them just as we expect to be treated." Keen's astonished reaction: *For the $2,000 prize of the Henry Phillips Legacy!*

In 1921, Dr. Adolphus Knopf proposed writing and publishing a biography of Keen in *American Medicine* and requested an autographed photograph "with a personal dedication" to adorn his reception room. The compliment and implied flattery had little effect: Keen said, *I replied requesting him urgently* **not** *to prepare or publish his proferred biography. I have not sent any photo or other material.*
When Knopf persisted, less than a week later, so did Keen: *I vetoed anything at all and did not send my photo.*

Keen's daughter Dora found the following notice in her Los Angeles hotel room:

> WHILE A GREAT MAJORITY OF GUESTS ASSIST THE ASSOCIATION OF HOTEL AND RESTAURANT OPERATORS IN CONVINCING THE AUTHORITIES OF THEIR CO-OPERATION TOWARD LAW ENFORCEMENT, THERE ARE YET A FEW WHO CAUSE SERIOUS EMBARRASSMENT BY OPENLY DISPLAYING LIQUOR ON TABLES AND IN ROOMS AND BY LEAVING EMPTY BOTTLES. WE TRUST WE MAY HAVE THE COMPLETE FRIENDLY CO-OPERATION

OF ALL GUESTS IN THE FUTURE, IN OUR ENDEAVOR TO COMPLY WITH THE LAWS.

IIis comment: *It seems an admirable example for other hotels to imitate. W.W. Keen*

The most expensive "stages" dinner I have ever been at, was Keen's account of the Annual Dinner of the Pennsylvania Bankers, January 8, 1925.

At the end of a letter Keen received, he inserted **Wm. Roscoe Thayer**, adding *He forgot to sign.*

Agnes Repplier's letter of April 27, 1909, says, "Mr. [Samuel] Clemens's letter came this morning. It is disappointing and it is unexpectedly intimate. I enclose it, but I think I may ask you to send it back to me, or tear it up. (Keen: *I returned it, of course.*) I did not ask Mr. Clemens to speak to the Club. I told him that you, as its president, wished to ask him to do so."

Keen received a telegram, in 1926, from *The Missoulian*, Missoula, Montana, requesting permission to reprint his *Woman's Home Companion* article on the conquest of scarlet fever. Keen assented, but added, **Please send me half a dozen copies.**

On April 5, 1922, Keen received from Cardinal Dougherty, of Philadelphia, a packet of religious souvenirs, on which he has inscribed, **To go with the duplicate of the nail used in the Crucifixion.**

Having read Keen's *I Believe in God and in Evolution*, the Men's League of a Congregational church asked how science accounts for the regaining of muscular brain cells, when gray matter is excised. Keen's holograph reply on the incoming letter says, **Nobody** knows. **We surmise that the neighboring cells may take up the work of those removed. W.W.K.**

I wrote a protest to the Ledger in regard to the non-enforcement of this law (regulating street processions to allow for periodic crossing at intersections). This note was added to the 1926 letter from the Bureau of Municipal Research which cited the appropriate ordinance [of 1873].

Keen's contemporary and good friend, Dr. Robert Fulton Weir, reflected thus on his early career (including in the War): "When I look back on my career, I am horrified at my misdoings & ignorances, but 'I meant well!'" Keen underscored the inner quote, perhaps recalling when he was getting his own on-the-job train-ing.

Yale economist Irving Fisher, chairman of the Hygiene Reference Board of the Life Extension Institute, tried to convince Keen of the fiscal and physical efficacy of preventive medicine. As with today's H.M.O., there was opposition from the A.M.A., and at the head of the rear guard was Keen. At the bottom of Fisher's final letter of appeal, May 27, 1922, is Keen's final dismissal: *May 29—Declined further discussion lest it should breed possible discord.*

6

—••⟨⟩⟨⟩••—

Family Matters

MY ENGAGEMENT AND MARRIAGE[1]

MY RESIDENT GRADUATE YEAR at Brown was the most fortunate of my life, for it was then that I met my dear wife.

Eudora Borden, her sister, I had known for a year or more, as she was at Mrs. Buel's School, in Providence. In the winter of 1859–60, her sister, Emma Corinna (or, as she was almost always called, "Tinnie") attended the same school. One afternoon, I went out to skate on Carpenter's Pond and was introduced to her. She was just 17½ and, as a result of a recent illness, had short hair.[2] Immediately upon being introduced to her, I asked her to skate with me, and off we went in high glee.

I had known many girls in Philadelphia and Providence, and I had had two short-lived and (fortunately) evanescent "love affairs." But this was a wholly different feeling. I fell deeply in love with Tinnie Borden, literally at first sight, deeply and truly in love, reverent love. But severe long, long years were to pass before my dreams were to be realized.

I began to pay her marked attention, but never was there a sign on her part of even the slightest character of anything beyond mere acquaintance.

At the same time, Kirke Porter, a senior at Brown and my dear friend, began to pay assiduous court to her. It was an entirely friendly, in fact a hardly recognized, rivalry between us. One day, Sarah Greene,[3] one of my most intimate girl friends in Providence, had quite a long and serious conversation with me about it. She thought that Kirke was better fitted to make Tinnie a happy life companion than I; and, moreover, she thought that Tinnie was in love with him and not with me.

My decision was made on the spot. Her happiness was by far the first consideration with me, and if Sarah was right (I dared not ask Tinnie herself), I ought to give up all hope of ever making her my dear wife. No break ever occurred

Emma ("Tinnie") Corinna and Eudora Sexton Borden of Fall River, Massachusetts, 1863

between either her or Kirke and me. In fact, I never exchanged a word with Kirke about this, but gradually ceased my attentions and left the field to him.

I left Providence, with an aching void in my heart, in June of 1860; began the study of medicine, in September; served in the Army; and went abroad *with Kirke,* in 1864, and did not return till May of 1866. Kirke and I still had never spoken a word on the subject of Tinnie. In the meantime, I saw her very rarely, practically only at Commencement. Infrequently, at long intervals, we corresponded, purely as friends.

But my love, instead of diminishing, grew stronger and stronger. I *longed* to make that dear girl my wife. But then I still thought that those two were fated and fitted to each other, and by no word or deed would I be untrue to my friend or to her.

By the winter of 1866–67 (I was then about 30), as they had never announced their engagement, I could not but surmise that it might never be consummated. What the obstacle was, I could not imagine. Finally, I resolved to find out from Kirke himself whether I might after all press my own suit, if his was hopeless.

And so, I paid him a visit in Pittsburgh. In the evening, we had a long, frank, and friendly talk, and he freely assented to my going to Fall River to see Tinnie herself and talk it all over with her. Together we knelt down and asked God's guidance for all three of us. Never were more sincere prayers made than we two made, that long wintry night.

Circumstances were such that I could not absent myself from my teaching until March of 1867. I made the excuse to my family that I had to go to New York to find and purchase some models, to aid in my teaching of anatomy and surgery in my Philadelphia School of Anatomy, and that I might be absent for several days. I *did* spend the day in New York buying my models; but then I hurried to the Fall River boat and landed in Fall River on the morning of the 4th of March. I had already written Tinnie of my visit, to assure myself that she would be at home.

That afternoon, in the little sewing room (where she was mending my glove), with a trembling heart and many misgivings of rejection, I told her of my visit with Kirke, of my deep love for her, which I had hidden even from her for those seven long years, and I asked her to be my wife.

To my utter amazement, she at once confessed to me that she too had concealed her love for me, all those dreary years, and had wondered if I ever would come. To say that I was wild with delight, and that I could hardly believe that I was to be so fortunate, is to put it mildly. My joy was so overwhelming that I could

Emma Corinna Borden Keen of Philadelphia, 1877

scarcely sleep. I walked in among the stars for the two happy, blissful days that I spent with her. Every moment I thanked God for His goodness—and her, for her dear love.

Before I broached the matter with Tinnie herself, I had seized a favorable moment after mid-day dinner, when Father Borden and I were alone, to ask his permission to propose to his daughter. He gave permission, but later, after Mother Borden (to whom Tinnie at once confided her joy) had told him of her acceptance, he told me that as I was a stranger—though he had seen me several times—he would have to consult a friend of his in Philadelphia, before he could assent to our marriage. The mails were suddenly slow beyond endurance, it seemed to me, but in a few days I received his and Mother Borden's full consent, which completed our joy. It turned out that the Philadelphia friend he consulted was David S. Brown, a lifelong friend of my father's! Mother Borden dubbed me "a burglar with good credentials."[4]

As soon as I received this consent, we announced our engagement. I told my own family first, of course. In a short time, dear Tinnie made a visit to my father and mother. When I introduced her, O so proudly, my father said, "So this is the model you went to get, is it?" She won all hearts at once (how could it be otherwise?) and was always a dear daughter, a solace, and a comfort to my dear parents in their declining years. (My mother died in 1877, at age 73; and my father in 1882, at age 85.)

Our wedding took place at noon on Wednesday, December 11th, 1867, in Father Borden's house. Amid many congratulations (Professor and Mrs. Lincoln even came from Providence), I always remember with especial pleasure the admonition of one of the guests, a dear old man whose name I immediately lost in the congratulating crowd: "Dr. Keen, take good care of this little girl. She's the flower of Fall River." He merely gave vocal expression to what everybody knew and felt.

We left at 4 P.M. for Boston, in a beginning snowstorm, which was so severe as to tie up boats and railroads, so that my father and mother (and quite a number of other out-of-town guests) were held prisoner in Fall River for several days. My dear mother was so feeble that she was scarcely able to travel, but go she would—and did. It was her last journey. Fortunately, there being no good hotels in Fall River, all the imprisoned guests were lodged in the homes of various members of the family.

In Boston, the next morning, the snow was three feet deep, and of course traffic was suspended. We did not venture out of the hotel until Saturday, when I took her for a fine sleigh ride.

On the following Monday morning, I went downstairs to look over the papers till dear Tinnie should be ready for breakfast. I finished the first page and turned over to the last, where in large letters I saw the headline GREAT FIRE IN FALL RIVER: AMERICAN PRINT-WORKS DESTROYED. I bounded up to our room, where I found Tinnie quite puzzled over a telegram just received, assuring her of everybody's safety. I showed her the paper, which explained the puzzle. As Father Borden was treasurer and manager of the Print-Works, and a large part of his fortune was in this corporation, we took a hasty breakfast and went at once to Fall River. This was the extent of our wedding journey—a sad end of a joyous beginning. Though Father Borden was over 66, the debris was being removed from the ruins by the time we reached Fall River. Unfortunately, there was no insurance. The storm had delayed placing it.

Before we were engaged, I had been in Father Borden's house in Fall River and knew that he was in comfortable circumstances, but I had not the least idea that he was a wealthy man until after my engagement, when his business friends in Philadelphia congratulated my father and described my father-in-law as rich. He was, in fact worth some two millions, the present equivalent, I suppose, of five or six millions. How glad I was to be ignorant of his wealth when it was so greatly diminished. I told dear Tinnie repeatedly, after I had learned of his wealth, that I married her for what she was, and not for what she might reasonably expect; and that the wealth that had never been ours, now that it was gone, made not the slightest difference, except to cause me to cherish her more dearly than ever. At the same time, I confess to a little feeling of pride that all I have, except for a modest inheritance from my father, has been the result of my own labor.

After two or three days in Fall River, we came to Philadelphia and settled in at 107 South 13th Street, where I had been since 1866. I had two parlors, one for a drawing room and waiting room (for the, alas, very infrequent patients) and the other for my private consulting room, plus a dining room. On the third floor was our bedroom.

Shortly before daughter Corinne was born, on November 4th, 1868, we moved to 1619 Chestnut Street, where we occupied the whole house. . . . It was a serious venture, for the rental was $1,500 a year, and my income for 1867 was very meager—and not much better in 1868. However, my father urged that I should shoulder the burden, especially in view of the eventual prospects of dear Tinnie's inheritance; and in the meantime, he promised to help me out. My income from teaching supplemented that from practice, and Father made up the balance. We had to practice economy, especially as the babies came along. When I sent out my bills, January 1st and July 1st, I had to use the money, for a number of years, to pay the incoming bills of the preceding six months. It was a heavy load, on not only my own shoulders but on dear Tinnie's too.

When Dora was just over six months old, we moved into 1729 Chestnut Street and have lived here ever since. Father Borden had this house built and gave it to dear Tinnie. The ground cost $13,350, I think, and the house cost about $25,000. There was a mortgage of $17,500 (*which was continued until the house was sold, in* 1922).[5]

In spite of her cares with three young children, dear Tinnie was a most active member of our own Church and in a number of other charitable and philanthropic organizations. The little volume *In Memoriam* tells the story in detail.

I shall never forget the feeling of gratitude and exultation I had when, some years later, I joyfully told dear Tinnie that I was at last square with the world and that the payment for my outgoing bills now would at last be available for the *coming* six months. Once out of debt, I never allowed myself to fall back in. But O how often, how often have I longed that she might have lived till I could have showered on her some of the luxuries of life! What a brave, self-sacrificing life she led! What a genuine helpmeet she always was! How she would have enjoyed my later success, not only financially, but far more, my professional success and the many honors that have come to me! How often have I longed to have had the privilege of laying them all at *her* feet!

In 1886, Tinnie and the girls were spending the summer at Osterville,[6] on Cape Cod, when my darling fell ill with a severe dysentery. I was still at work in Philadelphia, but I flew to her aid as soon as I learned of it. There was no good doctor there, so for a day or two I had to care for her myself. Then I became so anxious that I telegraphed Osler in Philadelphia. He came at once, but the next day she suddenly collapsed and died, after three or four hours. I have no doubt that it was from a perforation of the bowel. I had no instruments, dressings, antiseptics, nothing with which to save her. Even if I had been able to operate, it surely would have been futile. She was marked for her Heavenly Home.

It is now just twenty-six years since that dreadful day, but it is as vivid as if it had occurred only yesterday. Her virtues as a wife, a mother, and a Christian can never be adequately told. I speak of her but rarely, even to my children. Her name, especially her pet name, and her memory are to me too sacred to be uttered in ordinary conversation. They are treasured deep in my heart of hearts. How often, even now, after so many years, do my eyes fill with tears and my heart sink within me, when I think (and there are not many days when I do not think) of her, of her lovely character, and of my sorrow.

After having had the high privilege of being *her* husband, I could not possibly think of marrying anyone else. She is *the one woman in all the world that I have loved, deeply, reverently, and forever.* She was, is, and ever will be my idol.

My joy is that before very long we shall be reunited in that blessed home where, thank God, we shall never again be separated.

1619 CHESTNUT STREET

When I had to move from 107 South 13th Street to larger quarters, in 1868, I finally decided on 1619 Chestnut. My father had wished me to settle near him in West Philadelphia, where almost all of my friends lived. I pointed out to him that the circumference is always ready to seek the center, but that the center rarely goes to the circumference, for medical advice. I said to him that, frankly, immediate pecuniary success would undoubtedly be much more certain in West Philadelphia, but in the long run, when success did come, the rewards, in both income and moral and professional prestige, would be far greater, though delayed, in the center of the city.

When I took him to look at the house, he walked from 16th to 17th Street, counting the doctors' signs. "Why, son," he said, "there are already twelve doctors in this block!" I replied, "The very fact that twelve doctors have settled in this block shows, I think, that it must be a pretty good place for doctors or there wouldn't be so many here." This quite convinced him.

The rent was $1,500 a year, a fairly heavy burden for a doctor who could readily but approximately count his entire clientele on his fingers and toes. But my dear father, typical of his good sense and his generous affection, promised to stand behind me.

Corinne, Florence, and Dora were all born in that house. On December 31, 1871, when Dora was six months old, we moved into 1729 Chestnut Street, where we lived for just over fifty years.

In May of 1922, years after Corinne, Dora, and Margaret had set up their own homes, Florence and I moved into an apartment on the eighth floor of the Touraine, at 1520 Spruce.

1729 CHESTNUT STREET

Mottoes on the Children's Walls

Front Room

ORDER IS HEAVEN'S FIRST LAW

MORGEN STUND HAT GOLD IM MUND

A PENNY SAVED IS A PENNY EARNED

WHATSOEVER A MAN SOWETH THAT SHALL HE ALSO REAP

SOW ACTIONS, REAP HABITS

SOW HABITS, REAP CHARACTER

SOW CHARACTER, REAP DESTINY

A STITCH IN TIME SAVES NINE

LABOR VINCIT OMNIA

SOME BOOKS ARE TO BE TASTED; OTHERS TO BE SWALLOWED,

AND SOME FEW TO BE CHEWED AND DIGESTED

COUNT THAT DAY LOST WHOSE SLOW DESCENDING SUN VIEWS

FROM THY HAND NO NOBLE ACTION DONE

CE N'EST QUE LE PREMIER PAS QUI COUTE

FINE MANNERS ARE THE MANTLE OF FINE MINDS

SI DEUS NOBISCUM QUIS CONTRA NOS

GIVE EVERY MAN THINE EAR, BUT FEW THY VOICE

NIL DESPERANDUM

Back Room

A MERRY HEART MAKETH A CHEERFUL COUNTENANCE

NICHTS WIRD OHNE MÜHE ERLANGT

HE IS GENTIL THAT DOETH GENTIL DEDIS

NO CHANGE OF CIRCUMSTANCES CAN REPAIR A DEFECT OF CHARACTER

AIDE TOI ET LE CIEL T'AIDERA

A BEAUTIFUL BEHAVIOR IS BETTER THAN A BEAUTIFUL FORM

IT IS THE FINEST OF THE FINE ARTS

THAT LIFE IS LONG WHICH ANSWERS LIFE'S GREAT END

NULLA DIES SINE LINEA

WHAT CANNOT BE, LOVE COUNTS IT DONE

THEY ARE NEVER ALONE THAT ARE ACCOMPANIED WITH NOBLE THOUGHTS

PAS À PAS ON VA BIEN LOIN

COURTESY BEGETS COURTESY

NOTHING'S SO HARD BUT SEARCH WILL FIND IT OUT

TO ERR IS HUMAN, TO FORGIVE DIVINE

FIRE INSURANCE

The first fire insurance company established in Philadelphia (by Benjamin Franklin, in 1752) was the Philadelphia Contributorship for the Insurance of Houses from Loss by Fire. Every building insured by this company had an escutcheon mounted on the front, just below the roof. This consisted of four hands clasped as if to carry someone "Lady-of-London-style," as we boys used to call it. The company is now usually spoken of as "The Contributorship," but Old Philadelphians more often call it the "Hand in Hand," because of the escutcheon. The company insures only real estate, and not personal property, and then only in Philadelphia and its suburbs. It will insure only a certain amount on any one building (unless the fire hazard is too great), the rate varying with the risk, whether from the nature of the use of the building or from the danger of fire from the character of the environment. No more than a certain amount will be covered in one block. Most of its policies are perpetual; that is, not for a limited term. But either the company or the insured can, by agreement, terminate the policy or change the rate at any time.

On 1729 Chestnut Street, for example, I originally had $10,000 worth of insurance. I deposited two percent (two hundred dollars) with the company, so that at five per cent, therefore, I lose ten dollars per year, which is the cost of my insurance. Whenever the policy is terminated, the remainder of the two hundred dollars is returned.

By its conservative management (annual losses are very small—sometimes none at all), the company gradually has accumulated a large surplus, far beyond any reasonable loss. As a result, some fifteen or twenty years ago, an insurgent younger element among the policy-holders started a rival ticket for directors, in opposition to the official ticket. Old Philadelphia was stirred to its depths[7] and a long line of policy-holders (men and women alike) gathered for the contest. The old fellows won, but they could take a hint as well as Queen Elizabeth,[8] so that from then until now, a dividend of ten per cent on the deposit has been declared each year. I lose five per cent on my deposit, but I gain ten per cent in dividends, with the net result that I get $10,000 of insurance for nothing, while they pay me twenty dollars a year for the privilege of insuring my house.

They solicit business mildly, since their income from the invested surplus more than covers all expenses and dividends, leaving more or less to be added to the ever-increasing surplus. New insurance participates in the dividends only after ten years has elapsed. About twelve years ago, I increased my insurance from ten to fifteen thousand, depositing another one hundred dollars, so that for about two years, I have lost fifteen dollars a year in interest on my three-hundred-dollar total deposit and received thirty dollars a year as a dividend.

The "Hand-in-Hand," in the early days, would not insure houses with *trees* in front, since these hindered the firemen. After a time, a new fire insurance company was started which *would* insure such houses. Their escutcheon was the "Green Tree," but their legal name is the Mutual Assurance Company. This is a duplicate of the "Hand-in-Hand" in its methods, and a few years ago, it too adopted the plan of the annual dividend on the deposit. Both companies are purely mutual, with no traded stock.

THE DECLINE OF KEEN'S PARENTS

In the early '50s, Mother, although only about fifty years old, began to fall, at intervals of months, and later, of weeks. At first, we thought it was due to awkwardness and used to tease her about it in good humor. In my second year at college, she fell and broke her arm. After a while, we recognized the fact that her falls were due to a muscular weakness in her legs. She finally became chair-fast. Father had an elevator built from the northwest chamber to the parlor, and on to the basement dining room, but then she eventually became bed-fast. Gradually her arms, and especially her hands, became involved, so that she could not hold a teacup securely. She later had to use a glass tube, and finally had to be fed completely.

With the physical failure, dear Mother's mental powers were slowly failing as well, and for some years before her death, Miss Savage, our faithful Irish housekeeper, had complete charge of the house. For perhaps twenty years before her death, in 1877 (at seventy-three), she suffered over a hundred strange attacks of partial and temporary paralysis. While sitting at table, or in her chair, she suddenly would sink down in the chair, lolling over to one side, staring vacantly, and babbling incoherent sounds. She sometimes would recover herself in a few minutes, but occasionally, her attacks lasted for hours, even up to twenty-four hours, two or three times. Each attack was followed by a little loss, physical and mental. For the last year or two, she recognized only my father, and for the last six months, she recognized no one at all. Hers was a mere vegetative existence.

I saw her brain, at the post-mortem examination conducted by Dr. Sinkler. On a horizontal section, every little artery protruded slightly above the surface of the brain, which felt like a wire brush. This explained her attacks. The slowly spreading hardening of her arteries had cut off the blood supply of one small area after another, and each blockage of the blood supply caused one of her attacks.

They had been married fifty-one years. It was like an oak riven in twain. Father was a loving, considerate caretaker of Mother for years, as she gradually failed. He watched over her as a mother watches over her baby. When she was gone, his occupation was gone, but he lived on for over five years after her death. He too failed physically, slowly but surely, so that the elevator unexpectedly became necessary for his use as well. His sight was lost, first in one eye and then in both, so that he was almost totally blind for three or four years before his death.

I had never expected to see the day when I would thank God that my mother and father (and, I might add, both of my older brothers) had passed away, but it was true. My father died on August 4th, 1882, just thirty days short of his eighty-fifth birthday. My dear wife and the three older children all came down from the Adirondacks just before his death. The immediate cause was dysentery, but the precipitating factor was his age. Each of my brothers died at about seventy-nine, an age which I have just attained (1916). If I fail physically or mentally, I pray that I may quickly pass away. I wish never to be stranded—an empty wreck—a burden to myself and to my dear children.

FAMILY ANECDOTES

When Polly Butcher was just nine, I was there for dinner, in Ardmore. Sitting next to Polly, I had the following exchange with her:

"Polly, yesterday you were eight, weren't you?"

"Yes, Grandfather."

"And today you are nine?"

"Yes, Grandfather."

"The I suppose tomorrow you'll be ten."

"No, Grandfather, Nature doesn't do it that way."

When my oldest daughter Corinne was a child of eleven or so, she wrote a composition on Napoleon III that ended something like this: "Napoleon said that he abdicated for the good of the country, but I think it was because he had to."

When my youngest daughter Margaret was a small child, I had in my employ a colored man named Thomas, who was very swift-footed in answering the bell. One morning, I heard Margaret call him "Tom." Sitting in my office with her on my lap, I explained to her that "Tom" was too familiar, for a little girl talking to a man and that she must call him "Thomas." Just then, the front-door bell rang, and Thomas passed the open office door at full speed. Margaret turned around and greeted him again with "Tom." I said, "Margaret, I thought I just told you that you must not call him 'Tom.'"

"But Papa," she replied, quick as a wink, "He went so fast that I didn't have time to say more 'n 'Tom.'"

During the doll age of my daughters, I was "surgeon in ordinary" to all of the family dolls. To aid in these repairs, their dear mother instituted what, with her keen sense of humor, she dubbed the Morgue. In consisted of heads, arms, legs, torsos, and fragments of prior deceased dolls which might prove useful in effecting repairs.

On one occasion, I found on my desk a dolly and a detached arm, together with a note from Margaret addressed to "Dear Dr. Dollfix" reading as follows: "Won't you please glue my dolly's arm on, it's glued off."

One of my great-nieces had a burro sent to her from the West. It was in transit through various freight clerks, and an Eastern clerk, dictating the freight consist, pronounced it "bureau," in his ignorance of Western lingo. When it reached Philadelphia, the freight agent telegraphed back:

SOME MISTAKE. ONE BUREAU MISSING
AND ONE JACKASS OVER

When I told my son-in-law, Dr. Walter Freeman, of an ovariotomy of a young girl of fifteen, in whom a tumor weighed a hundred and eleven pounds, while the girl, after her recovery, weighed only sixty-eight pounds, he said, "Now Father Keen, you must be very careful or some day you might throw away the wrong piece."

And when a medical friend inquired of Walter the reason for my abdominal operation, in 1910, in which a suspected tumor turned out to be diverticulitis, he quickly replied, "A blowout of the innertube," an apt and accurate description.

Her uncle, Spencer Borden, gave Dora a lovely filly of pure Arabian blood, but born blind from cataracts.

I asked de Schweinitz, an eminent ophthalmologist, if we could not operate on her as we would on a human being. He smiled (no wonder) and sugggested that, in the first place, she would inevitably rub away the annoying dressing, and the eyes would be lost. In the second place, if we removed the lens, as we do in human beings, we should have to outfit her with a pair of spectacles.

This idea naturally set me to laughing at myself. "Why of course! Isn't it odd that this had never occurred to me. How stupid!" And I laughed at myself again.

7

—••₤ ₯₤ ₴••—

Medical Anecdotes

SPEECH AT THE ANNUAL DINNER OF
THE BRITISH MEDICAL ASSOCIATION,
LONDON, AUGUST 1, 1895[1]

[Recorded by B.M.A. secretary]

D R. W. W. KEEN SAID that they had been told by the Lord Chancellor that the most difficult thing for a speaker to do was to sit down. He found most certainly that the next most difficult thing for a speaker to do was to get up. It was bad enough to make an after-dinner speech in his own country, but in England, and with that distinguished assembly before him, he could assure them that it was with great trepidation that he rose to his feet.

They had heard the thanks presented to this noble association by their distinguished guest, Professor Stokvis, as representing the eastern hemisphere; it was his (Dr. Keen's) pleasant duty to return thanks for his brethren of the western hemisphere. Only the other day he met an American friend at dinner, at the hospital table of the president of their surgical section, who said to him, "I think I dine with you more frequently in London than I do in New York." This brought forth a remark from an English friend, that the Americans seemed to think nothing of crossing the Big Pond, to which Dr. Keen replied, as he justly might, "It is no wonder that we can come over here, and do so frequently, when we have such attractions on this side." Though a good many Americans were prodigal sons, somewhat over a hundred years ago, yet whenever they did come home, he noticed that Englishmen were always ready to kill the fatted calf, and by reason of it there was great danger—and he had found it so—to their digestion. He could assure them that nothing pleased an American so much as to come to the old home, Old England, to be welcomed by its capacious heart, big enough to hold all of them, yea, and all the world besides. The roast beef of

153

Old England had been celebrated, but it had given way, with Americans at least, to their appreciation of the old and great English heart. In saying "English," he meant not only England, but Scotland, Wales, Ireland, and the colonies as well. It was very much on the principle of the commencement of the church service which said, "Dearly beloved brethren" on the ground that it was not necessary to mention the sisters, because "the brethren" embraced the sisters.

Another reason why they should come over was that they had all been taught in the English school. When he was a student of medicine, he was cradled in Gray's *Anatomy*, and he hardened his gums on *Watson's Practice*, that admirable book by the Addison of modern English medicine. He was guided, in his first obstetric case, by the light of *Ramsbotham's Obstetrics*, whilst his surgical patron saint was Sir James Paget. He wished that the members of the association could come to America, where they would receive as hearty a welcome as the descendants of the Old English stock could show them. He was glad to know that there were many American physicians who were held in just as great esteem on this side of the water as distinguished English physicians were on their side. They all knew Gross, DaCosta, and others. Mr. Heath said of one of their Americans, at least, that his name was in all their mouths and his button was in their bowels.[2]

He had seen, in the *Boston Medical and Surgical Journal*, a proposal which out-Murphied Murphy by far. It was written under the name of Paul Pry Jr. and was dated in 1995. It related the procedure his ancestor, a century before, had introduced into American practice, and from that it had spread all over the world, an immense improvement, especially in celiotomy. At that distant time, it was not uncommonly necessary, after having made an abdominal section, when the bowels got tangled up, to make another in order to disentangle them. Paul Pry's grandfather had taken a hint from Nature and had improved the common practice greatly. The hint was a very simple one. There, thought he, as he was about to begin his operation, was the belly button; doubtless, thought he, the remnant of a row of buttons that ran up and down, and, thereafter, in order to induce a return to atavism whenever he had a celiotomy, he made a row of buttons and buttonholes and simply closed the abdomen in that way. Then, if the bowels got tangled and twisted up, he could readily reopen and disentangle them. In fact he narrated, as a remarkable proof at that time existing of the truth of Darwinism, that a number of children had been born of parents who had been operated on by his grandfather with a row of brass buttons all the way down the median line of the abdomen.[†]

He could assure them, speaking seriously, that he had brought to them most hearty thanks for the welcome that had been given to them, and that had been as cordial, as widespread, and as universal as the members of the British Medical Association.

† [Keen's postscript] "I met New York Professor W.T. Lusk, a year or more after giving the above address. He told me that his son had been present at the dinner, and that next to him sat an Englishman, drinking it all in until I came to the 'row of brass buttons,' at which he turned and said, 'Oh pshaw, he can't expect us to believe that anyway.'"

Among Keen's recorded anecdotes for his daughters, some fall into this category, some into "Humorous Anecdotes" (Chapter 10), and some could go either way. His lively correspondence, both professional and personal, has many examples of both that are omitted, some forgotten with the passage of time, no doubt, and some perhaps considered inappropriate for a memoir he wished to be a decorous inheritance. It's not my collection, of course, but I should not have overlooked the note of congratulation he received from his colleague Dr. Horatio Wood, in 1889, on attaining the Surgery Chair at the Jefferson: "Allow me to . . . express the wish . . . that you may carve human flesh to your heart's content, with your scalpel, bistoury, and catlin, hewing and hacking a clear road to fame and fortune." More medical than humorous, clearly.

A WOMAN SCORNED

One Sunday afternoon, I was hurriedly sent for to see a woman living not far from my office who had just attempted to commit suicide by swallowing broken and pounded glass, which she had drunk with, as nearly as could be ascertained, almost a pint of whiskey. She was raving drunk from the whiskey, but there was as yet no evidence of injury from the glass, which she had pulverized so fine that under the persuasion of mashed potato (which leaves a considerable residue in the bowel) and castor oil, she suffered no damage. As soon as she got sober, she was as well as ever. She then voluntarily confided her story to me, and after the lapse of so many years—and the death of all parties to the episode—the story may now not improperly be told.

When I first saw her, she was a woman of about forty-five who had at first been engaged by her employer, a well-to-do man, as a housekeeper and as an attendant on his sick wife. The latter was hopelessly ill of a slowly but surely mortal disease. Under a promise of marriage following the death of the wife, my patient became his mistress and even bore him two children. The man deferred the marriage, on various pretexts, following the death of his wife, and on the day before the attempted suicide, my patient read in a newpaper that her employer was soon to marry another woman, whose means and social standing were much above her own.

We had more than one conversation over the matter, and as a result, she promised me that she would not repeat the attempt to kill herself. A few weeks later, she came to see me again and said that the man had married her rival. She was present at the ceremony and described, with an almost demonic glee, how she had stood at the very door of the middle aisle, as they walked out of the church to the strains of Mendelssohn's "Wedding March"; how the skirts of the bride brushed against her own; and how she looked the man direct in the eye, never glancing aside to the right or left, from the moment when he could first see her till they had passed beyond the door.

My only wonder was that she did not shoot him, then and there. Her vindictive rage was equal to that, or to any other desperate act of violence. But a sweeter revenge was in store for her.

I did not see her again until a year or two later. It is so long since this happened that many trivial details have faded from memory, but the main facts are too deeply etched upon my brain ever to be forgotten.

Suddenly, during my afternoon office hour (fortunately, I was alone), a woman strode into my private consulting room, where I was seated at my desk. I did not recognize her at first, as her features were so distorted. Her eyes were all aflame with a hideous joy. Her clenched fists were raised aloft and then, with a downward chopping gesture, accentuated every outcry of her now exultant but sorely wounded soul. She exclaimed again and again (and fiercely), "I've seen him again, Dr. Keen, I've seen him again! Seen him in his coffin, *seen him in his coffin, IN HIS COFFIN!*" This last she fairly screamed. And so she passed out of my life.

Then I understood the adage that Hell hath no fury like a woman scorned.[3] Then I understood also those fearful words of Scripture that refer to the wrath of the Lamb.[4]

A TRAGIC POST MORTEM

Many years ago, Weir Mitchell asked me to make a post mortem in the following sorrowful circumstances. A charming young lady, perhaps twenty years of age and from a well-known Philadelphia family, went to Paris for the trousseau for her approaching wedding. For some years, she had been subject to frequent and severe headaches of unknown origin, and she was attacked by one of them while in Paris. Guéneau de Mussy, a very prominent medical man, was called in and gave her a hypodermic injection of a quarter grain of morphine—a frequent, if not the usual, dosage. She went to sleep and never woke up.

Her body was brought home dressed in her wedding gown. Only the brain was to be examined, so we did not disturb the body further than to move it far enough over the head of the coffin in order to prevent any soiling of her beautiful dress.

When the top of the skull was removed, the cause of death was immediately apparent, but a cause the like of which I have seen but this once in my fifty years of experience. The entire inner surface of the skull was peppered over with a hundred or so little bony growths, ranging in size from as small as a grain of sand to as large as a small pea. One of them (the only really large one) was like a mushroom in shape, with a slender stalk, about an eighth of an inch high, and an almost circular disk of bone about a third to a half inch in diameter. Inflammation of the brain's membranes had caused her death. The bony condition, which had caused her headaches, was absolutely impossible of diagnosis.

The fatal result was inevitable, and Guéneau de Mussy was wholly innocent of blame. By breaking down a part of the roof of the orbit, I removed the back half of the two eyeballs without changing the appearance of the features. Examination by Dr. William Thomson, I think it was, revealed that the optic disks (that is, the ends of the optic nerves in the retina) were choked and swollen. Had the eye-grounds been examined with an ophthalmoscope (a far less frequent procedure in those days than now), Guéneau de Mussy could have seen that there was a very serious disease inside the skull, though he could not have told what it was, nor where it was, nor what to do about it. Yet it would have led him to make the post mortem in Paris, and that would have exonerated him entirely, and at once.

A TYRO'S TEMPORARY PANIC

Two months after I had graduated from Jefferson Medical College, I entered the Army and was made Executive Officer of the Eckington Military Hospital, on the outskirts of Washington. The hospital had been a country residence, and I was assigned one room that served as both bedroom and office. There were a number of tents on the grounds for the patients.

At about ten o'clock, one Sunday morning, a soldier sought my advice. In order to make a diagnosis, I was obliged to make an instrumental examination, which caused him so much pain that I had to use an anesthetic. The only place where I could do this was in my room and on my bed.

At the Jefferson, I had been trained by Professor Gross to use chloroform. I called one of my assistants to give chloroform to the patient on a folded towel, as this was the most approved method. Just as I was about to begin the examination, my assistant suddenly said, "Doctor, he's not breathing!" I looked down at the patient's face and saw that it was getting purple; his chest was not moving, and his pulse could not be felt. I instantly seized a knife and cut across his temporal artery. Not a drop of blood escaped. We quickly began artificial respiration and continued it for over an hour, but it was all in vain. The man was stone dead.

On inquiry, in order to notify his friends, I discovered that he was a relative of an assistant postmaster general, a high goverment official who I naturally feared might be extremely hostile. At noon, I rode into Washington, feeling very blue and with all sorts of fears and much compunction of conscience, to see the assistant postmaster general and make a clean breast of the whole sad affair. I found him to be a most kindly and considerate man who, after I had explained everything in detail, said that I was not in the least to blame. He even consented instantly to my request for a post mortem in order to ascertain, if possible, the cause of death.

The post mortem was made at about five or six that afternoon. Since the death had been instantaneous, there was not the least rigor mortis: The body was as limp as though its owner had fainted. (When one dies slowly, muscular rigidity sets in soon after death.)

I should explain here how we remove the brain for examination. One sweep of the knife is made down to the bone, over the top of the head, from one ear to the other. (The hair is previously parted along this line, so that when it is brushed again into its normal place, the incision is completely hidden.) The whole front half and back half of the scalp are then detached from the skull, the first being drawn down as a flap over the face, and the other, low down on the back of the head. On the temples—a very important point in this narrative—are two strong muscles which pull the lower jaw tight up against the upper jaw. (By placing a finger on the temple while repeatedly chewing, one can feel it contracting and releasing.) As soon as they are uncovered, when the scalp is displaced, these two muscles are divided by knife, at the level where the intention is to saw all around the skull. This detaches the entire top of the skull from the lower part, making it easy to remove the brain.

My assistant (himself quite nervous, as he had been the one who administered the chloroform) was stooping to steady the head while I was using the saw. I had sawn all across the forehead and then swept the saw gradually towards the temple. With the first full sweeps of the saw, the patient loudly champed his jaws at us several times! My assistant instantly dropped the head and leaped backwards, holding up both hands in horror and exclaiming, "Good God! Isn't he dead?" I stood trembling and aghast with the same idea in my mind. A cold sweat broke out all over me. My heart gave one great convulsive leap, then stood still, then began to beat at race-horse speed, while I was gasping for breath. And no wonder.

Consider the circumstances: a callow youth, just graduated . . . his first fatality . . . the sudden death . . . the influential relative . . . the possibility of a civil or military inquisition, with an uncertain outcome . . . the scalp on the top of the head torn loose, and the top of the skull half sawed off (surely a mortal wound if the man had not really been dead). And now this seeming protest, by the corpse, at what I was doing. All this, and more, passed in an instant through my brain in frightful sequence. Is it any wonder that I had a fleeting sense of panic?

But a moment's reflection explained the matter. I had failed to completely sever the fibers of the temporal muscles, and as the saw caught them in its teeth, in its to-and-fro movement, the muscles tightened at the extreme ends of the excursion and relaxed at the middle. Since the body was limp, the lower jaw would drop, as the muscles relaxed, and snap vigorously against the upper jaw when the muscles tightened. In addition, there was no hemorrhage from the extensively divided scalp.

In a few moments, we had sufficiently regained our composure to realize that the man was surely already dead and to continue the post mortem, although with unsteady hands and perturbed minds. Finally, when I rolled the brain out of the skull into my left hand, my assistant said, with a sort of ghostly smile and a sigh of relief, "Well, doctor, at least he's dead now!"

The brain and the heart in our dead soldier both proved to be normal, and the chloroform, analyzed in the Surgeon General's laboratory, was found to be pure. The only explanation for the fatality is that it was one of those undoubted, but rare, cases of a particular, individual susceptibility to the effect of chloroform which kills in a moment and without premonition.

A BURST HOT-WATER BAG

One of my personal friends, a man well along in years, fell very ill and came under my care. His mind wandered so much that I told his daughter and daughter-in-law, who were devoted to him, that he must be watched closely lest he attempt to jump out of the window.

They had occasion to put a hot-water bag under his back. The water was very hot, and after a short time he screamed and started to get out of bed. The bag, an old one, had burst, and naturally he wanted to get out of the scalding water. Yet he was so dazed as to be unable to explain his plight.

The two women, mindful of my warning, thought that he wanted to get up to jump from the window. They threw themselves on him and held him down. In a few minutes they discovered the accident, but it was too late. He was blistered from the neck to the hips and died soon after.

HOW A DOCTOR TRIED TO PROVE TOO MUCH
AT A MURDER TRIAL

In a large town not far from Philadelphia lived a German butcher and his wife and children. The wife's sister, a lusty, muscular woman of about twenty, long accustomed to work in the fields, had been in America only a few months, I think, when the following tragedy occurred.

The two sisters went to a local dance, while the husband stayed at his shop. The married sister proposed, after a while, to return and look after the baby, but the unmarried sister prevailed on her to stay (since she had so many friends there) and she would go home instead. When the married sister returned home, an hour or so later, she found her sister dead on the floor of her room, with her throat cut.

The bed had not been slept in, and the furniture was not in disarray. Even the little rug in front of her bureau was flat and straight, though her bloody head lay on it. There was no evidence of an attack or of a struggle such as a strong young woman might be expected to put up. The husband was called from his shop, and he and the wife lifted the body. This accounted for the blood on his clothes and hands.

The police authorities believed that it was a case of suicide. Someone suggested that a prominent Philadelphia doctor be called in, since, as a coroner's physician, he had had wide experience in such cases. He suggested that the woman had been murdered. I suppose that he was influenced by the rather curious fact of the deep cut on the back of the neck. In addition, because of the sudden and profuse loss of blood (the left carotid artery and jugular vein had been divided), the seven gashes in the front of the neck could not have been made by the victim herself. *Why* anyone should want to kill her was wholly conjectural. But at all events, the butcher and his wife—there being no other obvious suspects—were arrested, charged with murder, and jailed.

The attorney for the defense asked me to make a second post mortem examination. I did this with minute care, making written notes of every fact observed. Among other things, I noted (1) that the cut on the back of the neck, though deep, had a distinct layer of muscular tissue at the bottom and that the vertebrae were not exposed; (2) that the left carotid artery and jugular vein were both severed; and (3) that the right carotid artery and jugular vein were intact.

A few days later, I received from the attorney the typewritten notes of the preliminary hearing before the committing magistrate. The statements made by Dr. X differed materially from the notes I had made. For one thing, he declared that the cut on the back of the neck not only exposed the bones but also showed the cartilage lining the joints between two of the vertebrae. Any anatomist or surgeon would know that this cartilage could *not* be thus exposed. I think his statement was calculated to show that an assailant, attacking her from behind, struck this blow first. He apparently believed that this blow so completely stunned her that she fell (causing some bruises), whereupon the assailant cut her throat seven times.

I was then face to face with a problem. The doctor would state certain facts, which I should then testify were not in accordance with what I had found. But he had made perhaps hundreds of medico-legal post mortems, while I had made none. Whom would the court and the jury believe? So I bethought me of a witness that both court and jury would *have* to believe, namely, the neck itself. On inquiring of the attorney, I learned that the body had not been re-interred, and as it was December, and very cold, there had been no decomposition.

The next day (I remember it was Christmas Day, because we had already distributed our presents), I went by train, met the attorney, secured the girl's neck, took it with me in a jar of alcohol, and returned to place it under lock and key in my office.

Shortly after the beginning of the trial, the attorney for the defense, in his opening statement, created great interest and curiosity when he said that the very body of the girl would be produced as a witness.

While on the train to present my testimony, I was amazed to read in the newspaper account of the previous day's session that Dr. X had sworn that *both* carotid arteries and *both* jugular veins had been severed. I could only assume that he wished to increase the emphasis on the sudden and voluminous loss of blood so that it would appear impossible for the woman to have made as many as six additional cuts across the neck.

I knew it was possible that seven cuts could be self-inflicted after one carotid and one jugular had been divided, because I had had, not long before, a case in St. Mary's Hospital, where the poor fellow confessed to the self-infliction of exactly similar wounds.

Had I been asked, before this trial, whether a person would not immediately collapse and die, with both carotids and jugulars severed, I surely should have answered in the affirmative. But this case led me to carefully research the recorded literature, and I found, among others, two surprising but authentic cases. (The notes I made on these cases have been lost, so I cannot give the references. My memory of the main facts, however, is very clear.)

First: A tramp slept in the hayloft on the second story of a barn. He had cut his throat, and the post mortem showed that, although both carotid and both jugulars had been severed, he climbed down the ladder and walked across a small yard, up some steps, then for some distance along an entry-way, where he fell exhausted by the loss of blood.

Second: A man who similarly cut his throat managed to climb a fence and walk a considerable distance to a shed, where he succumbed.

But to return to the trial.

After the usual preliminary questions, the attorney showed me a drawing, something like the following, and asked me to describe it.

I replied that it illustrated the carotid artery (C) on the right side of the neck, with its division into two branches, the internal carotid (I) going to the brain, and the external (E) going to the face. Also depicted is the jugular vein (J). The attorney stated that the drawing had been placed in evidence by the prosecution, and that the heavy transverse line represented the place where both of these great blood vessels on the right side had been cut across in the neck of the deceased. (It should be noted that this line is *below* the point where the carotid branches.)

He asked me if the carotid and the jugular on the right side of the neck were divided at any point, to which I replied, "No."

"How do you know that they were not so divided?"

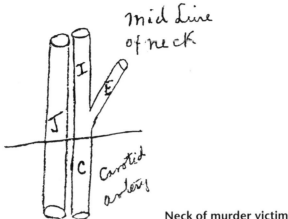

Neck of murder victim

"By notes I made during my post mortem examination, which state expressly that these two blood vessels were intact."

"Have you any other proof, and if so, what is it?"

"I offer in evidence the woman's neck."

I then demonstrated, by passing glass rods up through them, that the vessels on the left side were completely divided, whereas those on the right were not divided at all. (The neck in evidence included all of the blood vessels from a point at the bottom of the neck to a point well above the division of each carotid into its two branches.) I also demonstrated the fact that the deep cut on the back of the neck had *not* exposed the vertebrae, much less the cartilage.

The prosecution case collapsed, of course. *Falsus in uno, falsus in omnibus.*

The butcher and his wife were acquitted, but see the injustice caused by the hasty conclusions of one "expert" witness, an injustice for which society owed them a debt that could never be paid. The man's business was destroyed, and his wife became a lunatic. What became of them later I never knew. Whether it was a case of murder or a case of suicide, I could never even guess.

THE LOST SPONGE

To those unfamiliar with the reality and possibilities of an abdominal section, it would seem extremely careless—even criminal—for a surgeon to leave a sponge or an instrument sewn up inside the patient. But the published records of well over a hundred such cases at the hands of surgeons (among whom some of the ablest and most careful) should be sufficient evidence to the contrary. My personal experience is that a sponge, and even relatively small instruments such as forceps or scissors, may easily elude even the most careful search at the close of an abdominal operation. Moreover, one of the very best American surgeons had the following experience in the days when we were all using marine sponges.

At the close of the operation, instruments and sponges (twelve of the latter), were all counted and the count found to be correct. The abdomen was closed. By the third day, it had become very evident that something was wrong. The abdomen was reopened, and a thirteen-inch sponge was found! When recounting at the end, it had been forgotten that, in the heat of the operation, one of the marine sponges had to be torn in two, to meet an emergency hemorrhage, and this produced the thirteenth sponge.

In 1896, I operated on my sister-in-law, Mrs. George Dean,[5] for a very large abdominal tumor. As usual, every small instrument and twelve gauze sponges were counted and the numbers entered on a blackboard on the operating room wall. (I never trusted this to memory.) In addition, each sponge was sewn to a tape, ten to twelve inches long, and to be safe, a pair of forceps was clamped onto the tape whenever its sponge was inserted. At the close of this difficult operation, the operating-room nurse counted the instruments but could account for only eleven sponges. The nurse recounted the sponges, and I searched the abdomen with the greatest possible thoroughness. Still only eleven. We looked in the folds of the aseptic sheets, over the patient and under the patient. We turned out all the contents of the waste bucket and carefully picked them over. We re-searched the abdomen, re-examined the sheets, and recounted the sponges. Still, to my dismay, only eleven. It was evident that I could not keep the abdomen open any longer, so I was compelled to close it, trusting that if the errant sponge was really in the abdomen after all, it would declare itself sufficiently early—and that it would not be very dangerous.

My anxiety can readily be imagined. Here was a family patient I loved, upon whom I had done a highly dangerous operation for which I had made the most careful, painstaking preparation, planning every step beforehand with scrupulous exactitude. And now, possibly, there was a missing sponge in the abdomen! If it should cause her death, could I ever forgive myself? Would her husband and the family ever forgive such carelessness?

The first few nights, I slept hardly at all. The natural and expected rise of temperature after the operation my fears magnified into certain peritonitis and possible, if not probable, death. Then, as the days went by and her condition became more and more satisfactory, my dreadful anxiety began to lessen. Still, the specter of a *late* complication from that missing sponge would not wholly die down till weeks, and even months, later.

Now that fifteen years have passed, and the sponge has never been heard from, there is but one explanation: a miscount by the nurses. I so regularly used twelve sponges that they chalked down twelve, though they had only really prepared eleven.

But I never want to repeat that unique experience.

A LITTLE "SCRAP OF PAPER"

Many years ago, I was called into a neighboring state to operate in a case of an abdominal tumor. When my assistant and I arrived at the farmhouse, I found that the patient was a very stout woman of middle age. Her husband was at work, out ploughing in the field—which I thought was a little strange. Careful examination showed the existence of a large but obscure growth, which, if allowed to remain, would be a constant and augmenting menace to her life. Whether it could safely be removed was uncertain and could be decided only following an abdominal section. What was not doubtful, however, was that by reason of its size, extension, and adhesions—as well as almost certain hemorrhage (with which we could not so successfully cope in those days as we do now)—its removal would be both difficult and dangerous, a desperate chance. But balancing present danger against the certainty of a not-far-distant fatal conclusion, I recommended that the operation be attempted.

I explained the matter fully to the husband and told him that he must be the one to decide the matter. He turned on me and in a surly—almost savage—tone demanded, "Will you ensure her recovery?"

"Certainly not," I replied. "It is impossible to do more than to promise that I will do all in my power for your wife. What the dangers are I have frankly told you."

"Then I won't have any operation done," was his reply.

"Very well," said I, turning to my assistant. "We will then take the next train back to Philadelphia."

At the last moment, he relented but said that if she died he would hold me legally responsible for her death. Again, I began to pack up, but he consented for the second time.

"I shall operate only on the condition that you sign a paper which I am going to write out, if you will find me pen and ink."

Just what made me propose such a paper I do not know. It seemed like a sudden inspiration.[6] I had never done such a thing before in my life; nor have I ever done it since.But in view of the uncertainties of the case, and of the evident ugly disposition of the husband, I resolved, on the spur of the moment, to protect myself and thus drew up the following paper:

> I, _____ , hereby request Dr. W. W. Keen to operate upon my wife, and after having heard from him a full explanation of the difficulties and dangers of the operation, in case her death should be the result of it, I will not hold him in any way responsible.
>
> *[Signed]*

"Here," said I, "is a paper for you to sign, in the presence of your doctor and my assistant as witnesses. If you sign it, I will operate on your wife. If you do not, I will immediately return to Philadelphia. You are entirely free to sign or not to sign."

After some hesitation, he signed and we proceeded to operate.

All of my forebodings came true. The hemorrhage was furious. Though I did my best—and by that time I was no novice in surgery and had often been able to prevent death from hemorrhage—I was unable to staunch the blood. Neither before nor since have I seen a more profuse or uncontrollable loss of blood, and from so many sources. The tumor was finally removed, the hemorrhage controlled, and the patient replaced in bed, but in a terribly precarious condition. Instead of taking the next train, I stayed with her for several hours, doing all in my power to save her. It was all in vain: she was so weak that she gradually sank and died.

The husband was furious and almost attacked me physically. He poured out the vials of his wrath upon me, proclaiming loudly that he would have the law on me and get the biggest damages he could, that he would pursue me to the ends of the earth, etc.

As may well be imagined, I was glad to escape from such uncomfortable surroundings. (I should add, perhaps, that the children were most kind to me and did not show their father's rage.) But what comfort that little bit of paper in my inside pocket gave me can hardly be imaged. My conscience cleared me to myself of any professional delinquency, and that little piece of paper would clear me of any legal responsibility.

From that day to this, I have never heard from the husband. I have often wondered whether or not, in the eyes of the Law, that warrant was worth even the paper on which it was written.* Even if not, however, it served as a moral fetter upon one who might have given me a deal of trouble and anxiety.

* *A lawyer friend later told me that, from a legal point of view, the paper was worthless.*

THE DOCTOR DUMBFOUNDED

One of my very early patrons (in the days when another patient was as welcome as the cry "A sail!" to shipwrecked mariners) was a family in which there were several sons. One of them was a passionate young man who indulged, from time to time, in a wild spree. In due time, he married a fine young woman. Their means were limited, yet he persisted in his earlier habits, freely spending money, in his dissipations, that was needed for the household. When he sobered up, he almost invariably appeared, the picture of despair, in my office. His one fear was that he had contracted syphilis and might communicate it to his wife, to whom he was most deeply attached, in spite of his unfaithfulness. He often threatened suicide, and so earnestly that I warned his wife to take possession of his gun and knife and to make poisons unavailable. I hardly needed to lecture him. He saved me the trouble, as no one could blame, warn, entreat, or caution him more seriously—or more fiercely—than he himself.

He lost one position after another and was unable to support his wife and child, scarcely supporting himself with the neccessities of life. Her father finally compelled her to leave him and return to her parental home. The dissolute man drifted around the country, for a while, until one day the news came that he had at last carried out his threat and hanged himself. His body was brought home, and I had the unwelcome and sad duty of identifying it.

A year or so later, his widow called to see me. In the course of the conversation, she asked me the hardest question I ever was asked: "Dr. Keen, do you think that George went to heaven?" I was startled, dumbfounded, speechless. Happily for me, she went on to answer the question for herself. After a pause during which one could have heard a pin drop, she said, "Dr. Keen, I was devoted to George. I knew of his bad habits, his intoxication, his remorse, and even of his unfaithfulness, but it seems to me that if I, with my little heart, could forgive him again and again, then God, with His great heart, could forgive him also."

Reason as we might, theologically I believe she was right. But what a vast depth of a woman's love was revealed, by that question and by that answer! Only Divine love surpasses it.

A GRUESOME FIND

A client once sought attorney Benjamin Harrison (later president of the United States) and engaged him to search for the body of a relative that was reported to have been removed from the grave and taken to one of the anatomical study rooms in Cincinnati.

In the course of his search, Harrison came to the Medical College of Ohio, where Dr. Phineas Conner, an old friend during my college days, was a professor of surgery. As coroner, he was present when this incident occurred, and he related it to me.

Harrison, his client, Dr. Conner, and others sought diligently to find the body. They began the search in the cellar and ended it at the top story. Seeing a rope in one corner of the dissecting room, on the top floor, Harrison went over to it and shook it, and then, realizing that something heavy was attached to it, asked that it be drawn up. This was done, and the heavy object turned out to be a body. As the head appeared above the level of the floor, Harrison started back with the exclamation, "My God, that's my father!"[7]

It would be difficult to imagine a more dramatic situation than such a discovery, to say nothing of the fact that, in this instance, the body happened to be that of the son of one president and the father of another.

When I took charge of the Philadelphia School of Anatomy, in 1866, there was no anatomical law. All the medical schools and the two private schools then in existence, in addition to my own, were supplied by (1) the so-called body-snatchers, who took bodies from inconspicuous cemeteries, and (2) the unclaimed bodies from the coroner's office. It was an illegal traffic, of course, and if it had been detected, I could have been arrested and fined, or even imprisoned. But there was absolutely no other way of being supplied with cadavers for dissection, and so as a necessity, the practice was winked at by the authorities.

I do not remember the exact date, but a year or more before I discontinued the school, in 1883, the Pennsylvania legislature passed the best anatomical law in the country. All unclaimed bodies were delivered to an anatomical board, which consisted of professors and demonstrators of anatomy and surgery of the medical schools (and representatives of the private schools) throughout the state. We organized the board, and I was president of it for a good many years. The bodies were distributed on the basis of data furnished by the schools to Dr. Mears, the administrative officer. This obviated the necessity to encroach on cemeteries, and the scandalous situation ceased to exist.

The law was drawn up by Dr. William Forbes, and curiously enough, when he was a Demonstrator of Anatomy at the Jefferson, he was the first and only person to be charged under his own law. The evidence against him was complete, and he was arrested.

Fortunately for him, on the night before the date fixed for the trial, his father-in-law died.[8] This resulted in his obtaining a postponement of three months, in the next term of the court, by which time the public wrath had subsided. In the end, he was discharged, though I do not remember on what pretext.

TWO FAMILY CALAMITIES

In the middle of the night, many years ago, my night-bell rang furiously. I found my nocturnal caller to be an old medical friend with whom I had been a fellow student in Berlin. He was greatly excited, as he told me his tale of woe. He had just come from Washington, (where he held an important position in the Government). He was engaged to a lady who was one of two or three sisters of a family widely known both in literature and in public life. His fiancée had fallen ill with peritonitis and was under the care of a physician who was also her near relative. For some unaccountable reason, this physician had given her three or four drops of croton oil, which is a violent purgative that is rarely and cautiously used, usually in doses of a drop or less. As we drove to the house, my friend explained the situation and said, "Remember, you are to take command of the case. Spare the doctor if you can, but if this is impossible, save her life at all hazards, no matter what the consequences to him."

As soon as I saw her, it took but a glance to know that her case was absolutely hopeless. All I could possibly do was to soothe her suffering. I stayed by her all the rest of the night and saw her several times on the following day. The second night was a distressing admixture of sorrow and joy. The wedding reception of a young friend of ours was held that evening. I left the house of mourning and with my dear wife went to the house of joy. Afterwards, I spent the rest of the night with the dying girl and my desolate friend.

•

I had never been in that house before and had no occasion to go there again until some years later, when I was a witness to yet another calamity. A sister of the first patient had been sought in marriage by two young men. She really loved one, but, having had some quarrel with him, turned around, almost on the instant, and married the other. This was at noon. By seven o'clock that evening, she had become insane. When I saw her, some days later, I found her unwilling to talk or even to answer questions. Yet she was never still, save for short intervals of sleep. Walking, walking, walking the entire day, upstairs and down, in and out of rooms, and seizing food from the table when the family was at meals. She never sat down her entire waking day, so I was told. It was only exhaustion that made the *tramp, tramp, tramp* cease. My advice was that she be placed under the care of an alienist,[9] and I never saw her again.

Some time afterwards, her husband sought me, stated that her condition was unchanged, and asked me to give him a certificate to be used in court to proceed with a divorce. I refused to do this, reminding him that when he had married her, he promised to cleave to her alone, "in sickness and in health, till death us do part." I added that I neither could nor would help him to violate this promise. It was a very difficult case, and I have often since wondered whether or not my decision was righteous and just. On the one side, his solemn vow "in the presence of God and these witnesses"; on the other side, his ruined life. On the whole, I still think I was right. I never heard the later history of either the man or the woman.

PROFESSOR ELLERSLIE WALLACE AND HEMORRHAGE IN CHILDBIRTH

Ellerslie Wallace, Professor of Obstetrics at Jefferson, was a six-footer who weighed over two hundred pounds. A very dramatic lecturer, he always tried to illustrate the points he was trying to make.

When lecturing on hemorrhage in childbirth, he simulated the condition to perfection. He used a female cadaver and a baby cadaver. Employing some kind of artificial reservoir, he filled the uterus with a dark red fluid resembling blood. As soon as he delivered the baby, he carefully wrapped it up and laid it on one of the chairs in the arena of his lecture room and said most emphatically, "Be most careful of the baby and place it out of the way of any possible harm."

Then an assistant compressed the mother's abdomen, and blood flew out in the most lively and dramatic manner. As soon as Wallace, after stooping over and manipulating the patient for quite a while, had arrested the bleeding, he straightened up, braced himself with both hands in the small of his back, sighed with relief, and sank, exhausted, with all his weight on the chair on which reposed the newly delivered baby in its place of supposedly absolute safety!

That baby was surely a "spoiled child." And such a shout as went up from the whole class! For months afterwards, when Wallace met an old friend, he was often greeted with, "Hello, Wallace! Sat on any newborns lately?"

RISKS THAT DOCTORS, AND ESPECIALLY SURGEONS, CONSTANTLY RUN

Three times I personally have suffered from infection of my fingers, twice during surgical operations and once from a post mortem prick of a needle. The first two were mild infections, which soon yielded to efficient treatment, but the third nearly cost me my life.

A patient in my private hospital died from a perforation of the stomach from cancer. He died during the night, between Saturday and Sunday. My assistants did not report for duty on Sunday unless I had foreseen the need and asked them to come in. The family wished to have the body moved on Sunday afternoon, and as I was eager to have a necropsy (and they were willing), I performed it myself. The abdomen was full of pus, which I knew to be dangerous, and I was more careful than usual. I had completed the examination and had almost closed the abdominal incision when in some unknown way I pricked my right thumb with the needle. It was no more than many a woman inflicts on herself when hemming a handkerchief, and I barely felt the prick. I washed and carefully disinfected my thumb at once, but I hardly thought it necessary to make an incision and a prolonged, deep disinfection. In fact, I did not give it a second thought.

By about seven o'clock, I began to feel a little creepy and chilly. I lighted the parlor wood fire and decided not to go to church, especially as it was a stormy night, but to toast my toes and read instead. I went to bed early, feeling rather seedy, but I could not get to sleep. By one or two in the morning, my thumb began to throb, and this made me recall the needle-prick from the post mortem. I recognized the danger, and dressing partly, I slipped quietly down to my office to call Dr. Taylor, my first assistant. He lived on 18th, just below Chestnut. While waiting for his arrival, I got out the necessary instruments and dressings, some carbolic acid and bichloride tablets, plus a hypodermic syringe and a solution of cocaine. He injected the cocaine on both sides of my thumb, after which he made a deep incision, scrubbed and disinfected the wound very thoroughly, and dressed it. He then gave me an injection of a quarter of a grain of morphine.

I returned to bed and finally, towards morning, fell asleep for a short time. At eight o'clock, he saw me again and found my temperature to be a hundred and five. He called in Drs. Chalmers DaCosta and Joseph Hearn for consultation. Two days later, they etherized me and disinfected the wound anew. I was desperately ill for about a week and then gradually mended. It was some weeks before the wound was sufficiently healed for me to resume operating. Never shall I forget the kindness of my friends. Until I was quite well, I knew nothing of it, but they called and inquired, and telephoned, and left cards, messages, and dainties, almost without number. When I looked over the cards, I was astonished (and, I confess, gratified) to find many from almost complete strangers. Sickness often proves to us how many warm friends we have—often far more than we would expect.

One thing seems most providential. On Monday morning, Dr. Taylor discovered that his telephone was out of commisssion. My nocturnal message was the last he received. Had he not responded to my call, I should almost certainly have waited until morning. With only women (my daughters and the servants) in the house, I should not have asked them to brave the stormy night, and I certainly should not have wanted to venture out myself. Yet had I delayed until morning, I am convinced that the outcome would have been fatal.

While this was my only really dangerous illness contracted in the line of duty, I was constantly exposed to such risks. In my earlier professional life, from pecuniary necessity, I attended medical—and even a few obstetrical—cases. I suffered several times from a slight infection of diphtheria, especially in the cases which we then operated on by tracheotomy. (Thanks to the antitoxin and intubation, we hardly ever even *hear* of a case of diphtheria's being treated by tracheotomy these days.)

I have been exposed often to the danger of "professional" syphilis, but fortunately have always escaped it. This danger has been a tragedy in not a few of my professional friends and acquaintances.

I have known over a dozen men who for years have suffered the tortures of syphilis and the fear of communicating the disease to their wives and children, which is even worse. One of my friends told me that he had had several doctors under his care for syphilis who committed suicide, and I can hardly wonder at it. While I would be the last to do such a deed, I also would be the last to blame them. I am willing to believe that a merciful God would not judge them too harshly. Two of my medical friends died, utter wrecks, from cerebral syphilis.

Others also have been under my care who have had wide-spread surgical infections, followed by abcesses in many parts of the body, but who have weathered the gale, finally, and recovered.

I have referred elsewhere to the elder Dr. Gross's splendid example of courage when cholera broke out in New York. I have also referred to the young German bacteriologist who was studying the bubonic plague, accidentally became infected, and heroically died; and to the many unknown and unsung heroes who have lost their lives in epidemics of yellow fever. I have recited in some detail the extraordinary and deliberate attempts by doctors at self-inoculation with the germ of yellow fever in Cuba, and their success in demonstrating the only means by which the contagion is carried (the mosquito, of course), knowledge attained, alas, by the sacrifice of human lives. Had it been possible to conduct these experiments on animals, it would have been unnecessary to try them on human beings, but, unfortunately, man is the only animal liable to this disease.

So too, medical men have gone to Africa to investigate the fatal sleeping sickness, sometimes offering themselves as voluntary victims, for the benefit of mankind. Only a few months ago, Ricketts, one of our most promising young doctors, lost his life while studying typhus fever in Mexico, well knowing when he went there that his death might be the price of victory. As I write these lines, seventeen young men in Baltimore have just volunteered for experiments in cancer inoculation, an offer properly declined, since animals can be inoculated for this just as well.

No other profession can show such a record of self-sacrifice. It is any wonder, then, that I take just pride in the altruism of the medical profession?

A DISTRESSING NIGHT

One of the most distressing nights of my life was spent at the bedside of the daughter of a medical friend of mine. She was a sweet girl of fifteen or sixteen who had been ill for a day or two, but not so seriously that the family physician had been called in to see her. Her father, who was a specialist, was not familiar with internal medicine and had given her a preparation of opium.

I suspect that not only was it a larger dose than was wise, but also that the girl was one of those people who are particularly susceptible to opium.

She fell asleep, and after a while, her sleep seemed to be deeper than was expected. Her father tried to rouse her, but still she slept on. At last, becoming thoroughly alarmed, he called another medical friend and me. It was past midnight, and she had been asleep for several hours. All our efforts to waken her were in vain, and the pupils of her eyes were contracted almost to pinpoints, as is common in opium poisoning. Her respirations were gradually becoming slower and slower, and it was clear that her life was at stake.

Never can I forget the dreadful anguish of that father, as he paced up and down the room and into the hall and back. He was wild with grief and self-accusation, wringing his hands and groaning, "I've killed my daughter, I've killed my child!" Meanwhile, we were so engrossed in our effort to save the girl's life that we could give little attention to the poor distracted father. We used the stomach pump, though after so long a time it was of doubtful value. We administered various remedies, and in order to sustain the failing breathing, we began aritificial respiration, which we kept up for hours. At last, signs of more normal breathing and returning consciousness gladdened our hearts, and her recovery was finally assured. The reaction on her father, in the whole episode, was nearly more tragic than had been the hopelessness. He collapsed under the strain, and I almost feared for his life or his reason.

As I wended my way home, in the cheering rays of the rising sun, how fervently I thanked God that it was not one of my own children that had looked into that open grave. For years afterwards, I never gave one of them—or anyone else—a dose of medicine without asking myself, with some anxiety, if it was the proper dose.

THE RESPONSIBILITIES WHICH SURGEONS ARE OBLIGED TO ASSUME

I.

Two boys, twelve to fourteen years of age, got into an altercation in the street. One stabbed the other in the neck with a penknife, causing an immediate, furious hemorrhage. Had the victim not been directly opposite a doctor's office, he undoubtedly would have perished in a few minutes. The doctor rushed to his aid and placed a rather heavy bag of shot on the wound, retaining it in place by plaster and bandages.

The penknife had divided both the carotid artery and the jugular vein, which run parallel and directly in contact with each other. Fortunately, the boy recovered and was brought to see me at the Jefferson Hospital. The two openings had been quickly glued together, so that the blood passed from one blood vessel to the other, but chiefly the arterial blood into the vein because of the greater strength of blood in an artery.

On placing a stethoscope over the wound, I heard a loud blowing sound. The wall of the vein being thin, it was yielding to the increased pressure, and a large arterio-venous aneurism had formed and was growing. The blowing sound was also very annoying to the boy.

Some infection had occurred when the wound was inflicted, and as a result, all the tissues would surely be matted together. But I had to operate.

Note, now, the responsibility upon my shoulders. If the wounded boy should die, as a result of my operation, the other boy would be tried for murder, or at least for manslaughter.

The operation was one of the most difficult I ever did in the neck, because all landmarks had been obliterated and everything matted together as if by solidified glue. It took a long time to separate the artery and the vein from the surrounding tissue, so that I put a ligature on each—both above and below the opening—or four separate ligatures. I finally succeeded and immediately closed the wound. The lad promptly recovered.

The operation took two hours, the longest one I ever did. What a sigh of relief I released when he was safely in bed! I devoutly thanked God for my success.

2.

The case of Midshipman Aiken, elsewhere related.[10] Two good surgeons had already decided against an operation. His parents were on the way from New Orleans.[11] It was three days after the accident, and further delay meant death. I had to take the responsibility of the parents' possible disapproval. I opened his skull and removed two-thirds of a tumblerful of blood. He recovered, fortunately, and fortunately also, his parents wholly approved.

3.

A girl of about sixteen shot herself in the right side of the abdomen, just under the ribs. The ball could be felt under the skin in the left flank. She was evidently bleeding to death internally. As with Aiken, her parents were on their way to her bedside.

Again, I faced the same responsibility. As any good surgeon would, I decided that I was responsible for her life, even in the face of her parents' disapproval, certain in the case of her death. I opened the abdomen, found and closed two holes in her stomach and tied some large, bleeding arteries. I had to remove the kidney, as it had been seriously mutilated by the bullet. I then removed the bullet from under the skin of the left loin.

She did very well for several days. The right kidney balked for two or three days and then buckled down to work. There was every prospect for a speedy recovery, but about ten days after the operation, she suddenly died. The post mortem showed that a large blood vessel had been badly bruised, the bruised part had sloughed away, causing a fatal hemorrhage.

In spite of the outcome, the parents approved of the course I had taken.

THE CLEVELAND OPERATIONS

In the middle of June, 1893, I received a letter from my old friend Dr. Joseph Bryant, of New York, saying that he wished to consult me about a very important matter. As I was going on to the Commencement at Brown, leaving home on the afternoon of June 19th, I wrote him that I would leave early in the afternoon so that we could talk over the matter privately on the Fall River boat. He met me at the boat at about four o'clock, and we had the deck to ourselves. He told me that President Cleveland, who in March had been inaugurated for the second time, was suffering from a serious disease of his upper-left jaw, that he intended to operate on it soon, and that he wished me to assist him. I readily agreed, saying that I should hold myself in readiness for the moment when he needed me.

About ten days later, he wrote me full instructions as to the course to be followed to assure secrecy. I followed them to the letter.

The political and financial condition of the country made such secrecy essential. America was passing through a severe financial panic. The Democratic (and several in the Republican) Party were possessed by the silver craze, and the country was drifting toward a silver standard. Vice President Adlai Stevenson[12] was known to be an advocate of free silver. Only Cleveland, a sturdy champion of the gold standard, stood between us and wide-spread bankruptcy. He wished to repeal the Sherman Silver Purchase Act, and it would require all of his energies to bear down on Congress with this issue.

The only persons to whom I confided the facts were my brother Charles and my assistant, Dr. William Taylor, in both of whom I could place absolute reliance. Charles, as a broker, was profoundly interested and might be most adversely affected in his finances, should the president die—or even should a hint of a serious malady become public.[13]

If it had been suspected that Mr. Cleveland was suffering from cancer, the possibility that his life might be shortened or his considerable influence

The steam yacht *Oneida*, scene of the two 1893 operations on President Cleveland
[The Society for the Preservation of New England Antiquities]

diminished would cause the politicans to desert him (as the setting sun) and flock to the support of Stevenson (the rising sun); the Silver Act would never be repealed, and the direst possible consequences to the country would follow.

I did not even disclose my errand to my children, but simply told them that I had been called to New York for an important consultation and operation and might be absent several days. With characteristic good sense, they did not even ask for further information.

The president left Washington, openly, on the afternoon of June 30th, stating that he was going for a weekend cruise on the *Oneida*, the steam yacht of his friend Commodore E.C. Benedict, a New York banker. He reached the city after dark, repaired to one of the piers on the East River, and was rowed out to the yacht. With him was his friend Daniel Lamont, the Secretary of War. (Before leaving Washington, Mr. Cleveland had issued a call for a special session of Congress, three weeks later, for the purpose of relieving the financial panic by the expedient of repealing the Silver Act.)

Dr. Bryant and his assistant, Dr. John Erdmann, rowed to the yacht from other piers, as did Dr. Edward Janeway, Dr. Ferdinand Hasbrouck, and I, all reaching the *Oneida* between nine and ten o'clock.[14] A large operating chair, all of the necessary instruments, anesthetics (nitrous oxide, ether, and chloroform), dressings, and so forth, had already been put aboard.

The president and I sat on the deck for some time, smoking cigars and chatting. I had never met him before and was greatly interested in and impressed by his personality, especially concerning his high ideals about his personal duty to the country. As his own administration had followed a four-year term of Republicans, he was sorely beset by a horde of office-seekers, to whom he referred in terms of the utmost abhorrence. "They always follow me," he said, "and even assault me in my dreams." The yacht soon got under way, and all went to bed.

On Saturday, we were cruising slowly eastward on Long Island Sound. The weather was bright and the water smooth. Immediately after breakfast, all our surgical preparations were made, in the cabin where the surgeons and Dr. Hasbrouck, the dentist, were assembled. The chief steward was the only other person there. Colonel Lamont and Mr. Benedict were on deck.

The best and safest method of anesthesia was a question of the greatest importance. Mr. Cleveland was fifty-six years old, a corpulent man with a short, thick neck. His skin showed many warts and moles. I do not remember (I am writing this in February of 1912) what the reports were as to his heart and kidneys, but I am fairly sure that they were in "good" condition (though they may have been only "fair"). He had been through several periods of stress, as an attorney-at-law, as the mayor of Buffalo and the governor of New York, and, in a prior term, as president of the United States. Such strains would almost certainly have seriously taxed, and possibly impaired, the condition of these vital organs.

Therefore, Dr. Bryant had asked Dr. Hasbrouck to be ready to use nitrous oxide. It became immediately evident, however, that this could not be adminstered so as to keep the patient well under its influence, since the operation was within the mouth. Chloroform was substituted for the nitrous oxide. This was chosen because we would certainly be obliged to use the Pacquelin cautery, which would preclude the use of ether because of the danger of fire. I am quite clear in my recollection that Dr. Hasbrouck was wrong, in later newspaper interviews, in describing nitrous oxide as the only anesthetic used. On the contrary, it was quickly found to be unsatisfactory and was abandoned forthwith.

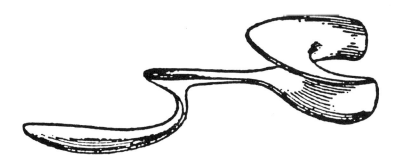

Cheek retractor Keen bought in Vienna; later used in Cleveland operations

Dr. Erdmann administered the chloroform, I think. Dr. Janeway watched the pulse, while Dr. Bryant did the operation, I acting as his assistant. We used my own silver mouth retractor, which I had bought in Paris in 1866, and which served admirably to give a wide and most satisfactory access, drawing back the cheek and exposing the jaw.[15]

The entire operation was done within the mouth, with no external incision whatever. The malignancy involved the alveolar border and extended some distance beyond. Dr. Hasbrouck removed two or three teeth. Then, with the rongeur forceps, considerable portions of the upper jaw, on its anterior and palatine surfaces in the roof of the mouth, were removed, as far as, and somewhat beyond, the visible limits of the disease. The excision extended nearly to the orbital plate and for a moderate distance on the palatine surface, though not so far as to reach the attachment of the soft palate. The antrum was opened very widely, of course. The hemorrhage was considerable, but not at all alarming. Pressure, and later an iodoform gauze plug, controlled it. I do not think a single ligature was used, but in this I may be in error. The raw surface was then cauterized, and the wound was re-packed. The operation was ended.

What the relief was to the surgeons no one can ever realize. Not only was a serious surgical operation complete on the chief magistrate of the land, but the patient had not died, or even collapsed, under the anesthetic, a possibility we had considered.[16]

For the country, the result was too momentous to be imagined. The fortunes of hundreds, nay thousands, of people were saved; the progress of the prevailing panic would be stopped, a stable currency would probably be assured, and the return to national prosperity would be certain.

Never did I feel such a deep, almost overwhelming, sense of responsibility as during that operation. In itself, it was nothing, as compared with many others I have done of greater difficulty and danger, but in its possible consequences for good or evil, none I ever was involved in could compare with it.

Mr. Cleveland was placed in bed, and in a short time revived from the anesthetic and soon became himself. Of course, he could talk only with great difficulty, as the wound had been packed with gauze to arrest the hemorrhage. When the packing was taken out, so much of the bone had been removed that his speech was entirely unintelligible, resembling that of a child with a severely cleft palate.

As we had had no communication with the shore for several days, the yellow newspapers spread the wildest reports as to a supposed presidential spree, reports which even today, many years after the event, make me fiercely indignant. For a large part of July 1st and 2nd, I sat at his bedside and, to occupy his mind, read to him. He had almost no stimulant. What little he did take (two or three tablespoonfuls) was necessary, after so considerable an operation, and even that he would have preferred not to take. He was one of the most docile and easily managed patients I ever cared for.

Dr. Hasbrouck was landed at New London on July 2nd; I landed at Sag Harbor on the 4th and returned directly home. The operation later became known, but the fact was never revealed that we did a second operation, about ten days after the first. Dr. Bryant wrote to me that he was not satisfied that we had removed all of the diseased tissue and thought it best, therefore, that we return to the scene. It can be easily understood that a touriquet cannot be applied around the mouth, as with an arm or a leg, so that it is very difficult, when the blood is flowing rather freely, to judge the exact limits of an unwanted growth.

At any rate, on the evening of July 14th, we all (except for the dentist, whose services were not needed this time) were again conveyed from the various piers to the *Oneida*, at anchor in New York harbor, and we again steamed out into the Sound. The next morning, Mr. Cleveland was again chloroformed, and in a few minutes the second operation was over. The same routine was followed as before, and everything went well. This time, though, I was landed at Newport, on the evening of the 18th, just before the Fall River boat arrived en route to New York.

In order not to betray my presence to my friends, I headed for my stateroom at once, intending to stay secluded there. But as I reached the head of the main stairway, whom should I meet but my brother-in-law, Spencer Borden, who was also on his way to New York. "Hello, Billy Keen," he said, "what are you doing here?" "Well, Spen," I replied, "I reached Newport from a nearby consultation only a few minutes ago and had just enough time to catch the boat, but no time to visit the family in Fall River." This seemed to satisfy him, but there was no stateroom for me until bedtime.

Meanwhile, the president had returned to "Gray Gables," his vacation home, and had been fitted with an artificial jaw by a very skillful dentist.[17] With it in place, his voice was perfect; without it, unintelligible. He received public deputations, very shortly after his operations, and made speeches to them. He went fishing and in all ways resumed his usual life. No one suspected the truth.

Though the story of the first operation got out, the president's evidently vigorous health—and Dr. Bryant's equally vigorous denials—quieted all public apprehension, and the scandalous stories of Mr. Cleveland's sprees on the *Oneida* also died down.

On August 4th, with Florence, Dora, and Margaret, I went to the World's Columbian Exposition in Chicago, and then to Lake Minnewaska, where I stayed until the 12th of September.[18]

The explosion came on August 29th, but fortunately too late to prevent or undo the action of Congress, which had met the third week in July. The House of Representatives repealed the Sherman Silver Purchase Act on August 28th, and the Senate followed suit on October 20th.

In the *Philadelphia Press* of August 29th, "Holland" (E.J. Edwards), their New York correspondent, published a long dispatch giving what was, to all intents and purposes, a full and fairly accurate account of the first operation, with dates, places, and names (excepting that Dr. Janeway's name was not mentioned). It was a great newspaper scoop. I don't know how the story got out, but I think that Dr. Bryant does. I have always suspected Hasbrouck, who was at the first operation but not the second, but I could be wrong.[19] He certainly talked a great deal more than he should have, after Holland's piece appeared, but I do not know whether he also talked before then. All the papers were then agog. Reporters flocked to see everyone whose name was cited, but especially Bryant. I have always thought that the steward and the crew of the *Oneida* received scant credit for their silence.

Only one reporter found me. A number of them came to my house, but Dr. Taylor met them with the statement that I was somewhere in the woods and he could not give them my address. One man, however, a reporter for the *World*, returned to the house after Dr. Taylor had left and tried to find out where I was from the servants. As they were not suspicious, they told him they thought I was in Fall River. He took the Fall River boat that night and learned from someone at the wharf, the next morning, that Mrs. George Dean was my sister-in-law. (I had been going to Fall River every year for over thirty years.) He immediately went there and told Dora (Mrs. Dean) a touching, if fictitious, tale. According to him, I had done him a great service, many years before, for which he had been able to thank me only by letter. Spending a short holiday in nearby Warren, Rhode Island, he had heard I was in Fall River and and wished to thank me in person. She, in guileless sincerity, told him that I was at Lake Minnewaska. He took the same boat back to New York and went the next morning to New Paltz. There, he learned that, as it was a Sunday, the Smileys did not allow the back-and-forth shuttle of the stages to town. Nothing daunted, he hired a team and drove across country. After supper, while reading in the lobby, I was handed his card and he told me his errand. I said that I was sorry to have to deny him any information, but that all of us had agreed that only Dr. Bryant should make any official statement. The only thing I did was to admit (as it had already been published) that there had been an operation on Mr. Cleveland and that I had assisted Dr. Bryant. Out of this, however, he wove quite a little story—chiefly fiction. I knew nothing until later of his perigrinations here or to Fall River. The newspaper account in the *World* in no way represented what I told him but enlarged and embroidered it.

When Holland's dispatch appeared in the New York papers, Spen read the account at home in Fall River. One can imagine his saying, "Effie, I'll bet a dollar that was where Billy Keen had been when I met him on the Fall River boat." As a matter of fact, he did not remember the exact date, for when he and I met in Newport, I was returning from the *second* operation, which even today, after nineteen years, is practically unknown.

(The newspaper clippings I have saved were not systematically collected but are only those which happened to come my way. A complete collection would have filled a very large scrapbook, for practically every paper in the land published dispatches and editorials.)

Dr. Bryant's policy to say nothing was undoubtedly the wisest, but I'm afraid he bent the Tenth Commandment rather badly. He had made careful notes of the operations, and all of their incidents, as or soon after they occurred. My own account may be inaccurate in some details, and thus should be corrected by his account, but the main incidents I have cited are certainly correct.

I often shudder to this day, when I think of the heavy risk we ran and of the terrible disaster which would have followed either the President's death or the premature disclosure of the extent and character of the operations.

(After the repeal of the Silver Act, the gold standard was finally inserted into the 1896 Republican—possibly even the Democratic—convention platform.)

For the next few months, I went to Washington, at varying intervals, to examine Mr. Cleveland's mouth. In spite of the fact that the pathologist made a diagnosis of, I believe, sarcoma, there never was any return or the slightest suspicion of it. (Certainly that was the clinical diagnosis.[20]) In these visits, I usually lunched with the family and saw Mrs. Cleveland and the children, who were charming young girls. I was angered almost beyond endurance at the villainous reports that one or more of them were feeble-minded. Whatever political opinion the paper (reporter or editor) held, as to the President's acts or policies, why strike a woman in the tenderest spot of her heart, her love for her children? Only a beast could do so.

Twice after that, I saw Mr. Cleveland in consultation with Dr. Bryant. He was then living in Princeton. He complained of attacks of abdominal pain, sometimes very severe. Owing to this excessively fat belly walls, it was impossible to examine the abdominal viscera with any accuracy. The first consultation was early in 1905, the second, at the end of the year. The symptoms seemed to point to recurring intestinal obstruction. Palliative, rather than radical, treatment was recommended, for to do an abdominal section, at his age and in his condition, both Bryant and I thought very injudicious. His death did not occur until 1908. I have never learned the results of a necropsy, if indeed one was performed, but I have always suspected that it would have disclosed a malignant growth. But that he had no local recurrence for over thirteen years was a triumph indeed.

8

———••⚎)(⚎••———

Personal Health

SMOKING

I NEVER SMOKED UNTIL the day I was twenty-one, in my junior year at Brown. I smoked a whole cigar, and without paying the usual penalty.

I was a moderate smoker—usually one cigar after my day's work was done—for I appreciated the disadvantage to me of auscultating the lungs of sick patients, especially of women, with the stale odor of tobacco about me. At a formal dinner party, I would often smoke two cigars. When cigarettes "arrived," I often smoked two to four in a day, in addition to my usual cigar.

I continued to smoke for about sixty-four years. Then suddenly, when in Boston at a surgical congress, I would take a few puffs at a cigarette, during a luncheon, and it was disagreeable to me, for some completely unknown reason, and I would throw it away.

After a few days, I said to myself, "Old Man, nobody compels you to smoke. If it is disagreeable to you, why don't you give it up?" From that day on, I have not touched tobacco in any form.

And I have no hankering for it. I have not been tortured by the urgent desire to smoke, as have so many men who swear off for a month or a year and are utterly miserable. The odor of smoke is still agreeable to me, but I have entirely lost the desire to smoke.

I have not the least suspicion of what caused my sudden dislike of smoking,[1] which happened about 1921, but it is now 1927 and I have never returned to it.

A story was told me by Mr. Stuart Patterson, vice president and later president in succession to Frederick Fraley, of the Western Saving Fund. Fraley was also president of the National Chamber of Commerce and president of the American Philosophical Society. He was one of the leading citizens—one might almost say the leading citizen—of Philadelphia. He died in harness at ninety-seven, I think. The following conversation took place in his office at the Saving Fund when Mr.

184

Fraley was over ninety. Mr. Stuart Patterson was present.

A representative of an anti-smoking organization came to get his opinion as to the evils of using tobacco.

"Well," said Mr. Fraley, in his quiet Quaker way, "I think it is a slow poison."

Encouraged by the tenor of the conversation, the caller urged him to say more, and Mr. Fraley obliged: He said, "I have smoked ever since I was fourteen years old. I think it is a *very* slow poison."

MY "ANNUAL" ACCIDENTS

I have rarely been sick. At about twelve, I had an attack of varicoid; when a medical student, I had a dangerous tonsillitis; in my early professional life, I suffered several times with other more or less threatening attacks of tonsillitis after attending cases of diphtheria—especially after doing a tracheotomy. I cannot recall any other serious illnesses. I presume that I probably had measles, whooping-cough, and scarlet fever, but I do not remember them.

I have always been nearsighted, but it has never been a problem, professionally or personally. On the contrary, my nearsightedness (of, I think, one-and-a-half diopters) has been of great use to me. All my near work I have done without glasses—reading, writing, and operating. Not seldom, as my near vision was very sharp, after my first assistant had failed two or three times to seize a small, spouting artery, have I said to him, "Suppose you let the old man try," and only rarely did I fail to seize it at once.

Then, too, if blood from a spouting artery hit me in the eye, two or three winks, or a quick wipe with sterile gauze, and I went on operating. No glasses to be cleaned, no hands to be disinfected again, and no time or blood lost.

For the last fifteen or twenty years, however, the muscle of one eye has become weakened, and I am bothered with double vision at twenty feet or more. One result is that I see two ministers and get two sermons—quite an unfair allowance. For reading without glasses, on the other hand, even with the rather small print of the *Ledger*, I have no difficulty as yet (1925).

But of accidents I have had eleven that I can recall—and my abdominal operation may well count as a twelfth serious surgical danger. A few years ago, one of my daughters warned me to be careful, as I had not had my "annual" accident for several years. I promptly fractured my left arm.

I began my series of accidents at about six years of age, when, as an amateur carpenter, I chopped off the tip of my left forefinger. My dear mother tried her hand as an amateur surgeon. Finding the piece, she washed it and bound it to the raw end, but her surgery was unavailing. The result of the accident is a bevelled end of a finger—which is about a quarter of an inch shorter than its fellow on the right hand.

I recall very vividly the next two accidents, both when I was probably between ten and twelve years old. I was fishing at the Maylandville Dam (about in the hollow of 49th and Woodland, but long-since drained), with a so-called "dipsy" (a pyramidal leaden sinker), and while casting, I caught one of the fishooks in my right thumb, and it was buried in the flesh. I had to walk all the way home, which was at 36th and Chestnut. My cousin, Dr. B. Rush Mitchell, a surgeon in the Navy, cut it out, and I yelled like a good fellow.

My third accident I well remember. The Evans house, across Chestnut Street, had a piazza in front under which was a quite free space. John Evans and I imagined this space to be a den for a band of bold robbers. One time, when I was one of the robbers and John one of the police, they chased us to the refuge of our den. The police seized clothes poles and tried to dislodge us by ramming our den with these weapons. The end of one of the poles struck me on the left cheek, about a quarter of an inch below the rim of the left orbit. Had it struck even a quarter of an inch higher, or more, it would have gouged out my eye—and very possibly have entered my brain. As it was, it made only a nasty cut, of which I still bear the scar.

During the Civil War, my horse stumbled and threw me. I fractured my nose and the outer wall of the frontal sinus. I also knocked out seven good teeth, so that ever since I was about 25 years old, I have had to wear artificial dentures.

While in Florida with Dora, many years ago, in jumping on board a sailboat, I received a severe blow over the left tibia. In a few days an abscess developed, and I had to return to Philadelphia, where Dr. Taylor opened it. I was kept in bed in my own hospital for several days.

In 1886, while Florence and I were riding before breakfast, in Osterville on Cape Cod, again my horse stumbled and threw me. I broke my right clavicle and a couple of ribs. I went at once to the Massachusetts General Hospital. (I arrived the day that Dr. Maurice Richardson opened a stomach, for the first time, and removed an artificial denture from the oesophagus. The patient recovered.) While I was there, my dear friends, Stephen Caldwell, Phillips Brooks, Dr. Bowditch, and dear Professor Bigelow all came to see me, in spite of the weather, with temperatures in the 90s. I did not know that I had so many friends, as was shown by the daily flowers (in fact, flowers in such profusion that Corinne, who was with me every day, sent the flowers of the preceding day into the wards). As a result of this accident, I learned to write with my left hand, almost—but not quite—achieving ambidexterity.

Ten years later, in the Keene Valley of the Adirondacks, I fell from a bicycle and seriously injured my left knee. I was laid up in bed for some weeks with a large effusion into the joint and had to wear a plaster cast for about three months. Occasionally, I still feel a twinge when I twist the joint a little, in coming down stairs.

On Sunday, January 9th, 1898, I made a post mortem on a patient who had died from a sudden perforation of the stomach. There was a lot of pus in the peritoneal cavity. As I was sewing up the incision, I barely pricked my right thumb. I washed it and sucked it and thought no more about it. By seven o'clock, my thumb began to pain me. I could not sleep and finally went down to my office and called Dr. Taylor on the telephone. By the time he came, about two or three o'clock in the morning, I had dressings and instruments, and so forth, ready. He laid open the thumb, under local anesthesia, swabbed it out with pure carbolic acid, and gave me a hypodermic injection of a quarter-grain of morphine. I had little sleep, however, and by eight o'clock, my temperature was 105°! I was laid up for three or four weeks—and barely escaped with my life.

In Burma, late in 1901, the horse I was riding stumbled and threw me (yet again!). The accident occurred on a rather steep hillside, and I rolled over and over for perhaps twenty or thirty feet, until I was stopped by a tree. I was amused by the fact that as I rolled, I recalled the anecdote of the learned butler who fell downstairs and replied, when asked by his master what was going on, "'Tis I, sir, rolling rapidly."[2] I broke my *left* clavicle, thus restoring the natural equilibrium.

In 1908, on my return from an absence of eighteen months in Europe, as I was going to bed, at about eleven o'clock, I stepped into a dimly lighted adjoining room and stumbled over a pail full of water. Involuntarily throwing out my arms to save myself, I promptly dislocated my right shoulder as my right hand hit the wall. Chalmers DaCosta immediately came around and reduced the dislocation by manipulation, but even today, while I have wonderful free movement of the joint, I have pain or sudden or extreme movement.

In 1916, I fell on the hard pavement and fractured the surgical neck of my left arm. Fortunately, complete healing took place, and, except being hampered in the extreme elevation of my arms, it is as good as ever.

I round out an even dozen, not exactly by a twelfth accident but rather by the serious abdominal section of 1910, described in my "Reminiscences for My Children."

A FALSE — BUT ALL TOO REAL — ALARM

(I feel such admiration and gratitude for and to Florence and Dora, for their splendid conduct in the summer of 1910, that I want especially to record it here.)

Early in July of 1910, Florence and I sailed for Glasgow. Dora had gone to Switzerland to climb in the Alps.[3] I took my auto and chauffeur with me, and it was arranged that Florence would stay with me until the end of August, when she would return, via Montreal, to attend the Conservation Congress in St. Paul; and that Dora would join me, a few days before Florence was to sail, and continue with me until sailing home from Bremen, on the eighteenth of October. Our more complete itinerary included a visit to Edinburgh, where we were to stay with Dr. George Gibson; then a visit in the Highlands with Dr. Peter MacLaren, followed by a leisurely motor trip down to London.

After a visit with [my nephew] Herbert and [his wife] Hattie, we planned to motor through Somersetshire in search of relics of my mother's family, the Budds. Then on to Penzance and Land's End; then Wales, Holland, and Germany, where I wanted to visit universities I had never seen, in Göttingen, Jena, Halle, and Leipzig, reaching Berlin by the first of October. (I was the delegate of the American Philosophical Society to the centennial celebration of the founding of the University of Berlin.)

Prior to the trip, I had attended the commencement at Brown (and the meeting of the Corporation) and from there went with Florence to visit Margaret's camp at Weekapaug. I intended to stay there until July, when Florence and I would sail, with the auto. But early in June, I began to suffer from diarrhea, without any apparent cause, and it did not yield to the usual remedies. I had no pain and did not feel sick. I had my usual appetite and my temperature was normal, but the diarrhea persisted, especially at night.

I left Weekapaug and consulted Fitz, in Boston, then later, just before we sailed, Janeway, in New York. Neither of them made a physical examination but both prescribed medicines, which I took without benefit. On the ship, Dr. Collins, of Providence, was my roommate, but he could throw no light on my continuing trouble.

In Edinburgh, I asked Dr. Gibson to make a physical examination, and he discovered a tumor in the lower left abdomen. I gave up our planned visit to Dr. MacLaren and motored directly to London, where I consulted Dr. Hale White, to whom Gibson had written. He too discovered the obscure tumor and said that at my age such a tumor might be very serious. He advised a sigmoidoscope examination—under ether, if necessary—and consultation with a surgeon, to both of which I immediately consented. The examination was made the next day by a Mr. Mummery, at a nursing home (without ether, as the pain was bearable), and while they made no comment to me, I learned later that Dr. White had told Florence, in the adjoining room, that I had an inoperable cancer of the bowel.

Naturally, the first question she asked was whether or not her father should be told the truth. They advised against undeceiving me, for to tell me would be to spoil my whole summer, causing me to give up our Berlin trip and go home or to lose all heart in the Berlin celebration. And even if I had wished to go home at once, it would have been difficult, if not impossible, to get berths, as the steamers were all full. Moreover, I eventually would spontaneously and inevitably discover the truth.

Meanwhile, Florence and Dr. White, at her suggestion (but without a word to me), wrote to Dr. Will Mayo, explaining the facts as they understood them. Florence also wrote fully to Dora and to Corinne and Margaret at home.

Dr. White and Mr. Mummery were kindness itself, and I appreciated their good intentions. As a surgeon, however, I feel that no one in the presence of such an obscure tumor (discovered only by sigmoidoscopy and a digital examination) ought to say positively that the case is inoperable. An abdominal section is the only way to reach a positive and correct opinion, as was later proved. Any surgeon can easily make a mistake in diagnosis, in such an obscure case, but to avoid a mistake in treatment, it is absolutely necessary to open the abdomen.

Florence and I left London as planned and motored down to Penzance, where Dora joined us. Florence left on schedule for St. Paul, and Dora and I continued the tour, sailing for home following the celebration in Berlin.

All through this period, for nearly two months, my two dear girls never once, by word or deed, by silence or unusual sympathy, by a tear or a sad face, betrayed that they knew I was fatally ill and should be spared to them for only a few months. I went along as gay as a bird, free from pain and anxiety, supposing that the obscure tumor had disappeared as a result of the free purgation I had had, and that the supposed "tumor" had been only an accumulation of feces.

How their hearts must have ached, and how constantly the joyous face was masking an anxious heart! Never can I be grateful enough to them, or appreciative enough of their self-effacement. I often think of their lonely hours of grief. "It was a hideous nightmare. Let's forget all about it," said Florence, a few days ago.

At the beginning of October, as a result of a secret conversation with Dora, I was examined by von Eiselsberg, of Vienna (who happened to be in Berlin). Up to this point, I did not suspect the truth. He found the same tumor as the others and said that at my age, "one must be suspicious as to its character." I agreed completely and was then quite convinced that the overwhelming odds were that it was cancer.

Within an hour of this consultation, I wrote to Mayo, asking for an exploratory operation, as soon as I could get to Rochester. We reached home on October 25th, and with coolness and an absence of fear or distress that even surprised me, I made some changes in my will and otherwise set my house in order in all earthly matters. Never did I feel so completely as then that God was my support—and was so very near to me. I was walking in the valley of the shadow of death, but I feared no evil.

Before the operation, I told Mayo that when he opened me, he had carte blanche to do anything needed, and that unless its removal involved a risk that no prudent surgeon would take, the tumor was to be *removed*. I would far rather die from the operation than die after months of suffering, a burden to myself and my children.

With Florence and Dora, I arrived in Rochester on November 7th and was operated on two days later. The tumor proved to be caused by a diverticulitis and was removed. When I awoke from the blessed sleep of ether, my dear Corinne was beside me and Margaret was in Rochester as well. They too had shown the same self-control as Florence and Dora, for they also had believed, during my previous week at home, that I was fatally ill. They never once flinched or by anxious sympathy tended to unnerve me. What a proud and happy father I am to have four such splendid daughters!

The day after I was operated on, I had only hot water to sip. The next day, I was allowed albumen water. Now if you could devise more tasteless stuff than that, you would deserve a leather medal, so I asked if I might have some albumenized milk. I had used it for years in my own surgical work and knew its virtues. This gave me great comfort. Naturally, the nurses discussed it among themselves, as it was new to them.[4] A patient in the adjoining room, hearing of it, asked if she could have some, and her doctor agreed. Her nurse was not able to ask my nurse (who was out) but went to the refrigerator and, finding the bottle with my name on it, poured out a generous dose. When her patient took a sip of it, she said, "Throw it out! If that's what Dr. Keen calls good, I pity him." When my nurse returned and heard the story, she laughingly explained that, as I had emptied the bottle during the night, she decided to wash it out thoroughly and had filled it with soapsuds.

I had but three days of bearable, though disagreeable, pain. I was sitting up, and out of bed, in twelve days. I left the hospital in three weeks and have been entirely well ever since. As the tumor was not malignant, there is no fear of its return. The Mayos said that the case was rare: Mine was only the sixteenth they had ever operated on.

We are all most grateful to our Heavenly Father and sing a thankful *Te Deum*.[5]

A KEEN REACTION TO LOBSTER

The method for testing what foods will agree or disagree is roughly as follows. First, extracts are made of the nitrogenous compounds in various foods, both animal and vegetable. The epidermis is then scraped off from the patient's skin over a half-inch spot, usually on the arm, but not so deep as to draw blood. With an aseptic piece of smooth wood, the extracts from the various foods are gently rubbed over this surface. If the food is agreeable, there is no reaction. If not, the spot reddens within a minute or two, and that is a food the patient should avoid.

About 1922 or 1923, I asked Dr. Kolmer, of the Graduate School of the University of Pennsylvana, to test my reactions. He applied the test at twelve places on each arm, twenty-four in all. Nothing happened. All of the twenty-four foods tested surely agreed with me. A few days later, I asked him to test me for lobster extract, and the redness appeared almost immediately. I thus knew that I should avoid lobster.

I had eaten lobster a few times, but had had to abandon it for many years because a piece as large as two fingers was the quickest emetic (after five or ten minutes) I could take. This seemed very curious, for all other shellfish—oysters, crabs, snails, clams, mussels—agreed with me. Indeed, I was accustomed to say that there were only two things I could not eat, lobster and ten-penny nails.

In Christiana, Norway, in October of 1865, I was visiting some of the hospitals, and friends invited me to dinner. When lobster appeared, I said to myself, "Here we are with the ocean at our feet. Surely the lobster is absolutely fresh, and Norwegian lobster may act differently from American lobster."

Soon after I had eaten a large piece, I was nauseated and had to leave the table four times during the evening, much to my mortification.

For fifty-eight years I had never eaten a particle of lobster, yet the idiosyncracy persisted.

So far as I know, we are not aware of the reason for such a curious personal reaction from one shellfish, in spite of the fact that all others agree with me perfectly.

MY PERCEIVED LOSS OF HEIGHT
AND IDENTITY IN MY OLD AGE

For life insurance purposes, etc., I frequently have had my height and weight measured. My height was consistently five feet four and a half inches. After I had passed the insurable age, I had no occasion to measure my height, but one day early in 1920, I had it measured out of mere curiosity. I had lost three inches and now measured only five feet *one* and a half inches,[6] and thus discovered the reason why I had to stand on tiptoe to reach the lights in the office chandelier. But even at that lower height, I surpassed Napoleon, who measured, I believe, only five feet, and was known as the "Little Corporal."

I mentioned it at the table, one day when the Freemans were with us, and said it was evidently due to the compression of the invertebral cartileges. "No," said Walter, my loyal oldest grandchild, "it is due to the weight of the ideas in your head."

When Jack Freeman, as stroke of the Yale varsity crew, and Norman, as stroke of the "combination" [i.e., the lightweight] crew, beat the corresponding Harvard crews, in June of 1921, I wrote them that I had gained an inch in height—"an inch that I desperately needed." I told them how L. Clarke Davis, long the distinguished editor of the *Public Ledger*, asserted that he was described in his early life as the husband of Rebecca Harding Davis and in his later life as the father of Richard Harding Davis, adding that now, when my name was mentioned, people would say, "Keen? Keen? Oh yes, the grandfather of those two Yale men who, in 1921. . ."

RETIRED?

One of the faculty of the Jefferson, more inclined to "slippered ease" than to hard work, I am told, said, "Yes, Keen has returned to make us all miserable by his restless activity." As an evidence of my good health and endurance at eighty-four and a half years of age, I may testify as follows.

While at Seal Harbor, Mt. Desert, in August of 1921, I was called away on an urgent case. I left the hotel in an auto at 7:45 A.M. and returned at 8:15 P.M. We lost half an hour by a blowout. Of the twelve hours, I spent four at luncheon and in a prolonged and thorough consultation with the patient's doctor. In the remaining eight hours, I had traveled two hundred and forty miles.

When I returned, I was as fresh as when I started and spent the evening with friends in the parlors of the hotel till ten o'clock.[7]

POST-MORTEM CARE

A Grim Proposal

Soon after we moved into 1729 Chestnut Street, in 1871, a neighborhood undertaker, who evidently appreciated my abilities more than the general public, according to my Visiting Book, called on me and, with much bowing and scraping, requested the privilege of leaving some of his professional business cards on the table in my waiting room. It was doubtless his desire to cheer up my infrequent and desponding patients by the assurance of gentle and appropriate care in preparing for and conducting the expected, or at least the possible, obsequies.

An Enticing Suggestion

A few days after the celebration of my 84th birthday had been in all the papers, I received a beautiful circular, with fine half-tone illustrations, containing an invitation which, in view of my age, seemed most appropriate. It was a folder from "The _____ Burial Company," and the first of the half-tone cuts was of a lovely auto-hearse. The rear double doors were open, disclosing a cool, clean, and inviting interior, while on each side stood a suitably garbed attendant, politely suggesting that I be carried in, for *ex natura rei*, as my old professor of Mathematics at Brown used to say, it would be quite impossible for me to enter on my own.

I could not refrain from replying to such a kind proposition. I thanked the company for their gentle hint that if I was not already dead, I surely ought to be very soon, adding that, "as I have some other plans in view at present, I must decline the offer."

A Curious Statement

I was soon involved in Act III of this continuing drama, when I noticed an ad in the *Weekly Roster of Medical Meetings in Philadelphia* in which the publisher was making a plea for "Our Advertisers: Their Products and Services."

The first "service" was in commendation of cremation, supported by "some of those in the [medical] profession who have expressed their preference for cremation and *"whose desires to be cremated have been fulfilled"* at the crematory. Among those who had been declared officially to have been cremated I found my own name.

I pinched myself to find out whether I consisted wholly of ambulant ashes. I seemed to be real flesh and blood, but there it stood: My desire to be cremated had been fulfilled. However, printed statements (such as many of those of my friends the antivivisectionists) are not always to be taken at their face value, and I concluded that I will continue to eat and drink, and at some suitable time in the future, I will be cremated again.

Recrossing the Bar

Towards the end of January 1922, I received a letter from a gentleman in British Columbia asking for certain information. It was addressed "To the son of the late Dr. W.W. Keen." I replied, giving the information sought, and added, "I beg to inform you that my sons are all daughters and I am yours truly, the late W.W. Keen."

9

—••❧ ❦ ☙••—

Medical Progress

PAIN

THE ABILITY TO ENDURE PAIN varies greatly. The more highly civilized races do not bear pain nearly as well as those lower in the scale of development. So too, man in general feels pain far more acutely than the lower animals. A horse with a leg so badly mangled that he had to be destroyed has been known to hobble around and quietly crop the grass as if nothing had happened, in the time interval before a suitable weapon could be obtained.

Many missionary surgeons have commented on the fact that Asiatics and Africans, even after extensive operations, suffer little from shock, which is almost always found after operations on Europeans and Americans.

One of my patients needed the removal of a considerable portion of a rib just over the heart, because the bone was irreparably diseased (or, in fact, dead) and threatened further mischief. On account of a serious valvular disease of his heart, I gave him cocaine, instead of ether or chloroform, but he was one of those rare patients on whom cocaine had little effect. He struggled so violently that I feared the possibility of my knife's penetrating his chest and puncturing his heart. I chose to run the lesser risk of using ether to avoid the greater risk of possible chloroform shock to his nervous system. The operation was then successfully finished, and he recovered nicely.

Observing this operation was Dr. Thom, surgeon at a mission hospital in Mardin, Turkey, who told me that if a Kurd had needed such an operation, he would have told him to lie down on the table and would have proceeded with the operation, giving no thought to cocaine or ether. The patient would never have budged or uttered a cry or moan.

Another man, exceptional in America, illustrated this same stoicism and indifference to pain. He was a man of about thirty who came to consult me, one evening, about a lump on his back. On examination, it proved to be a fatty tumor as large as two fists. When I told him that the only way to deal with it was to cut it out, he instantly threw himself down on the lounge and told me, laconically, to go ahead. I asked him if he didn't want ether, he said, "No, go ahead."

As soon as I could make my antiseptic preparations, I "went ahead." The incision was about six to eight inches long, and the tumor, by reason of fibrous adhesions, required considerable cutting—and not a little force—to be excised. He never moved a muscle or made a sound. It was more like operating on a cadaver than on a living, sentient human being. I sewed up the wound with silver wire (this was a good many years ago), carefully dressed it, and told him that if he had any pain, or if any bleeding showed through the dressing, that he was to come and see me in the morning. I added that he should come in to see me on the next day, and again a few days later, so that I could remove the stitches. Producing an encouraging roll of bills from his trouser pocket, he asked, "How shall I pay you?" As a young and impecunious doctor, I quickly recalled that a bird in the hand is worth two in the bush, and instead of suggesting that he wait until he was well, when he could pay me for the operation and any later care, I mentioned an amount. He willingly paid this and left the office. Who removed the stitches I do not know, but I never saw him again!

The introduction of anesthesia has, happily, abolished pain. Older surgeons have often described to me the horrors of the dreadful earlier days I never saw. As seen in pictures of the surgeries, a patient bent his knees and clasped his ankles, the ankles and hands being securely bound together by bandages. He was also kept in comparative quiet by strong assistants. His uncontrollable struggles and his screams must have been something terrible to see and hear. Meantime, as the means for controlling hemorrhage were very imperfect, the operating rooms were a veritable bloody shambles.

The careful and painstaking, long-lasting operations of today were impossible. In the first place, human nerves could not endure one or two hours of terrible pain. Also, the patient's struggles absolutely prevented the kind of fine and delicate operations that are now so common. The best surgeon (and one who was held in the greatest repute) could slash off an arm or leg, or extract a stone from a bladder, in five, ten, or fifteen seconds less than any other operator available. This developed great dexterity, but it was inconsistent with the exact and careful surgery of today. Before 1846, the stress was on speed; now it is on safety and success.

ANESTHESIA

One constantly sees, in the antivivisectionist literature, doubts cast on the absence of pain sensation in animals, because (according to them) the anesthesia is incomplete. They also state that so long as the corneal reflex exists, the animal may suffer pain.

Both of these assertions are untrue.

Everyone knows that the eye is exceedingly sensitive to the slightest touch. This is necessary for its protection. The instant the cornea is touched, the eyelids close. In fact, we can't keep them open. Nay, more: Even if you tell a person that you will aim a blow at his eye but will not actually touch him, he can't help closing the eyelids when the simulated blow is delivered, even though he trusts you completely and knows that you will not strike him.

This involuntary closing of the eyelids when touched is called the corneal reflex. When the etherizer wants to know if the patient is completely anesthetized, so that he will not move or struggle while the tissues are being cut, he lightly touches the cornea, and if the lids do not close, he knows that the pain of the knife will not be felt. In many cases this test is even too delicate. I have often begun to operate before this reflex was totally extinguished, and yet those patients did not struggle. When questioned after the operation, they said that they had suffered no pain. If this is true of man, whose nervous system is much more acute than that of other animals, the retention of the corneal reflex in animals is quite consistent with the absence of pain.

Anesthesia may be incomplete, and the patient may struggle—even violently—and yet no pain is felt. Very recently, in a case of an injury to the elbow, I was obliged to have nitrous oxide administered several times, while I forcibly flexed and extended the patient's forearm so as to prevent a "stiff" elbow. The patient struggled slightly and showed other *apparent* evidence of feeling pain (she groaned loudly, once, and writhed to such a degree as almost to fall out of the chair), yet on no occasion did she suffer any pain.

Such muscular struggles are frequent in the early stage of excitement from ether; many surgeons prepare for them by securing their patients to the operating table, in various ways. Most patients go quietly to sleep; a moderate number struggle, more or less; and a few are *very* difficult to control. Even those who do not struggle while being etherized will sometimes move when the knife first cuts the skin. They are completely etherized, but in order for the surgeon to be able to do careful, exact work, they must be anesthetized more deeply, in order that all muscular movement except respiration and circulation is eliminated.

My friend Dr. Weir, of New York, tells an amusing story of a patient he was once etherizing for Dr. Gurdon Buck. Touching the eye and finding no corneal reflex, he said that the patient was ready. At the first touch of the knife, the patient drew the leg sharply away. "A little more ether, Dr. Weir," said Buck. Again, after the same test, "the patient is ready now," and again, the leg was drawn away.

"Can't you give him enough ether so that I can operate, sir?"

"But sir, the corneal reflex is entirely gone."

"Which eye did you test?"

"The right eye, sir."

"Oh, that's a glass eye."

A patient is sometimes subject to the wildest delusions. No prudent surgeon will anesthetize a woman patient except in the presence of others.[1]

The same rule should apply in the case of male patients, because they sometimes have the delusion that they are being attacked by the etherizer and will turn furiously on him.

I never transgressed this rule but once, and that was early in my professional life. It was a lesson I never forgot. The patient needed only an instantaneous cut of the knife to open an abcess, and so I had expected to do it without an anesthetic, as the discomfort of the ether would really be worse than the pain of the knife. But the patient insisted on having ether, and as no assistant was available, I gave it to him myself. He had taken only a few whiffs when he was seized with the delusion that I was going to do something he didn't want done. He tried to get off the bed, while I tried to keep him there and continue the ether. He was several inches taller than I, and far more muscular, and he flung me aside. He grabbed a chair and raised it over his head, threatening to crush my skull with it. I could not possibly hold him. Agility had to replace strength, and for a few moments, we had a mighty lively time of it. Fortunately, he had had only a little ether, and as the muscular exertion quickened his respiration, he blew out the ether and inhaled enough oxygen to revive himself. Had it not been so, these lines might never have been written.

On another occasion, at St. Mary's Hospital, a young, splendidly developed fireman had been injured. Anesthesia was essential for me to be able to make a thorough examination to determine the extent of his injuries. Present were two residents, the orderly, the etherizer, and myself.

For a considerable time, the patient was perfectly quiet. We were standing to one side and discussing the possible diagnosis, so that the etherizer and the orderly were the only ones beside the table. The patient suddenly began to struggle, in an effort to escape from the etherizer. He rose up, flung the ether cone into the corner, brushed aside the etherizer, and tried to get at me. Fortunately, the orderly had been behind the patient as he sat up and was able to grasp him around the waist and hold him—though with difficulty. The man was so intent on reaching me that he didn't notice how or why he couldn't get off the table. In a moment, all of us were on him and held him down till the effect of the ether had worn off.

We sent for four of his fellow firemen, meantime tying each wrist and ankle to a table leg and passing a broad band around his body and under the table top. The firemen held his arms and legs, and the orderly held his head, while the ether was begun again. The same scene was reenacted. In spite of the thongs and the men holding him, he was so strong that it seemed he would either break his bonds as easily as Sampson broke those of the Philistines or reduce the table to firewood. Never before or since have I seen such strength in a man. (The only comparable exhibition of strength I have ever seen in a woman was in a case of puerperal convulsions in a rather frail and delicate woman, who almost overcame four ordinary men.) Our fireman finally succumbed and lay as quietly as a child while we examined him, fortunately finding only a passing injury.

One of the students in my Jefferson clinic brought in his father, a clergyman, for an operation on a small cancer of his lower lip. When his turn was near, I told an assistant to inject cocaine, a local anesthetic, into the lip. While waiting for it to take effect, I went on with another brief operation. The rising seats of the amphitheater allowed space for small rooms under the uppermost seats where patients were anesthetized and otherwise prepared for operation. Naturally, any loud noise in these rooms could be heard by the several hundreds of students usually present for the clinic.

Just before the prior operation had been completed, I heard some loud outcries, apparently from my clerical patient being prepared. As these continued, and increased in vehemence, I asked my assistant to finish the operation at hand and went into the room under the seats. I found that the clergyman belonged to the Church Militant, for he had cleared out the etherizing room and was monarch of all he surveyed. Recognizing me, he shouted, "They have made me drunk, Dr. Keen . . . and . . . I . . . am a . . . *Prohibitionist!*" One could sympathize with his indigation, while at the same time not wonder at the very audible laughter from the benches.

This was only one instance of the occasional effect of cocaine (and, indeed of most anesthetics), which can produce a state of excitement that is sometimes intense, and may even be dangerous.

I have often looked at patients in the deep sleep of ether and wondered at the temerity of Long and Morton, and the other early anesthetizers. A patient lies there absolutely motionless. Lift the arm or the leg and it falls like lead. Prick him, pinch him, strike him, cut him; he shows no evidence of feeling. He seems to be dead, except that he continues to breathe and his heart has not ceased to beat. But how soon will he wake up? In fact, will he ever wake up? And if he does not, may I not be adjudged guilty? These and similar questions must have thronged the minds of the pioneer anesthetizers, and they occasionally come into my own mind, even at this late date. Verily, it took enormous courage, in 1846 and '47, to give ether or chloroform. What if the first public case, in the Massachusetts General Hospital, had died on the table?

We would not dare to do today as they did then. We use anesthesia on human beings only after repeated, painstaking, and successful investigation of the immediate and long-range effects on animals. Sir James Simpson's first experiments with chloroform on himself and his friends, in 1847 (and so dramatically described by his daughter in the January 1894 issue of *Century Magazine*), were foolhardy and might easily have become lethal. Indeed, he narrowly escaped death when Sir Lyon Playfair refused to give him a newly discovered liquid until it had been tried first on two rabbits. (Simpson had wanted to inhale it immediately.) The rabbits were successfully anesthetized but expired soon afterwards from the after-effects of the poison.

Chloroform, about six times as dangerous as ether, is much more agreeable to inhale and is quicker in its effect. It seldom produces excitement, and it requires a far smaller quantity to produce insensibility. Simpson's immense reputation (and the slight esteem in which American science was held, in 1846), and the virtues just recounted, made chloroform *the* European anesthetic for many years. Under certain circumstances, we are still obliged to use it in preference to ether. Only a large body of statistics showing that ether was far less dangerous finally induced many German surgeons to routinely use it.

One single, sudden death on the operating table delayed its use in Germany for many years, thus probably costing many lives. Dr. Sands, a distinguished New York surgeon, was visiting the Berlin clinic of his friend Professor Langenbeck, probably in the late '60s. He so vigorously urged the greater safety of ether on his German friend that Langenbeck finally proposed that his American friend himself should administer ether at his clinic. To the consternation of everyone, and especially Sands, the patient promptly died on the table. If it could kill so easily, even in such skillful hands, the Germans were very naturally wary of it.

The danger even of ether has led to the most diligent search for safe, as well as efficient, anesthetics. Several have been introduced, but after extensive trials they have been found to be just as dangerous, or counterbalanced by other disadvantages, and thus have been either abandoned or used very sparingly. Nitrous oxide is the safest of all, by far, its mortality rate being only about one in two hundred thousand cases (versus one in sixteen thousand for ether, and one in two thousand five hundred for chloroform). For very brief operations, it is the anesthetic of choice. But until lately, it could be used only for a very few minutes without in turn becoming a threat to life. Recently, its combination with oxygen has made it far more useful for even very long operations, and eventually it may become the most widely used of all.

Local anesthetics, which abolish sensation only in the areas where they are injected, have begun to play an important role in surgery, with patients, though conscious, unable to feel any pain whatsoever, even during such serious operations as amputations or the removal of tumors.

Spinal anesthesia, the injection by lumbar puncture of various anesthetics into the sheath of the spinal cord, is also of increasing value, in the small porportion of cases in which neither chloroform nor ether can be safely used. All nerves below the point of the puncture are temporarily deprived of their normal ability to transmit pain, yet the patient remains completely conscious.

But the ideal anesthetic does not yet exist. I certainly hope and believe that it will be found before very long. It will *not* be an agent which produces insensibility to pain and leaves the patient conscious. It will render the patient unconscious, but *without danger to life or later health.*[2]

There are few operations done in which sudden emergencies, especially from hemorrhage, do not occur, sometimes very grave emergencies which instantly demand all the resources of the most experienced surgeons. Naturally, such emergencies produce some bustle and stir among the assistants, as well as sharp, quick commands from the operator. For the nervous or timid patient, to be conscious and aware of such incidents can be demoralizing, possibly producing a depressing shock or even sudden, restless, apprehensive movement, which could change a minor accident into a dangerous one.

The controversy over who should have the credit for the discovery of anesthesia was long and bitter.[3] Oliver Wendell Holmes was the only one whose wit enlivened the quarrel. When it was proposed to erect the Ether Monument, in the Boston Public Garden, how to word the inscription was an embarrassing question. The friends of Morton and Jackson were, each party, clamorous for its own hero. When they consulted Holmes, he said, "Nothing is simpler: Put up your shaft with the name of Morton on one side and Jackson on the other, and in between, the motto, 'To Ether.'"

Brains From Afar

When two of my daughters and I were on our way from Madras to Calcutta, near the end of 1901, we had on board General Sir Henry Ellis, Lady Ellis, and several of his staff including Maj. Gen. Richard Wace, director-general of Ordnance in India, on a visit of inspection to the Andaman and Nicobar Islands, which were a long way out of our direct route. I confess to a very dim knowledge of the geography of these islands, before this unexpected visit, but learned that a British penal colony is located on the Andamans. We did not land, but anchored off Port Blair, the capital, for quite a while, during which General Ellis and his party went ashore.

While in Calcutta, during the Christmas season, we were invited to all the public functions of the court, owing to the kindness of my old friend Dr. Harvey, Surgeon to the Viceroy of India. One evening, there was a large dinner party of perhaps fifty-odd, at the Government House. After dinner, we spent an hour or more in conversation. Lady Curzon was especially kind to us, as fellow Americans, and we had quite a long discussion as to the safety of our going to Persia. By Lord Curzon's advice, we went and were well repaid.

A year later, after our return home, Dr. Spitzka, the Professor of Anatomy at the Jefferson, happened to say to me one day, "What a pity it is that several races of mankind are dying out and their brains have never been examined," and went on to specify the dying races on the Andaman and Nicobar Islands.

"I'm not sure but that I can help you," I said, and told him of Lord Curzon's kindness to us the previous year, adding that I would write to him and seek his aid. In due time, Curzon replied to my request, saying that he had forwarded my letter to the prison surgeon at Port Blair with instructions to do his best to fulfill my request.

A letter from the Port Blair surgeon followed, in which he explained the serious obstacle: the superstitious native fear of burying a mutilated body. But he also asked for instructions, in case he should succeed in getting the brains.

Spitzka wrote out detailed directions, and about a year later, two brains, one of each race, were received in good order. He made a careful examination and presented the results in a paper read before the American Philosophical Society.

JEFFERSON MEDICAL COLLEGE AT 90

[My speech to the J.M.C. Alumni]

1825 . . . 1860 . . . 1915. What do these three dates mean? The first is the date of the founding of the Jefferson Medical College.[4] The second is the year I entered her halls as a student. The third is the present year of grace. In 1860, the Jefferson was only thirty-five years old. From 1860 until now, I have been connected with the college, as student, alumnus, lecturer, professor, and emeritus, for fifty-five years, or almost two-thirds of its entire existence.

In 1860, the faculty consisted only of the "sacred seven," plus one solitary demonstrator in Anatomy. There are now forty-nine active professors of various grades, and a hundred demonstrators and other assistants. Then there was only one laboratory, and now there are fifteen. In those days, one could walk right in from the anvil or the plow and after two so-called years walk out a full-fledged doctor. I say "so-called years" because all medical schools in those days spurned the Ptolemaic, the Julian, and the Gregorian calendars: they had their own. It might be called the Hippocratic (or perhaps hypocritic) calendar, in which the year consisted of five months, with a liberal allowance for official holidays, in addition to those required when our numerous grandparents had to be buried.

A capital operation was a rarity, and on each such momentous occasion (which was rumored for days), there was a great rush for the front seats. The blasé student of today hardly hastens his step for anything less than a suture of the heart or a hip joint.

The undergraduates were much less studious than those of today, and the number of roisterers, who often had differences of opinions with the police, was much larger. Scarcely a week went by when some member of the faculty was not routed out of bed to go bail for some student offender.

I remember a story told me by Dr. Weir Mitchell of a young man from Texas who wished to enter as one of his office students. (Every student had a preceptor, in those days.) After some conversation as to his education, Dr. Mitchell innocently asked him if he had any accomplishments. Whereupon the young man drew out a bowie knife and let fly, deftly planting the knife blade between two panes of glass near the top of the window. Mitchell complimented him on his high, if not to say accurate, aims but advised him to enter a more war-like office than his own, perhaps one in which students were prepared for the Army or Navy.

The first year was wasted, to a large extent, but the second year had to be one of more serious work. There was no examination at the end of the first, but what passed for an examination really did take place at the end of the second.

At the end of my first year, I coached a second-year student in Anatomy, Physiology, and Surgery. I sprinkled over him the thimbleful of knowledge I possessed, and some of it must have soaked in, for he passed.

This was the way in which alumni were made, half a century ago. I am not, as you perceive, a *laudator temporis acti*. I believe that the present is far better than the past and that if our honored ancestors were to return, they would gladly recognize the enormous progress we have made.

The only wonder is how the men of my time ever amounted to anything. The explanation, which will apply to you in turn, is simple: From the day of our graduation until now, we have had to work our fingernails off; we have had to "scorn delights and live laborious days"[5] (aye, and laborious nights as well); we have had to read books and journals (in French and German as well), and to card-catalog what we have read; and we have had to take full notes of our cases.

We have had to remember Bacon's dictum that "reading maketh a full man, conference a ready man, and writing an exact man."[6] From writing brief articles we graduated to the level of longer essays, finally coming to write systematic treatises or textbooks. The moment that, by study, observation, and experience, you know more than other doctors about a disease, symptom, or operation, in that moment you owe a duty to our profession—and to suffering humanity—to publish that knowledge. But never write or speak unless you have something to say that is *worth saying*, and then when you have said it, STOP.

Thus far, I have described the way in which our medical colleges made alumni, and how the alumni of those early years made up for the defects in our education. What has been the harvest? What have our alumni done?

Homer's catalog of the ships has always seemed to me an example of useful dullness. Any extended list of Jefferson graduates, including those identified with her as teachers, would be even more tedious. I therefore shall recite only a short list of the more eminent alumni, omitting, with two exceptions, the living. Each name will call up some memories, especially among those of you who have passed the half-century mark. I shall not list them in chronological order, but in the order in which their names occur to me.

George McClellan (the founder)

George McClellan (his grandson)

Nathan R. Smith

Joseph Pancoast

Thomas D. Mütter

Robley Dunglison

John K. and S. Weir Mitchell

Samuel D. and Samuel W. Gross

J. Marion Sims

Robert Battey

Levi C. Lane

Daniel Brainard

William Goodell

Washington L. Atlee

Thomas Addis Emmet

Charles D. Meigs

J. M. DaCosta

John H. Brinton

Roberts Bartholow

Only a score, and yet, how much they suggest, and how much they did! The number of our alumni who have founded other medical colleges (including Rush) and who have taught—and continue to teach—is too large to recount.

Two names among the living I feel I must speak of: Thomas W. Jackson and Victor G. Heiser, both students of my own.

You all know of the sad plight of Serbia, now involved in a third war in as many years and suffering from a severe epidemic of typhus fever, that age-old foe of armies often more deadly than the enemy. But when did men of our guild ever flee in craven fear before danger? Eighty-odd years ago, Gross hurried *into* New York when everyone else was hurrying *out*, because the cholera was daily slaying hundreds of victims. So now another graduate of the Jefferson, Thomas Jackson—his very name is an inspiration—has hastened with other doctors and nurses to aid that little nation in its heroic fight. God grant that they may win, without themselves falling victim.

Victor Heiser has had a fine record as Director of Health of the Philippines but is about to leave government service to undertake work for the Rockefeller Foundation, with no less a goal than to eradicate leprosy around the world. And I believe he can do it.

This school, which has produced an honor roll embracing the names of those men as I have read, has more than justified its existence. It has occupied a high place among the beneficent institutions of the entire country.

But what of the thousands of graduates who are among the undistinguished alumni? Have I not a word in their behalf? Yea, verily.

You remember Lincoln's fabled saying that the Lord must have loved the plain people because he made so many of them. To play a distinguished role in life is given to only a few. But the Great Father in heaven does not judge by man's standards. Those thousands of alumni who, in their daily rounds of arduous duties, are faithful, tried, and true, cheering the faint-hearted, bringing health to the sick and the maimed, consoling the dying and the bereaved, endearing themselves to patients and their families by the kindly sympathy that only a doctor can give, leading pure and unselfish lives before their Maker, such men and women, whether their lives be long or short, have lived complete and worthy lives. They are sure of the welcoming, "Well done, thou good and faithful servant."

THE ANTIVIVISECTIONISTS
AND THE ANTIVACCINATIONISTS

I have been the militant foe of both for over fifty-five years.

About 1870, Mrs. Caroline Earle White, the recognized head of the cult [of antivivisection], called to see me in order to convert me to her views. We had a two-hour conversation in my office. Before she left, I told her that I had patiently listened to all of her arguments and was obliged to give her my frank decision. I said, "I regard it as a scientific, moral, and Christian duty to obstruct and nullify, to the extent of my influence and ability, your efforts to hinder experimental research on animals," and I have kept the faith for almost six decades.

As Paddy might say, "Whenever I see an A.V. head I hit it," and I hit it as hard as I can. I have met their lies with denial and most abundant proof. In season and out of season, I have been ever on the alert to find a joint in their armor which I could pierce, and my efforts have not been altogether in vain.

I can point out only a few of the world-wide benefits from the discoveries made in our laboratories and clinics, and I record here again my profound conviction that research by animal experimentation has been the main factor in all this beneficial progress. I have been lied about, malignantly attacked, and called all manner of names, but the abuse has had no more effect upon me than the proverbial water on a duck's back. I have felt, like Luther: *"Hier stehe ich; ich kann nicht anders."*

Bacteriology has disclosed to us the causes of many formerly obscure diseases: plague, syphilis, cerebro-spinal meningitis, cholera, typhoid, leprosy, pneumonia, and tetanus, among others. Even the filterable viruses, such as infantile paralysis, have yielded up their secrets. As a result, we have developed antitoxins with which to cure (or even prevent) many of the maladies.

With some diseases, such as cancer, hydrophobia, yellow fever, and smallpox, plus children's diseases such as scarlet fever, we still are in the dark as to the cause, but happily, with yellow fever and smallpox we have the means for preventing them.¹ In a number of diseases (yellow fever, the plague, sleeping sickness, and typhus, for example), we have discovered the medium for their diffusion by various insects, and therefore can largely, or even entirely, prevent their spread, thereby averting the terrible epidemics which have wasted the world in ages past.

No other American research organization has done so much for the relief of humanity as the Rockefeller Institute, whose Foundation has undertaken (or soon will undertake) campaigns encircling the earth to eradicate leprosy, yellow fever, and hookworm disease. They have every prospect of ultimate success. What can stir the imagination more than such a prospect! What possibly could do more for the whole human race! And yet a few fanatics rail at the founder of the Rockefeller philanthropies as though he were the embodiment of cruelty.

Typhoid fever, hitherto the scourge of armies and the autumnal reaper of death, has now been entirely banished from the U.S. Army, has been only a minor factor in the Great War, and is rapidly diminishing (and on its way to disappearance altogether) among our civilian population. If only the public would demand—and obtain—clean water and clean milk, and employ broadcast the antityphoid vaccination. What a glorious time this is in which to live and to witness (and still more, to help bring about) such splendid results of research!

Yet I am *not* an experimental researcher. When the first experimental laboratory was established by Andrew Carnegie, in 1884, in connection with Bellevue Hospital, my career as a clinical surgeon was well established, and I had neither the time, the tools, nor the opportunity to do research work. I was born too early.

I have not experimented on so much as a single mouse—or even a frog. What I have done is to clinically apply the wonderful discoveries of others to many of my patients—and to thank God for the saving of untold suffering and of many, many lives. As a teacher, I have multiplied myself in literally thousands of students who were indoctrinated in the practice of antiseptic and aseptic surgery and to the value of experimental research.

Yet the attacks on me by the A.V.'s have been multiple and malignant. I have been called a "fiend," and even an "arch-fiend," and my sainted mother has been cursed forever for ever having given birth "to such a monster of cruelty."

In order to share the results of experience and discovery, I have been an ardent and conscientious friend of experimental research. Having begun my study of surgery in 1860, and having practiced, up to 1876, the dreadful septic surgery, and then from 1876 to 1907, having arduously worked my way up to the light, and to the glorious surgery of the present day, I speak now as an expert and of my own personal knowledge when I say that I *know* that most of the progress of modern medicine and surgery has been due, directly or indirectly, to such experimental research.[8]

The most important subject which brought me in touch with President Taft was the International Humane Congress, which met in September of 1910, in Washington. He was the honorary president of the Congress. Knowing that the antivivisectionists would try to secure a pronouncement for their cause, I wrote to him, calling his attention to this and expressing the hope that he would not take such an anti-scientific and anti-humane attitude. He wrote me at once, enclosing a copy of the letter he had written to Dr. Stillman, president of the American Humane Association, saying that if the antivivisectionists were to attempt any such maneuver, he could not countenance it by continuing to act as honorary president. Dr. Stillman replied at once, giving a pledge that no discussion of vivisection would be permitted at the Congress. Thus, fortunately, I was able to block their game. Dr. Stillman was true to his promise, but in their journals, the antivivisectionists fumed and frothed at being thus muzzled.

Many of my letters and papers, and especially my book, *Animal Experimentation and Medical Progress*, set forth in detail many of my various attacks upon these enemies of both animals and mankind.[9]

Conversions were rare, but not unheard of. Dr. James Wilson was my first "office student" (with Dr. Harry Landis) and later my colleague on the faculty at Jefferson. One day, he asked me to see Mrs. K., who he feared had cancer of the breast. I knew that she, and especially her daughter, were bitter opponents of experimental medical research on animals, and I expressed my surprise. "Yes," he said, "when I proposed you as a surgical consultant, she said, 'Anybody but Dr. Keen,' but I was rather insistent, and she finally yielded."

I operated on her in my private hospital, at 1700 Summer Street, and in a few days she was well. Before she left, she asked to see me to say goodbye. We talked for quite a little time, in the course of which she herself told me of her "Anybody but Dr. Keen" remark. She then said she had changed that to "Nobody but Dr. Keen."

She immediately acceded to my suggestion that she show her gratitude by endowing a bed in the Jefferson Hospital and forthwith wrote out a check for five thousand dollars.

NURSING

[My graduation speech, Allentown Hospital, May 27, 1915]

When I received the kind invitation to address you, I hesitated a good deal, at first, for I am no longer as young as I was seventy-eight years ago, and I have so much to do that I have had practically no leisure.

But when I learned what you are doing here, and how extraordinarily well you are doing it, I said I will surely *make* the time to go, for I want to see the place and encourage those good people—including the trustees, the doctors, the nurses, and the community at large.

Your last report shows 181 beds and 1,869 patients, during the year; that is, over ten patients in each bed, though not simultaneously but tandem, if I may so express it. Imagine what it must have been in the Hôtel-Dieu in Paris, 150 and 200 years ago, when there were two to six patients (and such patients!) in one bed—and simultaneously.

You reported also 1,035 operations, which meant almost six operations per bed. This quick turnover means quick recovery, which in turn means a well-adminstered hospital, an able staff, and devoted, competent nurses.

You could hardly imagine the state of affairs when I graduated, fifty-three years ago. The newly fledged doctor had never auscultated, or percussed the heart or the lungs, had never examined an abdomen, and had never even so much as touched a patient to find out if there was a fever. There were no thermometers in general use until the '70s. He had never looked through a microscope, handled a test tube, himself examined any secretion, and had never seen a necropsy.

The nurse (but there *were* no nurses as we now understand the term), or any woman (practically never a man) who wished to become a nurse, simply helped this doctor or that, or nursed a friend through typhoid or a maternity case, gradually becoming fairly skilled by mere practice; that is, learning how to nurse *you* by her mistakes on *me*—or the reverse, as I should much prefer.

When I opened my office, in 1866, I did not need any nurses, for I had no patients for many weary weeks. When the need arose at last, I knew not where or how to get one. So I obtained from one of my much older friends, who was in active practice, a list of names and addresses. Then when I needed a nurse, I gave a copy of this list to the patient's family, who spent from a few hours to a day or more, driving from place to place in a hired hack, only to find one nurse out nursing, another one shopping, another sick in bed, and so on, though finally they would get one. Happy was the family who got a nurse within the first few hours, or even during the first day.

Ever since 1882, at the College of Physicians of Philadelphia, we have had a directory in which certified nurses, both men and women, are registered, with lists of those who are at work and those who are at liberty, of those who specialize in accident or other surgical cases, or those who specialize in contagious diseases, and so forth. Rarely does one have to wait more than an hour or two, and often the nurse is secured (usually by telephone) within half an hour. In accidents, in cases of sudden delirium tremens, or insanity, or unexpected obstetrical emergencies, this is indeed a boon.

If you have no such directory of nurses in Allentown, this hospital should inaugurate such a service, not only for its own graduates but for all the nurses in town.

When you have patients like me, for instance, you will need unlimited patience. Twice I have needed the kindly services of a good nurse. The first time, I had a bad fall resulting in a broken collarbone and ribs and was generally shaken up from head to foot. The first night in the hospital, I ached intolerably and frequently asked to be turned. This "turning" often consisted in budging me half an inch one way or the other, I'm sure, but it relieved my mnd, if not my body, and it kept the night nurse busy and out of mischief. (Just to establish an equilibrium, I broke the other collarbone a few years later, by yet another fall.)

In the morning, my conscience pricking me, I said to her, "I'm afraid that I was a *very* troublesome patient last night." (She was one of that class of fine nurses whose winsome ways and attractive uniform make one, if well, half-glad to be sick, and if sick, half-loath to get well.) "Oh, well," she replied, in a cheerful and forgiving tone, "you did have to be turned rather often." Rather often? You bet. Excuse the slang, but it's the only expression that fits.[10]

The second time I required similar services was after a serious abdominal operation, and my day and night nurses were equally patient, tender, and, again, forgiving. Two events stand out, during that convalescence, one of which has given me great pleasure and the other great amusement ever since. One of the former graduate nurses of the Jefferson, to whom I had handed the gold medal of honor at her graduation, some years before, had risen to the responsible position of superintendent of a nurses' training school in a large hospital. Having heard that I was "so near," as she put it, she took a whole night's journey by rail to pay me a visit of congratulation on my recovery, and spent another night returning to her hospital. That was indeed the loyalty of an old friend.

Remember that, for doctors and nurses, the most important canal in the world is not the Panama, nor the Suez, nor the Soo, nor the Kiel, but the alimentary. Watch, therefore, with scrupulous care everything that enters it. Learn how to cook the little appetizing *bonne bouches* and (do not forget this) to serve them with the daintiness which stimulates or even evokes an appetite, just as slovenliness dulls or even destroys it.

I wish you all might read *Horae Subsecivae,* the delightful volumes of Dr. John Brown, of Edinburgh. I could also wish that the English title read *Leisure Hours,* rather than *Spare Hours,* which always suggests spare ribs to me. In those volumes you would find much homely wisdom bearing on medicine, including "Rab and His Friends," the most charming and pathetic of all medical stories.

In another story, I find this: "Pray, Mr. Opie," asked someone of the painter, "with what do you mix your paints?" "With brains, sir," was the crusty but illuminating reply.

If you wish to succeed in nursing, in medicine, in blacksmithing, in business, in anything, you must use your brains, something both volatile and valuable which will ensure success. Failing that, you may not starve, you may even get along, but more than "get along" you never will.

Among the uses to which you must put your brain is to make yourself one of the family, not drawing too rigid a line around yourself within which lie your duties and without which you ignore everything else. Remember the golden rule for nurses (and for doctors as well, for I have often done myself the not-always-agreeable work of a nurse): *Whatever is necessary for the comfort, well-being, and recovery of your patient, that is your duty.*

Don't expect to be waited on. To wait on yourself will be a necessity, in many cases, and when this is so, do it cheerfully, sometimes waiting not only on your patient and yourself, but oiling the machinery by waiting on others in the family, as well.

You will find many people unreasonable. They expect you to be made of Bessemer steel and vulcanized rubber, to know no such thing as weariness or sleepiness, but to be on duty twenty-four hours, every day. The doctor, in such a case, should be your confidant and succor. There are times, for a day or so after an operation, when prolonged hours are a necessity, but once this emergency is passed, the doctor should insist on good sleep, meals as regular as possible, and at least one hour in the open air every day. He should point out to the family that to them, sickness is a rare emergency, but to you, a constant companion; that to *nurse* well you must *be* well; and that proper sleep, food, and fresh air are prime requisites for good health.

If you should find that rare unreasonable family who will not heed the doctor and self-evident common sense, then you owe it to yourself and your health to give up the case. But if you should do this, always stay for at least twenty-four hours, longer if necessary, in order to afford time for procuring another nurse. To leave a seriously ill patient abruptly is a sin of the first magnitude for a nurse, unless the circumstances are wholly exceptional.

You will go forth from this hospital well trained in your honorable profession. You will be a comfort and a joy to many a patient and many a family. You will be the doctor's right hand. On you rest the honor of the profession, the responsibility of caring for your patient in the intervals between the doctor's visits, and often the recovery of your patient.

If you do your work faithfully, "as ever in your great Taskmaster's eye," each day's duty will be a joy to you and a blessing to your patients. I bid you farewell and Godspeed.

MEDICAL RESEARCH AND ENDOWMENTS

Until, say, twenty-five years ago, the opportunities for research in this country were very scanty. Anyone who aspired to this kind of work had to go abroad for European training, only to find on his return that there was almost no place where he could go to continue with this fascinating work. Within the last twenty or thirty years, laboratory after laboratory has been established, and of such high quality that many Europeans are now coming *here* to learn. When I entered on my duties as Professor of Surgery at the Jefferson, European surgeons at my clinics were rarely seen. Before I resigned, in 1907, they or their chief assistants were frequent visitors.

The Rockefeller Institute, the Carnegie Institution, the Pepper Laboratory, the Jefferson Laboratory, plus research labs at Harvard, Columbia, Cornell, Chicago, Rochester (both New York and Minnesota), and perhaps a score of others, are seething centers of ceaseless work—and good work, too. Our authors and experimenters are quoted abroad, and few journals are better or better known than the *Journal of Experimental Medicine*, *American Journal of Physiology*, *Journal of Medical Research*, *Journal of Infectious Diseases*, *Archive of Internal Medicine*, *Journal of Biological Chemistry*, and the *Journal of Pharmacology and Experimental Therapeutics*, all of them American, and none, I think, over twenty-five or thirty years old.

When I was president of the American Medical Association (1900), I took as the subject of my presidential address "The Endowment of Medical Colleges," in which I pointed out how little has been done for medicine, as compared with theology, literature, and departments of science. While the tide was then probably turning towards medical-school endowment, I have reason to believe, from what has been told me, that my address, one of the earliest on the subject, has had no little influence in that direction. Since then, truly magnificent endowments of Harvard, Yale, Columbia, the University of Minnesota, Washington University, Tulane, the University of Pittsburgh, and the splendid gift of the Mayo brothers have been achieved, amply justifying their existence.

10

——••❧ ❀ ❧••——

Humorous Anecdotes

THE PARIETAL BONE

Doctor X, the son of a famous surgeon, imagined himself his father's peer. He was, in fact, a reckless and almost dangerous surgeon, even though he occupied the Chair of Anatomy in a medical college.

Harry Landis, one of my office students, was a delight to me on account of his acute sense of humor. One day he appeared all aglow with a good story about Professor X. The professor, he said, had just finished describing the parietal bone (which is the principal bone on the side of the skull—one on each side).

Harry said that as he was holding up this bone, closed his description and his lecture by this apostrophe, "Such, gentlemen, is the parietal bone! Where would the genius of Shakespeare have been without a parietal bone?"

FICTION INSTEAD OF FACT,
ILLUSTRATED BY TWO FABLES

The Umbrella Story

How strangely fictitious stories will appear and re-appear is well illustrated by my umbrella story. I have been introduced several times to people who have opened the conversation by saying, "I'm very glad to know you, Dr. Keen: I've always wanted to know whether or not your umbrella story is true." I would sometimes astonish them by suggesting that I was hoping they would ask me about that.

As the story goes, a man who was walking down Broadway slipped and fell, breaking his leg. A crowd of curious passers-by quickly gathered, but the only action taken was a hurried call for an ambulance. While waiting for its arrival, the crowd gave way to admit a gentleman who seemed to have a clear idea of what needed to be done and set out to do it. Slipping his furled umbrella up the injured man's trouser leg, where it would serve as a splint, he called for handkerchiefs from the bystanders and secured the broken bone firmly to the umbrella.

Just as he had finished, the ambulance arrived, and the doctor made his way through the crowd. Looking at the well-splinted leg, he turned to its creator and said, "That was really well done. You must have taken some lessons in first aid." As the man was being lifted into the ambulance, the doctor asked the gentleman for his card so that he could return the umbrella to his address.

On reading the card, he exclaimed, "Great Scott!" and added some complimentary remarks which shall be unrecorded here.

Now as a matter of fact, I never saw a man fall and break a leg on Broadway and therefore never had occasion to use my umbrella there as described. The inherent improbability of the story is evident, I have always claimed, for I never would have used my own umbrella so long as I could have borrowed one.

The $75,000 Fee

A still more fictitious story, lamentably, is that of the seventy-five-thousand-dollar fee. As the newspaper had it, a friend entered the office of a Pittsburgh banker just as he was drawing a check. As soon as he had signed it, he tore it off and showed it to his friend, saying that it was the best buy of his life. The check, for $75,000, was drawn to *my* order!

The sad truth is that by some error of the post office, neither that check nor any other check representing a fraction of that delightful amount ever reached me. I have longed in vain for that elusive check!

THE LOST FORK

One winter evening, I was invited to the country home of Mr. DeWitt Cuyler, for a reception of the Junior Legal Club. While we were at dinner, I had started to lay down the fork on my plate when my arm was jostled and the fork fell to the floor. As I did not wish it to be trodden on, I looked and looked for it but could not find it. I concluded that it had gone under the table and would be found by the waiters after the dinner.

At the close of the evening, we all went up the station stairs together to take the train back to town. As I lifted my right foot, I suddenly found that the flexion of my leg was obstructed by something in my pocket. Inserting my hand, I pulled out the lost fork. Those around me immediately cried out, "Ben Butler!" "Ben Butler!"

The explanation was an easy one: I had on an evening coat, and as the aperture of the pocket gaped, the fork dropped into it unnoticed.

I venture to think that if a novelist included such an incident in a story, it would be pronounced most incredible. It was another case in which truth is stranger than fiction.

WHALE LIVER OIL

After our return from the North Cape and Spitzbergen, I was asked to give a public lecture for the benefit of our Sunday school. My daughters occupied seats in the front row so that they could lift warning fingers in case I passed from the realm of fact into that of fiction. But when the time came, they forgot to play their role, or else, moved by compassion (or amazement) they did not raise a finger

Among other things, I referred to a visit to Tromsø and related the remark of a friend who said he could never forget it because it "smells so." The cause of this, I added, was the cod liver oil industry.

Apropos of that, I told of our seeing four whales being towed into the harbor by a steamer for the purpose of making cod liver oil. I was as innocent as a child, in making that statement, and did not even perceive the titter which my daughters later insisted passed through the audience. How I roared with laughter, when they told me what I really had said.

Another amusing thing as to those four whales. We actually saw them, not at Tromsø but at Hammerfest, the northernmost town in the world. I took a snapshot of the steamer and the whales as we were approaching the town, though too far away to photograph the town. When nearer, I took another picture of the town itself, but, alas, I had forgotten to wind the camera and the pictures were superimposed, showing the whales in the water and the steamer paddling its way over the roofs of the houses.

MY LONG, MYSTERIOUS, AND FATAL CLINIC

I always had to change my underclothing, after my surgical clinics at the Jefferson Medical College, because they were so wet—a good evidence of how great was the mental strain involved in serious operations. Officially, my clinics lasted from twelve to two o'clock, but when I had selected more patients than I could operate upon in those two hours, or when earlier operations were more complicated and lasted longer than I had expected, I did not wish to disappoint those patients who had been antiseptically prepared and who had screwed up their courage to the sticking point, so I always continued until all the patients for each day had been operated upon. Not seldom, my clinics lasted until four o'clock, and sometimes still later.

At one of the Jefferson Alumni Dinners, Dr. J. Chalmers DaCosta told this story, which he admitted was a dream. He was passing the hospital in the evening of one of my clinic days, and, seeing the operating room all lighted up, he wondered who was at work so late; so he entered and peeped in. This was the picture he saw. There I was, still operating on the patient, while around me were the assistants and the nurses, all lying on the floor and all dead as doornails.

"MARY'S GHOST"[2]

1
'Twas in the middle of the night
    To sleep young William tried;
When Mary's ghost came stealing in
    And stood at his bedside.

2
Oh, William, dear! Oh, William, dear!
    My rest eternal ceases;
Alas! My everlasting peace
    Is broken into pieces

3
I thought the last of all my cares
    Would end with my last minute,
But when I went to my last home,
    I didn't long stay in it.

4
The body-snatchers they have come
    And made a snatch at me;
It's very hard them kind of men
    Won't let a body be.

5
You thought that I was buried deep,
    Quite decent-like and chary;
But from her grave in Mary-bone,
    They've come and bon'd your Mary.

6
The arm that used to take your arm
    Is took to Dr. Vyse;*
And both my legs are gone to walk
    The hospital at Guy's.

7
I vow'd that you should have my hand,
    But fate gave us denial;
You'll find it there at Dr. Bell's**
    In spirits and a phial.

8
As for my feet, the little feet,
    You used to call so pretty,
There's one, I know, in Bedford Row,
    The t'other's in the city.

9
I can't tell where my head is gone,
    But Dr. Carpue*** can;
As for my trunk, it's all packed up
    To go by Pickford's**** van.

10
I wish you'd go to Mr. P.,
    And save me such a ride;
I don't half like the outside place
    They've took for my inside.

11
The cock, it crows—I must be gone!
    My William, we must part!
But I'll be your's in death, altho'
    Sir Astley***** has my heart.

12
Don't go to weep upon my grave,
    And think that there I be;
They haven't left an atom there
    Of my anatomie.

---

* *Joseph Vyse (1757/8–1841)*
** *Charles Bell (1774–1842)*
*** *Joseph Constantine Carpue (1764–1846)*

**** *Pickford's: The famous "removals" firm dating from the reign of Charles I (1625 49).*
******Astley Paston Cooper (1768–1841)*

II

—••❊❳❲❊❳••—

Remarkable Encounters

SOME OF MY PUPILS

I BEGAN TEACHING IN THE Philadelphia School of Anatomy in the autumn of 1866, after my return from study in Europe. I taught Anatomy and Operative Surgery there until 1875, when the property was taken by the Government for the construction of the post office at 8th and Market.

Among a few of my distinguished pupils there I recall Professors James C. Wilson (later my colleague at the Jefferson), W.H. Parish, and James B. Walker; Dr. John C. Berry, now of Worcester, Massachusetts, who established the first School of Anatomy in Japan; Professor George McClellan; Thomas Eakins, the artist; Professor Juan Guiteras of Havana; J.C. Merrill, of the Library of the Surgeon General; Dr. Oscar H. Allis; Dr. Morris J. Lewis; Professor John B. Roberts; Dr. John K. Mitchell, Dr. Robert G. Le Conte; John J. Boyle, the sculptor; Dr. Joseph S. Neff, Philadelphia's able Director of Health; Professor A.P. Montgomery; Professor J. Collins Warren, of Harvard; Professor R.O. Cowling, of Louisville; Dr. Isaac Ott; Professor James W. Holland; Dr. Wharton Sinkler; Professor John H. Musser; Professor Henry W. Stellwagen; and Dr. L.L. Seaman.

Later, on the staff at the Jefferson, I recall Professors W.M.L. Coplin, F.Y. Dercum, J. Mendez DaCosta, K.F. Graham, John H. Gibbon, R.C. Rosenberger, Francis T. Stewart, W.M. Sweet, W.F. Manges, and A.G. Ellis, Professor of Pathology and Bacteriology in the Medical College in Bangkok, Siam; John M. Fisher, J. Chalmers DaCosta, Jr., F.J. Kalteyer, B.O. Thornton, T.C. Stellwagen, P. Brooke Bland, D.G. Metheny, and J. Torrance Rugh.

I have no list of my Jefferson students, and hence can recall but few, except for those from Philadelphia, and especially those now teaching in the college.

The present Surgeon General of the United States, Maj. Gen. Merritte W. Ireland; Dr. Royer, on the staff of the Pennsylvania State Commissioner of Health; Dr. Wilmer Krusen, Director of Health of Philadelphia; and Dr. J.J. Reilly, Chief Medical Officer at Hog Island. All these have been my students.

Dr. Victor G. Heiser, an old student, was for ten years the Director of Health of the whole group of the Philippine Islands and had a distinguished career there. Then he was lured from Government service by the Rockefeller Institute Health Board, which is doing wonderful work all around the world on leprosy, hookworm disease and malaria.

When in Siam, Heiser had an audience with the king (who was an Oxford graduate) that lasted for two hours, instead of a few formal minutes. On asking Heiser his truthful opinion of the hospital in Bangkok, the king was startled by the answer that it was the worst he had seen in the entire Far East. The king immediately sent his brother to examine the facility in Manila, and Bangkok now has an excellent hospital and medical school. Two of my pupils, Drs. A.G. Ellis and H.H. Radasch, have been appointed members of the faculty there, and Dr. Ellis has organized and directed the Department of Pathology of the Royal Medical College in Bangkok.

Another student, Dr. Babcock, of Haddonfield, New Jersey, was for some years the personal physician to the king of Siam, where he introduced vaccination and other health reforms. Moreover, Mr. William Potter, president of the board of trustees of the Jefferson, is an old friend of the king's and has provided him with two successive legal advisors. It would seem that the Jefferson has annexed Siam.

I taught as a special lecturer, and then as the Professor of Surgery, at the Woman's Medical College from 1877 to 1889, and among my students there, many have risen to eminence as practitioners, missionaries, and professors, in that college and others.

At the Pennsylvania Academy of the Fine Arts, I was asked to reorganize the Department of Artistic Anatomy, in 1878, just after the school moved to its present building at Broad and Cherry Streets. At every lecture there, I utilized the cadaver, the skeleton, and the living model. While teaching there, I collected what I judge to be the best library on artistic anatomy in this country. On my election to the Jefferson, in 1889, I resigned at the Woman's Medical College, and the next year, at the Academy, where my friend, Dr. George McClellan, was selected as my successor. On his death, Dr. H.B. Radasch, a former pupil, was elected in his place.

From 1878 to 1882, I also taught in the Pennsylvania Museum and School of Industrial Art. My course there covered especially the "Anatomy of Animal Forms as Applied to Decorative Art." This and the lectures at the Academy of the Fine Arts were delightful side issues which repaid the large amount of labor I gave to them.

I also was a regular lecturer, for a number of years, in the school of the Misses Bonney and Dillaye, first in Philadelphia and later at Ogontz.

My teaching covers forty-one years in all (1866–1907). As nearly as I can judge, I have had between nine and ten thousand students, all told. They are scattered all over this country. Many of them, especially as missionaries, are to be found in Japan, China, the Philippines, Egypt, Turkey, and at least one in Persia. Several times, in traveling in the United States, and in the East, some old pupil has reached a point where he could meet me, while the train was stopped, if only for a few minutes' conversation. Such encounters were always a sincere and great pleasure for both parties.

Joseph Shimoon was my sole student in Persia. He returned to his native land as a medical missionary and was laboring in Urumiah, when the Turks captured it during the Great War. They gave him the alternative, becoming a Mohammedan or death at the stake, and he suffered martyrdom by fire. His fine character and steadfast allegiance to Jesus Christ, even when tested by fire, proved to be pure gold.

Doubtless this list is very imperfect, for I have only my memory to aid me, and memory in the ninth decade of life is rarely comprehensive and none too accurate.

OLIVER WENDELL HOLMES

The first time I ever saw Dr. Holmes was in Frederick, Maryland, in 1862, shortly after the Battle of Antietam on the 17th of September. His son, later Associate Justice of the Supreme Court, had been wounded in the battle, and his father came down to find out where he was and, if possible, to take him back to Boston.

In November of 1857, the *Atlantic Monthly* had been founded, and by virtue of his contributions, collected and published in 1858 as *The Autocrat of the Breakfast Table*, Holmes was at the height of his fame. His portraits were everywhere.

I had been ordered from Washington immediately after the battle and was at Hospital No. 1 in Frederick. At about noon on September 20th, I had finished my ward work and had gone to the office, a room about twenty-five feet square.

The Officer of the Day, in full uniform, and I in undress uniform, were the only persons in the room. The door opened and a short gentleman appeared, quickly glanced from one to the other of us, and walked rapidly to the Officer of the Day (who, I may add, was not overly gifted with surgical knowledge).

"My name is Holmes, Dr. Oliver Wendell Holmes of Boston, and I am anxious to find my son, who was wounded at Antietam. I am told he is in a hospital in Frederick. Is he possibly in this hospital?"

Scratching his head as if to aid his memory, the O.D. said, musingly, "Holmes? Holmes? Seems to me I've heard of you before."

Holmes, in spite of his anxiety, could not keep back a smile while he repeated his request. Years afterward, when I reminded Holmes of this little incident, he had quite forgotten it—but we had a good laugh over it.

Holmes's quick wit was frequently observed during his lectures on Anatomy, at Harvard. During one of his lectures, one of the students, when Holmes's back was turned, threw a spitball, which struck the wall directly in front of Holmes. He paid no attention to it, but when a second spitball struck the wall, Holmes wheeled around and exclaimed, "Insatiate archer! Would not one suffice?"

MRS. CHARLES B. KEEN

Harriet Ide Keen was the daughter of Rev. George B. Ide, D.D., a former pastor of the First Baptist Church in Philadelphia. She died from pneumonia on November 8th, 1912, in her 79th year.

In 1852, Dr. Ide resigned his pastorate here and became the pastor of the First Baptist Church in Springfield, Massachusetts. It was there that, in November of 1856, his daughter Harriet was married to my brother, Charles Burtis Keen. I was a groomsman at their wedding.

Charles was formerly a member of our church, but then became a member of the First Baptist Church, West Philadelphia, which more recently has merged with the Chestnut Street Baptist Church. A few years ago, Charles and Harriet again became members of our church.

Harriet's intellectual attainments were of a high order. To a fair knowledge of Latin and French she added, many years after her marriage, a fluent reading knowledge of German and Italian. The latter was acquired without a teacher and after a severe shock,[1] nearly twenty years before her death, that paralyzed her left side.

Fortunately, this attack left her mind, her speech, and her right hand unaffected. For years, she was thus able to enjoy intellectual pursuits, to make beautiful embroidery, and to do exquisite china painting. She travelled extensively in Europe from 1907 to 1911, roaming over Sicily, Italy, the Riviera, Switzerland, France, and England.

Instead of bemoaning her disabilities, she counted her blessings and was always bright and serene, even when in deep sorrow. She lost a daughter, early in her married life, and a fine and promising son, at the beginning of a prosperous career in business. Her husband died several years before she passed away. Yet her faith and her faithfulness never wavered. She is survived by her daughter, Helen, and by her two sons, Herbert and Charles Barton.

In the spring of 1910, two years before her death, she decided to spend the summer at the Italian lakes. Her blood pressure was the highest I had ever seen, and her doctor and I were apprehensive of another apoplexy.[2] We urged her to stay home. I told her that with her very high blood pressure I was afraid that another stroke would almost certainly be fatal.

She listened to all I had to say and then replied, calmly but firmly, "Will, I can go to heaven just as easily from the Italian lakes as I can from Philadelphia. I'm going!" And go she did, with her daughter and her maid.

Back in Philadelphia, while ill of pneumonia, she suddenly sat up in bed one morning, and in a moment fell back dead.

I loved her dearly.

A SOLDIER OF THE FIRST NAPOLEON

While I was still a student at the Jefferson, in 1862, Professor Gross, my teacher of Surgery, took me to a house where I was to give chloroform for him for an operation. (He always used chloroform.) The patient, a man of over seventy, had been wounded just fifty years before, in the Battle of Borodino, during Napoleon's disastrous 1812 retreat from Moscow. The shot had buried itself in the calf of the leg and not emerged. A mere flesh wound at Borodino was not of much account: there were other fish to fry. After lying there, quietly embedded in the tissues for half a century, the shot had at last worked its way to the surface, finally causing an opening through the skin. The old fellow had pried it out with a pin, but the wound did not heal. There was a small but annoying discharge of pus, and some sort of hard substance could be felt deeper in the tissues.

Proposing to remove this, Gross laid out all his instruments and (as was often his custom) whetted his knife on his boot, a fine antiseptic procedure—but remember the year. He said to the patient, "Now, my good man, lie down so that my young friend Keen can give you a little chloroform."

"Do you suppose," replied the patient, "that a soldier of the first Napoleon wishes to take chloroform?"

At this, he stretched his leg straight out and concluded the discussion with an emphatic, "Go ahead!"

Professor Gross went ahead, and never once did the old soldier wince or budge. The lump cut out proved to be a bony mass, cup-shaped in form, which had been caused by the irritation of the ball during its long sojourn. He made an excellent recovery, in spite of the primitive preparation of knife on boot.

How near to me this incident brought the great emperor!

> *Note (1912)*: From the *Outlook* of October 26th: "Eight Russian survivors of the Battle of Borodino recently celebrated the hundredth anniversary of that bloody conflict between the Russians and Napoleon's *Grande Armée.* This seems incredible, but the newspaper reports give the names and records of those hoary veterans. One of them, at the age of 122, has recently been granted a pension by the Russian government. Another, Peter Laptyev, aged 118, actually met Napoleon face to face, during the campaign, and has a vivid recollection of the interview."

THE THREE WAYLANDS

Dr. Francis Wayland was one of the three great college presidents of the '40s and '50s, the other two being Nott, of Union, and Mark Hopkins, of Williams. (It was said that Hopkins at one end of a log and a student at the other constituted a university.)

Francis Wayland, citing his advancing years, resigned at Brown in 1855, the year I entered. He was only fifty-nine years old, but in 1850, a demi-centurian was spoken of as "venerable." In Lincoln Wayland's house, one time, I saw a portrait of his father, standing on the stage at Commencement. When I asked how old he was, I was told he was fifty-nine. "Why, I'm five years older than that now," I replied, "and I'm not thinking of resigning anything."

When I became a demi-centenarian, I remembered Dr. Lincoln Wayland's welcome to me, published in the *National Baptist*.

There was a story (probably fictional) about a student who told President Wayland that he did not believe in God. "Son," the president is supposed to have said, "you will believe in God before noon today or you will leave this college."

President Wayland was most kind to my beloved wife, when she was a student in Mrs. Buell's school in Providence.

Dr. Wayland's eldest son, also Francis, was a distinguished lawyer and for many years the Dean of the Yale Law School.

The younger son, Rev. Dr. Heman Lincoln Wayland, was the wittiest man I ever knew personally. At a New England Dinner in New York, he told the audience that, while walking down Broadway, he had seen a sign "Plymouth Rock pants for $2." He then said, "I appeal to this wealthy audience: Is there not only one but many with New England consciences who would contribute to this panting want, supplying that need of Plymouth Rock?"

Presiding at a similar dinner in Philadelphia, he introduced Secretary of State Evarts as "the gentleman farmer from Vermont who planted dollars and in prosperous seasons reaped sixpences."

He made two of the most delightful chemical jokes I have ever heard. The first was the assertion that "although the ancients said that Io died of love, modern chemists have discovered Iodide of potassium."

The second has been tarnished, to some extent, by the new chemical terminology. In my college days, the chemical formula for water was H.O. Modern chemists have changed it to H_2O. At our Brown University Alumni dinners in Philadelphia, we never had anything but water to drink. At one of them, H. Lincoln Wayland, in replying to a toast, pronounced a eulogy of water that would have done credit to John B. Gough himself. Then he suddenly stopped, and with a merry twinkle in his eye, he went on, "We are told by the chemists that Priestly discovered oxygen in 1774. Not so! It is a monstrous error. Ages ago, did not the prophet cry out, "H.O.! everyone that thirsteth, come ye to the waters."

A MEMORABLE STUDENT

A [Woman's Medical College] student who lives vividly in my recollection furnished me, in May 1887, a wholly unique surgical experience—unique, I fancy, even in the annals of surgery. The student referred to sought my advice for a number of tubercular glands in the neck. As they were on the point of becoming abscesses, I advised their removal. To this she immediately consented but added "upon one condition."

"And what is that?"

"That I shall not take either ether or chloroform."

"But, my dear child," I said, "surely you do not understand. This operation will last probably an hour and a half. I must make an incision from your ear to the breastbone and then along the clavicle nearly to the shoulder, raise both flaps over a large area and dissect the glands most carefully from the jugular vein, carotid artery, probably the great subclavian vessels and certainly from all the numerous nerves in the neck. If you jump from sudden pain, I do not know where the point of my knife may go."

"Yes," she said, "I quite understand. I will stand any amount of pain without budging, but I will not take ether or chloroform."

"Why not?"

"Because I have already had two operations for similar glands elsewhere, both done by Professor Henry Sands (in his day, the foremost surgeon in New York), one under ether and the other under chloroform, and I suffered so intensely from the after-effects that I prefer to endure the pain of the operation. If I can not have the glands removed without the anesthetic, I will not have the operation performed."

"Well," said I, seeing her absolutely fixed determination, "only within a few days I have seen an account of a new local anesthetic called *cocaine*, and if you are willing I will try that, but I can't promise how much it will dull the pain as I have never used it."

"Anything except ether or chloroform," was the quiet but decided answer. I got an ounce of cocaine solution (then so rare and costly that I paid five dollars for what I could now probably buy for ten cents), and we set the date.

A few days later I operated. As I had never used cocaine before, I am well aware that it was but partially effective, but she never so much as winced. Now, however, comes the additional and unique surprise. I had made my incisions and had begun to dissect the flaps when she said, "Would you mind if one of the residents . . . were to get me her hand glass and let me watch the operation?" For a moment, I confess I was—if I may venture to use the word—"flabbergasted." But I instantly made up my mind that anyone who could face fearlessly an hour and a half of pain without any anesthetic would be able to watch the operation without flinching. And so it proved. For over an hour, she held the glass and watched every stroke of my knife, even when shaving the great jugular and without a single movement of head, hand, or foot.

Her later history is interesting, instructive, and worthy of her. After a year or so of slum work in New York, Dr. Rosetta Sherwood Hall was sent to Seoul, Korea, as a medical missionary. There (for Cupid flings his darts in Korea as elsewhere) she married a young man with whom she had been associated in her work in New York. After the devastation of Pyonyang, in the Sino-Japanese War of 1895, they went up to attend the wounded of both armies, and it was there that her husband fell a victim to malignant typhus. She came home at once on a furlough and her second child, a daughter, was born in the United States. (Her first had died in Korea.) She later returned to Korea and twice built a fine large hospital (the second time, after its destruction by fire) for the mission by the late L.H. Severance, of Cleveland. Some years ago, she established the first school for the blind and later the first school for the deaf and dumb ever founded in Korea. They are two fine examples of the broad Christian charity which reaches out the helping hand to the defectives even more than to those who can help themselves. When her daughter was old enough, she efficiently aided her mother. About three years ago, both of them called to see me, and I was proud of their work, as well I might be. The Woman's Medical College of Pennsylvania, also, may count such a woman as one of many who have conferred honor upon the college, and benefits untold upon humanity.

A VERY INTELLIGENT HORSE

Of the several horses I have had, "George" certainly was the most remarkable. His judgment, memory, and reasoning power were astonishing.

He was a swift bay, whom I had to drive, as a rule, with my feet on the cross bar and the lines taut. He served me for years, therefore, as a gymnasium. He never needed the whip. In fact, some of my friends said I must have been a descendant of Jehu the son of Nimshi, and that when they saw (or, often, heard) us coming, they were wary till we had passed.[3] They also said that when I turned a corner, it was usually on two wheels. I drove George for, I think, well on to ten years, and then, when he failed physically, probably around the age of sixteen, I sent him to the zoo. He was useful even in death, for he was fed to the lions.

I always drove a buggy, and never a pair, because this was the swiftest method of locomotion. If I took along my boy or man, it was only to hold the lines, but for a number of years, I drove a good part of the time alone. Very commonly, I left George unhitched. As soon as he saw me coming out of a patient's house, he would turn either left or right, but always away from the curb for me to get in more readily.

He twice stood unusual tests. In one, he was standing, fortunately unhitched, facing west on Green Street, west of 19th. I happened to be looking out the window and saw a hack driving westward. The careless driver caught my hind wheel with his front and turned my buggy completely around so that it was facing east. George turned with it and calmly waited for me to drive to my next patient.

At another time, when the Centennial buildings were under construction in Fairmount Park, I had occasion to go out there for an interview with one of the officials. I left George facing a railroad track, not fifty feet away. In spite of the length of my call (fully half an hour), and the backing and filling and whistling of a switching locomotive in front of him, he never budged.

While standing facing east on Pine Street near 21st, one time, he played me a trick. My call was unexpectedly prolonged, and I was not able to leave till around eight, on that day in late autumn. When I came out, no horse and buggy were to be seen. He evidently disapproved of my late hour and wanted *his* supper, however careless I might be of my own. I went at once to the stable, at the northest corner of 17th and Sansome, and there he was, safe and sound. Later, I learned from a friend that he had trotted east on Pine to 17th, turned north on 17th, and gone straight to the stable. The horsecars on both streets ran in the opposite direction to his own, but he avoided all cars, as well as all other vehicles. The only damage done, according to the ostlers, who were startled at his arrival without his master, was that as the buggy turned in from the street, the hub of the front wheel grazed the brick doorway of the stable.

When nearing a cross street, he watched for horsecars when he heard the harness bells, and he could almost always immediately judge whether he ought to hasten to cross in front or slow down to pass behind the crossing car.

The quality of his memory is indicated by this incident. I drove up 5th Street to Thompson, turned west on Thompson, and stopped on the north side of the street near the middle of a block with a row of identical houses between 5th and 6th. This was a part of the city to which I was rarely called in consultation, and I had never before been called to this particular block. A year or more later, during which time I had never visited anywhere on Thompson, I was driving again up 5th, and when I got to the corner of Thompson, George evidently thought I was going again to the house where I had been before: he began to turn onto Thompson, and, instantly recalling my former consultation, I slackened the reins. George stopped on the north side of the street within one door of the house where I had called over a year before. Could there be a clearer indication of animal memory?

I have never had but one George. His successor was a light-spirited sorrel named "Colonel." Once, while passing the Union League (going south) on the way to a post mortem, I had an ugly accident. The front axle on my side broke, and the buggy toppled over, throwing Fuller, my faithful colored man, and me out onto the cobblestones. In the buggy, I had a two-gallon glass jar, half-filled with a solution of bichromate of potash, and a case of post-mortem instruments. It was winter, and I had had a gray fur robe over our knees. Everything was spilled into the street, and either the glass jar was broken or the top came off, I am not sure which. None of the acid touched either of us. One spot on the robe was stained yellow when a little of the acid spilled on it. The instruments were all right. We were not struck by the buggy nor injured by landing hard on the cobbles, though of course our clothes were soiled with dust and dirt.

I gathered up the impedimenta and went into the League to get washed and brushed up, but sent Fuller after the horse and buggy, for Colonel had not stopped for a moment. (George would have stopped, as he did on two occasions following more or less serious accidents.) Colonel ran down Broad to Spruce, turned east, and stopped. He had to stop. The buckle fastening together the ends of the reins had fallen and were caught in the apex of the V between two spokes, and the revolving wheel gradually wound up the reins around the hub, forcing the horse to stop.

I called a cab and got to my post mortem in time, minus only my jar.

ORATORS I'VE HEARD IN PERSON

I have been fortunate to have heard a considerable number of distinguished orators, both American and foreign. (Unfortunately, these did not include Webster or Clay, or Henry Ward Beecher.) Wendell Phillips and George William Curtis are the earliest two I can remember. I never heard Phillips in one of his fiery philippics against slavery, but only in his lectures on Toussaint L'Ouverture and "The Lost Art." Hence I can only attest to his powers of description, his broad knowledge, and his powerful delineation of character.

Curtis had the most charming, mellifluous voice I have ever heard. I first saw him at Brown, when we initiated him into our chapter of Alpha Delta Phi. Before the Phi Beta Kappa, I believe it was, during Commencement, he gave the oration, "The Scholar in Politics," and it was most charming. I never shall forget with what soul-stirring effect he quoted Mrs. Hemans's "New England Hymn." We were almost lifted from the pews, in the old First Baptist Meeting House, which was dedicated, in 1770, "For the Publick Worship of Almighty GOD and also for Holding Commencement in."[4]

We had initiated him the night before, and he had spoken to us as brothers. With what pride we shook his hand and claimed him as our own. The story by which he will always be known among Brunonians is his celebrated toast at one Commencement dinner. We always wanted him at these dinners and several times prevailed upon him to preside. He was a past master in the art of introducing various speakers, gracefully and with an apt quotation or reference for each. His memorable toast was, "The Brown-bred boys make the best-bred men."

I once heard Edward Everett deliver his celebrated address on Washington, which had been prepared to aid in the founding of Washington University in St. Louis. It is said that he delivered this address some two or three hundred times, all over the country. It was carefully prepared, and carefully memorized, but even after he had delivered it so many times, so goes the story, his memory began to fail him, and he had to re-memorize it.

I remember one sentence, and one gesture. The sentence described the Mississippi River, beginning with its origin at Lake Itasca, in Minnesota, following it downstream, receiving its several tributaries, and finally debouching into the Gulf of Mexico. The sentence was almost as long as the river, very possibly intentionally so. It covered two or three printed pages and contained more than three hundred words before the final period gave us breath at last.

The gesture was an elevated and long, trembling hand, which he shook as if from intense emotion. But it was too frequently repeated and at last became wearisome. Possibly this repetition and his too-florid style, especially when contrasted with Lincoln's simple, succinct, and immortal speech at Gettysburg, were responsible for the reduced effect. I write this with some reserve, however, since I have never read Everett's speech after first reading it in the newspaper, while I have often read Lincoln's address.

While in college, I heard Thackeray deliver his lectures on "the Four Georges." The one thing I remember of this series was his gradual disclosure of the mean figure of the real George IV, as he divested him of one garment after another, leaving before us a poor manikin.

I heard Charles Kingsley, and my impression is that his lectures were, on the whole, a failure. If this impression is accurate, I do not wonder at it, for I have a very clear recollection of this tall, gawky figure standing a few paces from the desk on the platform. He would stride from the desk to a nearby table, every few moments, take a sip of water, and then stride back again. I wondered why he didn't stay at the desk.

I had the great pleasure of hearing Tyndall's course of scientific lectures, and they were a treat. While his distinguished reputation made them a treat, I do not think he was the equal of Professor George Barker as a popular lecturer on any scientific subject. Barker's descriptions were models of lucidity, and his experiments were always striking and (what is often lacking in scientific lectures) brilliantly successful.

For side-splitting laughter and charming literary excellence, let me commend the joint readings of George Cable and Mark Twain. Both read from their own works. Cable not only read most charmingly, but also interspersed his reading with the most melodious singing of old Creole songs. I had read and merely smiled at some of Twain's works, but when he *read* them, with his drawl and his expressive face, I nearly "burst the buttons off my vest and fell in a fit." At the end of the evening, I was actually exhausted, tired and sore from the uproarious and continuous laughter. It took a day for my facial muscles to regain their normal condition.

I have been most fortunate to have heard, among foreign orators, Lord Rosebery, in addition to debates between Bismarck and Virchow and between Disraeli and Gladstone. The address by Lord Rosebery, on being installed as the new lord rector at Saint Andrews, in 1911, was a splendid effort, and a fine specimen of his learning, graceful wit, and charming English diction. Everyone was amused when he looked down straight at the premier, Mr. Asquith, who sat in the front row awaiting his honorary LL.D., and referred to the "ruins of the House of Lords." I suspect that Mr. Asquith rather chuckled, since he had successfully carried his bill for the reform of the House of Lords and in a moment would be awarded his honorary degree. Rosebery's lighter after-dinner speeches were beautifully suited to their several occasions.

Mr. Balfour, the former premier, spoke at the dinner that evening, but his speech was a great disappointment, worthy neither of the occasion nor of the man.

Of medical speakers, there are few who are eminent. I do not think I can well estimate French or German speakers, as a foreigner can scarcely appreciate the full flavor of what is being said. As a clinical teacher and speaker, Nélaton was by far the best I ever heard in France, as was Langenbeck in Germany.

Two among the British medical speakers and two Americans far excel the others I have heard. In his address as president of the International Medical Congress in London (1881), Paget was perfectly charming. And Moynihan, of Leeds, has no peer in a surgical debate, in matter, style, or manner.

In America, J. Mendez DaCosta was the easiest, clearest, most charming and scholarly speaker, both as a clinical teacher and in occasional addresses. His cousin, J. Chalmers DaCosta, along with George de Schweinitz, I would place in the front rank among living Americans.

I have heard only three from the pulpit whom I would place at the top: Edward A. Park, Phillips Brooks, and Francis Wayland (with Theodore Cuyler right behind). Never can I forget a sermon at a Brown commencement that Dr. Park delivered before the Missionary Society. His text was "I shall be satisfied when I awake in Thy likeness," and though the substance of the sermon is gone from memory, the effect, the uplifting effect, can never pass away.

Phillips Brooks was the most rapid speaker I ever heard and was the despair of all but the most rapid reporters. His sermons were read, as well as heard, a severe test of their merit. They are full of meat. But as a speaker he was an educational and inspiring force by the substance of the sermons, rather than by his manner of delivery. He was no orator. He spoke too fast to be impressive. The minds of his hearers were always on tension.

I was so fortunate as to hear Dr. Wayland every Sunday, after he had retired from the presidency of Brown and was filling in the long vacancy between the death of Rev. Dr. Granger and the arrival of Rev. Dr. Caldwell, at the old First Baptist Church in Providence (whose corporate name was, and still is, the Baptist Charitable Society). Wayland was no orator, in the sense of rhetorical flights of description or imagination, but he was eminently a logician, who having set forth the facts, drove them home and compelled his listeners to apply them to their own lives and consciences. It was a treat to hear him.

Two of my pastors at the First Baptist Church, George Dana Boardman and George Hooper Ferris, have also been notable preachers. Dr. Boardman was the greater master of the language, of imagery, of simile—in a word, a greater orator. He was simple of taste and almost timid in physical matters, but in spiritual affairs, he was of the stuff that martyrs are made.

Dr. Ferris is rather awkward of gesture and emphasizes his sentences too much by postures (sometimes seeming to be contorted) that border on the uncouth. Yet his views are large and wide, his convictions sincere, his knowledge extensive, and his diction admirable. He is one of the best preachers I have ever heard. He makes one think. He wears well, Sunday after Sunday.

CONSTITUTIONAL BY-LAWS

In 1873, or so, I attended an old lady for a fracture of the neck of her thighbone. She was then close to ninety years old.

She lived on the second story and regularly walked down to the basement for her meals. On the day of her accident, she had been out "shopping" for some time.

When she was complaining of her miserable health, one day, I remonstrated with her and recounted her physical achievements on the very day of her accident, saying in conclusion, "I think you should be proud of your good health at your advanced age."

"No, no," she replied, in the cracked treble of old age. "I've never had any constitution since that attack of yellow fever I had in '97."

I told my father (who was *born* in '97) that evidently she had been living on her by-laws for the past seventy-six years.

THE REEF OF NORMAN'S WOE

For several summers, when the children were growing up, we spent time as boarders with Mrs. Renton, at East Gloucester, Massachusetts.

The moors stretched all the way out from our cottage to Grapevine and the ocean. When the rain subsided, but before the winds and water had dwindled, we often went out to Bass Rock, in order to watch the high spouting of the waves.

In the quiet pools we sought the abundant marine life, including sea anemones, limpets, snails, crabs, and other small fry, and kept them in the inverted glass covers used to protect cake from flies, which we mounted on rings of wood with holes for the knobs. Reviewing the sea water daily, we learned not a little natural history.

The reef of Norman's Woe, on which Longfellow's "Wreck of the Hesperus" took place, was in full view. One evening, a dozen of us sailed out to the reef and climbed inside the lighthouse. The keeper had a piano in his sitting room, where also the rope from the fog bell was suspended. Our party included a fine baritone from Boston, and someone proposed that he sing the familiar poem while accompanied on the piano. The keeper was easily persuaded to toll the fog bell during the singing, and so the story became very vivid for us.

CHICKENS COME HOME TO ROOST

As I was walking up Chestnut Street towards the College of Physicians, I saw a sign that was totally new to me, "Dr. _____, *Napropath*." I stopped a moment, looked at it, and said to myself, "What in the world is a napropath?"

Looking into my Greek dictionary, I could find nothing to guide me to the derivation of *napro,* although *path*, of course, referred to a malady.

My curiosity drove me to write a note to Dr. _____ , saying that I had noticed the sign in the window and asking if he would not let me know the meaning of "napro," and tell me from which Greek word it was derived.

I received in reply a very kind letter saying that "napro" was not Greek but Slavic, and meant a ligament; and that in their branch of the profession, if I may so call it,[5] diseases were attributed to abnormal conditions in the ligaments of the various joints. The signature was that of a woman, who to my surprise concluded her note by saying: "I have always felt proud that you were my first anatomy teacher, at the Pennsylvania Academy of the Fine Arts," where from 1876 to 1890 I had been the Professor of Anatomy.

I then recalled the story of chickens coming home to roost.

THE VOICE TRIUMPHANT

Parepa-Rosa

In Boston, in 1869, Patrick Gilmore organized a gigantic concert-festival, the National Peace Jubilee, which lasted five days. A 50,000-seat auditorium was built[6] to accommodate an orchestra of one thousand pieces (six massed bands), a chorus of ten thousand voices, and an audience of thirty thousand.

A number of the best-known oratorios were presented, and among the singers was the acclaimed European soprano, Parepa-Rosa, who also sang solo the Bach-Gounod arrangement of "Ave Maria," accompanied by two hundred violins. Her voice, like that of a soaring bird, was heard by the entire audience.

All of that was accomplished by means of two little vocal cords, scarcely an inch in length! What a marvelous triumph![7]

Whitney

On the opening day of the Centennial Exhibition, in Philadelphia, May 10th, 1876, there was a concert by a chorus of four or five hundred voices, accompanied by a large orchestra and featuring a number of outstanding soloists. Myron

Whitney rendered a splendid bass solo, heard by practically the entire audience of a hundred thousand, even in the open air. It was a glorious triumph.

VOLUNTEER ALTRUISM

Among my letters will be found one or more from persons unknown to me, who have offered to undergo surgical experiments, even without anesthesia, if necessary, if there was any possibility of gaining thereby additional knowledge of anatomy, physiology, or surgery that would be of use to mankind.

I have received four or five such letters. I have always declined, of course, as it seemed to me wholly unjustifiable, since we can learn practically everything about humans from similar experiments on the lower animals (almost always done with anesthetics).

The most extraordinary offer I ever had of this kind was made in April of 1907, in Berlin. A young American of twenty-five or thirty made two visits to me at my hotel with the following proposition. He declared that he was absolutely sound and healthy in mind and body, and from head to foot. (He certainly looked it physically, though I confess I was a bit doubtful of his mental soundness.) He said that, since we doctors were consulted only by people who were ill, we were only able to observe and deal with bodies or organs that were diseased. On the other hand, he, being in perfect health, wanted us to open his abdomen (I think he offered his chest as well) so as to have the unique opportunity to study healthy organs in normal action, thereby learning far more than by studying the diseased.

I positively declined, showing him how useless such a sacrifice would be, and also how criminal it would be, for I should almost certainly destroy his life. He replied that he was perfectly willing to die if by so doing he could contribute to any lasting good. At his second visit, he was even more insistent, and I more resolutely refused. He left me a sadder (but scarcely wiser) man. That he was seriously convinced that such experiments would be of great use I have no doubt. What became of him I have never heard.

COMMODORE BENEDICT

On the deck of the *Oneida*, one night, after we had operated on Mr. Cleveland for the first time, Commodore Benedict reminisced about his own career.

He was the son of a Presbyterian minister who supported himself and his wife and seven children on seven hundred dollars a year! His father always carried his shoes to and from church, wearing them only during the service, in order to make them last.

"Now," he said, "I have a beautiful home in New York City, a beautiful summer home in Greenwich, Connecticut, and this yacht, which costs me forty thousand a year." And well it might, for I have never lived more sumptuously than on the yacht, with its elaborate table and every other luxury that money could buy.

The Commodore died in 1920. Dr. Erdmann and I are the only surviving yacht guests from those momentous days of '93.

NEGRO LINGUIST

Walking along the Nevsky Prospekt in Petrograd with Florence and Dora, toward the close of a day in 1902, we observed a splendidly lighted and apparently fashionable restaurant. We entered in order to have a real Russian dinner. Up to that time, we had always found menus in Russia printed in both Russian and French, but in this case it was entirely in Russian, printed in Cyrillic script. I said to the waiter, who evidently had asked to take our order, "I do not understand Russian."

He turned away at once, and a few minutes later, a Negro as black as the ace of spades came to us and asked in the unmistakable accent of an American southern Negro, "What would like to have, sir?" I said, "You are from America, are you not?" "Yes, sir," he replied. When I asked him where he was from, he answered, "Louisville, Kentucky, sir." I found out that he had been a waiter there and had known McMurtry, in addition to my old student, Cowling, and other medical friends. He was the polyglot waiter of the establishment and spoke seven languages: English, French, German, Italian, Spanish, Russian, and Swedish.

I suspect that his repertoire was limited to restaurant "lingo," but I had no opportunity to learn more, since he disappeared after he had taken our order.

He is the only Negro I have ever known endowed with a gift for foreign languages.

AN AUDIENCE WITH THE KAISERIN[8]

On arrival in Berlin, we came here, just across the street from the Friedrich-strasse Bahnhof. Dora and I have rooms on the street side, but it is so quiet that we should never know there was a station a hundred yards away.

We soon learned that we were in Deutschland, because alles ist *verboten*. In the cars, besides a map of the road, there were *eighteen* other signs, such as:

WARNUNG

NOTBREMSE

NICHT HINAUSLEHNEN, ES IST LEBENSGEFÄHRLICH

Surely one is cared for almost to death. Self-reliance and personal initiative are almost at a discount—except in the streets, where the autos and autobuses whiz by, and you must look out for yourself and step lively.

The imperial family have white autos with a special flag and a specially toned horn, and when they go by, *Donner und Blitzen!* all people and carriages have to get out of the way.

Professor Trendelenburg (Howard's friend "Trundle bed") is sick and can't come; nor can we visit them in Leipzig, as arranged. His son, Paul, came on Sunday at noon and was with us till Tuesday night. He was most kind.

We made our calls Monday and Tuesday, on Frau Kausch (geb. Mikulicz), the Ewalds, the Krauses, Professor Riedel (president of the Surgical Society) of Jena, the Hoffas, the Körtes, and some others to whom the girls had letters.

At one of the calls, I lunched with Riedel and about thirty others—a sort of preliminary canter. As I sat between Braun, of Göttingen. and Hildebrand (König's successor at the Charité Hospital here and the "Other" Kliniker—von Bergmann being the first), and they knew not a word of English, I was pitched headlong into the waters of German and *had* to swim. It was very good for my German, but a bit hard on *me*, and I fancy on them too, in spite of their good-natured fibs as to my *ausgezeichnete* German.

The Congress opened on Wednesday. Von Bergmann's portrait was draped, and at the conclusion of Riedel's presidential address, all rose in respect to his memory.

We all lunched with the Ewalds and with Professor und Frau Virchow (he is the Professor of Anatomy and a son of *the* Virchow) and our old friends, Professor und Frau Krause (whom Margaret will remember as our hosts in '99, at their villa on the Elbe, near Hamburg). We *like* the Ewalds more than any other of our Berlin friends. They are simply charming, and Frau E.'s English is faultless!

In the evening (5:30!), I dined with Professor und Frau Olshausen, at a delightful dinner for twenty. Again, Frau O.'s English was excellent. They know many of my friends at home, tho' they have never been in the United States, and he has had many pupils from there. The Ewalds were at the Congress in Washington, in 1903, and were well entertained.

Thursday, Hoffa called. He is just back from St. Petersburg, whither he had gone to see the little tsarevich, who is slightly pigeon-toed. I spent the day at the Congress (attended by half of the sixteen hundred members!) and in the evening went to the Fest Dinner at the Savoy, where there were more than two hundred present. We were bidden at 5:30 and sat down by six. By half-past eight (there were only six courses, besides cheese, fruit, and coffee) we were through, speeches and all, and by nine, nearly everyone had gone—most sensible.

The speeches were made in between the courses, and the waiters then waited. After the soup, Riedel gave the first toast, to the Kaiser, and he was followed by König, Küster, Czerny, von Eiselsberg, Rovsing (of Copenhagen), and me! I knew I would never have a more friendly and forgiving audience, so I plunged in headfirst and spoke in *German*, begging them to excuse my *zerbrochen Deutsch*. I did better than I had feared, tho' not so well as I had hoped. They at least seemed to understand me and even applauded a joke or two.

Friday, I was at the Congress all day. Von Eiselsberg was elected president for the next year—a capital choice. Some say that he *may* be appointed in von Bergmann's place, for they all recognize him as now the leading operator in Germany (which covers German Austria). They fear he made a mistake in going from Königsberg to Vienna. Had he stayed on German soil, his election would have been *sure*. He is an Austrian by birth, however, and all his family live in Vienna.

In the evening, I dined at the Körtes'. Frau Körte took my arm and placed me on her left, which I supposed to be the place of honor. Many old friends (there were thirty in all) attended, among them, Küster (of Marburg), whose son Margaret will remember as she nearly knocked off his nose (Paris, 1900). The son is a lawyer and in the Ministry of the Interior. This dinner was at 6:30, the usual hour, I think, and we left at ten.

The family is blossoming out in German! Last night, Florence and Dora went to dinner at Frau Kausch's (Mikulicz's second daughter), and Professor K. clinked his glass and said that, as I was not present, Fräulein Dora would respond for me—which she did in German, following my example of the night before. There's no telling to what we may come before we return!

Saturday, the Congress adjourned. At one o'clock, ten of us were asked to meet the president, who then gave us instructions as to an audience with the Kaiserin: Meet at the Schloss at 5:15 in full evening dress, including white tie and gloves, orders, and all. I went with von Eiselsberg, in an ordinary fiacre. I was *en grande tenue*, as prescribed, though I did not wear my orders.

We were present fifteen minutes before the appointed time, and after leaving our wraps (but by instruction carrying our hats; mine was an opera hat), we were ushered from one room to another, and finally to one on the second floor—all handsome but not especially noteworthy. We ended in a room about the size of our parlor and were placed in a semicircle, in the order in which our names had been handed in on the official list. The court chamberlain placed us, I being No. 1, as the only *Ehren Mitglied*. Then came Picqué (of Paris), Mr. Barker (of London), Rovsing, Eiselsberg, Braun, Kümmel, Rehn, Madelung, and Körte. The Kaiserin entered in a few minutes, first talked to the president, then came to me, and then went to each one, in turn talking with equal ease in English, French, or German, for probably three minutes each, so that we really had quite a nice little conversation.

I watched Riedel and, in turn, when she held out her hand, I took it, bowed over and kissed it (more Germanico), as if I were accustomed to do so every day. Of course, I waited for her to speak first, and, naturally, her opening question was whether this was my first visit to Berlin. I told her that I had been a student with Langenbeck, Virchow, and others, in 1865–66; that I knew many of the German surgeons; and that I had the honor to know the Princess Henrietta and Professor von Esmarch. She instantly responded, "Oh, yes, I remember their speaking of you and of the very pleasant dinner they attended in your home in Philadelphia." This broke the ice, and we talked very pleasantly about the von Esmarches, the German Surgical Society, etc., till she bowed and passed on to Picqué. I confess I was surprised at her remembering such a detail as a dinner thirteen years ago. I think your ball dresses must have so impressed the Princess Henrietta that she passed them on to her niece, the Kaiserin. I wanted dreadfully to tell her I would like to call on her distinguished and, I might say, well-known husband, but as she said nothing about him, I forbore.

Now as a model father, I carefully studied her dress and will try to describe it in detail. She wore a broad black hat with black ostrich feathers. Her dress was a high-neck, light blue-green satin (or silk?), and she evidently had been sitting down, for the skirt was creased transversely in several folds. She wore a lace collar and a string of pearls that reached to her waist. Her dress was adjusted to the bust, not by plaits but rather by being narrowed from the shoulders to the waist by seams pretty close together. It was then expanded from the waist to the hips by widening seams. It was bordered below by greenish velvet, four to five inches wide, and it had a short house train. The sleeves were puffed and slashed, and into the slashings were interpolated some figured stuff like velour.

The sleeves stopped at the elbow and were trimmed with a brownish lace. The same kind of lace trimmed the dress all over, converging from the shoulders to the center of the waist, front and back, and continued from the waistband of the same lace in a long streak down the front and back of the skirt. Where the back streak joined the waistband was a bow of the same lace. The lace also ran parallel to and a little above the velvet order of the skirt and rose in two or three points on each side, half-way to the hips.

She wore light-gray long gloves with two or three bracelets. She carried a fan (closed) but no prayer book.

Voilà! Now if you can't reproduce this dress in all its details, it will not be my fault.

Her gray hair was done up in a roll or knot. I think that it must have been a true lover's knot, at the back, but it was so shaded by her hat that I am a bit in doubt.

She is a little inclined to stoutness, but she has a very pleasing face and Shakespeare's proper woman's voice, low and sweet.[9] In her charm of manner, she reminded me not a little of Mrs. Cleveland.

In the evening, I went to the Anglo-American Medical Association, formed some years ago by Dr. Honan, a Chicago man in practice here for ten years. It is a most useful club (as is its counterpart in Vienna), in giving help of all sorts, professional and personal, to English and American students. It usually has fifty to eighty members and meets every Saturday night at 7:30 for an à la carte dinner, and at 8:30 for a lecture by some German professor or docent. Last night's was by Schleich—him of the "fluid." Walter, if you will keep your eye on the *Journal of the American Medical Association*, you will see a letter from me, describing the meetings here and the club. The boys *heartily* appreciated my coming, and I was *very* glad I went. It encouraged them to see that I took a timely interest in their welfare and wanted to help them. Of course, I had to make a little speech.

We expect Hilde Mikulicz (Frau Willy Anschütz) and Dr. A. to lunch with us, and at 3:30, we go by the Krauses' auto out to the Krauses' summer villa, forty minutes away. The Anschützes have a *Sprössling*, a year-old girl.

In order to let Dora see something of the schools here (they re-open on Tuesday), we shall not leave until Thursday morning at eight, reaching Vienna at nine in the evening, and probably leaving on Saturday morning for Trieste. On our way back, we shall probably stop for two or three days in Vienna, and for one or two days in Berlin, where we shall leave our storage trunks. After the first of May, these rascally Germans abolish *all* free baggage, as in Holland and Italy. Margaret's letters of the 23rd and 24th came three days ago, to our delight, and we were greatly pleased to hear once more from home (how good that word sounds, so far away!), and to know that all are well.

Now you see, like St. Paul, how long a letter I have written to you with mine own hand (how I long for the typewriter!) and told you all our doings. Repay me by others. No detail is too familiar or too petty to be without interest.

Most affectionately, Your loving father,

W. W. Keen

P. S. I have received here a letter from a florist in New York. The beautiful flowers came from a patient in Wheeling, West Virginia.

ADMIRAL PEARY[10]

I first Peary after his marriage, about twenty-five years ago, when his wife required my professional services. She was an unusually strong woman, and the two of them thought nothing of walking out to Chestnut Hill (ten miles or so) and back, when their quarters were near us at 1729 Chestnut Street.

They consulted me before the first time Mrs. Peary went with him to the Arctic. I told them that the chief obstacles were the continued severe cold, the prolonged darkness, and the dirt and discomfort of their surroundings. "If you can stand these three," I said, "I see no physical reason why you should not go"—and she went.[11]

In his penultimate expedition, Admiral Peary's toes were so badly frozen that most of them sloughed off, leaving painful and annoying stumps. He consulted me, and I amputated the stumps of nine toes, leaving one healthy little toe—"as a reminder," I told him, of his former full equipment.[12]

After that operation, he went North for his final attempt and walked several hundreds of miles to the Pole and back,[13] a very remarkable performance even for a man with ten good toes.

U.S. PRESIDENTS I'VE MET

LINCOLN

I saw President-elect Lincoln only once, when George Porter and I rode in the procession which escorted him from the Pennsylvania Railroad station in Kensington to the State House.[14] (In the carriage with him was John Hay, his assistant private secretary and our old college friend.)

GRANT

I also met President Grant only one time, at one of the Saturday-night receptions given at the home of Philadelphia philanthropist A.J. Drexel and his wife, but we barely exchanged greetings.[15] We, among thousands, saw him at the opening of the Centennial Exhibition in Fairmount Park.

CLEVELAND

I knew President Cleveland well, as a result of our operations on him, and after his death, there were still cordial occasional encounters with his widow.

McKINLEY

I also knew President McKinley well. When he was a congressman, his wife was a patient of Weir Mitchell's, and I had done a minor operation on her for Dr. Mitchell. At that time and during a later visit to Washington with my dear wife, I saw him frequently and formed a high opinion of his ability and personality. He was a loyal and devoted husband. Never did he miss writing to his wife at least one letter a day, when they were unavoidably separated. He sometimes wrote two, and occasionally even three letters a day. This she told me herself. When one remembers the exigencies of his public life, this is remarkable. When he was first a presidential candidate, his wife had an epileptic seizure in a department store in Cleveland. Mark Hanna, his campaign manager, was said to have advocated secluding her until after the election. He said that "if to become president of the United States I must shut up my wife, I will never be the president of the United States." A splendid rebuke.

I lunched at the White House en famille several times, with President McKinley, and on one occasion, Florence and Dora were with me. The president sat at the end of the table, and on his right was Mrs. McKinley. I was placed next to her, with another guest (a lady) on my right. In the midst of an interesting conversation with my right-hand neighbor, Mrs. McKinley was suddenly seized with an epileptic fit. She did not fall from her chair; nor were her convulsions so general or violent as to require her removal to a lounge or to the floor, and she apparently was in no danger of biting her tongue. She trembled rather violently and convulsively all over. In an instant, the president rose, threw his napkin over her head and face, and drew her body and head to his breast. He thus supported her for two or three minutes (which seemed an hour), and when the attack subsided, she was able to keep her erect position without help. Her face was deeply flushed, and she was quite dazed. The president resumed his seat.

Meanwhile, as Mrs. McKinley evidently did not need my professional assistance, I tried to continue the conversation, without cessation, embarrassment, or seeming to notice what was going on at my left elbow. Florence and Dora also did the same, and the incident was never alluded to. (Mrs. McKinley's malady was the result of the birth of one of her two children—who did not survive.)

What struck me most was McKinley's very evident growth in the presidency. When I saw him again, after an absence of several years, I found him a much larger, broader man. Great responsibilities, especially those of the Spanish-American War, had developed his powers, and he was a far stronger man. I respected him highly and deplored his death.

TAFT

When in Manila, in October of 1901, we were invited to lunch with Mr. Taft, who was then the governor-general of the Philippines. It was my first meeting with him, and he impressed me most favorably. I was one of his most enthusiastic supporters in the 1908 campaign. Soon after his inauguration, he consulted me about the health of his daughter Helen, who was then a student at Bryn Mawr. She evidently was in need of orthopedic treatment, and I placed her under the care of Dr. James Rugh, who did admirably for her.

Several times since then—in connection with the annual dinners of the American Philosophical Society, with the proposed establishment of a National Seismological Bureau, and with the re-establishment of the army canteen—I have met him, and always with pleasure and heightened esteem.

One of the noblest instances of patriotic altruism I have ever known was when, on two occasions, Taft was offered the blue ribbon of his profession, a seat on the Supreme Court. He declined it, saying that his duty to his wards, the Filipinos, was not yet completed. A man who could do that is made of the finest clay.

WILSON

And now (October, 1912), the next president will certainly be either Taft, again, or Governor Woodrow Wilson. I am sincerely puzzled to know whom to vote for. Mr. Roosevelt has forfeited my confidence by his deceiving the people, by breaking his pledge "under no circumstances" to accept another nomination, and by his wild vagaries as to the recall of judges and of judicial decisions. Governor Wilson I would trust personally,[16] but I do not like the platform and the tendencies of his party.

I shall probably vote for Mr. Taft, because he has been a very careful and conservative, and yet progressive, president. I think he is entitled to re-election as an endorsement of his course. He and the Republican Party have undoubtedly learned some wisdom and will be willing to institute the reforms that are greatly needed. Should either be elected, I should know the man well.

In the case of Wilson, I should again be in close touch with him. Only this last spring, I operated on Mrs. Wilson, and I operated on two of their three daughters a few years ago. One of the operations was very dangerous, as the furious hemorrhage was almost uncontrollable. Fearing a recurrence, I had Dr. Spencer sit up all night with her, lest it should recur and be quickly fatal unless skillful help was at hand on the instant. Such an emergency brings the surgeon and the family very closely together.[17]

A MOST REMARKABLE LINGUIST

While stationed at the Satterlee Hospital in West Philadelphia, I was a colleague of Dr. Frederic Louis Otto Roehrig, another Acting Assistant Surgeon—and a most remarkable man. He had *au fond* three areas of expertise: He was an able ophthalmologist, a noteworthy ornithologist, and an outstanding linguist. Beyond these three areas he was a simple child. He had married an able and thrifty American wife and was happy to pour his salary into her lap every month. It otherwise would have melted in foolish purchases.

When I first knew him, he read, wrote, and spoke over one hundred languages and dialects. I have heard him speak Turkish with our Turkish cook. He wrote a book (in Latin) on the affinities of the Finnish language—a very odd linguistic island among all of the alien languages surrounding Finland. I don't believe he ever published any other work.[18]

After the Civil War, I called on him while he was at Cornell as a professor of Sanskrit, Hindustani, Old Persian, Arabic, and other Eastern languages.

Between the end of the war and his appointment at Cornell, he had spent considerable time among the North American Indians and had several linguistic scalps hanging from his belt, adding to his antebellum collection.

He was an invaluable aid to the Government: When some missive arrived for the State Department which their own official translators could not decipher, it was referred to him. He was the arbiter as to the meaning of one of the treaties in dispute between Turkey and the United States, and as a result of his favoring the Turkish interpretation, he was designated a Chevalier of the Imperial Order of the Medjidiyeh.

I do not know when or where he died. In fact, I only suppose that he *is* dead because he was somewhat my senior.[19]

Rail Connections

In December of 1907, when Florence, Dora, and I were spending the winter in Rome, I had occasion to go to Vienna for a week. Both going and returning, I had a noteworthy fellow-traveler.

On the way to Vienna, a husky young fellow of about twenty-five occupied the upper berth in our compartment. We fell into conversation, in bad French. (I earnestly hope, though I would not be willing to assert, that both my lingo and my pronunciation were not as bad as his.) We soon exchanged cards, from which I learned that he was Prince _____ , one of the leading and most aristocratic families of Poland.

Our passage over the Semmering Alps was at night, and with considerable snow. When we awoke in the morning, our window was frosted over. I rose first, and finding none in the water closet, I called the porter and asked for four towels, two for each of us. Just after I emerged from the water closet, the prince began to yawn, and, seeing he was now awake, I told him of my request for towels. He stretched and yawned again, and after looking at the window he said, with a shudder, "It's too cold. I shan't wash this morning."

As he had only partially undressed, his dressing was quickly accomplished. He washed neither face nor hands and paid not even perfunctory attention to his teeth. He simply put on the few clothes he had taken off and went out into the corridor, where he began talking with some ladies! I was glad not to be a Polish prince.[20]

A few moments after our train had left Padua, on the return trip, a tall gentleman of about sixty entered the compartment, which I had had to myself all the way from Vienna. He bowed politely to me, and of course I bowed in return. After he had arranged his impedimenta, he sat down and opened a conversation, though in Italian. It was easy to discern by both eye and ear that I was a stranger, and one of the first questions he asked me was if I had ever been in Padua. I replied in the affirmative but added that in the forty years since my last visit, many of my impressions of the place had faded away. "But I can never forget," I continued, "that Padua is the home—and here I used the proper and customary superlatives—of the *celebrissimo e illustrissimo chirurgo* Professor Bassini. (Edoardo Bassini is known wherever surgery is practiced, because of "Bassini's Operation," but he also is Professor of Surgery at the University of Padua.)

He half rose and, putting his hand to his heart, replied, "Thank you. I am Professor Bassini."

The arrow, shot at a venture, unexpectedly hit the bull's eye.

We then exchanged cards and mutually recalled the fact that we had met before, but only casually. At the celebration of the Royal College of Surgeons of England, in 1900, we had both been made honorary fellows, but in the intervening seven years, the face of each had been forgotten by the other.

We chatted, on and off, all the way to Rome, and he dined with us, very pleasantly, the following evening.

MacEwen and Kelvin[*]

MacEwen referred to the boy's common trick with a "sucker," using a disk of wet leather, two or three inches in diameter with a string through the middle. When the boy places the wet leather on a brick and flattens it out with his foot to make it adhere, he can then lift the brick out of the pavement.

MacEwen then asked Kelvin what was the force which held the brick fast to the leather.

"The pressure of the atmosphere," said Kelvin at once.

"If you were to exhaust the air in a bell jar over the brick, the brick should fall, should it not?"

"Of course."

"But it doesn't fall."

"Have you tried it?"

"Yes."

[*] *Told to me by MacEwen himself, at the 6th International Congress of Surgery, in 1923* [of which MacEwen was president]

"What, in your opinion, is the restraining force?"

"Capillary attraction."

"Wait awhile. Let me figure it out mathematically."

In a short time, Kelvin returned and said, "Yes, I have proved by mathematical formulae that you are right. I don't need to try the experiment."

Whitlock and Hoover

At the very beginning of the Great War, two remarkable men, both Americans, stood out in bold relief for their extraordinary work in behalf of Belgium and the Belgians: Brand Whitlock, American Minister to Belgium; and Herbert C. Hoover, the head of the Commission for the Relief of Belgium, an organization (generally known as the C.R.B.), which he founded.

Whitlock's fine book, *Belgium*, is his personal narrative; and the reports of the C.R.B.—and still more the Belgians, especially the Belgian children whose lives he saved from starvation—are the monument to the herculean labors of Hoover.

When the Board of Fellows of Brown University met in December of 1915 to decide on those who were to be honored with degrees, the following June, I proposed the names of both of these men for an Honorary Doctor of Laws. Our strictly observed rule is that the nominee must be present to receive the degree in person, but I strongly argued the absolute impossibility of their leaving their work in Europe, and yet so emphasized their outstanding worthiness of such an honor that we finally agreed to confer the degrees on these two exceptional men in absentia.

Whitlock had five honorary degrees conferred upon him by other universities, and the legation to Belgium was raised to the highest rank, an embassy. Whitlock became the first ambassador.

Mr. Hoover has had the highest honors conferred upon him by twenty American universities, in addition to Oxford and eight others on the Continent.

But Brown led at the head of the procession.

"So Light On Her Feet"

I was called to attend a lady for a minor surgical operation. When she was well and I was about to take my leave from her, she suddenly said to me, "Dr. Keen, can't you help me further? When I was married, fifteen years ago, I weighed only a hundred and twenty-five pounds, and now I weigh three hundred and thirty." She looked every pound of it.

I told her that while it was not exactly in my line of surgical work, I thought it seemed to me very much a matter of common sense. When we wish to lessen the heat of the fire, we put on less wood or coal. "In your case," I said, "cut down the amount of food you eat, especially the starches, fats, and sugar," adding that she should regularly weigh herself on the same scales once a week and keep a written record. "If you are losing more than a pound a week, be less strict; if less, be more strict, and come to see me in three or four months."

At the appointed time, glowing with satisfaction and walking as if on springs, she returned, saying, "Dr. Keen, you can't imagine how light I am on my feet. I weigh only three hundred and one pounds."

A Soldier's Alternative

In 1915, I went to Allentown to give an address to the class of graduating nurses at the Allentown Hospital.[21] Seeing in the newspaper the notice that I was to be there, H.A. Mack, one of my old patients, had hunted up Dr. Schaeffer to learn where and when he could see me.

When we reached the hospital, at about four, I encountered a man who was pretty much my own age, but looking hale and hearty. He reminded me that he had been a patient in the Christian Street Hospital, which Drs. Mitchell and Morehouse and I had established specifically for the treatment of diseases of the nerves.

I had quite forgotten him and the incident, naturally, but he told me that when he himself had recovered, he was placed on duty as an orderly in the ward. Among our patients were a number of epileptics, and it was no uncommon thing to have as many as two hundred seizures in a night. He stood it for a few days, but then asked to be returned to the front. He couldn't stand the fits, and rather than face the contortions of our unfortunate patients, he preferred to face the bullets of the enemy.

12

—••꘎꘎••—

War and Peace

W HAT A TERRIBLY LONG LIST of wars I have seen!
In my youth, Indian wars in the West were almost continuous. I vividly
recall our Mexican War, Civil War, and Spanish-American War.

In Europe, I well remember the uprisings of 1848, which were put down
by the various national armies. Then followed the Crimean War, 1854–55;
the Franco-Austro-Italian War of 1859 (the year I graduated from college);
the Schleswig-Holstein War (1864), in which Prussia and Austria robbed
Denmark of those contiguous duchies; the Austro-Prussian War of 1866; the
Franco-Prussian War of 1870; the Russo-Turkish War of 1877–78; and finally
the cataclysm of 1914–16. (My father used to say, if the Devil doesn't get the
Kaiser, there's no use in having a Devil!)

In Africa and Asia there have been the Boer War (1899–1901); the Tai Ping
Rebellion, in China (1850–64); the Sino-Japanese War of 1895; the Boxer War
of 1900; the Russo-Japanese War of 1904–1905; and many military expeditions
(or small wars), as in India, Burma, Cochin, China, Java, Egypt, and the
Sudan. Africa has been partitioned among the powers of Europe. Included
in the efforts to establish supporting colonies were the Belgian atrocities in
the Congo, which were reported to me personally by missionaries who were
eyewitness to them.

Even now, it is not certain that the attempted spoliation of China by the
European powers, halted by John Hay, may not yet be carried out, once Europe
has recovered from the present war.

The maps of Europe, Asia, and Africa (and of the Americas, to a large extent)
have been made over and over, and soon will have to be re-made yet once more.
Thank God that the beastly cruel, unspeakable Turk will, in all likelihood, be
driven out of Europe, after nearly five centuries of misrule.

Politically, the unification of Italy and of Germany; the happy passing of the temporal power of the popes; the separation of Norway from Sweden; the changes from monarchy to republic, in France and in Portugal; the shrinkage of Turkey; and the kaleidoscopic changes in the Balkans are the most striking developments.

What effects the Great War will produce, no one now would venture to predict, though it *may* establish New York as the world's financial center and the dollar as the world's unit of monetary exchange. He would, of course, be a rash prophet who would declare that these things *will* happen.

THE GREAT WAR

There is ample evidence, from many sources, that Germany had been preparing for this war ever since 1870, much of it well documented in Paul Vergnet's *France in Danger.*

The German "White Book" acknowledged that there had been communication between Berlin and Vienna, in reference to the relations between Austria and Serbia, and that Germany supported Austria. Neither power has ever dared to publish the *text* of these conferences.

The favorite toast in German army circles was *Der Tag!* For a number of reasons, Germany judged that the day had come:

1. Great Britain was on the verge of civil war over home rule for Ireland, and the spreading disaffection in India would be likely to cause an uprising as serious as the Sepoy Rebellion of 1857.
2. France was about to lengthen the term of service to the colors from two to three years, and it was important to strike before the full effect of this change could be realized.
3. Russia was emerging from her defeat by the Japanese and would soon become too formidable.
4. The Kiel Canal had finally been widened and deepened, so that all German ships of war could pass through it between the Baltic and the North Sea.
5. The German navy had been strengthened until it was approaching equality with that of Britain's.
6. The German army had been notably increased several times by large additions to the peace force—with still more available in case of war. The excuse was that a new power had arisen in the Balkans and that all eventualities must be provided for.

The assassination of Archduke Ferdinand at Sarajevo was not the cause of the war but merely a pretext for it. The Austrian ultimatum was brutal and allowed no time for other powers to mediate or to halt the war. Germany and Austria were determined on war and would brook no interference or delay. Germany declared war on Russia, on the first of August, 1914, and the conflagration was ignited.

The brutal treatment of Cambon, the French ambassador to Germany (as related in the French "Yellow Book"), was in marked contrast to that of von Schön, the German ambassador to France. The latter was sent to the German frontier in a special train (which was promptly seized by the Germans). Cambon, on the other hand, suffered indignities which a spy or a servant would rightly have resented.

On August 4th, a few hours after the German minister had assured Belgium of her safety, German troops entered the country, simultaneously occupying all of Luxembourg. Germany had solemnly guaranteed the neutrality of both. It was impossible for Luxembourg to resist, since by treaty she was forbidden to have an army or fortifications. Thus were two treaties reduced to "scraps of paper." Since then, a third treaty has also been reduced to scraps of paper: In 1888, Germany, Austria, and Turkey (along with the other great powers) were cosignatories of a treaty guaranteeing that the Suez Canal should always be open, "in time of war as in time of peace, to every vessel of commerce or of war, without distinction of flag," Germany has never even attempted to defend her invasion of Luxembourg, though she has asserted that documents found in Brussels justified her invasion of Belgium. These "documents" were records of unofficial conversations among British officers indicating that *IF* Germany invaded Belgium, Great Britain would come to her aid. Even granting that German claim, the motives and acts of Germany on the 4th of August must be judged by what she knew at that time, rather than on what she pretends to have found ten days later in Brussels. But the frank avowal of von Bethman-Hollweg in the Reichstag is conclusive evidence that Germany had perpetrated a wrong on Belgium. The only reason given was that it was a "military necessity."

By terms of a treaty, Belgium was obliged to enforce by arms her own neutrality, and this was not considered a warlike act. Yet Germany has again disregarded this proviso and has committed unspeakable and barbarous cruelties on Belgium and her people. Lord Bryce's report, and the testimony of reliable witnesses I have known (or known of) personally, have set these forth with great force. The atrocities in Serbia and Poland are horrible beyond belief.[1]

Besides all this, Germany has ruthlessly destroyed cities and splendid monuments of the past, such as the library at Louvain and the cathedral at Rheims; has exacted enormous tribute from captured cities; has seized civilian hostages—sometimes shooting them on flimsy pretexts; and has made war more frightful than ever with her flaming shells and poisonous gases.

Submarine warfare has been waged by Germany with brutal disregard of not only international law, but also of the laws of humanity, taking the lives of Americans and other neutrals. The fine stand taken by President Wilson yesterday[2] expressed exactly the sentiment of the great bulk of Americans. His chief fault in the matter is that this note should have been delivered a year ago, when the *Lusitania* was sunk without warning. Our dead cry out to us, from the waters of the Atlantic, for the expiation of their murder.

The Germans whine over the inhumanity of the British attempt to starve them into defeat. Does anyone outside an insane asylum seriously believe that if the roles were reversed, so that Germany had command of the sea at the beginning of the war, she would have hesitated for an instant to blockade all British ports and thus starve *her* into submission? The food supply of Great Britain, as estimated by a number of writers, is usually sufficient for about six weeks only. Had not the British fleet commanded the seas, England would have been beaten almost before she began. Never were Admiral Mahan's views of the value of sea power in history more splendidly vindicated.[3]

In August of 1914, Belgium saved the day. But for her heroic resistance, the Germans would surely have invaded France and possibly have captured Paris.

After twenty months of war, the Kaiser's troops, halted on the Marne, have made little further progress. In the East, the Russians are gradually driving back the once-victorious Germans and Austrians. In Armenia, they have captured Erzerum and Trebizond and may easily threaten Constantinople. On the Tigris, the British bid fair to be victors. In Arabia and Egypt, the attacks on the Suez Canal have been halted. In the Balkans, the Anglo-French troops are almost ready for a drive against the Germans and the Bulgarians.

The Italians have not yet captured Trieste.

The miserable fiasco at the Dardanelles ought never to have occurred.

Meantime, the possible entrance of Holland and Rumania (as I hope) would hasten the inevitable victory of the Allies.

The titanic struggle is between two great principles:

I. Germany and Austria represent autocracy, military ascendancy, the state as sole arbiter, and the subservience of the individual, whose worth is negligible save as a small unit to be exploited by the state.

II. The Allies represent democracy, civil ascendency over the military, and the primacy of the individual, for whom and for whose welfare the state exists—though it has no right to infringe on the individual's life, liberty, or pursuit of happiness.

And where does my country stand? The bulk of the people, I believe, are loyal to our republican principles. They fervently hope for the success of the Allies, who are fighting *our* battle for *our* future freedom, and possibly even for our future existence.

Great fortunes have been made out of the war, and we are now the principal creditor nation of the world. I still believe that our ideals are our beacons and that we shall choose national honor and national duty to ourselves and to humanity, and fight and even die for them, if need be. We will not be recreant sons of the patriotic sires of 1776 and 1861.

Wholly apart from the money gained from making munitions for the Allies, we remember that to place an embargo on such exports would be a gross violation of international law, as well as a gross violation of the official neutrality to which we must adhere. Germany went into the war knowing that Great Britain had command of the sea. She voluntarily took the risk. As a neutral, we may by law sell to both belligerents, as Germany did during the Russo-Japanese War and the Boer War. To prohibit such sales to one belligerent because the other has lost command of the sea (or for any other reason) would be the greatest possible direct aid to Germany—which God forbid.

I feel such an aversion to Germany's conduct that, although I esteem my individual German friends as much as ever, I shall never again set foot on German soil, or on a German steamer. I shall never again buy anything MADE IN GERMANY, and never again trust a promise of the German government. (Of course, I include Austria, a mere tail to the German kite.)

My only regret is that we did not enter the war long ago as an ally of Britain, France, and Russia. We may yet bitterly repent that we did not. The positive demands of President Wilson's note, and his address to Congress yesterday, may result in our entering the war.

But no words can express my humiliation at our unpreparedness, or the failure of Congress—especially of the House—to appreciate the gravity of the situation and the need for prompt and adequate relief.

Our army has been on the Mexican frontier for four years. We might expect a raid, or possibly war itself, at any moment. Yet Villa's raid on Columbus, New Mexico, on the ninth of March, apparently caught our troops without even pickets to warn them. Our machine guns did not work, and we were so little prepared that we had no motor trucks ready to carry supplies to where they were needed. Of six aeroplanes, four were worthless. Our troops did not start after Villa until he had had a start of six days, and it was only on the eleventh day after his raid that the first fifteen auto trucks (of the one hundred ordered!) started with supplies. Practically our whole army at home is in Mexico or on the border, for this one little episode, leaving only about four thousand men available in case of any other emergency.

May we yet heed the warning and be ready when the call of duty is sounded.

THE PERFIDIOUS HUN

All of the world's achievements sink into insignificance in the light of the present horrible war. The history of its causes and its authors will only be known fifty, or even a hundred, years from now. Had Germany and Austria *dared* to publish *textually* the notes which passed between Berlin and Vienna (and that there *were* such notes is clear from the official introduction to the first German White Book), allowing the world to know how much of a hand Germany had, through von Tschirsky, her ambassador to Vienna, in framing the ultimatum to Serbia, it would be clear that the Kaiser was repsonsible for the war.

Had he lifted only his little finger, Austria would have called a European congress; or the ultimatum would have been preceded by conferences between the powers; or a reasonable time would have been given Serbia, during which the powers could have effected some arrangement to satisfy and protect Austria, while at the same time preserving world peace.

I hold the Kaiser responsible for all the sorrow, suffering, poverty, death, and destruction resulting from the war. He opened it by violating a solemn treaty (a mere "scrap of paper") and by desolating Belgium. This treatment of Belgium can be seen as a logical consequence of the Kaiser's speech to his soldiers, when he sent them to China during the Boxer Rebellion: "Spare nobody, take no prisoners. Use your weapons in a manner to make every Chinaman for a thousand years to come forgo the wish to as much as look askance at a German."[4]

Had the bungling, stupid German diplomacy sought, from pole to pole, anything which would have more firmly consolidated anti-German sentiment among the Americans—indeed of the whole civilized world—it could not have discovered a more efficient means than the destruction of the *Lusitania* and the *Ancona*. One shudders with revulsion at the violation of all international law (to say nothing of the laws of God and humanity) in this murder of innocent non-combatants on the high seas. Her scientists have devised means for the use of chlorine and bromine gases, diabolical weapons which place her beyond the pale of civilization.

Words fail to describe the utter detestation I feel, not for the German people but for the military autocracy and the army. As president of the American Philosophical Society, as well as the Fifth International Surgical Congress (which is to meet in Paris in September of 1917), I feel that I am not at liberty to declare my sentiments publicly. I therefore have carefully refrained from any expression of opinion which could reach my German or Austro-Hungarian friends, towards whom I feel as kindly as I ever did. Privately, however, I feel at liberty to (and do) express my abhorence of Germany's brutal methods. The report of Lord Bryce's commission (as well as numerous statements to me by friends of what they have seen and known) has convinced me of the truth of otherwise unverifiable rumors, even as though the Kaiser's admonition to his troops had never been uttered.

I would wish to eliminate such an enemy of civilization from my consciousness. May she drink to the dregs the cup of sorrows she has pressed to the lips of so many innocent sufferers!

GERMAN "DIPLOMACY"

(1) The rape of Luxembourg. In this case there was no question of found documents nor of any army. Luxembourg, by the treaty guaranteeing her neutrality, was prohibited from having an army and compelled to dismantle all the fortifications of the capital. She had only a police force. Yet Germany broke faith with her and has simply taken possession of the country.

(2) The rape of Belgium, with all its atrocities. The motives of Germany must be judged by what they knew when they sent the ultimatum to Belgium on August 4th. This shows that von Bethmann Hollweg was right when he admitted in the Reichstag that they had committed a great wrong.

(3) The atrocities in Poland.

(4) The atrocities in Armenia, where the ally of Germany has murdered over a million Armenians without even a protest from Germany.

(5) Germany complains bitterly of England's attempt to starve her civilian population. Is anyone so simple as to believe for a moment that if Germany had had command of the sea she would not have starved the civilian population of

Great Britain into a peace? I do not know anyone so naif as to think so. It is Great Britain's vulnerable point. Cut off her food supplies, and in six weeks, I have seen it stated, she would be starving.

(6) The interned officers at Norfolk. These men had given their parole of honor that they would not escape. They were given unusual and, as it proved to be, unwise privileges. They broke their parole of honor and escaped. The only course open to Germany was to return them to the United States to be interned until the end of the war. By not doing so, she has tacitly approved of their breaking their word of honor.

STARVING A NATION

The Germans and their advocate, Professor Harry L. Barnes (in the October to December, 1925, issues of the *Christian Century*) have made a great outcry against the starving of Germany by means of the blockade. Professor Barnes even calls it illegal.

Cutting off the food and water supply, as a means of compelling the surrender of any besieged city, has always been a legal and a well-recognized weapon.

Professor Spaight (in his *War Rights on Land*, published in London in 1911, three years before the World War and therefore free from the passions aroused by it) calls attention to what the Germans did during the siege of Metz. A walled town that had outgrown its limits, Metz had a large extra-mural population. When the Germans were about to bombard the city, not only did they refuse to allow the women and children, or the aged and the sick, to pass through their lines, but they drove all the extra-mural population into the city within the walls so as to exhaust the food supply so much the sooner and thus force their early surrender. As Spaight points out, this driving of the extra-mural population inside the city walls was utterly illegal. When these poor fugitives, as well as many deserters from the French army, tried to escape, the Germans drove them back again within the walls.

As everybody knows, the Germans starved Paris into surrender in 1871. It ill becomes them, therefore, to complain of the blockade on a larger scale. The principle is the same, whether in the case of the population of various cities or, as in this case, its application to a whole nation.

So too, cutting off the water supply to force an early surrender is a well-recognized legal procedure.

C'est la guerre!

It would be well also for Professor Barnes to read the terms of the Armistice. In one of these terms, Germany distinctly agrees to point out the wells and springs that they had poisoned. So far as I know, this is the first time that any supposedly civilized nation has confessed its resorting to such prohibited measures.

AMERICAN REPLY TO GERMANY, *LEDGER* MAY 9, 1916

"The note of the Imperial German Government, under the date of May 4th, 1916, has received careful consideration by the Government of The United States. It is especially noted, as indicating the purpose of the Imperial Government as to the future, that it 'is prepared to do its utmost to confine the operations of the war for the rest of its duration to the fighting forces of the belligerents,' and it is determined to impose upon all its commanders at sea the limitations of the recognized rules of international law upon which the Government of the United States has insisted.

"Throughout the months which have elapsed since the Imperial Government announced on February 4th, 1915, its submarine policy now happily abandoned, the Government of the United States has been constantly guided and restrained by motives of friendship in its patient effort to bring to an amicable settlement the critical questions arising from that policy.

"Accepting the Imperial Government's declaration of its abandonment of the policy which has so seriously menaced the good relations between the two countries, the Government of the United States will rely upon a scrupulous execution henceforth of the now altered policy of the Imperial Government such as will remove the principal danger to an interruption of the good relations existing between the United States and Germany.

"The Government of the United States feels it necessary to state that it takes for granted that the Imperial German Government does not intend to imply that the maintenance of its newly announced policy is in any way contingent upon the course or result of diplomatic negotiations between the Government of the United States and any other belligerent Government, notwithstanding the fact that certain passages in the Imperial Government's note of the fourth instant might appear to be susceptible of that construction.

"In order, however, to avoid any possible misunderstanding, the Government of the United States notifies the Imperial Government that it cannot for a moment entertain, much less discuss, a suggestion that respect by German naval authorities for the rights of citizens of the United States upon the high seas should in any way or in the sightest degree be made contingent upon the conduct of any other Government affecting the rights of neutrals and noncombatants. Responsibility in such matters is single, not joint; absolute, not relative."

MY EARNEST PROTEST TO THIS REPLY

I never thought it possible that even in nearly four score years, I should ever live to see the day when my country would be offered such an insolent note as that just sent by Germany. Apparently the President actually is willing to accept it. Is it possible that we have fallen so low as to become the official cat's paw of Germany to pull the English chestnuts out of the fire for her?

She has tried more than once to induce the President to obtain something from Germany by first influencing Great Britain to change her method of warfare. Happily the President has always refused to conduct negotiations with one nation conditioned upon the results of negotiations with another. I cannot believe that he will fall into this trap, or rather will be moved by this brazen threat.

That England has violated international law in some ways may very possibly be true. But there is this fundamental difference between the two countries. England has *seized our goods*. Germany has *murdered our citizens*. Shall we balance a bale of cotton against a human life?

Germany is said to have made "concessions" to us! Can a promise that hereafter she will conduct her submarine warfare "in accordance with the general principles of visit and search," that is to say, if I understand it rightly, in accordance with what have been the well-recognized principles of international law, possibly be called a "concession?" By this very statement Germany admits that she has been violating international law up till now. She now promises not to do so at present. But her letter, like a scorpion, has a sting in its tail. If our Government cannot compel England to do as Germany wishes, then forsooth Germany "must reserve for itself complete liberty of decision." That is to say she will revert again to her former self-confessed illegal methods and sink and destroy, slay and slaughter belligerents and neutrals, combatants and non-combatants, the innocent as well as the guilty. And this conditional promise is called a "concession"! Since when has it been a concession for my neighbor to allow me to exercise my unquestioned right to walk down the street without molestation? When, why, and by whom is it a "concession" if I am "allowed" to sail on a peaceful errand on the open sea, in safety from being torpedoed without warning?

On this memorable day when our dead of the *Lusitania* are still calling upon us—and alas so far in vain!—for reparation, for the utter abolition of similar future barbarous murders and for the establishment and enforcement of international law, it is right for an American citizen to utter an earnest protest against such a sinister threat. It is right for him to call anew for disavowal of that inhuman act and for punishment of the dastard who slew these innocent victims in cold blood.

A whole year has passed. The "Strict Accountability" note of William J. Bryan was followed by the note calling another such attack a distinctly "unfriendly act"—most serious words when used in diplomacy. Other and many similar murders on the high seas, in the Mediterranean as well as in English waters, have been perpetrated upon our fellow citizens and nothing has been done. Not so would Washington or Jefferson or Lincoln have accepted such multiplied indignities.

Moreover, what is the market value of German promises today? Nothing. She has guaranteed, i.e., pledged her honor, to support the neutrality of Luxembourg, and she overran her whole little territory without scruple. She had done the like for Belgium, and the whole world stands aghast at her atrocities. In 1888, Germany, Austria, and Turkey, with other Great Powers, guaranteed also the absolute neutrality of the Suez Canal, and for a third time she has broken her faith. (How wise we were to fortify the Panama Canal is shown by this incident.) "Punic" faith for centuries has been a by-word and a hissing. For the future, "Germanic" must replace "Punic."

Germany is constantly whining about the inhumanity of England in attempting to starve her into submission. Let me ask only one question. If, in August of 1914, Germany instead of England had had control of the sea, is there a single human being outside a lunatic asylum who believes that Germany's first act would not have been to starve England? In two to three months, England would have been brought to her knees. Would those who murdered the women and children on the *Lusitania*, who have starved Poland and Serbia, have balked at such a step? Even now, the very aim of her submarines is expressly to starve England in both food and munitions. Her barbarities, including starvation and worse in Armenia, through her honored ally, the unspeakable Turk, have been a disgrace to civilization.

That England is right even in stopping food for the civilian population of Germany is manifest when one remembers that to allow such food to reach the civilian population is only an indirect way of feeding the German army. Every bushel of American wheat that reaches the German civilian non-combatants replaces and releases a bushel of German wheat for the German army.

From time immemorial down to the Siege of Paris by these same Germans, in 1870, and to the surrender of the ten thousand of the English army at Kut-el-Amara, in 1916, starving a fort, a town, a country, has been a recognized method of warfare. For the advocates and admirers of Germany's campaign of "Frightfulness," to rail at starvation as inhuman is really ludicrous. What is sauce for the Belgian, Polish, Serbian, and Armenian geese should be also sauce for the German gander.

Her declaration of the so-called "War Zone" around Great Britain is distinctly illegal, and her mode of warfare by indiscriminate slaughter without warning is as inhuman as it is illegal. Submarine warfare should conform to international law, as in her last note Germany promises to do temporarily, and not international law yield to the submarine.

Germany's use of flaming bombs, of the horrible poisonous gases, of dropping bombs on unfortified places, in contravention of her own promise at The Hague, and the killing and wounding almost wholly civilians, and especially women and children, is simply devilish. The horrors of the Wittenberg camp for prisoners of war, under the infamous Aschenbach, repeat those of Andersonville during the Civil War, and the Reconcentration camps in Cuba under Wyler.

From the very beginning of the war, Germany has proclaimed the doctrine that "Might gives Right," that the individual is nothing, the state is everything, and the state is power.

Vergnet, in his *France in Danger* (published before the Great War broke out), shows from German evidence that Germany had been preparing for this war for forty years. That Germany egged on Austria, in the period preceding the war, is shown in the first German "White Book." Neither Germany nor Austria has ever dared to publish the *text* of those conversations between Berlin and Vienna.

The German Kaiser, by only lifting a finger, could have prevented war.

May 8th. It is but just to the President to record his reported rejection to the proposal and threat, at the end of the last German note. Thank God for so much.

But we ought to have joined hands with the Allies in the war a year ago. Not only our duty called us, but self-interest pointed the same way.

As Col. Harvey points out, in this month's *North American Review*, when the war is over—no matter what the result is—it will be easy for Germany to pick a quarrel with us, declare war, defeat us on the whole Eastern seaboard in less than three months, and exact blackmail from Boston to Washington to an amount which would recoup much or most—or even all—of the cost of this war.

And where could we find a friend or ally?

WILSON'S TREASON

I have just read, in Volume III of Page's *Letters*, the unbelievable account of Woodrow Wilson's treachery, as I conceive it, to his country.

Von Bernstorff asked permission to send to the German Government a package of documents in the official pouch of the State Department. These reached Mr. Gerard, our ambassador in Berlin. He found they were duplicates of financial transactions of the German embassy. They disclosed the fact that Von Bernstorff had paid five thousand dollars or less to several persons in the service of Germany for propaganda against the United States, and for cables to seven foreign countries for German propaganda against the United States.

Mr. Gerard did not dare forward them from Berlin, nor even to cable to Washington from Berlin, but sent them by one of his own secretaries to Page, who could safely cable to the Secretary of State from London. No wonder he took this precaution, for Mr. Gerard stated that he had made seventeen protests against the *opening of mail to our ambassador* by the German Government in Berlin! They were mostly ignored.

The five thousand dollars was paid to Archibald, whose papers had been intercepted and published. They caused the dismissal of Dumba, the Austrian ambassador to the United States.

Page sent the package to the State Department. They actually were returned to Gerard with instruction to deliver them to the German Foreign Secretary.

In Section 2 of Article III of the U.S. Constitution, it is enacted that "Treason shall consist only in levying war against them or in adhering to their enemies giving them aid and comfort."

Of course the Secretary of State would not do such a wholly extraordinary thing except on direct orders from the President.

Mr. Lansing was Secretary of State, in 1915. Surely an inquiry should have been made as to whether Lansing or Wilson was responsible for this treachery, and the culprit should have been exposed and placed on trial.

In view of Wilson's treatment of Lansing, the onus of this treachery must certainly rest on Wilson himself.

GERMAN DEVILTRIES

Several times during the World War, I tried to trace to their source and verify stories of German barbarities, but found most of them to be unworthy of credence. However, the following I have seen with my own eyes and heard with my own ears, and know them to be true.

1. At the kind invitation of Lt. Col. Michaud, of the French army, and under his guidance, this morning, I visited the Municipal Laboratory, where I saw the official drawings of the internal mechanism of what externally seemed an ordinary lead pencil. In its interior was a mixture which, when the pencil was used, would explode. It might not only disfigure the face but might easily blind the user—and even endanger his life.

2. I saw and handled a can, apparently of American make, but really a devilish counterfeit of German make. It was labelled COOKED CORNED BEEF, in English. Included on the label was MANUFACTURED UNDER THE PURE FOOD AND DRUGS ACT OF 1904 OF THE UNITED STATES. This too was filled with a powder which would explode and burst into flame when unguardedly opened by the casual finder. Its appearance would easily deceive anyone. In confirmation of this (if, indeed, any confirmation were necessary), on tour with us was an American woman working for the soldiers in France. She related a case that recently was under her own care. A man had found and opened such a can and was so severely injured that he died shortly afterward.

OCTOBER 12TH, 1918

At two locations in my "Reminiscences" (written in January and April of 1916), I have placed on record my views as to the real causes of the war and the cruel and detestable deeds of Germany. The barbarities perpetrated would be beyond belief, were it not that they are proved: (1) by Lord Bryce's and the Belgian and French reports; (2) from accounts related by or to my own friends; and (3) by the rules laid down in the official War Code of Germany (see *The Contrast Between the War Codes of Germany and Those of Great Britain, France, and the United States*).

This very day, while Germany is seeking peace through an armistice, she has just torpedoed the *Ticonderoga* and fired on and killed the crew and passengers escaping in open boats; she is looting, burning, and utterly destroying what is left of French and Belgian towns, even smashing the expensive embroidery machines; and she is deporting even the old and the children (whither—and for what purpose?). In Cambrai, a city of 56,000 persons in 1914, when our troops entered *not one single human being* was left in the ruins! These atrocities cause us to hate Germany, and indispose us to peace except by unconditional surrender.

Up to this time, war consisted in fighting the armed forces of the enemy. Civilians who got in the way suffered, of course. But the German troops have systematically destroyed all houses and agricultural tools, smashed furniture, defiled beds and floors, cut down fruit trees, poisoned wells, and taken back to Germany anything of value, leaving the entire country a waste.

Their taking of hostages, exacting enormous fines on communities, raping the women and girls—all are forbidden by international law. Even in their own country they are establishing polygamy in order to replenish their own population. For women of child-bearing age who have no husbands, they force strange men upon them as fathers of their illegitimate children, a fact well attested to me. The next generation of Germans, therefore, will consist largely of "official" bastards. All these outrages excite our utmost horror and detestation.

As to Germany's having deliberately plotted the war, that is now well established. The pamphlet by Thyssen describes the industrial preparation (confirmed and extended by Mühlen, a Krupp director in Essen: see his *Vandal of Europe*) under way months before the war. The statement of Lichnowsky, the German ambassador in London, as well as the statements to Morgenthau (our ambassador) in Constantinople by von Wangenheim, the German ambassador to Turkey, make it clear that war was decided upon on July 5th, 1914, at a famous conference in Potsdam. The Kaiser, the Chancellor, the foreign minister, high-ranking military officers, and representatives of the great banking firms were present. The Kaiser asked each in turn if he was ready for war, and if not, how soon could he be ready. All were ready except for the bankers, who asked for a delay of two weeks so as to be able to dispose of their securities. On July 23rd, only eighteen days later, Austria sent her ultimatum to Serbia!

In the Italian parliament, Giolitti disclosed the fact that in 1913, Austria asked for help in an attack on Serbia, but Italy refused, as the treaty of the Triple Alliance was for purely defensive purposes.

At last, thank God, our patience was exhausted, and on April 6th, 1917, we entered the war. We bungled the thing weakly at first, but finally we struck our pace and have done magnificently.

We barely got in in time. At the peak of the German offensive, last summer, Paris was so seriously endangered that all plans had been made—once again—to transfer the government to Bordeaux. Pershing pleaded, at first in vain, but at last was allowed to put 50,000 of our troops (only half-trained) into the trenches, and Paris was saved.

Now we have about two million men in France, and the Germans are retreating almost in a rout. Thank God! Thank God! Civilization will be saved from the Huns.

Bulgaria has made an unconditional surrender. Austria and Turkey seem to be on the verge of similar action, and Germany *must be compelled to do the same*—and to spew out her Hohenzollern crew.

I have hopes that at the peace table the robbery of 1864 will be suitably punished by a compulsory retrocession of Schleswig-Holstein—with its splendid harbor of Kiel—to Denmark. Two years after it was stolen by Prussia and Austria, following their war with Denmark, the duchies were stolen by Prussia, following her war with Austria. Now Germany should be made to disgorge it all.

I have set these views before some of our most influential men in Washington, and the ideas have had a friendly reception. I have also recently written to the same effect to Mr. Arthur J. Balfour, the British foreign minister, with whom I was brought in touch when he was in this country officially. (He was elected to membership in the American Philosophical Society during my presidency.)

We shall be a new country, after the war. We are the world's creditor nation. We have learned to think in world-terms. We have cast aside our former isolation, abandoned the fear of "entangling alliances," and thrown ourselves body and soul into the war for Freedom and Right. *Our* freedom, *our* independence were at stake for nearly three years, while Great Britain, France, and Italy were fighting *our* battle. The British fleet saved us. Never can we be too grateful to it. Had Germany won control of the sea, Great Britain would have been starved in a few months. The war would have been won by Germany.

In our political life the war has wrought havoc with "State Rights." A Democratic Congress, at the request of a Democratic President, has given to the national government (as represented by the President) greater power than is enjoyed by any other ruler in the world. He has seized almost everything for the nation and is running everything on national lines. Scarcely a protest has been heard—a wonderful and momentous fact. It is a fact that conscription was cordially adopted with almost no opposition and following a brief debate, instead of after a long debate and great opposition, as was the case in Great Britain.

But above all else, I feel the greatest pride in the vindication of what I have often asserted, the idealism and altruism of the American people.

We have recognized our duty to be loyal to Freedom, to Justice, and to

Right—as against Might. That loyalty has taken our troops to France and made them willing to die for others. No finer heroes have ever gone forth to fight for the Right than our soldiers. I have the most profound admiration for them.

We are on the eve, it seems, of the climax of the greatest war in all history, and it will be settled, thank God, in the right way.

I thank God that my life has been spared to see these great days and to see my countrymen showing such exalted, heroic patriotism.

May the Great Peace right the wrongs inflicted by Germany, and may those who arrange it have wisdom given to them to establish a League of Nations to enforce Peace and Justice and realize Tennyson's splendid ideal of

The Parliament of Man,
The Federation of the World.[5]

THE ARMISTICE

At noon on Thursday, November 7th, 1918, the news came over the wires that an armistice had been concluded and that hostilities had ceased—i.e., that practically the war was over. At once, without waiting for confirmation of the news, the whole people went wild. All the brokers' and other offices poured their army of clerks—and the members of the firms too—into the streets. No further business was done, the stock exchange closed, everybody tore ticker tapes into small pieces, and a snowstorm of these little white paper fragments filled the air and covered the streets and sidewalks. All the means for producing noise were called into play to celebrate the Peace through Victory.

Later, it was found that while the Germans had asked for an armistice and negotiations were proceeeding, they were not yet concluded.

But on the following Monday morning, I was awakened at 3:20 A.M. by whistles, bells, sirens, *hoorahs*, and shouts. I knew then that the news was true and that peace was soon to follow. Meantime, the fighting was to cease and the Armistice begin at 11 o'clock of the 11th day of the 11th month of 1918.

The streets soon filled, the crowds being especially dense on Broad Street from City Hall to Locust Street. Someone started the long-meter "doxology." Everyone in the crowd uncovered and sang—not only this but "Nearer, My God, to Thee" and other appropriate hymns. It was the most solemn scene this city had ever witnessed.

Then everything again broke loose as it had on the preceding Thursday.

One of the terms of the Armistice is the most terrible indictment a nation ever acknowledged to be true, viz.: that the Germans must point out the *poisoned springs and wells*, thus admitting one of their own damnable acts.

NOVEMBER 30TH, 1918

Germany again, thank God, has completely collapsed. The danger now is that she may dissolve too far for us to collect the indemnities she must pay.

I have stated previously my belief that Germany knew all about the Serbian ultimatum and did not *dare* (as I wrote to von Eiselsburg, in Vienna) to publish the *text* of the notes which passed between Berlin and Vienna. Nor did Austria. Later, as I have already noted, various authors have proved that Germany was responsible for the war. Now come official documents, published by Bavaria, which further confirm these facts.

The astounding cruelties and barbarisms of Germany have been freely confirmed. Even in retreating to Germany, in accordance with the Armistice, the vandals are thieving and destroying as before.

The real underlying reason for our entering the war was the idealism of America. We believed in the sanctity of plighted faith in treaties; we believed in the rights of Humanity; and we foresaw that, in spite of President Wilson's statement (so amazing!) that the causes and the results of the war did not interest us, we *were* interested; that the *whole world* was interested; and that Justice and Right should prevail—and by the ultimate forces, rather than by Force and Frightfulness.

True, as neutrals we profited largely, at the beginning of the war, by our munition and other contracts, but what are these millions compared with the billions we have spent—and gladly spent—in upholding our ideals? No! America is, I believe, the most altruistic and the most idealistic nation in the world. Not even the French excel us.

I have just written to Depage, Lorthioir, Sir Robert James, and others, as to the International Surgical Congress, and urged an early consultation as to the date and place. I have suggested September of 1920, in order to give time to organize it. I have also offered unhesitatingly to withdraw from being considered as president, in favor of any of the heroes who have done the actual fighting and have suffered its horrors and sacrifices.

The International Surgical Society, which manages the International Surgical Congress, took the first step, on November 3rd, 1917 (see *Journal of the American Medical Association,* March 23rd, 1918, p. 865), when delegates from the Allies met and decided to organize the Inter-*Allied* Surgical Society, which in turn will establish the Inter-Allied Surgical Congress.

Then followed the action of the French Academy of Sciences (see *British Medical Journal,* November 2nd, 1918, p. 492) in deciding to cast out all representatives of Germany and her three vassal states. On October 3rd, under the auspices of the Royal Society (see *Science,* November 22nd, 1918, p. 509), representatives of the scientific academies of the various Allied nations took similar action and referred the matter for final consideration to the various constituent academies.

I am glad to see that our International Surgical Society was the first to act.

DEVASTATED FRANCE

Immediately after the close of the Fifth International Congress of Surgery, over sixty of us, a large party of surgeons with their wives, and with a few of their children, left Paris for Rheims by rail. Under Cook's management, there were over sixty of us on a melancholy excursion to see the ravages of the war.

In Rheims, we were told that seventy-five thousand people already had returned to the city, living in the cellars of their old homes and shanties. The mayor there greeted us amid the ruins of the Hôtel de Ville. As President of the recent Congress, I responded, but after a few words, I confess that, after seeing the terrible wreckage of the bombardment and the half-ruined cathedral, my feelings so overcame me that I completely broke down. Professor Mayer quickly retrieved the situation by calling for three cheers for the United States, and by adding a few words in reply to the mayor.

We set out from Rheims for Verdun in three large *char-a-bancs*, stopping at various places to see the ruin wrought by the cursed Germans—inexcusable ruin, ruin for the sake of ruin, and wholly unnecessary from any military standpoint. We spent the night at the Coq Hardi, in Verdun, where we had very fair rooms and meals. The next day, we visited the forts at De Vaux and Donaumont. Near the former we saw a sign in a large field of only grass and bare ground, without the vestige of a building: It said "Here *was* Fleury," formerly a prosperous little village, now *spurlos* [i.e., without a trace] destroyed. There were houses with no roofs and only partial walls, with great breaches that made them uninhabitable. In Fort Donaumont we went into the trenches and dugouts where the French resisted the Germans, making good their assertion that *"On ne passe pas."* My grandson Howard found an old rifle, which he took home as a trophy.

The bark was stripped for three or four feet from the fruit trees to kill them. Their destruction was not a military necessity, of course, but they stood as gaunt witnesses to German brutality. Never in my life have I seen, nor could I have imagined, such an abomination, such desolation.

The fields were so full of buried shells that they had to be abandoned for tillage on account of the danger of explosions.

We returned to Rheims by another route, thence back to Paris by rail. (On two occasions during these outings, a little merriment was provided when two major generals insisted on carrying my suitcase—and I a mere major. One was J.M.T. Finney, of Johns Hopkins; the other was M.W. Ireland, Surgeon General of the U.S. Army and my former pupil at the Jefferson.)

The following year, through the kindness of Miss Anne Morgan,[6] we had another visit to devastated France. She had more than a hundred villages under her care, and we spent three days and two nights visiting some of them. At one, Coucy le Chateau, the village surrounded the old chateau, whose torn and blackened walls were witness to the German destruction. Amid the ruins, a Frenchman had put up a frame building for a restaurant with a few beds at the back, his sign proclaiming, with supreme irony, "Hôtel Bellevue."

Miss Morgan had a frame hospital, with medical and surgical wards, a children's ward, a maternity ward, and a dental clinic, in the charge of a wide-awake young American woman dentist. Illustrated cards showed the population the need for sleeping with the windows open, of taking a bath at least once a week, of cleaning the teeth, and so forth.

The people were "living" in old trenches, in quarries under stone overhangs with vertical boards at the ends, with no light except daylight through open doors, and with a primitive cook stove for heat for the approaching winter. Any makeshift, such as the German corrugated-iron arched trench covers, would shelter a family. Fortunately, the past winter has been relatively warm.

In Paris and other cities, the straits to which the people were reduced to meet the monetary situation reminded me vividly of the "shinplasters" during our Civil War.[7] Many of the municipalities issued little notes good for a franc, 50 centimes, etc., and even large establishments, like the Bon Marché, did the same. Of course, they were only good in the city or the store of issue. Four 25-centime postage stamps were folded up in paper and given in change, even at the post office. In La Rochelle, where Florence went to visit some of her French godchildren (including Jean, Simone, and Marcella Rolland) in the villages nearby, they had tin token money.

Paris was dark at night. Where there had been one gaslight in each arch of the Rue de Rivoli, there was now one in only every third, fourth, or fifth arch, and where there had been clusters of four or five lights, only one was now burning.

But the streets were spotlessly clean. In over five weeks, driving or walking over a large area, I saw only three or four bits of waste paper in the roadway or on the sidewalk.

Many of the buildings were "smallpoxed" with plaster chipped away by bullets or fragments of exploding shells. We saw the damage to the Church of St. Gervais, in which over forty people had been killed by a Big Bertha shell that exploded during a service on Good Friday. (I saw a photograph of a seven-seated auto entirely engulfed in the shell hole excavated by the explosion of one of these bombs.)

One day, we lunched with the Jusserands and met Dr. Albert Calmette, of the Pasteur Institute, and his wife. Mme. Calmette told us of her personal experience as one of a dozen wives of prominent citizens of Lille (her husband had been director of the Institute) who were taken as hostages for their husbands, contrary to the rules for civilized warfare. They were deported and confined for eight months, including an entire winter, in a barrack near Berlin. For companions they had a number of Parisian prostitutes, who were unclean in person, thought, and speech. One blanket was allowed for each "bed," which was merely boards set two or three feet above the floor. They were allowed no reading matter, no writing material, and no artificial light. They had scarcely enough water for drinking and none for bathing. Although her husband sent her food every week, she did not always get it. How she managed to live through it, I can hardly imagine. I wonder that she did not go crazy.

Dr. Calmette gave us a two-hour inspection tour of the Pasteur Institute, during which we saw a lot of persons undergoing preventive treatment against hydrophobia. Two little girls of seven or ten ran off giggling and laughing.

We visited the U.S. cemetery in which Vincent Dearing was buried, placing a U.S. flag and some flowers on his grave and taking a photo of it. Had I lost a son in France, his body should lie forever in that sacred soil. The cemetery was laid out in regular, numbered sections. Each grave had an oaken cross at the head, with the name, rank, regiment, and the date and place of birth of the occupant. On the back of each cross there was a strip of tin with the same information *stamped* on it, along with the section, row, and number, assuring perpetual accurate identification. In the center of the cemetery, which was scrupulously cared for, there was an open circle of grass, perhaps thirty feet in diameter, with an American flag flying from a tall flagpole.

We left Paris in August and went to Brussels, where the Mayers had insisted on our occupying their house while they were visiting her parents a few miles away. The Lorthioirs insisted on our taking lunch and dinner with them, and it was a most agreeable five days. The Lorthioirs drove us down in their auto to Louvain, where we saw the gaunt walls of the library propped up lest they fall and injure someone.

The Hôtel de Ville, midway between the cathedral and the library and about two hundred feet from each, was untouched, though the library was utterly destroyed. The cathedral was burned at various isolated places in the interior, indicating that each fire had been separately and intentionally kindled. All the buildings along a street leading to the station, an eighth of a mile or so beyond the cathedral, had been destroyed and were now all rebuilt in stone. The Germans evidently spared the hotel for their own use while occupying Belgium.

We dined one day with Professor Antoine Depage, whose wife had been murdered by the Germans, in 1915, by the sinking of the *Lusitania*. Mme. Lorthioir served as our gracious hostess. I was placed on her right, Depage on her left. Near the end of the meal, Dr. Depage rose and, after a complimentary little speech, handed a medal to Mme. Lorthioir and asked her to pin it on my breast, by order of King Albert and the Belgian Minister of War. The decoration was that of Officer of the Order of the Crown of Belgium, and after she pinned it on, she added, "Sir, I think it is proper for me to give you a kiss," which she did on both cheeks. In a few sentences, I acknowledged the kindness of the King, as well as that of M. Depage and Mme. Lorthioir.

(Earlier in the year, also by order of the King, M. Hagemans, the Consul General of Belgium, awarded Florence the Medal of Queen Elizabeth, in recognition of her services during the war.)

We next went by boat to Dover, and on our way out of the harbor at Ostende, we saw the *Vindictive*, which the British had sunk so as to create an obstacle for the German destroyers and submarines. It was a thrilling sight, and I badly wanted to cheer. But as there were so many British on board, I waited for *them* to lead the cheering. Not one took the initiative.

After a month or so in London, including a day in Sussex at the country place of Lord Bryce and a day in Sidcup with Mr. Gillies at his hospital for deformities resulting from wounds, we sailed for home from Liverpool.

13

—••✦){ ✦••—

Keen the Baptist

DUTY AND CONVICTION

MY SINCERE EFFORT, over the years, has been simply to do each day's duty to the best of my ability, and this effort has met with its final rich reward. I say this not from vanity (my children will recognize the truth of this) but as a lesson and a call to others to duty, especially to my grandchildren. My children, each in her own way and in differing sphere of action, have been ever faithful to this high ideal, as I am glad and proud to testify. I hope and believe that my grandchildren, and their children in turn, will be equally faithful, and if so, they may be sure that they will be equally successful. Even in the humblest sphere of life, duty faithfully done meets with its due reward. High and influential public station may be the goal reached. Or it may be simply that the only achievement is a clean, upright life, faithful to high ideals but without attaining any conspicuous place, as the world counts it.

In my "Reminiscences," especially for my children and later descendants, I have traced the path along which I believe my Heavenly Father led me to the un-dreamed-of distinction of the Professorship of Surgery in the Jefferson Medical College, a position of such eminence and influence that in my early professional life, I had never considered it as a possibility.

For the Chair of Anatomy, I had intentionally prepared myself, and when it was denied me, I felt sorely disheartened. But I came to see that this rejection was most fortunate for me. Had I been elected, I should have been a surgeon teaching Anatomy as a side issue (as it was, until about 1897), rather than as the profession now rightly demands, an anatomist teaching anatomy and making it his life's work. I should have become an anachronism, and my career would have become much less satisfactory than it has in the department I really loved.

But in 1873, as I pondered my future, seeking God's guidance, the one thought I had was to do each day's duty as well as I possibly could, even if my career was to be that of a humble practitioner of surgery confidently leaving the rest in His hands. It is not the amount and importance of the work done, but the spirit of devotion to one's work that counts. If preferment and influence came to me, because I had worked hard and successfully, well and good: I would take what came, with a certain inward satisfaction, because in trying to do my duty, I should have deserved success.

My father had given me a good education, my health was unusually and almost continuously good, I was tough, rather than strong, and I loved work. In addition, I had long formed the habit of doing my work as thoroughly as I could. "Prosaic," you say? I admit it, but I add that the diligent performance of prosaic daily duties is the sum of successful human life.

My highest ideal in life has been to be of service to my fellow man, and thus to serve my God. To this end, I have honestly and earnestly tried to give my patients my best service, and to make these services more valuable by close and constant study; to arouse in my students an enthusiasm for good true work, as well as the highest moral and professional standards of life and conduct, thus multiplying myself through them and extending an ever-widening circle of good influences; and to share in the work of diffusing knowledge by writing and editing books and papers, sharing the results of experience and discovery.

I have always been a firm believer in the Christian religion. My ideas have been liberalized, as time has gone by, but I have not followed the modern trend of the almost total secularization of the Sabbath, in fact the total neglect of its religious duties and pleasures. Were the attendance on Sunday services to be given up entirely, organized Christianity would wholly disappear, and the influence of the churches would be eliminated. What a disaster this would be to the world is hard to assess.

The future life is, to me, a logical necessity, even apart from revelation. I cannot possibly believe that such master minds as those of the sages of Antiquity, or the later instances such as Dante, Shakespeare, Goethe, Kant, Huxley, Tyndall, Darwin, Kelvin, Holmes, Whittier, and thousand of others—great poets, authors, scientists, historians, anthropologists, preachers, lawyers, doctors, orators, artists, statesmen, and philosophers—all should be capable of development to such wonderful heights of intellectual achievement and then be snuffed out by death and vanish. It would be like a man who could construct the most perfect telescope, spectroscope, steam engine, telephone, or wireless (and the mind of man far exceeds all of these), and then throw them all, unused, onto the scrap heap. I do not believe that God is so illogical. There *must* be another and a better world. Otherwise, God (or Nature, if one prefers it) would be a monumental bungler.

Never did I feel more absolutely convinced of the existence of the other world than when I personally had to face it prior to my abdominal operation at the Mayo Clinic, in November of 1910. A few days before I left Philadelphia, I met with several members of the American Philosophical Society (of which I was still president) and told them of the seriousness of the operation, and of the possibility, which I believed to be a probability, of my death, so that they might not be taken by surprise.

I heartily enjoyed the dinner party I had given for the guest speaker at our monthly meeting, and I left for Rochester on the next day.

As I took the ether, I do not think that my pulse was quickened by even a single beat, surely evidence of what comfort a supreme faith in religion, and in God and my Saviour can be in such a time of trial.

I have recorded my reminiscences as an incentive to my children to do the humble, and often irksome, tasks of daily life as faithfully and thoroughly as possible, being sure that God is expecting just such work of us, and that if it is best for us, He will give us a high place, or if it is best for us, He will give us a lowly place. But wherever He places us, He will give us His blessing, and our final reward, according to the *spirit* in which we have rendered our service to our fellow and to Him.

THE ARGUMENT[1]

My darling,

I send you with this some flowers, with my very best and warmest love.

Does it not seem to you a natural miracle that from a hard dry black and apparently dead seed such beauty in so changed a form should arise? Is it not far beyond your "reason"? Can you understand a single one of the wonderful processes that produce the transformation of the seed into the plant and then the flower?

Is it any more wonderful that Christ should come into the world by a miraculous birth or that he should go through the same process of burial and resurrection that a flower does?

Surely we close our eyes, or rather our minds, to the said miracles of nature that a loving Father has given us as figures of the miracles of grace.

Your affectionate father

W.W. Keen

CHURCH VS. STATE

State

The summer of the Spanish-American War I spent in Europe, sailing for home from Antwerp in the autumn. The very day I left Antwerp, Dr. George Spencer, my assistant, received a long telegram from President McKinley, nominating me to a commission to investigate the alleged misconduct of the war, especially regarding unsatisfactory food and sanitation, unnecessary mortality, and general inefficiency. Not knowing what to do, Dr. Spencer took the dispatch to my brother Charles, and together they went to the office of the Red Star Line to see if it would be possible to reach me. Fortunately, I was a few hours out to sea. Had I received the dispatch, I should have been in a serious quandary. On the one hand, I could not keep the President of the United States waiting for ten days, until I reached New York. On the other hand, I knew nothing of the reasons for the appointment of the commission, of its scope or personnel, or of the time that probably would be required for the investigation, et cetera.

My first knowledge of the matter came on landing at the dock. I bought all the New York and Philadelphia newspapers, and on the train to Philadelphia I read everything about the commission, in order to post myself as much as possible. On reaching home, I talked with Charles, and at seven o'clock, I called the President's secretary to say that I was obliged to decline the appointment on account of other engagements. At nine, he asked me to come to Washington for a conference with the President. I went early the next morning and spent an hour with Mr. McKinley.

He begged me to accept the appointment. I told him about our church history, which had to be ready by December 11th, only two months away, and of which not one word had been written. He promised me all the stenographers and other help I needed. He said he wanted one medical man on the commission, a man of good sound judgment, one who would bring in a verdict absolutely free from bias or prejudice in favor of—or against—any person, high or low, who had been guilty of neglect, and a man who would be governed only by the facts elicited and fearless enough to state his honest conclusions. He was kind enough to add that, from his previous knowledge of me, he believed I was the person eminently fitted for this purpose.

I agreed to think over the matter, to sleep on it, and to let him know of my final decision the next day. In the end, I declined the President's offer and recommended as a substitute my old friend from college days, Professor Phineas Conner, of Cincinnati.

My refusal was fortunate. The commission lasted for several months, traveled extensively, heard many witnesses, and published its report. They were harried and grossly abused by those whom they condemned. Had I accepted, the First Baptist Church centennial would have been a failure. My time would have been wasted, and my practice would have suffered greatly. I should have been belabored by one side or the other and have obtained little, if any, credit with the general public, however much my conscience—and those whose judgment I really valued—had approved.[2] Had I been free of my obligation to the church, I should certainly have accepted the appointment as a public duty, accepting the abuse as an inevitable aspect of that duty.

Church

The Bi-Centennial History of the Founding of the First Baptist Church of the City of Philadelphia, 1698–1898 could not have been properly written by anyone else. By virtue of nearly two years' work, I had made myself familiar with the details of the history. This included reading many of the large volumes of minutes and other church documents spanning two centuries; reading of the lives of our ministers, the deacons, the trustees, and some of the more notable members; and reading the histories of all the various churches, institutions, and religious movements with which our church had been in contact, for two hundred years. It was impossible, of course, for me to personally read all of the volumes. This was undertaken by a Committee of Six, who made notes of the more important matters, with references to volume and page. I read all of these references—and re-read two or three times the records of the period of strife and contention in the Spruce Street Baptist Church. I made an honest and, I believe, successful effort to write with impartiality and accuracy.

The proofreading was done by me, but as the book was published with the imprint of the American Baptist Publication Society, the *page* proof was also read by Dr. Philip L. Jones, who had been pastor of the South Broad Street Church, but who then became the book editor of the Publication Society.

He called my attention to the fact that on page 108 of my book, I mentioned his election as pastor, but, since I omitted mention of his resignation, in January of 1889, it would be assumed that he was still the pastor. On page 109, the text read: "In 1886, they erected the church building (Fig. 32). Since then they have had an uninterrupted career of prosperity."

An examination of page 109 will reveal that there was very little space for any additional next, not over half a dozen words. Therefore, I inserted the words, "Dr. Jones resigned in January, 1889." Alas, I evidently did not read the amended text, which is as follows: "In 1886, they erected the church building (Fig. 32). Dr. Jones resigned in January, 1889. *Since then they have had an uninterrupted career of prosperity[!].*

I was mortified beyond expression. I begged him to let me have the entire leaf properly changed and reprinted to replace the original leaf in all of the unsold copies and to trace, as far as possible, the copies already sold and insert the new leaf. Dr. Jones was one of my warmest friends. He was amused by the mistake and said, "No, dear Dr. Keen, let it stand. A hundred years from now it will make no difference."[3]

EVIDENCE OF GOD'S GUIDANCE THROUGH KEEN'S ENTIRE LIFE[4]

NOTE: Some of the following facts appear in my "Reminiscences," but I repeat them here in order to make a complete chronological record of the various steps in the guidance of my dear Heavenly Father, to whom I can never be too grateful. Even my disappointments and apparent hindrances have conspired to promote my happiness and welfare.

My Happy Marriage

In a separate manuscript, I have recorded the manifest guidance of God, after apparent impossibilities covering eight years. This was the greatest blessing of my life.

The Choice of a University

I entered the Philadelphia Central High School in February of 1849, when just one month over twelve years of age (the limit was twelve), and graduated in February of 1853.

I next attended the school of Professor E.D. Saunders, which was situated at the bifurcation of 39th Street, north of Market. Here I practically wasted more than a year. Professor Saunders was an erratic genius, to whom I owe part of my love for the classics (though far more to Professor Lincoln, of Brown), but who was a poor teacher. Had I known of the New England "fitting" schools, such as Phillips Academy of Andover or Exeter, or the Boston Latin School, I could have entered the university in September of 1854. As it was, Professor Saunders considered me not ready until the following year, but the delay was providential, for had I entered college a year earlier than I did, I should never have met my dear wife.

Then came the question of which university. Should I enter the recently established University of Lewisburg, in Pennsylvania, or Brown University, in Providence, Rhode Island? In June of 1855, with a large party of Baptist ministers and a lot of young folks, I attended commencement at Lewisburg. My father had been a liberal contributor to the founding of the school, as well as an early trustee. I have already recorded the primitive method of reaching Lewisburg, seventy years ago. The university was evidently very primitive—scarcely out of its swaddling clothes—and I decided to go to Brown.

I knew no one at Brown or in Providence, but I was deeply impressed by the "new" system introduced in 1850 by that prince of presidents, Francis Wayland. He had brought the sciences into the curriculum, giving them equal rank with the humanities; and he also introduced the system of electives, long antedating that of Eliot at Harvard.

My decision to go to Brown was a providential factor in my life, for had I gone to Lewisburg, I should never have met my dear wife.

As soon as I began my studies at Brown, in September of 1855, I became painfully aware of my insufficient preparation. Compared with the boys from the New England fitting schools, I was not in the game. They were classical athletes, and I was only a novice. There was only one thing to do: buckle down to my work as hard as I could—and I began to revel in the *gaudium certaminis*, as I gradually caught up with the others. Until the appointments were made for the Junior Exhibition, I was unaware of my exact comparative standing. Being given the Latin Oration meant to me the thrilling fact that in scholarship I led the class. I was sure that my next competitor was almost treading on my heels. During the senior year, for the first time, I deliberately determined to win, and at Commencement I was the valedictorian by a very good margin.

In the meantime, however, I had also a delightful social life, with my fellows and many fine girls in Providence, especially among the students in Rev. Dr. and Mrs. Buel's School for Girls. We knew where the trailing arbutus blossomed the earliest, and where the laurel was the most abundant.

Richard Olney was a senior during my freshman year. Though the college was very small, I had only a speaking acquaintance with him, but John Hay entered with me in '55, he as a sophomore and I as a freshman. We roomed opposite each other on the second floor of University Hall, in rooms which had sheltered both American and French troops during the Revolution—not a bad patriotic atmosphere!

Toward the end of my senior year, I had to decide definitely on my vocation and chose Medicine. Although no medical college then required any pre-medical study, I decided to spend a resident graduate year at Brown. (Adoniram Judson and I were the only post-graduate students.) How thankful I have always been for this decision. I gave my mornings to Medical Chemistry and Physics and my afternoons to English literature. Had I omitted this latter collateral study, I never could have caught up: Before I graduated in Medicine, in March of 1862, the Civil War had broken out. I went at once into the Army, then abroad, and, on my return in 1866, I plunged at once into teaching and had no time for English literature. Whatever virtues of grace or force in the use of English I may have I owe to that post-graduate year under that accomplished scholar, Professor Dunn. It always made me critical in observing, and therefore avoiding, faults in the use of the language.

Here once more appears God's guidance. In Mrs. Buel's school, I knew Miss Eudora Borden, of Fall River. During my resident graduate year, I met her sister, Miss Corinna (or as she was always called, "Tinnie"—her own early attempt to pronounce Corinna) Borden. I should never have met her, so far as human probability goes, had I not spent the extra fifth year at Brown.

Thus, three times my decisions were guided by my dear Heavenly Father, so that I met my dear wife—although we met only for a few months of that one post-graduate year.

My Association with Weir Mitchell

I began the study of Medicine in Dr. Brinton's office, at 1003 Walnut Street, in the first week of September, 1860, and have elsewhere described how I made the acquaintance of Dr. S. Weir Mitchell, three days later. This was yet another wholly unsuspected instance of the guiding hand of God in my life.

The influence of Weir Mitchell was paramount and most potent, in the shaping of my *professional* career. This I have repeatedly acknowledged in various publications. His was the most stimulating mind I have ever been in contact with. He gave me the scientific stimulus and guided my early studies and writings. From 1860 till his death on January 4th, 1914, for over fifty-four years, we were intimately associated in his researches on snake venom; in the Hospital for Wounds and Injuries of the Nervous System; as a mutual colleague with Dr. George R. Morehouse; in the College of Physicians; in the Directory for Nurses; and in many other good causes. His generosity in making me his colleague—a "medical cub," I might say—and placing my name first in some of the papers which I wrote but which were published as our joint contributions (of course my name was last in some other papers), was as gratifying as it was rare. For years after the war, I did his neurological surgery at the Orthopedic Hospital. In every way, he was an uplifting, stimulating force.

My first, and I might say a casual, military service, was for the month of July, 1861, as Assistant Surgeon of the Fifth Massachusetts Infantry. I have recorded, in the *Transactions of the College of Physicians*, how extraordinary this was, in view of the fact that I had only begun the study of Medicine the previous September: I was commissioned an Assistant Surgeon before I was a doctor.

In May of 1862, my friend and classmate George L. Porter and I, having graduated in March, went to Washington and passed the examination for the United States Army. There were seven in our class. He and I ranked the others and were recommended for the Regular Army.

By the time my commission reached me—probably a month or more later—I had thought over my future and decided that, as I did not wish to make the Army my career, I had better decline any commission and ask for an appointment as an Acting Assistant Surgeon, U.S. Army. This surprised my friends and the Examining Board, for it was a distinctly lower position. (The regulars called us "damned contract doctors.") The salary was $1,200, while for the regulars I feel sure it was much higher. But it was again, though I did not know it at the time, the guiding hand of God. Had I accepted the commission in the regular army, I should have been made the head of various hospitals, during the war, and would never have fallen under the spell of Weir Mitchell. No "regular" would have been made subordinate to Mitchell, who was also only an Acting Assistant Surgeon. We would have drifted apart, and, while doubtless we would have been friends in Philadelphia, I never would have been so very closely associated in his work as I soon became.

Dr. Hammond, the Surgeon General of the Army, was an old friend of Mitchell's, and the latter suggested to him the founding of special hospitals for diseases and injuries of the nervous system, for diseases of the heart, for the eye and ear, and so forth. Early in 1863, Mitchell asked Hammond to transfer me to the hospital in which he and Morehouse were already installed. Years afterwards, he told me why he had asked for my transfer: In our entire work on snake venom and other researches he had found out that he could never kill me with hard work—a cherished compliment, as I have rightly called it.

Our "firm," Mitchell, Morehouse, and Keen, when it was very rare for papers to be written by more than one author, through Mitchell's wide reputation here and abroad, made my name well known, when I was a "kid," and it very decidedly aided my later career.

The Philadelphia School of Anatomy

On my return from Europe, in 1866, the head of the Philadelphia School of Anatomy—a remarkable "School of the Prophets," founded in 1820—desired to sell out and remove to Pittsburgh. After consulting with Drs. Mitchell and D. Hayes Agnew (the latter had been the head of the school when I was a student; I learned Anatomy from him), I purchased the meager good will and fixtures and started in as a teacher of Anatomy. I did this partly because I needed the means of support and partly because it apparently opened a door to me as a possible successor to Professor Joseph Pancoast, the aging Professor of Anatomy at the Jefferson.

I soon had the largest private school of Anatomy ever assembled in the United States. Curiously enough, my ticket was accepted by both the Jefferson Medical College and the Medical Department of the University of Pennsylvania, in lieu of that of their own demonstrators. The Jefferson was then, as now, at Tenth and Sansome streets; and the University of Pennsylvania occupied two large buildings at Ninth and Market streets, on the lot where the Post Office now stands. One building was the college, the other was the medical school. The tail wagged the dog.

The Anatomy Chair at Jefferson; An Opening at Harvard

In 1873, Pancoast resigned at Jefferson, and a lively campaign ensued in competition for the position, involving William H. Pancoast, his son; William S. Forbes; and me. Forbes was the head of another private anatomical school (also on Chant St., at the rear of St. Stephen's Episcopal Church, which is still on 10th St. below Market). I made a stiff fight for the place, but Professor Pancoast's son won the election, of course. I had the satisfaction, at least, of knowing that practically the entire profession in Philadelphia were of the opinion that I deserved the position.

I was bitterly disappointed by my defeat. I knew I could teach Anatomy. I knew that I deserved the place, if it had been decided by merit, and yet I lost it. Never for a moment had it occurred to me to aspire to the Chair of Surgery.

I had too low an opinion of my surgical attainments and ability to think of it. Hence my disappointment was the more acute.

After a while, I pulled myself together and made up my mind that my happiness and my usefulness ought not to depend upon a professorship of Anatomy. I said to myself, "Your duty is to go ahead and do the best possible work as one of the surgeons to St. Mary's Hospital (then a small Catholic hospital over two miles away in Kensington), and let God take care of your future."

Little did I know that these "defeats" were the most fortunate factors of my whole professional life! Had I succeeded in obtaining the Chair of Anatomy at the Jefferson (or a position at Harvard), I should have been a surgeon at heart, but teaching Anatomy as a means of obtaining a surgical practice, in which lay my heart's desire. The hour was just at hand when Anatomy, instead of playing a subordinate role leading to surgical practice, was to become a stalwart science, absorbing the whole life and enthusiasm of a real anatomist, to the exclusion of surgery. I should have become a "back number" from the very start.

The International Congress of Medicine in 1876, and the Introduction of Antiseptic Surgery into Philadelphia

In July, 1876, an International Congress of Medicine was held in connection with the Centennial celebration in Philadelphia. Mr. Lister (British surgeons are always called Mr.), then Professor of Surgery in Edinburgh, came over to attend it and was elected president of the Surgical Section. His presidential address was on "Antiseptic Surgery."

By some curious omission, I was not familiar, save in a general way, with his work in Glasgow or later in Edinburgh. During that period, he published several papers (his first having appeared in 1867) on his new method of treating wounds by carbolic acid.

I listened intently to his address and to the discussion which followed. Like his British colleagues, most of the American surgeons were cool or cold, or some even hostile, to his views. I became a convert at once. When I came on duty at St. Mary's Hospital, on the first of October, I found no spray, no carbolic, no gauze protective, in fact none of the means for the then complicated ritual to defend the patient from the germs in the air. We disinfected our hands with carbolic acid (1:40) and also applied carbolized dressings; we used carbolized catgut and ligatures, etc.; but the germs in the air were deemed our worst foe. I gathered all the necessaries and began to treat every wound antiseptically. I was amazed at the remarkable results. From that day on, I always followed Lister's principles (founded chiefly on Pasteur's researches), although I modified the methods to the aseptic as time went on. My colleague and successor at St. Mary's, Dr. J. Ewing Mears, followed me on January 1st, 1877, and continued the same practice. Thus was antiseptic surgery first introduced into Philadelphia.

The Revision of Gray's *Anatomy*

At a time when my fortunes seemed at their ebb, with the death of my darling wife, publisher Henry Lea invited me to undertake a new edition of Gray's *Anatomy*. It was just the kind of absorbing work needed to take me out of myself and my grief.

The Chair of Surgery at the Woman's College

I had been elected to this chair in 1883, in order to fill a vacancy. Here I learned to give clinical lectures, to operate on cases before the class, with running commentary, to think on my feet, and to increase my knowledge of surgical history. I had the ordinary run of surgical cases, in addition to a few cases of cerebral surgery. Two of the latter, in particular, naturally aroused a good deal of interest.

The earliest published account of the removal of a tumor from the brain, located purely by neurological data, was that of Sir Rickman Godlee (Lister's nephew), in 1885.

In May of 1887, when I was a surgeon at St. Mary's Hospital, a 26-year-old epileptic patient, Theodore Daveler, was sent to me from Lancaster. I had just finished re-writing the chapter on the nervous system for Gray's *Anatomy*. After obtaining a very careful and minute history of his case, including an account of an accident—apparently a very trivial one —which happened when he was three years of age, I was convinced that he had a tumor in the center of the brain which controlled the right arm.

Had this patient sought my advice before I had re-written the chapter on the anatomy of the nervous system—especially on the localization of function in the brain—I should have been utterly at sea as to the diagnosis, missing the sharpest turning point in my active surgical life.

Never having done any such operations, I felt it my duty to have a consultation both with good neurologists and with good eye specialists. I took him to Dr. Weir Mitchell's office, where he was examined by two other skilled neurologists as well, Drs. Morris Lewis and Horatio Wood, and by two skilled ophthalmologists, Drs. George Harlan and Charles Oliver. They all concurred in the conclusion that my diagnosis was not clear enough to warrant opening the patient's head. They thought that his epilepsy and other symptoms might be due to another cause and recommended a course of treatment to last several months.

I could not venture to do such a dangerous and vital operation in the face of their united opinion. I was so convinced of the correctness of my diagnosis, however, that I told Daveler that if he was not better by autumn, he should return and I would operate upon his head. My colleagues made no objection to this. Still suffering with headache, the patient returned and I removed the tumor (which weighed a fraction less than a quarter of a pound) on the 15th of December. At the time, it was, with one exception, the largest brain tumor ever removed. This case, so unusual and so successful, soon brought me two other cases of epilepsy. I operated successfully on both, and both promptly recovered.

A chubby four-year-old boy, a patient of the late Dr. George Strawbridge, was suffering terribly from headache, the result of an inoperable tumor of the cerebellum. The optic nerves on both sides were greatly swollen, and the child had been totally blind since Christmas of 1888. I resolved to drain a lateral ventricle, in order to diminish the pressure inside the skull.

Accordingly, operating on January 9th, 1889, I made a small opening in the skull, tapped the ventricle, and inserted a horsehair drain. About two to four ounces of cerebro-spinal fluid escaped daily. By the ophthalmoscope we could watch the diminishing swelling of both optic nerves. A week later, I inserted a rubber tube, instead of the horsehair, and the escaping fluid increased to from four to eight ounces daily. Early in February, as the headache was still severe, though less, I tapped the opposite ventricle. On February 12th, I irrigated both ventricles from side to side with half a pint of warm boric acid solution (4 grains to the ounce). The moment the warm fluid began to pass from side to side, the suffering child settled quietly into a position of complete comfort. But of course, though greatly relieved, the boy died soon afterward.

Preparing this case had led me to make some thorough studies, by a number of careful dissections on the brains of cadavers, as to the shortest and safest route to the ventricles, while avoiding doing damage to the central controlling motion on the surface of the brain. I then published a paper laying down the rules for this novel and useful operation, which now is constantly done in relevant cases. This case and the related paper naturally attracted a good deal of attention, both here and abroad. In London, some time afterwards, Mr. Mayo Robson also drained the ventricles.

The First Triennial Congress of American Physicians and Surgeons

The next step in the Providence of God, this Congress brought to Washington, in May of 1888, all of the country's medical specialists, such as those in Anatomy, Medicine, Ophthalmalogy, Otology, Physiology, Surgery, etc.

I took my three patients—and the three tumor specimens—to Washington and presented them, with a full account of the operations, before the American Surgical Association.

Cerebral surgery was the chief topic of the Congress, as it was, by far, the newest and most important topic. The Congress had a full-dress debate on cerebral surgery and cerebral localization in which Horsley and Ferrier, of London, and Mills, Seguinn, Park, Weir, Starr, and I took part.

In the debate, I pointed out the different view we have come to take of the contents of the skull, as contrasted with the contents of the chest and the abdomen-pelvis—heart, lungs, liver, stomach, intestines, pancreas, kidneys, bladder, uterus, etc.—a large number of discrete organs. In the past, we had been accustomed to thinking of the brain as a unit which functioned, somewhat like the liver, as a whole. In fact, we now see it as a most complex organ, with parts related to smell, sight, touch, hearing, thought, as well as motor centers for the back, the shoulder, the arm, the forearm, the hand, and for corresponding segments of the leg—but all fused into one mass. If the distinct viscera in the chest, and again those in the abdomen-pelvis were all fused into two masses, one in the chest and the other in the belly, it would be similar to conditions in the brain.

This was a wholly new and impressive view of the contents of the skull and the various cerebral functions.

The Vacancy in the Chair of Surgery at the Jefferson

When the elder Gross (Samuel David) resigned, in 1882, the Chair of Surgery at Jefferson was divided between his son (Samuel Weissel), who was my senior by just fifteen days, and Dr. John H. Brinton, one of my old preceptors. They divided the teaching as they thought best—and the trustees divided the salary between them.

Along with other chairmen's salaries, that of the Chair of Surgery had been $4,000, while those which did not lead to practice—Chemistry, Pathology, etc.—were $5,000. During all of my service as one of the professors of Surgery, my salary was $2,000, and I never thought of asking for any increase. (Of course my rapidly growing surgical practice was most satisfactory.)

The younger Gross fell ill of a severe pneumonia and died on April 16, 1889. He was a more brilliant man—but a less learned man—than his distinguished father and an abler surgeon, in my opinion. His death was a great loss to the school.

Not very long afterward, I was asked by a friend, an intermediary between the faculty and me, what my attitude was as to being Gross's successor. I replied that if I were assured of election, without any canvassing on my part, I would feel it an honor to accept. I would make a courtesy call upon each trustee at a time when he presumably would be out and would leave my card. I would not make any other form of canvass; nor would I ask any of my friends to make any efforts on my behalf. In due course, I was elected and began my duties in the autumn of 1889.

I was then within four months of fifty-three years of age, very late to begin a career, but so it proved to be. I served on the active faculty until the end of the session of 1907, when, at the age of seventy, I resigned. To break up all practice, I went abroad for eighteen months.

On my return, I seriously considered the question of a purely consulting practice, but I quickly decided against it: A consultant should be a surgeon *fully up to date* as to all the newest discoveries, novel operations, etc. This would mean that I must have my nose to the grindstone, just as I had had while I was teaching. If I did not keep abreast with the progress of surgery, I might easily give bad advice because I would be behind the times. So I decided one must be "in the swim" with full vigor or wholly out of it.

Friend after friend solicited me, "Now that you have nothing to do, why don't you come and help me?" To many of these appeals I have gladly responded and have done all I could to help not a few good causes.

My pen especially has not been idle, as my numerous papers and addresses show. I have tried to be not only a helpful doctor but also a helpful citizen.

Both my professional and other friends have showered honors upon me, far more than I have ever deserved. I say this advisedly, for I think I appraise my abilities and my services far more clearly and exactly than these over-generous friends have done.

I have taken great pleasure, and not a little pains, to support the religious life of the community, from time to time.

My "Cheerfulness of Death," first published in *The Outlook* on October 24th, 1903, and later by the Baptist Publication Society, has brought me many, many letters of appreciation and thanks, often from strangers. Of late, my *I Believe in God and in Evolution* and my *Everlasting Life* have done the same.

I hope also that, as many letters warrant my saying it, they have materially helped to solve the doubts of many honest searchers after truth and comforted many heavy hearts.

That "the time of my departure draweth nigh" I am well aware. I await the summons with a clear and absolute belief that human evolution does not cease at death but goes on to the next world. That will be a world of bliss unspeakable, when the separations of earth—especially from my dearly beloved wife—will cease, and we shall all, parents and children, praise God for His mercies and come to know our Lord Jesus Christ as our Saviour and the Holy Ghost as our Comforter. Amen!

BAPTIST HELPMEET

In the year 1885, I was teaching in the Wellesley Preparatory School for Girls at 2027 Chestnut Street, Philadelphia. One afternoon, I received a call from Mrs. Keen. I can never forget the impression which Mrs. Keen made on me. I was fresh from college and more or less ignorant of missionary work. Mrs. Keen told me that she had called to get me to write a paper to be presented at the Missionary Society. Its nature was to be a birdseye view of the mission situation. She said she could give me all the literature that I would need in preparation for writing. I could not withstand her winning personality and consented to write the paper. Later, she brought me over a great package of missionary magazines and leaflets, which I read.

I remember I was thrilled with the new information which I received. I gave the paper at the missionary meeting in the Fifth Baptist Church. I imagine it was an Associational Meeting, though I am not sure of that. Subsequently, I was invited to repeat the paper at two or three other Baptist churches.

The following year, I resigned my position and returned to Rochester, where I was married, but the missionary enthusiasm which the writing of that paper wrought in me did not wane, but rather increased with the years. I entered into the missionary work in our own church and Association, and ultimately in the state and national societies. I always felt that the pains which Mrs. Keen took to inform a young teacher and inspire her to write led to a turning point in my life. I have never ceased to be grateful to her, nor to remember her wonderful and persuasive personality. I believe that it is thus, by the touch of one life upon another, that the missionary cause grows and increases.

This is the story as first ever told at the time of the Pageant and the Celebration of the 110th Anniversary of the Women's Baptist Foreign Missionary Society of the First Baptist Church, Philadelphia, April 7, 1921, the oldest Women's Foreign Missionary Society of any denomination in the United States.

The writer of this tribute, Mrs. Helen Barrett Montgomery, has been for many years a world figure in Women's Foreign Mission work and as a speaker at meetings for men and women. She has almost no equals—men or women—and no superior.

The human touch thus given, late in 1885 (Mrs. Keen died on July 12th, 1886), has borne an abundant harvest—a hundredfold.

W.W. Keen

Philadelphia, April 22, 1921

KEEN'S STATED OBJECT IN LIFE[5]

My good friend Frederick Southgate Bigelow, who is an associate editor of the *Saturday Evening Post*, does not know, of course, of my personal and professional relations. What he says in the issue of June 30th is written with partial knowledge. Moreover, it is couched in much more complimentary terms than I would have used.

He cannot know, for he has not heard, the oft-spoken word, nor has he read the many letters which I have gladly preserve for my descendants to know how my contemporaries have regarded me.

The one word which recurs most often is "Inspiration."

That is what I have aimed to attain, and so far as I can judge by the many letters referred to, I have been able to accomplish in many cases, namely: to inspire the highest ideals and motives in my students, who number, I am sure, no fewer than eight thousand. In all of the institutions where I have taught, I have striven to implant in the minds of the students the highest ideals of their duties to themselves and to their fellow men. This is the "inspiration" I have hoped to communicate.

Many of the letters to which I have referred use exactly that word, and when I see it, I always feel a thrill of pleasure. I have preserved for my descendants to read at first hand many of the letters which have recognized an "Inspiration" from my life and my teaching.

Happy the man or woman who can so serve his day and generation and also serve our Heavenly Father.

14

—••⊰)(⊱••—

Eyewitness

L IFE WAS RATHER PRIMITIVE IN 1837, when I was born. The population
of the United States was about sixteen million, and of Philadelphia,
about two hundred thousand.

One could not walk a block—a square, in Philadelphia parlance—even
when I was a young man, without meeting the Quaker dress, including drab,
"coal-scuttle" bonnets and drab dresses for the women, and drab, "shad-bellied"
coats, with no lapel or turn-over collar, and broad-brimmed hats for the men.
One now has to go to the 5th Street Meeting or the 12th Street Meeting on "First
Day" (the Quaker Sunday) to see them still.[1]

The limits of the city of Philadelphia were Vine Street on the north,
Cedar (now South) Street on the south, and the two rivers. Outlying suburbs,
though continuously built up, were called the liberties, such as Moyamensing,
Southwark, Spring Garden, and Kensington, for example. If a criminal was
chased beyond the city limits, he could snap his fingers at the police in pursuit.
This anomaly was ended, in 1854, by the consolidation of the city and its
neighboring districts.

It was estimated that the opening-day crowd at the Centennial Exhibition of
1876 numbered as many as a hundred thousand. President Grant initiated the
program, which was held in the open, though his address could not be heard
by many in the audience. My dear wife and I were both in the chorus of the
Centennial Choir, which numbered four or five hundred voices.

Politically, the changes during my lifetime have been very marked. The
United States has grown enormously. In 1837, the population was small, and
the West was scarcely settled.

Territories beyond the Mississippi River, Iowa, Missouri, Arkansas, Louisiana,
and Texas, have all attained statehood since then. A large territory was added

following the Mexican War. The Panama Canal was undreamed of. We had no colonial possessions then, but now have Puerto Rico, Hawaii, Guam, and the Philippines. We are showing that, like the English, we have the colonizing instinct (if the wretched Philippine policy of the Democrats does not destroy it).

In 1842, Marcus Whitman, a missionary at what is now Walla Walla, Washington, learned that his missionary board back East had ordered the closing of two local missions in the territory. After riding horseback all the way to Boston, through the winter of 1842–43, to protest the abandonment, he then went to Washington and urged President Tyler to strengthen the nation's interest in the area. British competing interests were on the rise, and Secretary of State Webster was negotiating a treaty to exchange the territory for some paltry fishing concessions in the Atlantic.

The President assured Whitman that if he could lead a significant number of immigrants across the Rockies to settle the area, the proposed treaty would not be signed. The following spring, Whitman took a thousand immigrants over the mountains and into the fertile valley of the Willamette, and that great empire in the Northwest was saved to the United States. News of the Cayuse massacre of 1847 led to the organization, in the following year, of the Oregon Territory.[2]

Alaska was a Russian possession, on the map of 1852, and as uncharted as mid-Africa. Not even the great Yukon River appears on it. "Seward's Folly" has proved to be a vision of farsighted statesmanship. It has already repaid a hundred-fold the $7.2 million it cost, and it is only just beginning to be developed.

Public lands were deemed so inexhaustible that one could buy a parcel for $1.25 an acre, and great land-grants were given out to aid in the construction of the various railroads, some all the way to the Pacific, in the '60s and '70s. In 1862, Senator Morrill introduced legislation giving a large grant of land to one university in each state in order to encourage the establishment of scientific agriculture. It was remarkable that this could be done while we were in the throes of the Civil War, and at its most serious stage. This was a great help to a few universities, especially Cornell and Minnesota (the latter now probably valued at $100 million!), but many of the schools, unfortunately, mismanaged this splendid gift.

The wonderful irrigation projects, again made possible only by great dams of concrete, have been devised and built practically entirely since about 1900, I think. The Great American Desert of my boyhood geography lessons has been made to blossom like a rose, by the magic touch of water.

When I was a child, the sewing machine did not exist. I remember well an evening when we were reading around the center table in the parlor (by the light of a sperm-oil astral lamp) that my father looked up from his newspaper and said to my mother, "Sue, I see in the paper a statement that a man has invented what he calls a 'sewing machine.' What an absurdity! Surely no machine can ever do the work of a woman's deft fingers!"[3]

The first bathtub in the United States was installed by Adam Thompson in Cincinnati, Ohio, on December 20th, 1842, according to records of the manufacturers of plumbers' materials. "At a Christmas party, Thompson exhibited his tub for his guests, four of whom later took a plunge." The incident and the new invention, which was lined with mahogany and sheet lead, aroused considerable criticism. Some papers called the innovation an epicurean luxury, while others thought it undemocratic. After seeing the original bathtub, however, President Fillmore was said to have had one installed in the White House.

My father never used any other than a quill pen, shaping it himself and cutting the nib on his left thumbnail. In England, I have often been annoyed, in the coffee room, by the *scratch, scratch* of such pens, and in 1915, I read that members of Parliament would no longer be supplied with them. Steel pens, at least those made by Gillott, in Manchester, were introduced only during my late boyhood. A popular conundrum asked, "Why is Gillott a corrupter of morals?" The answer: "Because he makes people steel pens and tells them they do right." The typewriter appeared towards the end of the 19th century.[4]

In the *Public Ledger* of March 4th, 1916, "Girard" (Herman Collins) writes: "Things they didn't find in Philadelphia, forty years ago, when President Grant opened the Centennial: Half our present population, one ten-story building, a trolley car, a telephone, a foot of street paved with wood or asphalt, a wireless station, a typewriter, a typesetting machine, a phonograph, a national bank or trust company with $5 million deposits (compared with about $95 million today), an automobile, an electric light in the street, an electric-propelled train, an electric fan, a "movie" theater, a City Hall, filtered water, an aeroplane, a million-dollar hotel, a man with a million income, a school or college with a thousand students."

I have seen the invention of the air brake; the X-ray; the movies, from the earliest attempt by Muybridge to the present pervasive degree; and the whole development of wireless telegraphy and the telephone.

Hoe's and other fast power-printing presses are probably less than forty years old. Compressed air, as a powerful motor in riveting, drilling, and mining, is a novelty probably not over twenty-five years old.

The whole modern development of electricity has taken place within the last forty years. At the Centennial Exhibition the *sole* electrical exhibit was one arc light, installed on the main bulding by inventor Moses Gerrish Farmer. Progress has produced the dynamo, the hydroelectric plant, and the trolley system, together with all the varied uses for electricity for obtaining light, power, heat, telephone, and telegraph.

The automobile as a common vehicle scarcely antedates the 20th century. Rural Free Delivery and Parcel Post are quite recent, the latter within the last three years. Articifial ice, that great boon to the tropics (and even to the temperate zones), dates back only thirty-five years or so.

Skyscrapers have become necessary because of the increasing value of land and have been made possible by the development of cement, reinforced concrete and steel construction, the elevator (a vertical railway), and by steam- and hot-water heat, as well as by forced-air ventilation.

In engineering, the progress has been no less astonishing. The skyscrapers have already been mentioned. Instead of walls' being built on a perimeter foundation supporting the floors, a forest of steel girders now rises from a central foundation bearing up the floors, which in turn carry the walls, whose only function is to keep out the weather. The walls begin on any story, instead of from the ground up.

The great bridges, the long tunnels, and the viaducts and canals of the last fifty years are exceeded only, perhaps, by the pyramids.

The Suez Canal, the Soo Canal, the Kiel Canal, and the Panama Canal are a few of the greatest artificial waterways of the world. Lesser canals are so numerous as to be impossible to catalog. The Panama, the greatest of all, was made possible only by, first, the prior conquest of yellow fever; second, by the development of cement and concrete construction; and third, by the invention of huge steam shovels. When we visited the canal, the last time, the walls of the great locks were nearing completion, and Colonel Sibert told me that if concrete and cement had not been available, there could have been no canal: The only substitution could have been dressed granite, and the prohibitive cost (and the much longer time required) would have made the work impossible.

Of mining and metallurgy, so successfully prosecuted in the United States, South America, and Africa, I can say only that chemical discoveries and the inventive genius of man have wholly revolutionized these entire industries.

Slavery has at last been abolished, thank God, from the United States, the only civilized nation in the world which practiced it so long, and it is gradually vanishing in the few other spots where it still exists.

Anthropology, archaeology, and philology are all cooperating to uncover the history, civilization, and manners and mores of the past, and to give written languages and dictionaries to the benighted races and peoples of the present.

Philanthropy and education in the United States have forged ahead, hand in hand, at an accelerating pace. The stupendous gifts by Rockefeller, Carnegie, and scores of other multi-millionaires have endowed colleges, universities, boards, institutions, institutes, and foundations, which are doing splendid service to God and man.

In medicine, I have witnessed all but one of the great modern discoveries. Vaccination was introduced by Jenner in 1796. But since I was born, anesthesis came in (1846) and antisepsis began with Lister's first paper (1867) and was well established a dozen years later. These three discoveries have revolutionized both surgery and medicine, in all their branches.

The new science of Bacteriology struggled for thirty years to gain acceptance, but it was not given its name until 1884. The medical secretary, the typewriter, the telephone, and the automobile, all products of the last twenty-five years, have doubled or tripled the efficiency of every doctor. How much more may our successors be able to accomplish!

Women's colleges, beginning with Vassar, and co-educational colleges have multiplied and have done a world of good.

In literature and art, painting, sculpture, and music, plus the domestic arts and crafts, we have progressed only moderately well, but we are improving. Some outstanding names appear, but in bulk we have lagged far behind in the race. But we have been busy, first of all, in getting a living, in subduing forests, in building railroads and cities, and gradually in accumulating the means for a leisure class, some of whose members (and in time, many) will give themselves to the things of the spirit, rather than to the things of the flesh.

The most remarkable achievement in amusements, of the last five or six years, is the development of the cinematograph, usually called the cinema or ciné, in Europe, and the movies, in this country. The first I ever knew of this was the work of Muybridge in photographing the movements of men and horses, which he described in his book *Animal Movements*, I think. As I recall it, he stationed a series of cameras at short intervals with strings stretched across the path of the animal. As these were broken, successively, the shutters were instantly open and shut. When placed in a zoetrope, with slits opposite each picture, the photographs blended, by the persistence of vision, into a continuous moving picture.

In science, the most wonderful discovery has been that of radioactivity, by which our views of physics and chemistry, and even the constitution of matter itself, have been wholly revolutionized. This alone has made the last fifteen years or so a time of extraordinary progress.

Chemistry has advanced as never before. The growth of modern applied chemistry, within almost every industry, is best seen in the complex programs of the Congresses of Applied Chemistry. Whether scientific or theoretical, chemistry seeks the quieter atmosphere of the American Philosophical Society, the National Academy of Sciences, and the American Academy of Arts and Sciences, as well as other technical scientific societies.

The synthesis of urea, one of the many substances believed to be obtained only as the result of the vital forces of plants or animals, has led to the production of a number of marvelous substances in the chemist's laboratory, which is replacing Nature's vital laboratory.

Synthetic rubber, indigo, gasoline, and many other substances are either commercially profitable now or doubtless will be soon. The multitude of new colors and medicines of the coal-tar groups show what can be done in this area. Often the by-products are more valuable than the product initially sought.

Astronomy, of which I can give only a few details, has progressed in marvelous fashion. The wonderful discovery of Uranus, by Adams and Verrier, using mathematical calculations based on planetary disturbances in the orbits of Neptune and Jupiter, reads like a fairy tale, as its location was so accurately predicted that the planet itself was found immediately.

The extraordinary development of astronomical instruments, as at the Mt. Wilson Solar Observatory, and the results obtained, almost outstrips the imagination. Bauer, of the Carnegie Institution, using the world-wide voyage of the non-magnetic ship *Carnegie*, has been able to correct large errors in the sailing charts and marine tables, making the seas far safer.[5]

When I was in college, Fraunhofer's lines in the solar spectrum were only a curious phenomenon, entirely unknown as to their cause or meaning. The spectroscope has now shown by these lines the chemical composition of the sun, the planets, the stars, and even of the nebulae and the comets. It has revealed the composition of the whole visible universe to be almost identical, in the essential elements, and new elements have been added to those already known.

Travel, in my youth, was far less common, more costly, and less comfortable than now. It took four hours to get to New York and cost four dollars. Now it takes but two hours and costs but two dollars. There were two routes by rail from New York, the Pennsylvania and the Camden & Amboy, which is now a part of the Pennsylvania system. (The Reading had no New York line, when I was young.) With the one, the traveler went by ferry from New York to Amboy, then by railroad to Camden. With the other, the ferry connection was at Jersey City, but the line did not extend to Philadelphia itself, at first, but only to Tacony, where passengers and freight had to transfer to a boat which brought them to the Walnut Street wharf (or was it Market Street?). There were no sleepers of any kind, so night journeys were infrequent, most uncomfortable, and usually made only on compulsion.

The railroads were few and short. The Pennsylvania was not a continuous line, even to Pittsburgh. Its depot, as we then always called it, was on Dock Street; later, successively, it was on Market Street at 8th, then 11th, then 13th, where Wanamaker's is now. Each long car (day coach, we now call it) was drawn by a string of six or eight mules from the depot out to 32nd and Market, where it was hooked up into trains and where the engine was added. There were inclined planes over the Alleghenies, as no lomomotive then made had power enough to scale those mountains. The cars were pulled up and let down by ropes actuated by a stationary engine based at the summit. An overland journey was supplemented by canal boats for the waterways.

When I returned from Europe, in 1866, not a mile of railroad track existed west of the Mississippi. Professor (afterward, Senator) N.P. Hill, my old Chemistry teacher at Brown, had to tote all of his heavy mining machinery by wagon, from St. Louis to Denver, a trek of over a month. A network of railways has now bound together the East and the West, and the North and South.

The Pullman and the sleeping car have arrived during my adult life. (It was a characteristic remark of a few German surgeons attending the Fourth International Surgical Congress in New York, in April of 1914, when asked how they liked the sleeping cars, said that they were satisfied, although they added that their wives "did not like the upper berths.")

The first line for streetcars, horse-drawn, was the Fifth & Sixth Street Line. It required quite a long fight (as it did later, with the introduction of gasoline) before they were allowed to displace the old omnibuses. This and the other early lines were encouraged by the most liberal franchises, with no compensation to the city, and the stockholders all grew rich. The fare was six cents—or possibly six and a quarter cents.

The first steamer from Europe, the *Great Western*, arrived the year after I was born, I think.[6] Her voyage was remarkable in more than one way, one of which was that it brought to America the first copy of a new volume in *Lardner's Scientific Library*, in which it was conclusively shown that no steamship could ever cross the Atlantic. The voyage usually occupied fourteen days or more; the scanty news was transferred to a pilot boat off Cape Race[7] and thence telegraphed to New York. We received European news only twice a week, and every steamer's name and probable time of arrival was well known in advance.

In my early years, the most common change in small silver were the old Spanish coins, the "fip" (short for fipenny—or fivepence—which equalled six and a quarter cents) and the "levy" (short for eleven pence, which equalled twelve and a half cents). The dime was seldom seen, and there were no nickles. Copper cents, "pennies," were as large as today's quarters. Out West, the dime was the "short bit," and the levy was the "long bit."

Paper money was not, as now, a national currency, freely circulating across the country and rarely counterfeited. There were no national banks, only state banks.[8] We knew, in Philadelphia, all about our local city banks, but when it came to banks in other parts of the state (or worse, in far-distant states), we were completely in the dark. Counterfeits abounded. In order to guard themselves, shopkeepers and bankers, among others, subscribed to regularly issued bulletins of counterfeit-detectors in order to learn the peculiarities of each counterfeit bill. We always expected to have to compare a one-, two-, or five-dollar bill issued by any bank from Maine to Texas with its counterfeit. The annoyance, trouble, and delay can hardly be appreciated except by those who experienced them. Salmon Chase, Lincoln's Secretary of the Treasury, was the happy father of our national banks.

Equally great changes have occurred in business. The factory system and co-partnerships, combining the capital, the skill, and the energy of two or more individuals, have given way to corporations (gigantic ones of late), and these in turn have given way to trusts, which, when rightly managed, are a boon to both capital and labor. All these I have seen develop. Labor unions, too, have arisen, and again, if rightly managed, are to be encouraged.

Financial panics have been bothersome to the national progress, and seem to have made me feel personally unwelcome. Born in the panic year of '37, I was a sophomore in college in the panic of '57. Others followed in '73 and '93, and again in 1901, just after we started around the world. There was yet another in 1907, just after we went abroad for an indefinite stay.

The meals served on the boats of the Fall River Line[9] demonstrated the table manners at the time. At supper, the ladies with their gentlemen escorts went down to table first, through the ladies' cabin. Then the waiting horde of men entered. The whole meal, including the dessert (for it was really dinner), had been placed on the table. Each man helped himself, and the nimblest eater got the most complete meal. Some were down to the dessert by the time the laggards were only half through with the meats. The uniform price, I think, was fifty cents.

At Saratoga, I was much impressed, as a boy, with the state and style of the service at dinner. Practically everyone was first seated. The waiters were all colored. The headwaiter rang a bell or blew a whistle, the doors opened from the kitchen, and the long line of waiters entered, with almost military precision. There must have been some semblance of courses, for I remember that at the sound of the bell or whistle, the plates were removed, and in a short time, the waiters returned with other viands, finally ending with the dessert.

When I took my first long journey, I went as far as St. Paul, then a small town. There was no Minneapolis, but only a straggling collection of houses around Fort Snelling, and at the Falls of St. Anthony. In fact, when I was born, even Chicago did not exist. On its site was Fort Dearborn, with a few houses around it.

The explorers have been busy. In America, the great deserts of the Southwest are now manageable, and the Rocky Mountains, once believed to be an impossible barrier, even in 1842, have been conquered.

Postal facilities were primitve indeed. We had no postage stamps, and for all of Philadelphia there was only one post office, at 3rd and Dock streets. My father took letters with him to town, in the morning. We did have one house delivery every day, however. Each letter was weighed at the post office, and the amount paid was written, in the upper right-hand corner, by the clerk. This amount varied for the city and for various distances, each, say, of 50, 100, 300, 500, and 1000 miles (though I am not sure that *any* letters were sent beyond 500 miles), or some such scale. When I was in college, a letter to England cost 25 cents for each quarter-ounce (fully equivalent to 50 cents now). No wonder that we always used *very* thin paper—and wrote all the way across each page![10]

The telegraph was so costly, and thus so rarely used, that when a telegram came, all hearts were aflutter, for the message must be something *very* urgent or important, usually concerning a death or other misfortune.

The first transatlantic cable was initiated in 1858, though after several hundred messages or so (the first exchange was between Queen Victoria and President Buchanan), it failed.[11] Only by the persistence of Cyrus W. Field was a new cable laid, in 1866, and it has been a success ever since.[12] The laying of the first cable was celebrated with great rejoicings and illuminations.[13]

At the beginning of February, 1915, one of the officers of the Bell Telephone Company in Philadelphia asked me to give him the name of a prominent surgeon in San Francisco. His object was to arrange that the surgeon would be present at the telephone office in San Francisco so that we might talk with each other by telephone all the way across the continent, a distance of thirty-four hundred miles. I gave him the name of Dr. Thomas Huntington, with whom Mr. Crosman made an appointment for the appropriate day and hour.

On February 11th, I went to the telephone headquarters, at 12th and Arch, and at five o'clock I was among approximately two hundred gentlemen gathered for the inauguration of this wonderful feat. We were seated on rows of chairs, and to each chair was attached a small, watch-size receiver. On a platform in front of us were Mayor Blankenburg, ex-Governor Stuart, Mr. Stotesbury, John Wanamaker, and three or four other prominent citizens.

In front of the mayor was an eight-inch-high replica of the Liberty Bell, accompanied by a small hammer. When we were notified that everything was ready, complete silence reigned in the room, and every man held his receiver to his ear. The mayor struck the bell three times with the hammer. This sound was carried by telephone to the custodian of the Liberty Bell in Independence Hall. He in turn struck the bell three moderate blows with three separate hammers, which I presume were to serve as souvenirs.[14] In front of our miniature Liberty Bell was a large receiver, very much like a megaphone. This carried the sound to the telephone, which transmitted it to San Francisco. The moment it was heard there, a bugler began "The Star-Spangled Banner." We immediately stood up for the anthem, which was heard as clearly as if it had been played only a block away. At its conclusion, we all burst into a wild cheer.

Following this, the mayor and several others at the platform table talked easily over the wire with their counterparts in California. Following the official conversations, I talked for three or four minutes with Dr. Huntington and heard him with the same ease as with an ordinary city telephone. There were similar conversations between the other gentlemen present and their San Francisco friends and associates.

In 1876, Mr. Alexander Graham Bell called his assistant for the first time over a wire. The assistant was in the same building, but in a room on the floor below. When Mr. Bell called, "Mr. Watson, come here, I want to see you," his assistant rushed in, with his eyes almost starting out of his head, and said, "I heard every word you said, as distinctly as if we were talking in the same room."

A few days before our long-distance conversation in Philadelphia, Mr. Watson, in San Francisco, was again called by Mr. Bell (in New York or Washington, I seem to recall), and the two conversed with greater ease and efficiency than thirty-nine years earlier. Remarkably, Mr. Bell used the receiver he had used in 1876 and found it still suitable for conversation.

There was but one polling place, the State House (now universally known as Independence Hall, just as the State House Yard is now known as Independence Square). The polls were open from seven in the morning till nine at night, I think. With the long queues of impatient voters (my father often waited for an hour or more), in the gathering dark, and with the rough and rowdy methods of those days, it is not surprising that belated voters often left, or that there were not seldom broken heads and broken ballot boxes. Our present methods, bad as they may be, are a big improvement of those of sixty years ago.

The volunteer fire department was not abolished until some time after I had graduated from Central High School. It was a surviving relic of the day when every gentleman had his fireman's hat, cape, and boots, as well as leather fire buckets with his name and address painted on them. The early engines had two long handlebars which were worked up and down to pump water.

Later, there were a number of celebrated local fire companies, such as the Moya (for Moyamensing) Hose Company and the Southwark Engine Company. Each engine required a large hose reel, on a separate vehicle drawn by the men, not the horses. The personnel consisted chiefly of the rougher element of the city, and there was great rivaly between certain companies. The State House bell signaled the district in which the fire had broken out, and the competing companies, in their effort to outrun their rivals, often collided at intersections. Fights, sometimes serious, frequently followed.

The paid fire department was finally established. Then came horse-drawn vehicles, hose reels, hook-and-ladder companies, and now the motor vehicles, the fire towers, and separate high-pressure service in some parts of the city. The political uses of this department—and of the police—are a modern scandal, which will be eliminated in time, I have no doubt.

Indian wars were nearly always going on. They usually began with the revolting massacre of settlers, only too often their cause being the no longer endurable wrongs done to the Indians by these same or other settlers.

I well remember the Mexican War, and the rejoicing and illuminations following the victories at Resaca de la Palma, Monterrey, and Chapultepec, and the capture of Mexico City. In celebration, my father placed a wooden bar across every row of window panes in the front of the house, with a hole opposite the center of each pane and a lighted candle at each hole. In my opinion, there never before had been such victories, such illuminations.

On the ocean, I have seen the wooden sailing ships give way to ships of iron and steel. In war, they are now armored against enemies and propelled by steam from coal (and latterly by oil). The frigate has been replaced by the battleship, the dreadnought, and the superdreadnought. The small guns, with projectiles weighing a few pounds, have given place to enormous cannon and twelve-, fourteen-, and sixteen-inch shells, the largest of which weigh over half a ton and cost, I believe, half a thousand dollars each. By smokeless powder, they can be hurled over twenty miles, and by modern hgh explosives they are shattered into a thousand deadly fragments at their target, wrecking forts and regiments alike.

The barbarous practice, introduced by the Germans in the present war, of using asphyxiating gases is a new and devilish invention worthy only of German *Kultur* and efficiency.

Yet so far as forts and ships are concerned, the great guns of the latter can destroy the former, while a mine or a torpedo, of relatively small cost, can destroy in a moment the proudest and costliest ship afloat. Young Hammond's torpedo, dirigible by wireless as far as six miles off shore (or even by wireless from an aeroplane), is the latest most wonderful—and most terrible—development of maritime warfare.

The mine, the torpedo boat, the torpedo-boat destroyer, the submarine, and various aerial means of attack (especially the last two) immediately preceeded, or have been developed chiefly during, the Great War now raging (alas!) on the most horrifying and gigantic scale the world has ever seen.

While other arts and sciences which can increase man's power of destructiveness are utilized in this war, I thank God that *my* profession exists, even in war, only to heal and to help.

15

—•+⊱〉⊰Ӡ+•—

Just Deserts

CENTENARY CELEBRATIONS

IT HAS BEEN MY GOOD FORTUNE to take part, whether as a beneficiary, actively participating delegate, or spectator, in a number of centenary celebrations. I have medals and other mementoes, as well as a number of diplomas, from some of these celebrations. I have given the diplomas from the Royal College of Surgeons of England and the German Surgical Society to the library of the College of Physicians of Philadelphia, since they are of special interest surgically.

My first centennial celebration was at Brown, in 1864, when we commemorated the first one hundred years of the university. We are now (1911) engaged in planning for the sesquicentennial, in 1914, and I hope to be present to enjoy this as well.

In 1887, I attended the first centenary of the College of Physicians of Philadelphia.

In 1893, I attended the sesquicentennial of the American Philosophical Society. The chief recollection I have of it is the delightful way in which Mr. Frederick Fraley, the president for many years, presided at the dinner. Though he was then eighty-eight years old, his incisive wit and his easy, gentle, and charming remarks in introducing the speakers, were remarkable, especially as coming from one so aged, and one whose occupation was not that of a scholar but of a businessman.

Thirteen years later, the Society celebrated the bicentenary of the birth of Benjamin Franklin (an early president) and with great success. The state contributed $20,000 towards the expenses. Congress voted that a commemorative medal be struck in bronze, and I have one of the many that were distributed. A replica in solid gold was presented to France, through Ambassador Jusserand, who himself is one of our members. A striking and pleasant episode during this celebration was the awarding of the LL.D. degree to Miss Agnes Irwin, dean of Radcliffe College. She ascended to the platform of Witherspoon Hall[1] clad in a black academic robe. She was escorted on the one side by Dr. Howard Furness in his scarlet robe of Oxford, and on the other by Dr. Weir Mitchell, in his scarlet robe of Edinburgh. The contrast of colors was picturesque indeed. The degree was conferred on her by Andrew Carnegie, Lord Rector of St. Andrews. His own purple and red robe added further to the mise en scène. This degree was particularly apropos in that Miss Irwin was a great-grandaughter of Franklin's, and in that St. Andrews was the first university to recognize Franklin's eminence by awarding a degree to him. The addresses by Secretary of State Elihu Root, President Eliot, Dr. Furness, and others were delightful and made the event a memorable occasion.

In 1898, we celebrated two hundred years of the First Baptist Church, as well as the publication of *The Bi-Centennial Celebration of the Founding of the First Baptist Church of the City of Philadelphia, 1698–1898*, of which I was the editor.

In 1900, the Royal College of Surgeons of England celebrated the first centenary of their new charter, and with great pomp and success. The original college charter had been granted by Henry VIII, in 1540, but in 1799, by some legal action (or want of action), that charter was forfeited. The new charter was obtained the next year, under George III. During this celebration, they were authorized to create as many as fifty honorary fellows, whereas until now, they had had only fellows, members, and licentiates. The Prince of Wales was privately made their first honorary fellow. At the public function, in July of 1900, Lord Salisbury and Lord Rosebery (leaders of the Conservatives and Liberals) and about thirty-five surgeons from a number of countries joined as honorary fellows. The four Americans so honored were J. Collins Warren, of Harvard; Robert F. Weir, of Columbia; William S. Halsted, of Johns Hopkins; and I. Florence, Dora, and Margaret were with me. I am certain that Margaret will not forget how Dr. Osler (now Sir William Osler, Bart.) mystified a lot of English ladies by introducing her as Mrs. Osler.

In 1901, the University of Glasgow celebrated its 450th anniversary, and though I had received a personal invitation to attend, I could not, since Florence, Dora, and I were on a two-year world tour.

In 1905, I received a personal invitation to the quatercentenary commemoration of the founding of the Royal College of Surgeons of Edinburgh. I was doubly honored on this occasion, as the University of Edinburgh conferred an honorary LL.D. on me, and I was made an honorary fellow of the college.

In 1906, the University of Greifswald celebrated its 450th anniversary. I was traveling in Europe that summer, when I received some letters from home congratulating me on my new German degree. I had heard of none and supposed it to be a false report. On my return, however, I found that this venerable institution had given me an honorary M.D. at their celebration. I knew no one on their faculty, so I acknowledged the honor to Professor Friedrich, the dean of the medical faculty (who is now at Marburg).

In 1907, the University of Upsala celebrated the two hundredth anniversary of the birth of their most distinguished alumnus, Carolus Linnaeus.[2] Since he had been a member of the American Philosophical Society, we were invited to send a delegate, Harvard being the only other American institution so honored. Botany professor William Gilson Farlow was one delegate, and I the other. Florence and Dora went with me. I received a medal; the laurel wreath, which was placed upon my brow (!); a beautiful ring, which was placed on my finger; and a diploma attesting to my Ph.D., the highest honorary degree they bestow.

In 1911, I was not a little surprised to receive, at the end of May, a formidable document, in Latin, inviting me to the mid-September quincentenary celebration of the founding of Saint Andrews. As I had already planned to go to Brussels for the Congress of the International Surgical Society, the last week in September, I immediately accepted, and Florence and I left for London on the 27th of August. Meanwhile, in July, while in Weekapaug, Rhode Island, I received a notification that I would be receiving an honorary LL.D. during the celebration. This was done, on September 14th, by Lord Balfour, the Chancellor, following the rectorial address by Lord Rosebery, the new Lord Rector. The most striking thing about the anniversary dinner, apart from the distinguished guests (who included the Gaikwar of Baroda, Ambassador Whitelaw Reid, Columbia president Dr. Nicholas Murray Butler, Sir William Turner, and Lord Reay—the principal), was the extraordinary number of speakers (twenty-five) following the traditional loyal toasts. As Florence and I were staying at Sinclair Henderson's, in Dundee, we had to take the special train before midnight. When we left, there were still fourteen speakers to be heard. I spoke very briefly at the luncheon in Dundee, the following day.

In 1912, I was invited personally to the tricentennial celebration of the founding of Trinity College, Dublin, but I was unable to go.

Post Script (1914):

In October, Brown celebrated, with great pomp and circumstance, the 150th anniversary of her founding. A new and worthy history of the university, by Professor Bronson, a new historical catalog, and a volume containing the addresses were published. It was a notable success in every way.

The next centenary I am planning to attend is my own. Since I have attended so many others, it would surely be amiss (or a miss, if you prefer) for me to omit this. After all, "Moons" (Moses) Keen, a collateral relative, lived to be 106 years old.

CUSHING TRIBUTES

(Cushing's references to me in his "Studies in Intracranial Physiology and Surgery," in the Cameron Prize lectures, University of Edinburgh, 1925)

PAGE 6. "Probably none of the younger generation of neurosurgeons can appreciate the trepidation felt when, for the first time in the course of an operation for cerebellar tumour, a needle was inserted into the occipital horn of the lateral ventricle to reduce tension and diminish bleeding. Corning must have had a similar sensation when he first pricked the spinal meninges for the purpose of introducing drugs (1855); Keen when he first deliberately tapped the ventricles (1889); Quincke at the time of his first lumbar puncture (1891); von Bramann on his first callosal puncture (1909); Ayer when he first tapped the cisterna magna in man (1920). Contempt of these procedures has come only with familiarity, and we soon forget that they were once so novel that their performance took courage."

PAGE 112. "Operative surgery is little more than a composite of devices; whosoever is most ingenious in using them is apt to be not only the most resourceful and skillful operator, but the one who secures the best results with the least damage to his patient. And though their therapeutic purpose may be clear, even comparatively simple operations, such as those designed for the limited purpose of a cerebral decompression, may go wrong in the hands of one who does not know the tricks of the craft, however clear may be his understanding of the principles involved. So, when it comes to the slow, painstaking enucleation of a tumour with as little loss of blood, as little damage to the brain, as inconspicuous a scar as possible, craftsmanship is really put to the test, and it is not a job for the inexperienced.

"I would like, therefore, to doff my cap to the sole survivor of the pioneers in this work, my fellow countryman, W.W. Keen, who was one of the very first (1887) successfully to localize and remove a large meningeal tumour, yet had neither bone wax to use, nor muscle to implant, nor hypertonic saline at his command; no knowledge of intra-pharyngeal narcosis, far less of local anaesthesia; no instrument of precision with which to follow the patient's condition from moment to moment; no provision for transfusion in case of need,* and who simply made a sufficiently large hole in the skull, removed the exposed tumour with his finger, ligated the bleeding vessels; drained the wound; and in spite of a subsequent fungus cerebri, the patient, with the same help that Paré relied upon, ultimately recovered. But both Dr. Keen and this celebrated case, the end result of which he recorded thirty years later,** are exceptions to all rules; neither is likely to be duplicated."

---

* No electrical drills and burrs to quickly make the flap of bone.

** As models of vivid case reporting, I would recommend the reading of Dr. Keen's two accounts of this case, in the *American Journal of Medical Sciences for 1888*, vol. 96, p. 329; and in the *Journal of the American Medical Association, 1918*, vol. 70, p. 1905.

KEEN'S PRESIDENCIES

The Philadelphia County Medical Society—1889 - 90

There is nothing special to record except the following little incident.

In lectures on epilepsy, it was impossible, of course, to give students a really vivid idea of what an epileptic seizure looked like. Fortunately, I had a friend in Berlin, a Dr. X, who was able to fill this need for all neurologists. Movies had just arrived. In New York, there was an Epileptic Farm Colony for men. Dr. X, not being in active practice and having ample means, spent a month or more in the summer at this farm. On the recreation field he erected a movie camera, focussed on a marked circle on the grass, and was all ready for instant action.

The patients wore only a light blanket. If anyone had a warning of an oncoming seizure, he threw off his blanket, ran to the circle, and lay down. (If he had no warning, his friends would carry him to the proper place.) The camera would do the rest. The films were so good that the movements of the eyeballs showed very clearly. All the phases of the attacks were accurately shown. The professor had epileptic fits "on tap."

Dr. X stayed with us, and at dinner I asked him how long it would take to show his films to the Society. He put his hand to his forehead and musingly said, "Let me see, I have fifteen hundred feet of fits," which he then said would take a certain number of minutes. All of us at table shouted with laughter at his "fifteen hundred feet of fits."

I need hardly say that this novel and accurate demonstration was a great success.

The American Surgical Association—1899

The only thing to note is the title of my presidential address, "The Technic of Total Laryngectomy." In it, I described the various steps of the method I had devised to remove the entire larynx in a case of cancer. My patient had made an uninterrupted recovery.

The American Medical Association—1900

In the presidential address, after noting a number of matters of passing interest, I urged the following:

A. That a section of pathology and bacteriology should be established, and that a pathological and bacteriological exhibit should be installed, in addition to the usual commercial exhibit of books, instruments, and so forth. Dr. Frank B. Wynn, of Indianapolis, at my suggestion, had already gathered a fine scientific exhibit on these subjects. For years afterward, and with commendable zeal, he continued to make these exhibits more and more interesting and valuable.

Dr. Ludwig Hektoen and a number of others, also at my suggestion, had already informally organized the proposed section on Pathology and Bacteriology. The Association accepted both.

B. That, as our financial affairs were in excellent order, we should follow the example of the British Medical Association in making annual grants-in-aid to scientific research. This suggestion was also adopted and has been in successful operation ever since.

The main topic of my presidential address was the "Endowment of Medical Schools." I backed this up by showing that medical education was becoming more and more expensive. New laboratories had to be built, and many more assistants had to be provided and paid.

Also, the first steps were taken in the reorganization of the Association to make the county medical society the unit, membership in which made one a member of the state society, which in turn made one a member of the national association. It was a great pleasure for me to cooperate with Dr. George H. Simmons, editor of the *Journal of the American Medical Association*—and a great editor, I should call him—and a number of the most scientific and progressive members of the Assocation, in this reorganization, which has proved a wonderful success.

When I was president, there were only about 9,000 members. There are today (1925) about 91,000.

The College of Physicians of Philadelphia—1900 - 01

Founded in 1787, this is the oldest medical organization in the United States. It is a purely scientific body, giving no instruction and granting no degrees.

It functions in four ways: by its monthly scientific meetings; by special lectures on special foundations; by the Mütter Museum; and by its splendid library, which is excelled only by that of the U.S. Army Surgeon General, in Washington.

When I became president, I found that we had a very scanty library fund with which to purchase books. Accordingly, I solicited my friends to establish book funds and to mention the college in their wills. All in all, I added $80,000 to the endowment of the library, and there are, at my suggestion, legacies in at least two wills that have not yet been probated—though possibly these legacies may fail us.

It has been a great pleasure not only to establish a $5,000 Library Fund, but also to keep our wants ever in mind. I added twenty incunabula (and books bought in Europe in 1907–08) by funds I begged and gave, and have ever borne the college in mind for books, portraits, memorabilia, and so forth.

I was chairman of a committee that included Drs. Weir Mitchell and Wharton Sinkler and two women as colleagues, which in 1882 organized a Directory of Nurses. This directory, besides being a great boon to the public, has added $2,000 a year for over forty years to the Library Fund, as we furnish the secretary with rooms for herself and family, which may be regarded as an equivalent.

The usual term of the president of the college is three years, but on account of a projected world tour in 1901 and 1902, I caused my term to be cut back to two years.

The Congress of American Physicians and Surgeons—1903

While on my world tour, I was elected president of this Congress, which was first organized in 1885-86. Meeting in Washington every third year, it consists of all the special societies—anatomists, physicians, physiologists, surgeons, etc. In the two years between the meetings, each society is peripatetic. Its value is not only in the published *Proceedings* of each society, as well as the whole body, but also largely in the personal and social contacts of the leading members of the profession all over the United States.

The title of my presidential address was, "The Duties and Responsibilities of Trustees of Public Medical Institutions." In it, I pleaded for great care in the selection of their own new colleagues as vacancies occurred, as these boards are usually self-perpetuating bodies; that they should elect the staffs of medical schools and hospitals purely on professional standards, casting aside social, religious, and other affiliations; that they should establish a fixed retirement age, which in a very few cases will retire a good man who is still an able teacher, but in many cases will avoid hard feelings when a man who, after long and faithful service, has outgrown his usefulness and has to be told that he must step down; and that they should raise sufficient funds for their purposes.

Dr. J. McKeen Cattell requested this address for re-publication in a volume entitled *Medical Research and Education*, which was published in 1913 by the Science Press.

The American Philosophical Society—1907-17

I was in Europe in 1907, when I was elected to the presidency of this, the most ancient of American learned societies. It is the highest American honor I have received. To sit for ten years in the presidential chair occupied by Franklin, Jefferson, Wistar, and others scarcely less distinguished; to preside over a body from whose membership, from Washington to Wilson, eight members have been elevated to the country's presidency, is indeed an honor.

When Woodrow Wilson was elected, the society passed some congratulatory resolutions. I went to the White House by appointment, and with David Jayne Hill, Elihu Root, Fitchener of the Coast and Geodetic Survey, and Walcott of the Smithsonian Institution, presented the resolution, handsomely engraved, to President Wilson, who made a felicitous response. We then had an informal luncheon. In chatting with the president, I remarked on his being our eighth member to be elected to the presidency, adding, "Sometimes, Mr. President, I shake in my shoes myself."

In my final presidential address, when I retired, I have given somewhat of a sketch of my happy ten years in office.

I increased the resources of the society by a gift of $5,000 and by begging $15,000 more for the Publication Fund.

I also assisted in a movement, not yet realized, to move from an inconvenient location and from a building which is not fire-proof to one located on the Benjamin Franklin Parkway. We have a contract with the city to exchange our old building for a lot on the Parkway at 16th and Cherry Streets. We hope before long (written in December, 1925) to effect this change and have our treasures safe from destruction.

Many of us regret moving from our location, which was given us by the state, and from the building, which was erected in 1787. But the lot is only 80 by 60 feet, which is too small by far, and the safety of our priceless collections must come first.

The Fifth International Congress of Surgery—1920

Towards the end of the 19th century, I had considerable correspondence with British and Continental surgeons as to the establishment of an international congress of surgery, and I had made considerable progress in this matter. Yet obstacles arose which I could not overcome.

Finally, in 1904, the Belgian surgeons invited a large number of the best-known surgeons to unite with them in forming an International Congress of Surgeons. The sessions have been held every three years, the first three convening in Brussels. The first, in 1905, was presided over by Kocher, of Berne; the second (1908), by Czerny, of Heidelburg, and the third (1911), by Lucas-Championnière, of Paris. In 1914, we met in New York, in April, under the presidency of Professor Antoine Depage, of Brussels. "Military Surgery" was the perhaps portentous topic for his presidential address, although no one dreamed that in four months, the world would be in arms.

Toward the close of the Congress, La Conte, of Philadelphia, and one or two others came to me and said that there was a general desire for me to serve as president of the next Congress, scheduled to be held in Paris in 1917. I demurred, saying that while I was gratified by their consideration of me for the post, I would be eighty years old—or possibly not here at all. They persisted, and in such a kindly way that I finally yielded my consent and was elected unanimously.

Then came the Great War, and in 1917, anyone worth listening to was in the field and the Congress was an impossibility. Soon after the Armistice, correspondence was restored and thoughts revived as to when the Fifth Congress should be assembled. It ultimately was fixed for July 19th to 23rd, 1920, and the Secretary General, Professor Leopold Mayer, of Brussels, and Professor Auvray, of Paris (Secretary of the Local Committee of Arrangements) and Mme. Auvray got busy and carried the whole plan through with admirable skill and energy. They deserve great credit. I left all of the arrangements in their hands, as I could not possibly have managed from three thousand miles away. In addition, the Auvrays' auto was practically ours.

President Keen, 5th Congress of the I.S.S., Paris, July 19–23, 1920

The opening was inaugurated officially by M. Hounorat, the Minister of Education, since the Premier, M. Millerand, who had intended to open the Congress, was busy with the Germans at Spa. I read my presidential address in English, but I had several hundred copies printed in a French translation, which was published in the *Gazette des Hôpitaux.*

Herbert and two others tried to dissuade me from taking up the two issues of Alcohol and the Single Standard of Sexual Morality, reminding me that a large part of the revenue of France was derived from the sale of wine and champagne, and that Paris would resent an American lecture on French morality. I was pleased at the

Keen, with scroll, on second step; immediately behind him is Henri Hartmann, Pres., Univ. of Paris; front far left, robed, is Prof. Georges Roger, Dean of the Med. Faculty, Univ. of Paris.; in front of left column is Leopold Mayer, of Brussels; to his left is Davide Giordano, of Venice

Front Row *left to right*: **2**. Fritz de Quervain (Pres. 9th Congress, 1932); **3**. Davide Giordano (Pres. 7th Congress, 1926); **4**. Henri Hartmann (Pres. of the 8th Congress, 1929); **6**. Keen; **8**. Jules Lorthioir (Treas. 5th Congress, 1920); **10**. Leopold Mayer, Gen. Sec'y. of I.C.S. (1912-1938)

applause which greeted my remarks on both of these topics, and I received an ovation at the close. Dr. Robert Lovett, of Boston, told me afterwards that he carefully watched the audience and said that I certainly carried them with me.

Madame la Comtesse de Béarn lent us her house, and it was a jewel. It included a theater, seating three or four hundred people, that was filled to overflowing for the reception. She herself was most courteous to us and spoke English admirably. Her husband was replacing Jusserand as the Chargé d'Affaires in Washington. Florence and I had begun to receive in white kid gloves, but as no one else wore gloves, we quickly hid them.

The theater was decorated in exquisite Byzantine style, so that I could easily imagine myself in Ravenna. In a recess on one side was a large mural of *The Last Supper*. On hand were artistes from the Theatre Français, who recited; others from the Grand Opéra, who sang; and still others from the Odéon, who provided the most beautiful and graceful dancing. The Society for Ancient Music furnished players of fine music who were accompanied on the harp, the spinet, and other antique instruments. There was also a comedian, who amused us by his jokes, which were really good—and with no taint of double entendre. There was an excellent refreshment table.

It was altogether the most enjoyable and unique reception in the history of our five congresses, and Sir William MacEwen, my successor as President, will find it difficult to excel—or even to equal—it.[3]

KEEN'S SEVENTY-FIFTH BIRTHDAY

On the day before my birthday, I had had to go to New York, where I spent the night, leaving at noon and arriving home at about half-past two. As soon as I came in, the girls sent me upstairs to spruce up, reminding me that at three o'clock the whole family was coming in to greet me.

Downstairs, at three, it was not only the whole family but about two hundred others. There were flowers on all sides, in the parlor and the library, and there were many presents. I later learned that Florence had sent out cards to a number of friends, including members of the American Philosophical Society and the Franklin Inn Club, inviting them to a surprise party, "from 3 to 6," on my birthday.

Professor and Mrs. Newbold sent a "debutant" bouquet, with long ribbons, which I carried all afternoon. We had scarcely enough vases to hold the flowers, to say nothing of the basket upon baskets, all of which made the house into a veritable conservatory.

Robert Vonnoh's 75th-birthday portrait of Keen as president of the American Philosophical Society. Scarlet robe from Saint Andrews; chair used by Benjamin Franklin (bust on pedestal).

The greetings were all so cordial and sincere. To say that I prized and enjoyed such a friendly tribute is saying little. It touched my heart and helped me realize how far more generous and kind my friends were than ever I had deserved.

At 4:30, Mr. Rosengarten read a "round robin," hastily got up by the members of the American Philosophical Society, congratulating me on my birthday and inviting me to sit for a portrait to be hung in the hall of the Society. I accepted, in a very informal speech, later sending a more formal written acceptance. Robert Vonnoh was selected to paint the portrait, and with the approval of the committee, he selected my Saint Andrews robe as the costume. The choice was appropriate: I was to be seated in Franklin's chair (the president's chair at the society meetings), with a bust of Franklin (the one in the Metropolitan Museum) pictured behind me; and Franklin received his first honorary degree from Saint

Andrews, in recognition of his distinguished service to science. Yet clad in its brilliant scarlet made me almost self-conscious.[4]

It turned out to be a wonderful portrait, and Mr. Vonnoh considered it his very best work. In April of 1913, it was presented, at the general meeting, to the American Philosophical Society.

The one underlying note of regret, in the celebration for me, and a diapason of sorrow, was that my dear wife had not lived to see that happy day.

THREE MOST APPRECIATED COMPLIMENTS[5]

During Civil War, I was stationed for some months at the Satterleee Hospital, at about 45th and Spruce. It had three thousand beds, and sometimes there were an additional two thousand or more tents.

One dark, late, winter afternoon, I was approaching the gate, where there was a guard, of course. Three or four of them were sitting on a nearby bench. As I approached, I heard my name mentioned, and, in spite of the adage about eavesdroppers, I slowed my pace and heard one of them say, "Why, Keen can hit a joint as well as a butcher"—a sincere compliment that I appreciated.

During Commencement at Brown, in June of 1922, instead of staying at the Hope Club, as I often did, I was the guest of Mr. Theodore F. Green, where I enjoyed the hospitality of him and his sister. Earlier that month, I had given the Commencement address at Crozer Theological Seminary, entitled "Science and the Scriptures." It was published in the *Public Ledger,* and the scientific parts of it were published in *Science* magazine.

At dinner, one day, Mr. Green told us that once, when he had had occasion to stop at the Hope Club, one of the bell boys said to him, "We're sorry that Dr. Keen is not at the club this year. We all like him. He is a very interesting man. Have you read his address in *Science?* I uderstood nearly all of it. It was very interesting." That I had been able to describe such technical matter so that a "Bell Hop" (Mr. Green used this recent expressive slang) could understand me was very gratifying.

On the way home from the International Congress of Surgery, in Paris, Florence and I stayed for ten days or so in London. One day we went to Lord Bryce's country place in Sussex for lunch. Lady Bryce was, unfortunately, absent. I had known Lord Bryce for a number of years in the Philosophical Society, and

Bust for Keen's 84th birthday, 1921, by Samuel Murray

he had been my guest two or three times. He was always a diligent seeker after knowledge and "pumped dry" his friends whenever he got the chance.

On this occasion, he asked me all sorts of questions as to the progress of Medicine and Surgery, especially since our Civil War. Finally, as we were leaving, he took my hand in both of his and said, earnestly, "I wish you would stay with me for a week."

KEEN'S EIGHTY-FOURTH BIRTHDAY

On my return from the International Congress of Surgery, in September of 1920, I found, to my surprise, that a large committee had been formed to greet me with a large public dinner. The date had been fixed for November 18th, the ballroom of the Bellevue-Stratford Hotel had been engaged, and the arrangements were all well advanced.

Among other things, a circular letter had been sent out to my friends asking that letters of appreciation be addressed to me, but sent to the chairman of the committee, Dr. William Duffield Robinson. He was the moving spirit, ably seconded by Dr. William Taylor. The full list is in print. They apparently sent out to the four quarters of the globe to friends whose names and addresses they found out in some way unknown to me. Not a suspicion of the matter reached me.

But my son-in-law, Dr. Walter Freeman, was evidently so desperately ill that it seemed as if his death would occur about that time, and I told them that if his death had occurred or was imminent, I could not possibly attend any such public function. So they changed the date to my birthday, January 19th, when I should achieve eighty-four years. Dear Walter died by mid-December, beloved and mourned, as I had almost never known before, by so many friends and patients whose regard was sincere and almost beyond belief.

Letters soon began to pour in on me; on and after January 19th, they came by the hundreds. Eventually, they were beautifully bound in four thick volumes.[6] The bookbinder said there were about thirteen hundred letters and telegrams. They are a wonderful evidence of affection, which I prize beyond what words can express. I discount the too-extravagant praise, both in these letters and in the speeches at the dinner, but I do not discount the expressions of affection and esteem.

When the change of date was made, the ballroom had already been engaged for the 19th of January, so they selected January 20th, the first day of my 85th year, instead of the last day of my 84th.

Besides these letters, a fine bronze bust, the admirable work of Mr. Samuel Murray, was presented to me, and a photograph of me was given to each guest.

There were six hundred guests, including my four daughters and all of my descendants, except for W.W. Keen Butcher and Florence Butcher, who were too young. There were also in the galleries some four hundred ladies, making about a thousand all told. In all my dreams, I never could have imagined such a tribute, nor the various honors which have come to me, far beyond my deserts. No man ever had kinder or more appreciative friends. I might well have sung my *Nunc Dimittis*, but I hope God still has some good work for me to do. What I find to do I must do with all my might and speed, for I can hardly expect to live much longer.[7]

Chapter Notes

—••**E**}(**3**••—

CHAPTER 1: *The Early Years*

1. Much of this historic area of Philadelphia, Society Hill, has been restored to its residential character. The name, derived from the Free Trade Society of Pennsylvania, now capitalizes on the tone—presumably higher—implied by the word "society."

2. It is *still* standing (1999), now occupied by professional offices. The distinctive decorative wrought-iron balcony has been retained, but the neighbor to the north is now a vacant lot.

Keen's birthplace *(right)*, 232 South 3rd St., Philadelphia,

315

3. In a later footnote to his original manuscript, Keen questioned his own memory as to whether this was the Willing Mansion or the Bingham Mansion. It was the Willing. Thatcher Freund's *Objects of Desire* (1994) traces the history of Thomas Willing's two-century-old, million-dollar card table—which was once valued at fifty cents.

4. Probably the forerunner of "Anne Page," a trademark registered in 1920 for the use of the Great **A**tlantic & **P**acific Tea Company.

5. When nothing happened in '43, the date was set back to '44. Still no Second Coming, but Miller was established as the founder of the Adventist movement.

6. Ignorance and credulity concerning comets still flourish, late in the twentieth century, and are certainly not limited to youth.

7. I.e., berries given a bed of straw to keep them out of the dirt while ripening.

8. Hercules Fuller, Keen's latter-day "faithful colored man."

9. These sketches were made from memory some six decades later.

10. Large blocks, one on either side, framing the steps to the piazza.

11. Forerunner to one of today's inanimate New Year's Eve noisemakers.

12. Decades later, land occupied by Drexel University.

13. Andrew Hamilton willed the Woodlands to his grandson William (1762 valedictorian at the University of Pennsylvania), at whose death it contained six hundred acres, including "Hamilton Village," an early speculative real estate development whose streets were named for members of his family and friends. The mansion, where Hamilton had hosted the first Class of '62 dinner, became the headquarters for Woodlands Cemetery, final resting place for Keen, his wife, and thirty-five of his relatives.

14. An 1849 map of the area reveals the Keen property as well as the school, the church, and the residences of several neighbors mentioned.

15. "Slave to no sect, who takes no private road / But looks through Nature up to Nature's God." Alexander Pope's *An Essay on Man* (Epistle iv, line 331).

16. Evans was responsible for the promotion abroad of the revolutionary painkiller nitrous oxide. His personal crusade for painless dentistry began at home, in Paris, but led him throughout Great Britain as well. Gerald Carson's *The Dentist and the Empress: The Adventures of Dr. Tom Evans in Gas-Lit Paris* (1983) gives a lively account of his dramatic life abroad.

17. John Henry Evans, taught by his Uncle Tom, became a Paris dentist also. Pope Pius IX made him a hereditary marquis of the Holy Roman Empire (under the name d'Uyley, after Doyle, his mother's name).

18. The evolution of many of the children's games cited may be found in Larry Freeman's *Yesterday's Games* (1970) and in two works by Iona and Peter Opie: *Children's Games in Street and Playground* (1969) and *The Lore*

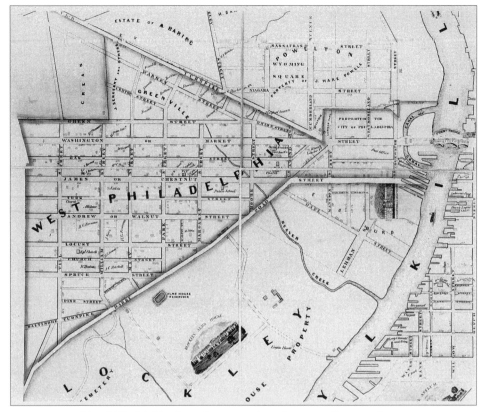

West Philadelphia. Keens' property is on James or Chestnut Street

and Language of School Children (1959). Stephen Nissenbaum's *Battle for Christmas* (1996) describes the holiday's evolution from primitive orgy to current-day extravaganza.

19. This decimated the city's population.

20. Kyn was not a Swede. See Appendix A for the source of Keen's confusion.

21. The *Kühn* to *Kyn* to *Kien* to *Keen* transformation of the surname is more felicitous than that of the given name: *Jürgen* to *Jöran* to *Jur[r]iaen* to *Urine* (on his deed of 1687).

22. Suspended from the ceiling of this charming little church are models of the *Fogel Grip* and the *Kalmar Nyckel*, the vessels on which the first group of Swedes arrived in this country, in 1638. When the church was built, in 1700, these settlers might have felt comfortable with the immediacy of the waterway: It was at the river's edge. Subsequent landfill has provided commercial piers and an eight-lane highway, but the church and cemetery, now at a remove from the shoreline, form a shaded, secluded sanctuary.

23. Keen was thirty-six; brothers George and Charles about a dozen years older.

24. In his original manuscript, Keen blamed this miscarriage of justice on George Jeffreys, who was notorious for his role in the 1685 assizes (when more than three hundred prisoners were hanged and some eight hundred were transported), but daughter Florence Keen pointed out that Jeffreys was only eighteen years old when Budd was jailed. It was a period when "persecution for opinion's sake raged in England." See Appendix B for an account of the precipitating circumstances.

25. "Ambition should be made of sterner stuff." *Julius Caesar* III, ii.

26. Now Budd Lake, of Morris County. Another settlement became Buddtown, in Burlington County.

27. See Appendix C for a 1912 journalist's review of the December 26, 1851, Kossuth reception, and the book containing the students' welcoming speeches.

28. Both institutions were founded by Baptists, the former in 1846, the latter in 1764. Each was renamed for a benefactor: The University of Lewisburg became Bucknell; Brown started out as Rhode Island College.

29. Also, Lewisburg in the decade before the Civil War possibly appeared a little *too* rustic, too monastic, for the city-bred Keen, intending though he was to train for the ministry.

30. Keen errs: His manuscript cites "Harkness," but Harkness's first Greek grammar was not published until 1860, after Keen had graduated. The recalled anxiety is accurate, no doubt.

31. In 1929, Keen noted the lackluster academic performance of his undergraduate Alpha Delta Phi brothers, surely a disappointment to the class valedictorian of seventy years earlier.

32. Built up from the keel with full-length overlapping planks.

33. A Fellow of Brown University, he was the father of Marshall Woods, a grandfather of John Carter Brown Woods, and an uncle of Mrs. George Dana Boardman.

34. The titles of more than two dozen of Keen's college essays are listed in Chapter 5, "Author and Editor."

35. Keen's mathematics examinations, red ink and all, are preserved in the John Hay Library.

36. Keen noted elsewhere that President Sears was fined two dollars, during the first term of his presidency, for not clearing the snow from his sidewalk.

37. Contemporary lingo for "flat broke."

38. Giles was a Unitarian minister and a popular lecturer. Antislavery was a favorite topic.

39. Donati's Comet and its tail occupied a heavenly arc of 60°, and when its orbit brought it to within a mere 46.5 million miles of Earth, it was measured at a magnitude 1 of brightness.

40. Startled, in 1914, to read in Guild's "History of Brown University" that 1859 valedictory honors were awarded to Edward Lawton Barker, "who declined them," Keen got librarian Harry Lyman Koopman to correct Guild's account. Keen noted that Barker, from a rival fraternity, was a good scholar but somewhat of a recluse, whose friends were jealous of Keen's socializing with faculty families and "broadly hinted partiality." These friends thought that Barker should have had the Valedictory, and they refused to participate in the Commencement other than to receive their diplomas. Barker refused to give the Latin Salutory and was replaced by Potter. There was no Classical Oration in Greek, originally intended for Potter. (See Appendix F for the net result.)

41. Will's senior-class portrait reveals a self-assured young man, but his father, like all fathers, could not resist a comment on the picture's contemporary hair style: "Good, very good indeed, but what have you done with your ears? We can't find them." Keen's next portrait, prior to entering Jefferson Medical College, reveals a more conventional cut.

Senior portrait of Keen at Brown University, 1859 *[Archive at Brown]*

Keen on entering Jefferson Medical College, 1860

CHAPTER 2: *My Career*

1. This comment reflects the anti-German sentiment engendered by the war (the time in which this reminiscence was written), a turnabout from Keen's prewar enthusiasm for the mutual cordiality and esteem with German practitioners and institutions—and the Kaiser. See "The Opening of the Kiel Canal," in Chapter 3, "On the Road", and "An Audience with the Kaiserin," in Chapter 11, "Remarkable Encounters."

2. According to Nigel Rees's *Cassell Companion to Quotations* (1997), this is almost certainly apocryphal.

3. ". . . and gifted with an egotistical imagination that can at all times command an interminable and inconsistent series of arguments to malign an opponent and to glorify himself." The full quote is from the *Times* of 29 July 1878, as cited in Rees (above).

4. Again, very similar earlier quotes have been attributed to others.

5. Now stored in the Hay Library at Brown.

6. O Keen, o tempora, o mores!

7. Keen's positions and awards are listed in Appendices H and I. Books and papers are listed in Chapter 5, "Author and Editor."

William Williams Keen Jr., M.D., **1902 oil portrait by William Merritt Chase** *[Thomas Jefferson University]*

8. Its new home, designed by Frank Furness and open for the Centennial of 1876, was beautifully restored, inside and out, in time for the *Bi*centennial.

9. For which students paid ten dollars each.

10. Thomas Eakins, who had studied anatomy at the Jefferson, was Keen's prosector at the Academy, preparing the cadavers for his lectures. Later, Eakins did several portraits of doctors (including his 1875 masterpiece, *The Surgery Clinic of Doctor Gross*), and the question arises as to why he never did one of Keen—who was not loath to sit for a variety of graven images. I speculate that as Eakins—now the director of the Academy—became increasingly controversial (mixed life classes!), Keen became increasingly distant. More to Keen's liking was the equally renowned but more conventionally respectable William Merritt Chase, whose portrait made the 5'4" doctor appear taller, for one thing. Such flattery would have been anathema to Eakins.

Incidentally, Eakins's portrait of Gross is enshrined at the Jefferson, though occasionally it goes out on loan for major exhibitions. Chase's portrait of Keen hangs at the Jefferson as well, but it's never invited out, in spite of the renown of both artist and subject.

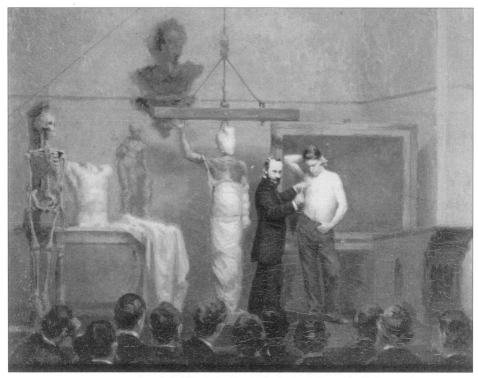

Anatomical Lecture by Dr. William Williams Keen, **by Charles H. Stephens, c.1879**
[The Pennsylvania Academy of the Fine Arts]

11. This trio, conducted by Keen, was captured by Charles H. Stephens in his painting *Anatomical Lecture by Dr. William Williams Keen,* which he donated to the Academy.

12. When the Female Medical College of Pennsylvania held its first graduation, in 1851, awarding M.D. degrees to women, "the action was so controversial that 500 medical students . . . protested the ceremonies and threatened to interrupt them," according to the account in John Francis Marion's *Philadelphia Medica.*

13. Keen's resignation at the Woman's Medical College evoked the resolution that constitutes Appendix J.

14. Still living, yes, but with a crater two inches deep in his skull. Keen later commented: "To protect the brain against injury, I bent a piece of tin to fit the surface of his head, covered it with black silk, and sewed this to the inside of a skull-cap, which he always wore." Daveler died in 1917; Dr. Aller Ellis performed the autopsy in Lancaster.

15. "We were the first that ever burst / Into that silent sea." *Rime of the Ancient Mariner,* Part II.

16. The scope of inquiry in medical research, even in those days, might be indicated

by the following: "In 1879 . . . Brown-Séquard started an international rage by announcing that he had rejuvenated himself with a 'liquid extract of fresh guinea pig and dog testicles.' His claims of increased strength and alertness, better digestion, and a longer urinary arc couldn't be replicated." Geoffrey Cowley, "Attention: Aging Men," in *Newsweek,* 16 Sept. 1996.

17. The Sultan of Turkey owed the Bordens' Fall River Tool Company thousands of dollars for rifles already shipped, but since he was on the losing side in the war with Russia, he could not pay. In 1877, unable to meet current liabilities, the company declared bankruptcy.

18. The family financial strain apparently caused two of the Borden sons-in-law to crack. In 1879, the *New York Times* ran episodic accounts of defalcations by Ellen's husband Walter Paine and Eliza's husband George B. Durfee. Each was treasurer of a Borden mill and, unauthorized, used mill funds to speculate in the cotton market. They lost significantly, when cotton futures dropped two cents a pound.

19. Jefferson Borden and older brother Richard collaborated on a number of successful ventures in Fall River and environs, among which was the establishment of the rail link between Boston and Fall River by the Old Colony Railroad Company. The eulogy for each contained abundant praise for their business acumen, irreproachable ethics, and contributions to the local economy, as cited in the *History of Bristol County, Massachusetts, with Biographical Sketches of Many of Its Pioneers and Prominent Men*, compiled by D. Hamilton Hurd (Philadelphia: J.W. Lewis, 1883).

Picture on a stock certificate of the old Colony Railroad Company showing the connection with the Fall River Line, 1876

20. Keen, recently retired from surgery and on an extended vacation in Europe (during the Panic of 1907), exhibited some Vanderbilt-like apprehensions about his "stack," writing home daily about his investments.

21. As described in Chapter 10, "Humorous Anecdotes."

22. According to Digby Baltzell, in *Puritan Boston and Quaker Philadelphia* (1979), Keen's successful practice and his congenial associations are typical of the magnetic forces which keep the conservative middle class of Philadelphia strongly attached to its roots—and its creature comforts. "Abroad" is used here in the sense that any place other than Philadelphia might as well be a foreign shore.

23. Designed by Louis and Augustus St. Gaudens.

24. "Under the direction of President Theodore Roosevelt."

25. *The American Commonwealth* (1888).

26. *The Government of England* (1908).

27. Bryan's views on evolution aroused in Keen a natural antipathy, which evolved into disdain over Bryan's endorsement of silver, and eventually appeared to stabilize at full-fledged contempt. Keen wrote a letter to the editor of the *New York Times* in reaction to the news that the secretary of state, following his resignation, was going to continue to speak out on national issues. Keen said that, in view of his mis-management of the State Department, he wondered whether it might not be more appropriate for Bryan to seek "the obscurity which he so richly deserves."

28. In his *"One Grand Pursuit": a Brief History of the American Philosophical Society's First 250 Years, 1743–1993*, A.P.S. librarian Edward C. Carter II does not discuss Keen's fund-raising efforts, but he does record that various factors "caused the Society effectively to abandon [the Benjamin Franklin Parkway project] by the end of 1933." Among the obstacles—other than the Depression—appears to be the opposition of many members to the surrender of their historic site adjacent to Independence Hall.

29. For an earlier Carnegie-Mitchell collaboration, see page 336

CHAPTER 3: *On the Road*

1. This was not disaffection: George and Charley were a half-generation older than the 18-year-old Will.

2. Keen acknowledged, later in life, that this earlier "clairvoyance" was wishful thinking. Such optimism was typical in the North, perhaps left over from the earliest days of the war, when many were convinced that it would be over in a matter of months. (Discovering in '61 that he was to be stationed in the South—i.e., Washington—Keen wrote to his mother to ask if he should take dress clothes suitable to the climate.)

3. In 1864, the Vatican proclaimed the Pope's "Syllabus of Errors," denouncing naturalism, communism, socialism, liberalism, freemasonry, and indifferentism. (For more on Pius IX, see Garry Wills's "The Vatican Monarchy," in *The New York Review* of Feb. 19, 1998.)

4. As cited in Note 1 of Chapter 2, the Great War caused Keen's approval rating of the Kaiser to plummet.

5. Published in the September 25, 1897, edition of the *British Medical Journal*.

6. Now more commonly known as a hookah; in either case, a pipe that includes a water chamber to cool the smoke.

7. At the end of the nineteenth century, the Antikamnia Chemical Co. of St. Louis marketed a full line of medicinal tablets designed to treat a wide range of maladies. The line (along the lines of snake oil) included Antikamnia & Codeine; Antikamnia & Heroin; Antikamnia & Quinine; and Antikamnia & Salol.

CHAPTER 4: *Citizen Keen*

1. On December 8, 1837, Boston's Faneuil Hall was the scene of a public meeting of outrage at the November 19 murder of editor Elijah P. Lovejoy (an advocate of emancipation), in Alton, Illinois, by a proslavery mob. Abolitionist Wendell Phillips said, in part, "Sir, when I heard the gentleman lay down principles which place the murderers of Alton side by side with Otis and Hancock, with Quincy and Adams, I thought those pictured lips [pointing to the portraits in the Hall] would have broken into voice to rebuke the recreant American,—the slanderer of the dead." [Great applause. . . .] Editor, educator, and orator George William Curtis ranked Phillips's speech as one of the three greatest by an American, the other two being Patrick Henry's at Williamsburg and Lincoln's at Gettysburg. Keen's glancing reference to it suggests that his daughters knew of the speech and the details of its occasion.

2. Today's cliché has had a surprisingly long life.

3. Keen, Weir Mitchell, and John Billings read papers to the College of Physicians of Philadelphia, on April 5, 1905, just four decades after the war. Keen's account of the war merits some attention, inasmuch as it was not included in his original "Reminiscences." (In all likelihood his daughters were familiar with his war stories and needed no recounting in print.) See Appendix M.

4. Even in 1993. Famed neurologist Oliver Sacks, in correspondence on another matter, recognized me as Keen's namesake and enclosed a reference to this early work.

5. The Military Order of the Loyal Legion was awarded to all Union officers who served in the Civil War.

6. Keen's speech, May 13TH, 1913, at the banquet to the foreign delegates to arrange for the Celebration of the Centenary of Peace Among English-Speaking People, in 1914–1915.

7. John Milton to Lord General Cromwell.

CHAPTER 5: *Author & Editor*

1. George W. Jacobs published Keen's *Selected Papers and Addresses* in 1923.

2. This book was an important Keen effort to counter the considerable efforts of the antivivisectionists.

3. Among the titles in this series (1879 and 1880), were: "Long Life and How to Reach It," "Our Homes," "Sea-air & Sea-bathing," "The Summer and Its Diseases," "The Throat and the Voice," and "Winter and Its Dangers." Forty years later, another title appeared: "Brain-work & Overwork."

4. Hercules Fuller was a long-time servant in the Keen household.

5. In 1859, Robley Dunglison edited the first American edition of Henry Gray's *Anatomy, Descriptive and Surgical,* with drawings by Dr. H. Van Dyke Carter. Keen's edition was the first to use color illustrations of blood vessels and nerves. This innovation possibly was inspired by Hyrtl's colorful models of the ear, bought by Keen in Vienna in 1866 (see page 33).

6. Keen added two more volumes by 1921.

7. Box 17 of Keen's letters and papers in the John Hay Library at Brown is filled with the editorial correspondence (1917–19) relating to vol. 7 alone. They reveal the extraordinary amount of work this octogenarian editor put into his pursuit of excellence.

8. Keen may be referring here to Harvey Cushing, who, when asked to write a chapter on "Surgery of the Head" for vol. 2, submitted a 700-page manuscript. He was the country's preeminent successor to Keen in neurosurgery, but declined his proposal to come to Philadelphia. (A Cushing tribute to Keen is reproduced at page 302.)

9. The titles do not suggest a premedical course, but they do provide evidence of a liberal arts education—a source of the many literary allusions that pepper Keen's lifelong writing. Consider this excerpt from his Commencement address at Rush Medical College:

> Make it a point not to let your intellectual life atrophy through nonuse. Be familiar with the classics of English literature in prose and verse; read the lives of the great men of the past, and keep pace with modern thought in books of travel, history, fiction, science. A varied intellectual life will give zest to your medical studies and enable you to enter not unequipped into such social intercourse as will beget you friends and will relieve the monotony of a purely medical diet. Let music and art shed their radiance upon your too often weary life and find in the sweet cadances of sound or the rich emotions of form and color a refinement which adds polish to the scientific man.

10. Less clinically, perhaps: ". . . in the porches of mine ear. . . ." *Hamlet* I,v.

CHAPTER 6: *Family Matters*

1. Letter from Weekapaug, R.I., dated July 12, 1912.

2. From correspondence between Will and Tinnie (almost daily, when they were apart for the summer), it must be concluded that her health was always less than robust.

3. Later the wife of Rev. Dr. Samuel W. Duncan, Brown Class of '60.

4. It is virtually impossible to mention the Bordens of Fall River without evoking some mention of Lizzie, who was accused in the 1892 slaying of her father, undertaker Andrew Borden, and his second wife, Abby Durfee Borden. Writing of his shock at the news of the murder, Keen told daughter Florence that he thought Andrew "was a cousin of your grandfather's." In fact, Jefferson was a generation older than Andrew: Lizzie was Tinnie's second cousin once removed. Too close for comfort, in family circles.

5. This note was appended to the letter in 1926.

6. Tinnie and the children escaped Philadelphia summers by vacationing in a variety of New England resorts—including with her Fall River family—always on the lookout for fellow Baptists, cultural stimulation, and safe recreation. The search culminated in Keen's 1885 purchase of six small lots on which to build a house of their own, a short block in from the beach, in the Cape Cod village of Osterville. Tinnie died the next year, and in 1888, he sold the lots—which today accommodate a million-dollar house.

7. In retrospect, shallow waters indeed.

8. This contemporary catch phrase refers to the fabled—and spurious—"Act of Parliament" decreeing that the Queen must "bathe once a month, whether she need it or no," but as Nigel Rees points out, in his encyclopedic *Cassell Companion to Quotations*, any famous person is fair game for such mockery; "Indeed, it is quoted as an anti-semitic joke by Freud in *Jokes and Their Relation to the Unconscious* (1905)."

CHAPTER 7: *Medical Anecdotes*

1. Published in the August 10, 1895, edition of the *British Medical Journal*.

2. In 1892, Chicago surgeon John Murphy introduced his eponymous "button" as a facilitator to surgery amidst the intestines. (See Appendix L.)

3. "Heav'n has no rage, like love to hatred turn'd / Nor Hell a fury, like a woman scorn'd." Congreve, *The Mourning Bride* I,1.

4. Rev. 6:16.

5. Tinnie's closest sister, Eudora.

6. Typical of Keen's many pioneering efforts, this would seem to be a precursor of malpractice insurance.

7. Charles Calhoun, professor of History at East Carolina University, slightly amended this episode during a C-SPAN telecast, August 19, 1999, about Benjamin Harrison. He noted that John Scott Harrison's body was stolen 24 hours after burial, in spite of elaborate anti-grave-snatching precautions. Also, although the entire family was involved in the search, it was not Benjamin but a younger brother who witnessed the actual recovery. ("My God, that's my father!" is still accurate, of course.)

8. Every cloud has a silver lining.

9. A physician legally qualified to determine mental competence, a psychiatrist.

10. On November 15, 1902, during a football game at Annapolis with Bucknell (who won, 23–0), Midshipman Hugh Kerr Aiken was kicked in the head, resulting in a serious brain injury. Keen, called in for consultation, accurately predicted the exact location of a blood clot and removed it. In the national spotlight, what might have been a fatal injury to Aiken—further fueling the fire in favor of the suspension of intercollegiate football—turned out to be a recovery instead. Keen reminisced about this incident in a later paper, "How I Saved College Football."

11. His mother may have been on her way. According to the *Army and Navy Journal* of November 22, his father, Dr. Gayle Aiken, was in the building during the operation, which was observed by navy surgeons F.W.F. Wieber and George Pickrell—and J.M.T. Finney, Johns Hopkins luminary and close Keen friend.

   (An ironic footnote: In 1909, Ensign Aiken, serving aboard the USS *North Carolina* in Naples, was killed by a gas explosion in the coal bunkers.)

12. Grandfather of the presidential candidate in 1952 and 1956.

13. If this fraternal confidence had ever precipitated actual stock-market buying or selling by brother Charles, it might have surfaced, eventually, with an aura of insider trading.

14. This roster omits White House physician Robert Maitland O'Reilly, who had examined the president's "bothersome mouth" two weeks earlier. For the latter half of the first operation, it was O'Reilly who administered the anesthesia.

15. This instrument, along with the excised malignancy and section of Cleveland's jaw, is occasionally exhibited in the College of Physicians of Philadelphia.

16. "Chloroform collapse" was an all-too-frequent hazard of the operating room. It led Keen into pioneering work in cardiopulmonary resuscitation through the massaging of the heart. (See page 64)

17. New York prosthodontist Kasson Church Gibson made the artificial jaw from vulcanized rubber. (A note to Gibson from Cleveland, three years later, commented that his recent loss of a gold filling should indicate how completely he had been committed to the gold standard.)

18. Lake Minnewaska and Lake Mohonk were two upstate New York family resorts owned and operated by the Smiley family. Lake Mohonk still thrives as a resort, while Minnewaska has been promoted to the status of a state forest preserve.

19. Persuaded by Holland that the story was already public knowledge, at least in outline, Hasbrouck confirmed it in full detail. When the doctors denied everything, the reporter was repudiated as a scandal-monger and discredited. The truth came out, in Keen's 1917 account in *The Saturday*

Evening Post, and Holland was vindicated. Since then, it has been virtually impossible for a president to drop out of public sight for a week with no verifiable explanation.

20. "The Final Diagnosis of President Cleveland's Lesion," by John J. Brooks, Horatio T. Enterline, and Gonzalo E. Aponte, lists the opinions of the principals as follows: Bryant, epithelial cancer; Keen, sarcoma and epithelioma; O'Reilly, epithelioma; and Erdmann, carcinoma (*Transactions*, College of Physicians of Philadelphia, 2:1 1980).

CHAPTER 8: *Personal Health*

1. Keen's daughter Florence appended the following note of explanation: "It was probably the abominable quality of the cigars to which he descended in those years. It was insufferable! Its 'aroma' penetrated from the first to the fourth floor."

2. Among Keen and his contemporaries, this popular play on words was based on the last line in a stanza of Thomas Campbell's 1802 poem, "Hohenlinden":
   > On Linden, when the sun was low
   > All bloodless lay the untrodden snow,
   > And dark as winter was the flow
   > Of Iser, rolling rapidly.

3. Inheriting her father's vigor, Dora Keen was driven to climb. (See Appendix R for more on Dora.)

4. Keen supplies the recipe ("from an old experienced nurse"): "Shake together for five minutes three ounces of lime water and the whites of three eggs. Add a half-pint of hot (not boiled) milk and shake it again for five minutes. Add sugar or sherry to taste. Use more or less lime water as needed. Give in hot or cold doses from a spoonful to half a tumblerful." (Keen often seems to use the word "tumbler" as a standard liquid measurement, though it has quite disappeared as such. I find it interesting that a tumbler was originally a glass without a stem, and with a rounded, pointed, or convex base, that would tumble unless supported until empty.)

5. At the same time, a measure of gratitude must have been acknowledged for the professional courtesy extended to Keen of Philadelphia by Fitz of Boston, Janeway of New York, Collins of Providence, Gibson of Edinburgh, White of London, von Eiselsberg of Vienna, and the Mayos of Rochester.

6. The loss is confirmed by his description on passports issued in 1901 (5' 4½") and 1919 (5' 1½").

7. While it is not germane to the thrust of Keen's "testimony," and since it might have violated his standards of doctor-patient confidentiality, he does not mention that this "urgent case" concerned Franklin Roosevelt's polio attack at Campobello. (See page 359.)

CHAPTER 9: *Medical Progress*

1. Keen presupposes a male surgeon, among other things.

2. Exposure to anesthesia has proven to be hazardous to the anesthetist, as well. See "A Compelling Intuition," by Paul Brodeur, which appeared in the "Annals of Chemistry" of *The New Yorker*, Nov. 24, 1975.

3. Congress voted to award an honorarium of $10,000 to the discoverer of anesthesia. Applicants for the prize included (1) Crawford Long, who in 1842 used ether in surgery but didn't tell anyone—and who once needed a renewed supply for recreational use, when two young ladies were coming to call; (2) Horace Wells, who in 1845 demonstrated the use of nitrous oxide, but in an almost carnival-sideshow atmosphere; and (3) William Morton, who in 1846 demonstrated ether, as suggested by his teacher (4) Charles Jackson, who was in the habit of inhaling it himself. The controversy raged unabated for many years, until Congress finally withdrew its offer. Crawford returned to his small-town practice, Wells committed suicide, Morton died a pauper, and Jackson went insane—all frustrated in their attempt to get recognition. In 1870, the American Medical Association resolved "that the honor of the discovery of practical anesthesia is due to the late Dr. Horace Wells of Connecticut." *Dentistry: An Illustrated History*, by Malvin E. Ring, includes a detailed account of the origins of anesthesia and some illustrations of the cumbersome early chambers used for its application.

4. The proposal for the school's original charter was effectively blocked by the well-established neighbor, the University of Pennsylvania. Undaunted, George McClellan persuaded Jefferson College, of Canonsburg, to open a medical branch in Philadelphia.

5. From Milton's "Lycidas."

6. "Of Studies," in *Essays*.

7. Irish intellectual G.B. Shaw was vehemently opposed to vaccination, according to biographer Michael Holroyd, because infant immunization had failed to protect him from a case of smallpox as an adult, during the 1881 epidemic. Holroyd said, "It was less his helplessness as a smallpox patient that Shaw hated than the revoltingness of the disease itself into which, he felt, he had been medically tricked." In 1906, Shaw called vaccination "nothing short of attempted murder."

8. See Appendix O for Keen's 1912 list of specific benefits.

9. Not averse to showmanship in a righteous cause, Keen included in this book a picture of granddaughter Mary Louisa ("Polly") Butcher with her mouth propped open like a laboratory animal. See Appendix Q for an ironic antivivisectionist letter to the editor.

10. "Slang" has come a long way in eighty years.

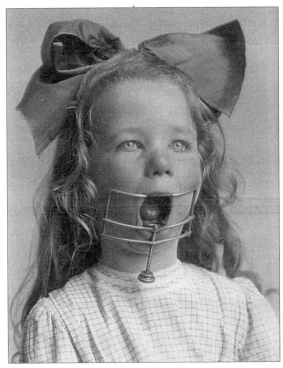

**Keen's granddaughter Polly (Mary Louisa Butcher),
demonstrating for his book *Animal Experimentation and
Medical Progress* that laboratory work is not necessarily
sadistic.**

CHAPTER 10: *Humorous Anecdotes*

1. General Benjamin Franklin Butler, appointed military governor of New Orleans, was dubbed with the nickname "Spoons" for pocketing silverware in the process of confiscating the property of those who refused to swear allegiance to the Union. (In *Profiles in Courage*, John F. Kennedy noted that Butler, a "talented but coarse and demagogic Congressman from Massachusetts," was the chief prosecutor for the House in the impeachment of Andrew Johnson.)

2. In his "Early History of Practical Anatomy," Keen commented: "Poetry has lent its aid to perpetuate the legend of the 'Invisible Girl,' whose ghost was believed to haunt Sir Charles Bell's anatomical rooms, where she had been dissected alive on the night preceeding that appointed for her marriage." Thomas Hood's poem "Mary's Ghost" (included in his *Whims and Oddities*) does not follow the legend as to the dissection's being ante mortem. Critics have suggested that Hood's success in writing amusing verse and ballads of social protest may have forestalled a career in the top rank of poets.

   I am grateful to British scholars Nigel Rees and Jeffrey K. Aronson for their help with the poem's historical references. Rees added the information that Pickford's Removals is mentioned in Dickens's *Our Mutual Friend*. (I have followed the published orthography and punctuation.)

CHAPTER 11: *Remarkable Encounters*

1. In context, this appears to be a stroke.

2. Ditto

3. "[T]he driving is like the driving of Jehu the son of Nimshi; for he driveth furiously." 2 Kings 9:20.

4. This dedication was carved into the cornerstone, which is now preserved inside. Each graduating class at Brown troops down the hill for Commencement in the meetinghouse, though there is no longer a Baptist affiliation with the university.

5. It has always been difficult for the A.M.A. to recognize alternative medicine.

6. On the south side of Copley Plaza.

7. The success of this concert led impresario Gilmore to stage a *World* Peace Jubilee, in 1872, with a chorus of *two* thousand, an orchestra of *twenty* thousand, and artillery-supplemented in the "Anvil Chorus" from *Il Trovatore* by a hundred Boston firemen hammering out the rhythm on real anvils. When Gilmore lost control of the gargantuan orchestra, he covered the resulting musical mayhem with artillery fire, using controls at the podium. (The artillery tradition seems to be firmly entrenched, at least in Boston, for the musical fireworks of the July 4th performance of Tchaikovsky's 1812 *Overture*.)

8. Letter to daughter Corinne and her husband.

9. "Her voice was ever soft, gentle, and low—an excellent thing in woman." *King Lear* V, iii.

10. Written in 1921.

11. Coldness, darkness, and dirt and discomfort were assumed—but so was the risk, which kept the public captivated by the latest dispatches. In a family letter of January 1892, Keen comments that "the Academy of Natural Sciences is stirring in the matter of sending a relief expedition to rescue Lt. and Mrs. Peary in the spring. I hope they will get home alive."

    An implied emotional reason for her going was the support of her husband and their new marriage. A daughter, Marie Ahnighito Peary, was born in the Arctic—but so, eventually, was a semi-sibling, the result of Peary's liaison with a friendly native. This is recorded by Robert M. Bryce in his monumental *Cook & Peary* (1997).

12. Bryce cited Peary's statement that one toe was amputated but he decided to keep the little ones. He kindly sent me a copy of Keen's letter of Sept. 30, 1902, with its surgical recommendations (at odds with Keen's memory of the surgery two decades later).

13. *Cook & Peary* authoritatively and exhaustively documents the decades-long drama of polar priority, principally between these two antagonists who started out as colleagues. Because of the inaccuracy of geographical measurements of bygone days, claims of attaining the Pole (i.e., 90° North latitude) have always been questioned—though not by the *National Geographic*, which periodically will update its support of Peary with yet another feature article on its protégé.

14. The railroad line did not yet extend to the center of the city.

15. It might be supposed that following a formal introduction, in such a social gathering, Keen the teetotaler and Grant the imbiber would naturally drift apart.

16. In his sustained agitation over the Great War, Keen drastically depreciated his esteem for Wilson. The after-and-before contrast is clear in Wilson's appearances in chapters 12 and 15, respectively.

17. In a handwritten memo dated Dec. 11 1929, listing "Public men whom I know," Keen included President Hoover, ex-President Coolidge, and Governor Roosevelt.

18. He published seven other books, all concerned with foreign languages.

19. He died in 1908, in Pasadena, having retired from teaching at Stanford.

20. Or one of the ladies!

21. See Chapter 7 on "Nursing."

CHAPTER 12: *War and Peace*

1. In 1915, when Turkey formally sided with Germany, the Imam declared a Holy War, and an international commission later determined that between May and October of that year, the Muslims killed more than a million residents of Armenia, the world's oldest Christian nation. Keen publicly lamented the immolation of Joseph Shimoon, a former student who would not renounce his Christianity.

2. Chronologically, this followed by two days Keen's former collection of reminiscences, when Wilson was reported to be about to speak to Congress "tomorrow."

3. Mahan's relevant works were *The Influence of Sea Power Upon History* (1890); *The Influence of Sea Power Upon the French Revolution and Empire* (1892); and *Sea Power in Its Relations to the War of 1812* (1905).

4. Quoted in von Schierbrand's *Kaiser's Speeches* (1903). Wolf von Schierbrand came to America in 1872 for a career in journalism. Of the books he produced, probably the best known was *Germany: The Wielding of a World Power.*

5. *Locksley Hall*, line 128.

6. Anne Morgan, daughter of John Pierpont, was an extraordinary friend to France, which recognized her efforts as the head of the American

Committee for Devastated France with a Legion of Honor award. Not resting long on her laurels, she was back, in her seventies, to help France pick up the pieces after the *Second* World War.

7. "Shinplasters" was the derisive name given to paper currency issued by the government in denominations of less than a dollar, starting during the Civil War.

CHAPTER 13: *Keen the Baptist*

1. A letter written on November 14, 1892, to daughter Florence, who had told her father that she "did not believe in miracles or the Virgin birth."

2. Conner's expression of gratitude to his old college friend for his recommendation has not yet come to light.

3. Quite true!

4. Written prior to Keen's 90th birthday (January 19th, 1927), this summing up was received by Brown's President Faunce, whose response is reproduced as Appendix K.

5. Written July 29, 1928, while at Lake Mohonk.

CHAPTER 14: *Eyewitness*

1. Declining attendance at the 12th Street Meeting made the Society of Friends amenable to the surrender of its prime location to commercial interests. A benefactor preserved the historic brick meetinghouse from demolition by having it dismantled, transported, and reassembled on the campus of the George School, a Quaker secondary school in suburban Bucks County.

2. Whitman and his wife were killed in this massacre, but he is memorialized, in a way, by the official mascot of Whitman College, of Walla Walla: "The Fighting Missionaries."

3. Keen's manuscript includes a list from the December 1916 *National Geographic*, contrasting epochal inventions by Americans with those by others. (See Appendix D.)

4. Keen received a typed letter in 1875. Always striving to be up to date, he advanced the twin causes of speed and legibility by typing much of his own correspondence. He also wrote shorthand.

5. Dava Sobel's *Longitude: The True Story of a Lone Genius Who Solved the Greatest Scientific Problem of His Time* (1995) tells of John Harrison's invention of the marine chronometer, which enabled mariners to be much more accurate navigators. She also chronicles the Establishment's opposition to Harrison's earth-shaping invention. As is often the case, a financial reward was at stake.

6. Her first crossing, in 1838, took fifteen days.

7. Avalon Peninsula, Newfoundland.

8. The Metacomet Bank of Fall River, Massachusetts, issued a three-dollar bill, which depicts a Metacomet Indian, spear-fishing from his boat; the *Bay State*, the first steamship of the Fall River Line, and Jefferson Borden, president of the line.

Three dollar bill, issued by (and useful on) the Bordens' Fall River Line.
[Courtesy of Mrs. Jefferson Borden IV]

9. Launched in 1847 by Jefferson and Richard Borden, the line featured a daily sailing in each direction between New York and Fall River (with connections to Boston, Providence, and Newport) for ninety years. It was the premier service on the Long Island Sound and was frequently employed by Keen and his wife (J.B.'s daughter), following their marriage in 1867. Roger Williams McAdam's *The Old Fall River Line* (1955) chronicles the life and death of the service, and his pictorial *Floating Palaces* (1972) provides evidence of the luxuriousness of the accommodations.

10. The first adhesive stamps were issued in 1847. Prepaid postage became compulsory in 1855, when the rate for a half-ounce letter was three cents for a distance of less than three thousand miles, ten cents for more. In 1863, the domestic rate was fixed at three cents, twenty years later, at two cents; in 1885, two cents covered a full ounce.

11. In *The Great Iron Ship* (1953), James Dugan presents a vivid history of the *Great Eastern* and her adventures with the transatlantic cable.

12. Field hoped and prayed (by cable) that Keen's surgical treatment of his daughter would be successful. It was. Part of the *cable*'s success might be attributed to Keen, a frequent user. Always eager to economize, he set up code words to shorten messages, personal and professional. (His home cable address was PAKEEN.)

13. By 1858, "illuminations" had come to mean fireworks. One such display destroyed the cupola atop Manhattan's city hall. It was replaced by a cupola of a different design, but fortunately, following another fire in 1917, it was reconstructed according to the architects' original plan.

14. The Liberty Bell was for many years encircled by the stairway and landing between the first and second floors of Independence Hall. Over time, so many visitors had "nicked" it for souvenirs that it had to be moved to a more secure shrine of its own, a block away. The bell, now closely watched, is available for all to touch but not to sample.

CHAPTER 15: *Just Deserts*

1. The Witherspoon Building, cheek by jowl with City Hall, Philadelphia, was the site of John Witherspoon's founding of the Presbyterian Church in America, in 1706, coincidentally the year of Franklin's birth. Witherspoon Hall was a large and useful second-floor auditorium.

   According to Dr. Norman H. Reid, Keeper of Manuscripts and Muniments at the University of St. Andrews Library: "Agnes Irwin (only the fourth woman in its history to have been awarded an LL.D. by St. Andrews) actually graduated *in absentia*. Sir James Donaldson would have 'capped' Miss Irwin had she been present." In 1934, Agnes Repplier, Irwin's biographer, said: "A parchment sent across the seas and presented in a dreary hired hall loses much of its savor, though the honor remains." Weir Mitchell, a long-time friend of Carnegie's—and delighted to see Irwin so honored—may have promoted this Philadelphia ceremony, with the philanthropist in the leading role. (Carnegie was the titular Lord Rector of St. Andrews—though Donaldson did all the work.) In 1909, Mitchell precipitated an eleemosynary Carnegie urge on behalf of the College of Physicians (see page 74).

2. The fame of the Swedish botanist was derived from his definitive taxonomies of plants and animals, but in *Birds, Beasts, and Men* he was more ingenuous than ingenious: He categorized wild man as "four-footed, mute, and hairy." American man, "erect, choleric, obstinate, gay, free," lives by custom; European man, "gentle, clever, inventive," is governed by rites; Asiatic man, "melancholy, rigid, severe, discriminating, greedy," is governed by opinions; and African man, "crafty, indolent, negligent" is governed by caprice.

3. Keen later noted, "We met in London, in 1923, when the Prince of Wales opened the Congress. We are called to meet in Rome in April of 1926, but I fear my health will prevent my undertaking so long a journey."

   Wm. Osler

4. The scarlet robe and portly figure led one observer at a latter-day commencement at Brown to comment that Keen looked like an adorable lobster.

5. A fourth compliment, surely appreciated, appeared on the front page of *New York Times*. A lengthy article by Lyman P. Powell, under the headline WILLIAM OSLER AND OLD AGE, included an invitation for Osler to name the seven greatest doctors in America. Osler's framed holograph response:

XIII.6.02

Dear Mr. Powell

I think you might leave me out of the list of seven sages! I should put Mitchell, Welch, Billings, Keen, Bowditch, Senn, and McBurney.

Yours sincerely,

Caricature by Wyncie King *[Franklin Inn Club]*

6. These four beautifully bound volumes, one intended for each daughter, are shelved in the John Hay Library at Brown. In a letter that was *not* included, a Missouri surgeon who had studied under Keen sent a birthday greeting to which he added that he would never forget when Keen, while operating on a large woman, suddenly stood back, raised his index finger, and said, "Gentlemen, I'd give fifty dollars for another inch on this finger."

7. Eleven years to go! In 1927, a celebratory dinner, with speeches and tributes, was given for Keen at the Bellevue-Stratford Hotel for his 90th birthday. His reminiscence, written for the occasion, is a paean for "God's Guidance" throughout his life. It is reproduced in Chapter 13, "Keen the Baptist."

Portrait of Keen for his 90th birthday, 1927

Appendices

— ••£){ ¾•• —

Appendix A

Gregory B. Keen's exhaustive family genealogy, published by the Swedish Colonial Society (Philadelphia, 1913) begins with the statement that "Jöran Kyn . . . was born in Sweden about A.D. 1620." He may have made this assumption on the basis of the Swedish source of the colony, and this may have taken root as family folklore, in the intervening 270 years. He apparently did not give enough weight to his own footnotes—or did not have access to Printz's *Monat Gelder Buch* (monthly account book), in which Kyn's account was captioned "Jürgen Schneeweiss von Sachsen." In the Governor's report from "Kihrstina, June 20, 1644," Snöhuitt is mentioned as a soldier in his life-guard, but Gregory Keen guessed that the name snow-white was a nickname, "possibly, in consequence of some physical peculiarity, such as the lightness of his complexion."

According to Peter S. Craig's 1693 *Census of New Sweden* (1993): When the Swedes had decided to establish a foothold in the New World they found that the Protestant countries of northern Europe constituted a fertile recruiting ground for their colonizing army, during the Thirty Years War. When Jürgen Schneeweiss of Saxony signed on, he was given the more bellicose name of Jürgen Kühn (i.e., from "George Snow-white" to "George the Bold"), which was *transliterated* into the Swedish as Jöran Kyn.

Once established in New Sweden, he left the army and took up farming on four hundred acres in Upland. Noted for his "singular gentleness of disposition and great excellence of character"—more snow-white than bold after all—he was the only one of the original colony to be on hand when the English authority replaced the Dutch—which had replaced the Swedish. (The English changed the settlement name from Upland to Chester.) Kyn deeded a portion of his land, in 1687, to certain persons in trust "to the use and behoof of the Chester meeting of the people of God called Quakers and their successors forever." This deed-signing constituted the last mention made of Kyn as living, and since his name does not appear in the May 1693 census of Swedes living on the Delaware, it is likely that his death occurred during that interval of time.

Gregory Keen's cousin Will accepted the presumed Swedish ancestry with pride, but back in 1878, he made an effort on his own, through a professional friend, to trace "Kyn" in official Swedish records. His daughter Corinne undertook the same quest, in 1929, through a professional genealogist. Both of these efforts, unavailing, proved only that "Kyn" was not naturally a Swedish name.

The majority of Keens living in the United States came—*as* Keens (or Keenes or Keans)—from the British Isles. But Kyn was a singular root, "the ancestor of eleven generations [in 1913] of descendants born on American soil." Saxon or Swede is almost a moot point.

APPENDIX B[*]

On the 7th of the month called April, in the year 1657, [there] was a meeting at the house of Thomas Budd, in the parish of Martock, to which five priests came, attended by a rabble furnished with staves, cudgels, pitchforks, and such like rustic arms.

They rushed into the meeting with so much confusion and noise that the preacher could not be heard. Their coming indeed made it a riotous assembly, which the moment before was a congregation of grave serious Christians of sober and virtuous conversation, and some of them of considerable estates.

However, the priest who brought the mob and caused the riot complained to the magistrates that the meeting at Thomas Budd's was a riotous assembly, to the destruction of public peace.

Whereupon one Captain Raymond, with his soldiers, was ordered to disperse the next meeting that should be held there.

Accordingly he went thither, on the 23rd of the same month, when Thomas Salthouse was preaching, and took him, together with Thomas Budd, into custody and conducted them next day to Robert Hunt, Justice of the Peace."

---

[*] Excerpt from Joseph Besse's "Sufferings of the People Called Quakers in 31 Counties in England, the Isle of Mann, and Wales from 1650 to 1688," published (London 1685) in *Good Order Established in Pennsylvania and New Jersey in America*, by Thomas Budd II, who had settled in Burlington County, New Jersey. It was republished (New York, 1865) by William Gowans with a new title: *The Introduction and Historical Notes by Edward Armstrong, a Member of the Historical Society of Pennsylvania and Dedicated to the Memory of William Penn.*

APPENDIX C

"Men and Things"

[*Philadelphia Evening Bulletin*, October 2, 1912]

An odd little relic of the enormous enthusiasm which Louis Kossuth excited when he visited Philadelphia has been placed in my hands [by Keen]. Men who remember the journey of the Magyar orator, statesman, and warrior in the United States have said that, almost as were the greetings to him everywhere, there was no other city, with the exception of New York, in which this feeling was so intense as it was in Philadelphia. On one or two occasions in past years, we have cited here some of the unusual facts which attested the delirious state of the public mind in its welcome to the eloquent champion of Hungarian freedom. . . .

The spirit of this popular admiration is reflected in the relic which I have just mentioned. It is a book of small or pocket size that was published in Philadelphia in the early part of the winter of 1852, under the editorship of Dr. P.H. Skinner, and bearing the title of *The Welcome of Louis Kossuth, Governor of Hungary, By the Youth, December 26, 1851*. It was intended to be a memento of the part which the pupils in the public schools of the city had played in the great reception. In the plans for that event, it appears that pains had been taken that the juvenile population should be represented and that the educational authorities had given their consent to a competition among the pupils for the honor of composing an address which the author would personally deliver in the presence of the illustrious guest. A committee of clergymen, which included David Martin, John Chambers, and A.D. Gillette, had been appointed to examine the thirty-eight youths who prepared compositions for that purpose. These were read by them before the committee;

the ages of the competitors were between twelve and sixteen; at least one, perhaps a few of them, are still living among us, in their three score and ten, and the addresses which all of them submitted to the consideration of the clergymen are preserved in this little book. . . .

Of course, they bear the marks of youthful greenness, and one smiles at the extravagance of much of the sentiment. But it may be doubted whtether the pupils in the public schools at the present time would present, on the whole, a better average in both the sense and the graces of expression, notwithstanding the prevailing belief that this branch of education is conducted with more facility than it was then. Perhaps the influence of John S. Hart, who himself was the author of textbooks of grammar and rhetoric and whose own style as a writer on moral and educational themes was an admirable example of ease and lucid flow, had not a little to do with the attention given to English instruction, for he was, at this time, the head of the High School, and apparently it was from the High School that most of the competitors were drawn. Two of its pupils were winners of the foremost honors—one Master Malcolm A. MacNeill, aged thirteen, and the other, Master John L. Painter, also aged thirteen and credited to West Kensington—and these lads were therefore chosen to act as spokesmen in conveying to Kossuth the sentiment of regard in which he was viewed in Philadelphia. . . .

The time for the presentation ceremony was the day after the Christmas of 1851, and the place the hall of the Chinese Museum, which was situated at Ninth and Sansome streets—a large part of the site of the Continental Hotel—and which contained the most capacious auditorium in the city at that time. After each of the two lads whom the committee had selected had received a gold watch as a prize for his address, Kossuth made his appearance on the platform and they were introduced by the Rev. Dr. Lyman Coleman. Master Painter then began his address, saluting Kossuth with "Welcome! Great Chief," comparing him to Washington, declaring that Hungary would eventually rise from its oppression, assuring its champion that there was not an American youth who would not "rather be the defeated Magyar than revel in the halls of a despotic autocrat." There was a bit of gallantry, too, in the boy's allusion to Kossuth's spouse. "Sir," he said, "we have read of the toils and hardships of your dear beloved wife who, in disguises, escaped the vigilant eye of the monster Haynaun. With such examples of female heroism, Hungary must be free; for by the virtues of our Mothers we are taught from infancy to lisp our detestation of tyranny; for disguise it as you will, a noble mind must be free and independent, and the minds of American youth are becoming brighter by education (for our public schools are as free as the air we breathe); every boy is taught that which is truly republican—Liberty of Speech, of the Press, Liberty to worship God as he pleases. In behalf of the youth of Philadelphia, whom I represent, I conclude as I began: Strike for your firesides, your altars, and your homes; and may the God of Battles guide the arm and hand of the Magyar hand."

At this point Kossuth, we are told, advanced to young Painter, placed his arms around his neck, and, in a most affectionate manner, imprinted a kiss upon his brow, amidst rounds of applause. Then came the turn of MacNeill, who had been chosen to speak for the girls of the public schools. He described the patriotic enthusiasm of every American schoolboy, congratulated Kossuth on his appearance in the very birthplace of liberty, and bade him welcome to the protecting shade of the Star Spangled Banner. "And be assured, Sir," he said, "the schoolboy is not alone. No: the schoolgirl, too, does join him. For the same spirit which prompted America's daughters to raise floral triumphal arches to receive Washington and to throw themselves upon the protection of him who had been the defenders of their mothers, still burns within their breasts, and they now unite with us in cordially and heartily welcoming him who fain would have proved himself to be a Washington to Hungary. Into our midst, then, most worthy Sir, you have the most sincere welcome of the schoolboy and the schoolgirl; and in every act you undertake for the advancement of liberty, their unceasing wish to you, Sir, is Godspeed." The lad then brought forward a small volume containing the Declaration of Independence and the Constitution of the United States, and this was presented to Kossuth with the assurance that it was from its pages, in simplified and comprehensive form, that the Constitution was studied and committed to memory by the American schoolboy. . . .

Kossuth, after having kissed young MacNeill as he had young Painter, proceeded to make his reply. It was probably extemporaneous in the main, if not altogether so, although it was not only keyed to the high pitch of fine feeling that marked all his public speaking, but the diction was more expressive than that of many a native orator. Indeed, Kossuth's mastery of the English language, which he had begun to study only a few years before, was marvelous; and he was known to hold the uninterrupted attention of American audiences for three or four hours at a time. On this occasion, his reply related largely to public schools and their value to the cause of national freedom. He thought that there two marks which a man carries on his character throughout his life and which cannot be erased from it—the mark which the mother has imprinted upon his heart and the one which the teacher has imprinted upon his mind. He hoped that the hearts of men would become as pure as those of children in their love of liberty. "Indeed," he went on to say, "our Saviour, who pointed out the children to humanity in such a way, is the great teacher of the principle of brotherly love—of that brotherly love of which your city bears even the name. I hope that every man will remember that by sentiments of children the principles of mankind are sanctified and that there is a halo of piety attached to that action of mankind which is conformed to these principles." Kossuth then placed his arms around both the Painter and MacNeill boys. "My own children," he said, "I have kissed you: take it for a father's kiss. And when you grow up to be men, though you may forget me personally, forget not that the man who represents the oppressed liberty of Europe, pleading for it before the great tribunal of the people of the United States, has imprinted a kiss upon your brows; and may that be a link for you and your companions which shall bind you through every vicissitude of life ever and ever to be warm-hearted, generous protectors and maintainers of those principles for which you feel now, in your childhood, a warm sympathy. God bless you. . . ."

Today there are Philadelphia households in which the memory of the tradition of that Kossuth greeting is still cherished from one generation to another.

PENN

Appendix D

Invention	Inventor	Year
Telephone	Bell	1876
Typewriter	Sholes	1878
Cash register	Patterson	1885
Incandescent lamp	Edison	1880
Electric furnace-reduction	Cowles	1885
Talking machine	Edison	1878
Electrolytic alkali production	Castner	1890
Transparent photograph film	Eastman	1888
Motion-picture machine	Edison	1893
Buttonhole-sewing machine	Reece	1881
Carborundum	Acheson	1896
Calcium carbide	Willson	1888
Artificial graphite	Acheson	1896
Split-phase induction motor	Tesla	1887
Air brake	Westinghouse	1869
Electric welding	Thomson	1889
Type-bar casting	Mergenthaler	1885
Chain-stitch shoe-sewing machine	French & Myers	1881
Single-type composing machine	Lanston	1887
Continuous-process match machine	Beecher	1888
Chrome tanning	Schulz	1884
Disk harrow (modern type)	Hardy	1896
Welt machine	Goodyear	1871
Electric lamp	Brush	1879
Recording adding machine	Burroughs	1888
Celluloid	Hyatt	1870
Automatic knot-tying harvester machine	Appleby	1880
Water gas	Lowe	1875
Barbed-wire machine	Glidden	1875
Rotary converter	Bradley	1887
Automatic car-coupler	Janney	1873
High-speed steel-maker	Taylor & White	1901
Dry-air blast-furnace process	Gayley	1894
Railway block signals	Robinson	1872
Trolley car	VanDepoele & Sprague	1887
Harveyized armor plate	Harvey	1891

Inventions by Foreigners During the Same Period

Electric steel	Heroult (French)	1900
Dynamite	Nobel (Swedish)	1867
Artificial alizarin (dye)	Graebe & Lieberman (German)	1869
Siphon recorder	Thompson (English)	1874
Gas engine, Otto cycle	Otto (German)	1877
Wireless telegraphy	Marconi (Italian	1900
Smokeless powder	Vielle (French)	1886
Diesel motor	Diesel (German)	1900
Centrifugal creamer	De Laval (Swedish)	1880
Manganese steel	Hadfield (English)	1884
Electric transformer	Gaulard & Gibbs (English)	1883
Process for extracting metal	Arthur DeForrest (English)	1888
Mantle burner	Welsbach (Austrian)	1890
Coke oven by-product	Hoffman (Austrian)	1893

APPENDIX E

In the *Outlook* for yesterday [March 15, 1916], there was an article entitled "Opportunity," by Lyman Abbott, and it reads, in part, as follows:

"Three elements combine, in successful achievement: opportunity, equipment, and courage. A few persons go through life unsuccessfully because they have no opportunities, more because they have no equipment, and a great many because, with opportunity and equipment, they lack the courage.

"Edward L. Trudeau, at 17, had contracted tuberculosis as a result of nursing his brother. He later took refuge in the Adirondacks because of his delight in the free wild life of the wilderness.

"It was while he was there that Koch's discovery that tuberculosis is due to a death-dealing germ in the human body was published. Dr. Trudeau saw in this discovery a possible opportunity to fight this dread disease, and he was inspired with the purpose to undertake the fight, by his brother's untimely death, his own illness, and his sympathy with thousands of patients similarly affected. His equipment for this audacious attempt was very slight.

His medical education had consisted of three years in an American medical college and six months in a hospital. He had no laboratory experience, no knowledge of the use of the microscope, and no money to fit up a proper laboratory for his studies in the Adirondacks. [There follows a description of the beginning of New York's Saranac Laboratory and its meager equipment.]

"Out of this humble beginning have grown the great Adirondack Sanitarium and the splendid campaign carried on throughout the United States against the White Plague. A great opportunity, meager equipment, and a great heart of courage—and behold the result.

"There have been many men in the world better equipped for such a campaign, but there was only one Dr. Trudeau; many women in the Civil War better equipped for nursing, but only one Clara Barton; many men at the end of that war better equipped for the education and moral emancipation of the Negro race, but only one Booker Washington. Most of us have had many more advantages than we have taken advantage of. We have passed doors of opportunity; sometimes we have not seen them, and sometimes have felt ourselves unequipped to enter them. Many times we have not had the courage to make the venture."

APPENDIX F

Brown University, Class of 1859

Aldrich, Samuel Nelson (1839–1908)
Allen, Crawford (1840–1894)
Andrews, Theodore (1835–1909)
Ansley, Joseph A.
Arnold, Thomas Clay (–1883)
Bailey, Samuel Slaughter (1838–1860)
Bancroft, Timothy Whiting (1837–1890)
Barker, Edward Lawton (1835–1889)
Bolles, Lucius Stillman (1837–1873)
Bowen, Lewis H. (1839–1921)
Bowen, William Erastus (1834–1886)
Bredell, Edward (1839–1864)
Brown, Charles Henry
Brown, James (1838–1902)
Chase, Charles Baylies (1828–1906)
Colburn, Isaac Davis (1831–1907)
Cowles, Edwin
Davis, Wade H.
Dockray, James Robinson (1834–1912)
Douglas, Robert W.
Dunnell, Jacob (–1874)
Eberly, Daniel (1834–1910)
Eddy, William (–1879)
Ely, Frederick David (1838–1921)
Ely, William Grosvenor (1836–1906)
Farr, Eleazer D. (1816–1899)
Fielden, Robert S. (1831–1863)
Freeman, Zenas S.
Fry, Richard G. (1834–1857)
Fuller, Oliver Payson (1832–1893)
Hathaway, William H.
Holbrook, Silas Pinckney (1837–1917)
Hutchins, Benjamin Tucker (1836–1889)
Jenney, William Henry Harrison (–1920)
Jones, William B.
Judson, Adoniram Brown (1837–1916)
Judson, Elnathan (1838–1897)
Keen, William Williams (1837–1932)
King, William Dehon (1838–1914)
Kneass, William H.

Manly, Francis Edward (1830–1898)
Mitchell, Edwin William (1837–1873)
Morris, Edgar R.
Nash, Stephen Sydney (1829–1896)
Newbold, Louis Henry (1836–1867)
Olcott, Egbert (–1882)
Perkins, Charles H.
Perkins, Joseph
Perry, Charles Homer (1835–1908)
Phelps, Henry (1837–1924)
Plumer, Joseph Trask (1837–1910)
Poinier, Samuel Thane (1837–1909)
Porter, George Loring (1838–1919)
Potter, Albert Knight (1833–1887)
Potter, Walter McDuffie (1836–1866)
Pratt, Joseph Porter (1834–1863)
Ransford, Hascall
Reed, Nathan A.
Short, Chester Fitch (–1864)
Smith, Aaron
Smith, Charles Morris (1838–1917)
Smith, Joseph (1837–1876)
Smith, Virgil Clarendon (1832–1865)
Southwick, Daniel
Stuart, John Franklin
Thurston, Robert Henry (1839–1903)
Tobey, Thomas Fry (1840–1920)
Tyler, Henry E.
Varnum, Atkinson C.
Warren, Henry C.
Washburn, Henry Homer (1839–1921)
Waterman, Richard (1839–1888)
Weston, David (1836–1875)
Whipple, Jeremiah (1838–1871)
Whitney, Solon Franklin (1831–1917)
Williams, James
Wood, Jonathan M. (1830–1896)
Wood, Reading
Wrenn, George Lawson (1836–1908)

Appendix G

Faculty Records
1849–70

Standing and Assignment of Parts
Class of 1859

1.	Keen, William Williams	19.76	Valedictory
2.	Barker, Edward Lawton	19.65	Latin Salutory
3.	Walter McDuffie Potter	19.25	Classical Oration in Greek
4.	Tobey, Thomas Fry	19.10	Philosophical Oration
5.	Weston, David	18.79	Oration of the First Class
6.	Brown, William Erastus	18.30	*Ditto*
7.	Whitney, Solon Franklin	18.20	*Ditto*
8.	Smith, Virgil Clarendon	17.89	*Ditto*
9.	Poinier, Samuel Thane	17.776	*Ditto*
10.	Short, Chester Fitch	17.771	*Ditto*
11.	Smith, Charles Morris	17.74	*Ditto*
12.	Bowen, William Erastus	17.69	*Ditto*
13.	Bancroft, Timothy Whiting	17.55	*Ditto*
14.	Holbrook, Silas Pinckney	16.78	*Ditto*
15.	Pratt, Joseph Porter	16.62	*Ditto*
16.	Judson, Elnathan	16.33	*Ditto*
17.	Colburn, Isaac Davis	16.28	*Ditto*
18.	Potter, Albert Knight	16.25	*Ditto*
19.	Judson, Adoniram Brown	15.10	*Ditto*
20.	Perry, Charles Homer	14.97	Oration of the Second Class
21.	Porter, George Loring	14.96	*Ditto*
22.	Ely, Frederick Davie	14.92	*Ditto*
23.	Bolles, Lucius Stillman	14.67	*Ditto*
24.	Jenney, William Henry Harrison	13.66	No appointment
25.	King, William Dehon	12.08	Oration of the Second Class

J.B. Angell, Secretary

Appendix H

Positions Held by Keen — Medical

1. Assistant Surgeon, 5th Massachusetts Regiment, July 1 to July 31, 1861.
2. Assistant to Surgical Clinic, Jefferson Medical College, 1861–62.
3. Acting Assistant Surgeon, U.S. Army, 1862–64.
4. Chief of Medical Clinic, Jefferson Medical College Hospital, 1866–69.
5. Lecturer on Pathological Anatomy, Jefferson Medical College, 1866–75; Professor of Principles of Surgery and of Clinical Surgery, 1889–1907; Emeritus, 1907.
6. Surgeon to St. Mary's Hospital, 1866–89; since then, Consulting Surgeon.
7. Lecturer on Anatomy and Operative Surgery, Philadelphia School of Anatomy, 1866–75.
8. Secretary, Pathological Society, 1869–72.
9. Professor of Artistic Anatomy, Pennsylvania Academy of the Fine Arts, 1876–90.

10. Consulting Surgeon and Lecturer on Clinical Anatomy, Woman's Medical College, 1877–83; Professor of the Principles and Practice of Surgery, 1884–89.
11. Lecturer on the Anatomy of Animal Forms as Applied to Decorative Art, Pennsylvania Museum and School of Industrial Art, 1878–82.
12. Corresponding Member, Therapeutic Society of New York, 1880.
13. Member, American Society for the Advancement of Science, 1880 and 1908.
14. Consulting Surgeon, Philadelphia Home for Incurables (and several similar institutions).
15. Constituent Member, American Surgical Assocation.
16. Vice-president, American Surgical Association.
17. Constituent Member, Philadelphia Academy of Surgery.
18. Member, Philadelphia Obstetrical Society.
19. Constituent Member, American Anatomical Society.
20. Secretary of the Section on Anatomy, 9th International Medical Congress, 1885.
21. Surgeon to St. Agnes's Hospital, 1888–92; since then, Consulting Surgeon.
22. President, Philadelphia County Medical Society, 1889 and 1890.
23. Board Member and Trustee, Pennsylvania College of Dental Surgery, 1889–1900.
24. Consulting Surgeon, Philadelphia Lying-in and Nurse School, 1889.
25. First Vice-president, Philadelphia Academy of Surgery.
26. Attending Surgeon, Philadelphia Orthopaedic Hospital and Infirmary for Nervous Diseases, 1890; resigned, 1898; elected Consulting Surgeon, 1899.
27. Honorary Chairman, Section on Surgery, Pan American Medical Congress, 1892.
28. Consulting Surgeon, St. Christopher's Hospital, 1893.
29. Member, Philadelphia Neurological Society, 1893.
30. Honorary Fellow, Rhode Island Medical Society, 1893.
31. *Membre Correspondant Etranger de la Société de Chirurgie de Paris*, 1894.
32. Consulting Surgeon, Pennsylvania Training School for Feeble-Minded Children.
33. Honorary Member, Altoona Academy of Medicine and Surgery, 1894.
34. Consulting Surgeon, Wernersville Asylum for the Chronic Insane, 1894.
35. Corresponding Member, Cumberland County Medical Society, 1894.
36. Honorary Member, Cleveland Medical Society, 1894.
37. Consulting Surgeon, Kensington Hospital for Women.
38. *Membre Honoraire de la Société Belge de Chirurgie*, 1895.
39. Honorary Member, Tri-State Medical Society of Illinois, Iowa, and Missouri, 1897 and 1908.
40. Consulting Surgeon, St. Joseph's Hospital, Lancaster.
41. President, American Surgical Association, 1898.
42. Honorary Member, New York Medical Society, 1899.
43. President, Anatomical Board of the State of Pennsylvania, 1899–1906.
44. President, American Medical Association, 1900.
45. Honorary Fellow, Royal College of Surgeons of England, 1900.
46. President, College of Physicians of Philadelphia, 1900–01.
47. Honorary President, First Egyptian Medical Congress, 1901.
48. *Ehrenmitglied der Deutschen Gesellschaft für Chirurgie*, 1902.
49. Honorary Member, Clinical Society of London, 1902.
50. President, 6th Congress of American Physicians and Surgeons, 1903.
51. Honorary Fellow, New York Academy of Medicine, 1904.

52. Honorary Fellow, Royal College of Surgeons, Edinburgh, 1904.
53. Honorary Member, German Medical Society, 1907.
54. Honorary Fellow, Italian Surgical Society, 1908.
55. Honorary Fellow, Palermo Surgical Society, 1908.
56. Honorary Fellow, Royal Academy of Medical Sciences, Palermo, 1908.
57. Lieutenant, Medical Reserve Corps, U. S. Army, 1909.
58. *Ehrenmitglied der Berliner Medizinische Gesellschaft*, 1910.
59. Honorary Fellow, American College of Surgeons, 1913.
60. Honorary Fellow, Philadelphia Academy of Surgery, 1916.
61. Member, National Research Council, 1916.
62. Member, Medical Section, Council of National Defense, 1916.
63. Major, Medical Section, Officers Reserve Corps., U. S. Army, 1917–1919.
64. Honorary Fellow, American Surgical Association, 1920.
65. President, 5th International Congree of Surgery, 1920.
66. Honorary Fellow, Royal Society of Medicine, London, 1920.
67. Honorary Fellow, Royal College of Surgeons in Ireland, 1921.
68. Foreign Associate, *Académie de Médecin*, 1921.
69. Honorary Member, Boston Surgical Society, 1922.
70. Academic Correspondent, *Reale Accademia Medica di Roma*, 1923.
71. Honorary Member, Massachusetts Medical Society, 1924.
72. Vice-president, Fellowship of Medicine and Post-Graduate Medical Association, London, 1924.
73. Honorary Member, American Neurological Association, 1924.
74. Honorary Member, Philadelphia Neurological Society, 1924.
75. Honorary Foreign Member, *L'Académie Royale de Médecin de Belgique*, 1925.

Positions Held by Keen — Nonmedical

1. Member, Alpha Delta Phi, Brown University Chapter, 1858.
2. Constituent Trustee, Crozer Theological Seminary, 1867.
3. Trustee, Brown University, 1873–95; since then, Fellow.
4. Manager, American Baptist Publication Society.
5. Member, American Association for the Advancement of Science, 1880 and 1908.
6. Trustee, Shaw University, 1883–95.
7. Member, American Philosophical Society, 1885; President, 1908–18.
8. Member, Pennsylvania Academy of Natural Sciences, 1885.
9. Deacon and Trustee, First Baptist Church in the City of Philadelphia.
10. Vice-president, University Club: 1893–1901; 1906–12; and 1917–21.
11. Member, Board of Visitors, United States Military Academy, 1894.
12. Member, Genealogical Society of Pennsylvania, 1899.
13. Associate Fellow, American Academy of Arts and Sciences, Boston, 1901.
14. *Ehrenmitglied der Schlesische Gesellschaft für Vaterlandische Kultur*, 1903.
15. Manager, American Baptist Missionary Union, 1906.
16. President, Baptist Social Union, 1906.
17. Member, Franklin Inn Club, 1906.
18. Trustee, Vassar College, 1906–11.
19. Delegate, American Philosophical Society to Linnaeus Festival, University of Upsala, 1907.

20. President, Contemporary Club, 1909–10.
21. Member, Sigma Chi.
22. Member, National Institute of Social Sciences, 1913.
23. Corresponding Member, Rhode Island Historical Society, 1915.
24. Member, Hoover's Local Committee in Philadelphia for Relief of Belgian Children, 1915.
25. Honor Roll, Order of Founders and Patriots of America, 1917–18.
26. Honorary Member, Welsh Society of Philadelphia, 1920.
27. Member, National Security League, 1920.
28. Chairman, Board of Trustees, Philadelphia Award, 1921.
29. Life Member, Association of Army and Navy Stores, Inc., 1921.
30. Councillor-General, General Court, Order of Founders and Patriots of America, 1921–24.
31. Member, Medical Veterans of the World War, 1923.
32. Honorary Member, Redwood Library, Newport, 1925.
33. Commander, Commandery of the State of Pennsylvania, Military Order of the Loyal Legion of the United States, 1925.
34. Member, Tau Epsilon, 1929.
35. Chevalier, American Society of *Légion d'Honneur,* 1931.
36. Member, Pennsylvania Academy of the Fine Arts, 1932.
37. Member, Pennsylvania Museum of Art, 1932.
38. Member, Republican Men of Pennsylvania, date unknown.
39. Member, Science League of America, date unknown.
40. Member, Simplified Spelling League, date unknown.

Appendix I

Degrees, Earned

1853	B.A.	Central High School, Philadelphia
1859	A.B.	Brown University
1860	A.M.	Brown University
1862	M.D.	Jefferson Medical College

Degrees, Honorary

1891	LL.D.	Brown University
1903	LL.D.	Northwestern University
1903	LL.D.	University of Toronto
1905	LL.D.	University of Edinburgh
1906	LL.D.	Yale University
1906	M.D.	University of Greifswald
1907	Ph.D.	University of Upsala
1911	LL.D.	University of Saint Andrews
1912	Sc.D.	Jefferson Medical College
1919	LL.D.	University of Pennsylvania
1920	Sc.D.	Harvard University
1920	Dr.	University of Paris

Decorations

1. Loyal Legion Medal. For service as a commissioned officer in the Union Army during the Civil War, 1861–65.
2. Minute Men Medal. For service in the Three Months Regiment, April to July, 1861.
3. Victory Medal. For service in the World War, 1917–18.
4. Officer of the Belgian Order of the Crown, 1920. (Awarded by King Albert.)
5. Henry Jacob Bigelow Medal, Boston Surgical Society. For contributions to the advancement of science, 1922.
6. Cross, Diploma, and Medal, with the rank of Officer, French Legion of Honor, 1923.
7. Dr. I. P. Strittmatter Award, Philadelphia County Medical Society, 1923.
8. Susan Colver Rosenberger Medal of Honor, Brown University, 1925.

Appendix J

RESOLUTION OF THE FACULTY
OF THE WOMAN'S MEDICAL COLLEGE
on Dr. Keen's retirement from the Chair of Surgery, in 1889

—Medical News, May 25, 1889

WHEREAS the Faculty have learned with deep regret of the resignation of Professor Keen of the Chair of Surgery in this College;

AND WHEREAS Dr. Keen's enthusiasm as a teacher in a Department for which he is eminently qualified, and his unhesitating surrender of time in doing a generous share of Faculty work has made his connection with the College conspicuously valuable and helpful;

THEREFORE IT IS RESOLVED that the Faculty desire to express their sense of personal loss, in the severance of relations which have ever been most harmonious and agreeable, and to proffer their congratulations to Dr. Keen, in view of his new appointment, with warmest wishes for success and happiness in his future work.

Appendix K

PRESIDENT'S OFFICE
BROWN UNIVERSITY
PROVIDENCE, RHODE ISLAND

December 3, 1925

Dr. W. W. Keen
  1520 Spruce Street
    Philadelphia, Pa.

Dear Dr. Keen:—

I thank you for sending me the very intimate and deeply interesting sketch of your life as you see it at the evening time. Few men living have so much to thank God for, and that you do thank Him is obvious in every line. I return it to you with my thanks for having allowed me to see it.

The greatest blessing that God has given you lies, it seems to me, not in any external efforts, not in any outside pressure compelling you to go in this direction or in that, but in the inner aspiration after things that are excellent, the inner energy and the inner soundness of judgment which have enabled you to take advantage of the opportunities which come to all, if men have the insight and the energy to seize them. In other words, it is God within us rather than God without us that really is meant by "divine Providence." At least so it seems to me. More and more I turn away from the idea of a God moving us around like helpless pieces on the chessboard to the thought of a God dwelling within, as the sap in the tree, or as that directive energy, for which we have no name, that gives character and development to every growing thing.

Sincerely yours,

/s/ W.H.P. Faunce

Appendix L

Murphy's Button

On April 3, 1893, Keen read the following paper before the Philadelphia Academy of Surgery (published in the June 1893 *Annals of Surgery*):

"A Case of Cancer of the Hepatic Flexure of the Colon Producing Intestinal Obstruction; Temporary Relief by an Artificial Anus; Later Re-Establishment of the Continuity of the Bowels by Ileo-Colostomy by Means of Murphy's Button."

The previous year, John B. Murphy had introduced his eponymous "button," and its utility in resectioning abdominal organs was quickly recognized by fellow surgeons.

The button consisted of two small circular bowls. Into a circular opening in the bottom of one bowl was "sweated" a cylinder with female screw-thread on its entire surface. This cylinder extended perpendicularly from the bottom of the bowl. There was an opening in the male bowl in which was "sweated" a similar and smaller cylinder of a size to slip easily into the female cylinder. Two brass springs were soldered on either side of the inner surface of the lower end of the male cylinder, which extended almost to the top, where small points protruded through openings in the cylinder. These points were designed to catch the screw-thread when the male cylinder was pressed into the female cylinder, and thus the bowls were held together at any desired point. A small brass ring, with a thin but not a cutting edge, to which was attached a wire spring, was placed in the male bowl and retained in position, projecting one-eighth of an inch above the edge of the bowl. This was for the purpose of keeping up continuous pressure until the entire tissue between the edges of the bowls was cut off. The two hemispheres of the button were inserted in slits or ends of the particular organ to be operated upon. A running suture was placed around the opening in the bowl, so that when it was tied, it drew the cut edges within the clasp of the brass bowl. A similar running suture was applied to the other portion of the bowel to be anastomosed, and the button was pressed together. The pressure atrophy at the edge of the bowl was produced by the brass ring supported by the wire spring. The opening left after the button had liberated itself was exactly the size of the button used.

Loyal Davis, *J.B. Murphy, Stormy Petrel of Surgery* (1938)

Appendix M

Centerville church near Bull Run *[Alexander Gardiner photograph.
Brady-Handy Collection, Library of Congress]*

The overriding impression Keen leaves is one of an army in disarray. He said, "It was like those days when 'there was no King in Israel, and every man did that which was right in his own eyes.'"

On August 30, 1862, the second and last day of the Second Battle of Bull Run, he was ordered to "proceed to the battlefield near Manassas and render such services as may be required" and return with the wounded to the Ascension General Hospital in Washington. He left with a train of thirty-six wagons, eleven of which contained whiskey, all or in part. ("May I not disclaim," he said, "any responsibility for being at the head of what might be called 'a traveling saloon?'") When the train was shelled from a parallel road, before arriving in Centreville, they realized that this was not going to be the "Glorious Victory" that Pope had proclaimed. The drivers were held to their posts only by Keen's pistol and the rifles of the escort soldiers who guarded "from attack from without and fright from within—both of which were quickly realized." The first enemy officers to gaze on the stored supply of liquor agreed that its volume was greater than that which could be found in the city of Richmond. Virtually the entire contents of the train were comandeered by Colonel Fauntleroy of the 6th Virginia Confederate Cavalry.

In Keen's words: "After the battle, I passed such a night as I had never before experienced. The suffering of the wounded is awful. Those who were ambulatory followed the army in retreat. Others are on the field, lying there since last Friday, eating nothing and drinking scarcely anything save what they obtained from the haversacks of dead comrades in their neighborhood. Those with abdominal wounds had to be left on the field, since there was no appropriate surgery available in those days; an abdominal wound meant sure death. Those who had a chance to live had to be picked up first. But as I found a hundred severely wounded men in a little church, I saw my duty well marked out. One of us started with a pail of water and a tin dipper to supply the first want of all, another, as quickly as we could heat some soup (humanely provided from the Confederate commissariat), started on a similar round to abate the hunger, while I took a bottle of morphine and my pocket knife and did not worry over any superfluous exactitude in doling out the blessed relief that morphine brings to men in pain. Upon a few mattresses and with almost no other conveniences or comforts the men lay in rows across the floor. Most of them had, in fact, not even a mattress but only a little straw under them, and as this became soiled it had to be diminished, until finally the poor fellows lay on bare boards. The bedsores that followed were something frightful, often larger than an entire hand. Add to all this the secondary hemorrhages—which often soaked the floor before they could be arrested—to get some idea of the suffering. Added to the gloom was the misery

Acting Assistant Surgeon Keen, 1862

of the field-hospital conditions: almost complete darkness (2 or 3 dim lanterns), drizzling rain, and six inches of Virginia mud. Fortunately, two or three of the Christian Commission and the Sanitary Commission (forerunners of the Red Cross) were on hand and helped, working twelve to fifteen hours a day or more.

"A long [mule] train of a hundred ambulances arrived to carry our wounded from the field

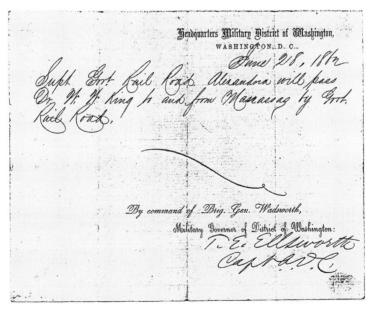

R.R. pass, following Keen's "technical capture" after the Second Battle of Bull Run
[Historical Collection, the College of Physicians of Philadelphia]

of battle back to Washington (over a corduroy road), and there were but four surgeons to look after them and their many imperative needs."

Keen also cited *Vanity Fair*'s headline summary of the battle: BULL RUN, THEY RUN, WE RUN.

Released from "technical capture" (see Appendix N) and returned to Washington, Keen was then sent to Hospital No. 1, in Frederick, Maryland, to gather war data. They included various mortality rates: pyaemia, 97.4%; hospital gangrene, 45.6%; tetanus, 89.3%; more deaths from patients' refusal to allow amputations than from amputations; abdominal wounds, almost 100%; hip-joint operations, 83.3%; trephining, 61%; shoulder-joint amputations, 28.5%; ligations of the femoral artery, 75%.

Appendix N

C O P Y

U. S. Naval Hospital
Washington, D.C.
January 18, 1916

Dr. W. W. Keen
1729 Chestnut St.
Philadelphia, Pa.

Dear Doctor Keen:

Dr. Bell, of the League Island Navy Yard, has just written me concerning your technical capture after Second Bull Run by a Colonel Fauntleroy and asked me if I could identify him. I don't think that there is the slightest doubt that he was my grandfather, who became a general in the Confederate army before the war closed but was badly wounded, about a year before Lee's surrender, and died about one year later. He had two sons on the Confederate side, one who was my father, an assistant surgeon (afterward a medical director of a group of hospitals with head-quarters at Danville, Virginia), and another son who was a captain in the Navy.

The reason that I am sure it was my grandfather is that there was only one family of that name on the Confederate side, and he was the only one who held the rank of colonel. I am very glad to know that you received one of my reports on the European war, as I had your name down on my list to send you one as soon as the second installment was received from the Government Printing Office.

With the highest respect and esteem, believe me,

Faithfully yours,

A.M. Fauntleroy

Appendix O

Some Achievements of the Friends of Medical Research in 50 Years

[Written in 1912]

1. Discovered and developed antiseptic surgery.
2. Made possible abdominal surgery and brain surgery
3. Made possible modern surgery of the heart.
4. Almost abolished lockjaw following operations and accidents.
5. Abolished yellow fever.
6. Reduced the mortality from compound fractures: 66% to less than 1%.
7. Reduced the mortality from ovariotomy: 66% to 2.3%.
8. Reduced the mortality from hydrophobia: 12–14% to 0.77%
9. Reduced the mortality from cerebro-spinal meningitis: 75–90% to 20%.
10. Reduced the mortality from hernia, mastectomy, and tumors: now negligible.
11. Reduced the mortality from diphtheria: less than ¼ of previous rates.
12. Reduced the mortality from tuberculosis: by 30 to 50%.
13. Enormously diminished the ravages of malaria.
14. Devised a method for the direct transfusion of blood.
15. Made operating for goitre almost perfectly safe.
16. Reduced Malta fever in the British army and navy: 1,300 cases to one case, in four years.
17. Reduced puerperal fever following childbirth: 10–57% to less than 1%.
18. Discovered a remedy for syphilis.
19. Discovered a vaccine that totally abolishes typhoid.
20. Discovered the cause of infantile paralysis.
21. Discovered the cause, method, and transmission, and the means of treating sleeping sickness.
22. Enormously benefited animals by discovering the cause of—and in many cases, the means of combatting—tuberculosis, rinderpest, anthrax, glanders, lumpy jaw, and hog and chicken cholera.

Note: In every case, these achievements have been made through animal experimentation.

Appendix P

Facsimile page (reduced) from Keen's Autobiographical Sketch," which was included in his four unpublished bound copies of "Reminiscences for My Children" (1916)

A list of the positions I have occupied and of the honors so generously given me and of the books and papers I have written and edited numbering over 300 (see list) will be found in the drawer of the table in the front office, and to some extent are given in "Who's Who in America". Of two of the highest professional distinctions, one European and one American, I only learned while traveling in India in 1901-2. In 1901 I was elected one of the eight Honorary Fellows at the German Surgical Society, the largest and most distinguished Surgical Society in the world. I am the only *when Halsted was Elected* American surgeon who, up to 1914, has ever received that honor. In 1902 I was elected President of the Sixth Triennial Congress of American Physicians and Surgeons to be held in 1903--the blue ribbon of the American Profession. The list of Presidents is a very distinguished one; viz,- (1) 1888, John S. Billings; (2) 1891, S. Weir Mitchell; (3) 1894, A. L. Loomis; (4) 1897, Wm. H. Welch; (5) 1900, Henry P. Bowditch; (6) 1903, W. W. Keen. Following me have *1916 W. S. Thayer* been (7),1907, R. H. Fitz; (8) 1910, E. L. Trudeau. *1913 Zen. W. C. Gorgas*

In the late '90's I think it was I made a serious effort to initiate a movement for an International Surgical Congress. *Billings* I corresponded with Czerny, Kocher, Gussenbauer, vonBergmann, *Lister the E.S.* and other leading surgeons in Germany, France, Great Britain and Italy. They all approved on the idea and it would have materialized but for the attitude of the British surgeons. They had no Surgical Society with scientific meetings, transactions, etc. The Royal College of Surgeons of England is a Society charged with (1) The examination (with the Royal College of Physicians of England and the Society of Apothecaries) and granting of degrees in medicine; (2) The care of the Hunterian Museum and (3) Certain funds for stated courses of lectures

Appendix Q

PLEA FOR RATS AND FLIES[*]

To the Editor of the Public Ledger:

Sir—We zoophilists . . . have greatly rejoiced at the splendid exposition of the law . . . as to cruelty to animals. Judge Bregy charged the jury that "the law of Pennsylvania does not allow pain and suffering . . . to be inflicted upon dogs for any purpose except for the relief of the suffering of the dog itself"—"dog" meaning, of course, any "animal."

Now I beg to call the attention of the District Attorney . . . to most flagrant and cruel violations of the law as thus expounded by Dr. Richard H. Harte, the Director of Public Health, and to pray that a stop may be put to his "crimes," as they may well be called.

Doctor Harte has insistently incited the whole community to kill all rats. We must poison them, drown them, smoke them out, starve them out, or give them to the ravening terrier or the stealthy cat. And why all this illegal and barbarous cruelty? Because the rat and his fleas spread the bubonic plague. But are these wanton tortures of the rat for the "relief of suffering of the rat itself"? Ask even the least intelligent rat! If they are then not for the benefit of each and every rat thus tortured, they are by the law of Pennsylvania illegal and puinishable as a "crime."

The same is true of the cruel and insensate campaign against the harmless though annoying fly. We zoophilists do not believe in bacteriology, and therefore do not believe that flies can spread typhoid. But even if they could, it is clearly illegal cruelty to catch them in traps and on tanglefoot paper and slowly starve them to death. Such conduct is surely not for the "relief of the fly itself." Moreover, this campaign of cruelty is demoralizing to children and cultivates those base instincts which develop into the barbarism of war.

But Doctor Harte goes further. He provides lymph—which we believe to be foul poison—and insists on introducing it into the clean, pure bodies of our dear healthy babies to prevent smallpox. In fact, we believe that the cause of the continued existence of smallpox is vaccination itself. We therefore refuse to be vaccinated.

Still worse, sir, Doctor Harte spends thousand of our good dollars annually on a bacteriological laboratory. Now bacteriology has again and again been proved to be false. We utterly reject the doctrine that any germ causes any disease. Typhoid, lockjaw and diphtheria are caused not by germs but by dirt and the neglect of sanitation. Our common and correct explanation of how pneumonia or consumption began is that a patient "caught a cold." If those horrid bacteriologists are right, we ought to say "he caught a germ," or, perhaps better, "a germ caught him."

We object energetically to the contamination of the blood of ourselves and our children by inoculating them with those filthy poisons—the antitoxins. It is true that the deaths from cerebro-spinal meningitis have much decreased since the use of that disgusting and dangerous antitoxin of Flexner was begun; that the mortality of diphtheria has greatly diminished since Behring's antitoxin was introduced, and that

---

[*] Keen was beleaguered by *Zoophilia* and its editor. This letter, published in the Philadelphia Ledger, possibly was written by Keen himself, who was a regular, published contributor to the paper.

typhoid has disappaeared from our army since anti-typhoid vaccination was made compulsory; but these and other similar facts are merely deceptive coincidences. The real causes of the improvement are better sanitation and wiser diet. Indeed, it is not too much to hope that a proper diet alone would eradicate most diseases.

I hope that the District Attorney will get out an injunction to prevent Doctor Harte from vaccinating anybody; close his bacteriological laboratory and save many thousands of our taxes; but, above all, that he will indict Doctor Harte on account of this criminal cruelty to the poor, unoffending rat.

ZOOPHILIST.

Philadelphia, September 6, 1914.

APPENDIX R

In July 1911, the *National Geographic Magazine* published Dora Keen's description and pictures in an article entitled "A Woman's Climbs in the High Alps."[*]

In 1912, she became the first person to succeed in the ascent of Mt. Blackburn (5,036 m), accompanied by one guide, George W. Handy, after six other guides had turned back. In 1916, four years after that climb, she and George were married. A possible impediment to the nuptials: Handy had immigrated from Germany, and Germany was distinctly out of favor with her father following the outbreak of the war. A week after the wedding, Keen asked Florence (the bridesmaid) for details and added, "I wrote D[ora] to send his fotograph and if he had none to fotograph him herself. I didn't suggest that she 'develop' him. That would be a work of supererogation."

A year later, when the couple were settled in Vermont, Keen wrote to Florence that "George is certainly a capital farmer," though it was still an embarrassment to have a son-in-law with a heavy German accent.

A dramatized account of the Mt. Blackburn climb, "The Romance of the Seventh Man," appeared in the *New York World* of August 6, 1916. Eighty years later, editor Bill Sherwonit included Dora's own nuts-and-bolts narrative in his *Alaska Ascents: World-Class Mountaineers Tell Their Stories.*

"Aunt Dodie" died in Hong Kong while making another trip around the world—alone—at age 91.

---

[*] Her other published articles include:

"A Woman's Ascent of the Matterhorn," in *Outlook,* May 28, 1910.

"Arctic Mountaineering by a Woman: Mount Blackburn," in *Scribner's Magazine,* July 1912.

"How I Climbed a 14,000-Foot Mountain," in *Ladies Home Journal,* August 1913.

"First Up Mt. Blackburn," in *World's Work,* November 1913.

"Exploring the Harvard Glacier," in *Harper's Monthly Magazine,* December 1915.

"Climbing the Giant's Tooth," in *Scribner's Magazine,* October 1916.

APPENDIX S

Dr. Eben Bennett had been brought over by motorboat from Lubec, Maine, the day after the attack, and diagnosed the ailment as a bad cold. In spite of more serious symptoms, the doctor persisted in his diagnosis, and Eleanor felt compelled to get a second opinion. Bennett and Louis Howe (Franklin's personal secretary) crossed to Eastport, "where they checked around by telephone to see who could be located." In Bar Harbor, a hundred miles down the coast, they found Keen, who agreed to go back with them.

Keen determined that the paralysis had been caused by a blood clot or a spinal lesion and prescribed vigorous massaging of the paralyzed legs. This was so painful to the patient that Howe wrote for help from [Uncle] Frederic Delano, who sought advice at Boston's Peter Bent Brigham Hospital and got a "certain"—though sight-unseen—diagnosis of polio from Dr. Samuel A. Levine, who urged the immediate end of the massaging, suggesting that it might actually aggravate the damage at that stage of the attack. Eleanor then sought a polio specialist and got Dr. Robert Lovett, who confirmed Levine's diagnosis and took over.

Keen's reputation, bolstered by Harvard's honorary S.D. the previous year (in which Keen was dubbed the "Dean of American Surgery"), must have seemed secure, and his availability heaven-sent. But he was 84 at the time and much more comfortable with neuropathology than with virology. (Somewhat ironically, he had once witnessed a quick cure of infantile paralysis by his mentor, Weir Mitchell.)

He was solicitous about the patient's recuperation, and among the incoming letters in the Keen papers at Brown are several from both Franklin and Eleanor, reporting the recovery of the invalid's spirit and inviting Keen to drop in whenever he was in town. Noblesse oblige, of course, especially in view of the mis-diagnosis—and the $600 fee.

In the *What if* department: It has been speculated that F.D.R.'s rehabilitation therapy at Warm Springs brought him in touch with similarly afflicted people, possibly sensitizing him to the plight and suffering of those not blessed with the multiple advantages of his own inheritance. Could a correct diagnosis and expeditious recovery have abbreviated his political career?

APPENDIX T

Profile of Keen in bronze by physician and sculptor R. Tait McKenzie, 1909

The original (65 x 113 cm) hangs at the top of the stairs in the John Hay Library at Brown University. Four copies (41 x 71 cm) of this handsome bronze were cast for Keen's daughters, and a miniature accompanies the certificate for each recipient of the

Brown Medical Alumni Association
William Williams Keen
Medical Alumni Service Award

"honoring an alumnus/a or member of
the Faculty of Brown University
who has exhibited oustanding service
to medicine, to the community, and
to Brown." Recipients to date include:

1975 Irving Beck '32, M.D.	**1980** Robert G. Petersdorf '48, M.D.
Ernest Daland '12, M.D.	**1981** Alexander M. Burgess '06, M.D.
Fiorindo Simeone '29, M.D.	(Posthumous)
William Williams Keen 1859, M.D.	**1982** Stanley M. Aronson, M.D.
(Posthumous)	**1983** Henry T. Randall, M.D.
1976 Herman Bumpus '12, M.D.	**1984** John T. Barrett '39, M.D.
Marshall Fulton '20, M.D.	**1985** Milton W. Hamolsky, M.D.
Elisha Bartlett 1826, M.D.	**1986** Kenneth G. Burton '27, M.D.
(Posthumous)	**1987** Walter C. Quevedo, Jr. '56, Ph.D.
1977 Arthur Holeb '41, M.D.	**1988** Pierre M. Galletti, M.D., Ph.D.
Harold Calder '02, M.D.	**1989** John R. Evrard, M.D., M.P.H.
Charles V. Chapin 1876, M.D.	**1990** Sanford W. Udis '41, M.D.
(Posthumous)	**1991** Levi C. Adams
1978 George Waterman '15, M.D.	**1996** David S. Greer, M.D.
1979 Frederick W. Barnes, M.D.	**1997** David C. Lewis '57, M.D.
J. Walter Wilson '21, Ph.D.	**1998** Judi D. Braman
(Posthumous)	**1999** Pardon R. Kenney '72, M.M.S., M.D.

APPENDIX U[*]

Front Row (L to R):
> **Florence Keen [2]**
> Mary de Forest Freeman
> Virginia Freeman James
> William Williams Keen James
> Wynne James III
> Marjorie Lorne Freeman
> **Corinne Keen Freeman [1]**
> John McGaw Foster
> Corinne Freeman Foster
> Duncan Graham Foster Jr.
> William Williams Keen
> Florence Butcher
> Elizabeth Bull Freeman
> Susannah Budd Freeman
> Paul Freeman
> Marjorie Franklin Freeman
> Franklin Freeman

Back Row [L to R]:
> William Williams Keen Butcher
> Margaret Butcher
> John Freeman
> Wynne James Jr.
> Walter Jackson Freeman III
> Walter Jackson Freeman Jr.
> George W. Handy
> **Dora Keen Handy [3]**
> Howard Butcher III
> **Margaret Keen Butcher [4]**
> Howard Butcher Jr.
> William Williams Keen Freeman
> Charlotte Elizabeth Hume
> Norman Easton Freeman
> Richard Borden Freeman

Not Shown:
> Dora Keen Butcher, Mary Louisa Butcher

---

[*] *Keen daughters in boldface*

Keen's family (spouses and espused included), Christmas, 1929.

Index of Names

—••❦❦❦••—

KEEN AND KIN

Book designed by Henry James and Sarah Bauhan
Typeset in Granjon
Printed by Thomson-Shore, Dexter, Michigan